AMSTERDAMER BEITRÄGE ZUR ÄLTEREN GERMANISTIK

Begründet von
Cola Minis†

In Verbindung mit
A.D. Kylstra†, A.H. Touber

herausgegeben von
Erika Langbroek, Arend Quak
und Annelies Roeleveld

Band 66 — 2010

Amsterdam - New York, NY 2010

Anschrift der Redaktion für Beiträge   Editor's address for submission
und Besprechungsexemplare: of articles and books for reviews:

                          Prof. Dr. Arend Quak
                          Instituut voor Oudgermanistiek
                          Scandinavisch Seminarium
                          Spuistraat 134
                          1012 VB Amsterdam

Hinweise zur Manuskriptgestaltung   Please also apply to the editor for
können bei der Redaktion   submission guidelines for articles
angeforderd werden   and reviews

The paper on which this book is printed meets the requirements of "ISO 9706: 1994, Information and documentation - Paper for documents - Requirements for permanence".

ISSN: 0165-7305
E-ISSN: 1875-6719
ISBN: 978-90-420-2933-0
E-Book ISBN: 978-90-420-2934-7
©Editions Rodopi B.V., Amsterdam - New York, NY 2010
Printed in The Netherlands

INHALT

Tette Hofstra, A.D. Kylstra 1920-2010	1
Elena Afros, Gothic Relative Clauses Introduced by *izei* and *sei* revisited	5
Guus Kroonen, Færoese *ta* and its relevance to the Germanic *Auslautsgesetze*	21
Frederik Kortlandt. Vestjysk stød again	29
Elżbieta Adamczyk, On Morphological Restructuring in the Old English and Old Saxon Nominal Paradigms	33
Arend Quak, Hintergründe eines altniederländischen Textes	63
Michael P. McGlynn, Bergþór's Voice: Orality in the Homicide Laws of the Old Icelandic *Grágás*	75
John M. Jeep, Heinrich von Veldeke's *Eneas* and the Tradition of the Alliterating Word-Pair	103
Helmut Beifuss, Wirnts von Gravenberc *Wigalois*. Ein Artusroman konzipiert als dichterische Auseinandersetzung mit den politischen Wirren seiner Zeit	137
Annelies Roeleveld, The Holy Rood in the Netherlands and North Germany. A comparative study of nine Middle Dutch and two Middle Low German recensions of the legend about the Provenance of the Cross	175
Erika Langbroek, Die Kreuzholzlegende im 'Hartebok' und ihre Verwandten	205
Elly Vijfvinkel, Lehrer und Propheten im Luzerner Osterspiel	249

BESPRECHUNGEN

Christian Schneider, *Hovezuht. Literarische Hofkultur und höfisches Lebensideal um Herzog Albrecht III. von Österreich und Erzbischof Pilgrim II. von Salzburg (1365-1396)*. (Beiträge zur älteren Literaturgeschichte). - Universitätsverlag Winter, Heidelberg 2008 (Albrecht Classen) ... 263

Martin Schuhmann, *Reden und Erzählen. Figurenrede in Wolframs* Parzival *und* Titurel. (Frankfurter Beiträge zur Germanistik, 49). - Universitätsverlag Winter, Heidelberg 2008 (Albrecht Classen) ... 266

Heinric van Veldeken, *Sente Servas. Mittelniederländisch, Neuhochdeutsch.* Herausgegeben von Jan Goossens, Rita Schlusemann und Norbert Voorwinden mit Stellenkommentar, kritischem Apparat, Namenverzeichnis und Bibliographie (Bibliothek mittelniederländischer Literatur 3). - Agenda Verlag, Münster 2008 (Michel van der Hoek) ... 267

R.B. Bremmer, *An Introduction to Old Frisian. History, Grammar, Reader, Glossary*. - John Benjamins Publishing Company, Amsterdam-Philadelphia 2009. XII, 327 (Yasushi Kawasaki) ... 270

Jakob Ruf: Leben, Werk und Studien. Konzipiert und herausgegeben von Hildegard Elisabeth Keller in Verbindung mit Linus Hunkeler, Andrea Kauer, Clemens Müller, Seline Schnellenberg Wessendorf, Stefan Schöbi und Hubert Steinke, unter Mitarbeit von Anja Buckenberger. 5 Bände im Schuber mit 2 CD-ROM. - Verlag NZZ Libro, Zürich 2008 (Cobie Kuné) ... 272

Sylvia Weigelt (Hg.), *Johannes Rothe. Thüringische Landeschronik und Eisenacher Chronik.* (Deutsche Texte des Mittelalters herausgegeben von der Berlin-Brandenburgische Akademie der Wissenschaften, Bd. LXXXVII). - Berlin 2007 (Erika Langbroek) ... 278

Karl G. Johansson and Maria Arvidsson (eds.), *Barlaam i nord: Legender om Barlaam och Josaphat i den nordiska medeltidslitteraturen.* (Bibliotheca Nordica 1). - Novus forlag, Oslo 2009., **und**
Robert Volk, *Historia animae utilis de Barlaam et Ioasaph (spuria): Einführung.* (Die Schriften des Johannes von Damaskos VI/1. Patristische Texte und Studien 61). - Walter de Gruyter, Berlin/New York, 2009. (Valentine A. Pakis) ... 283

Klaus Düwel, *Runenkunde.* 4., überarbeitete und aktualisierte Auflage (Sammlung Metzler 72). - Verlag J. B. Metzler, Stuttgart-Weimar 2008 (Arend Quak) ... 288

Yasushi Kawasaki, *Eine graphematische Untersuchung zu den* HELIAND-*Handschriften.* - Iuducium Verlag, München 2004 (Arend Quak) ... 288

Der Codex Vindobonensis 2681 aus dem bayerischen Kloster Wessobrun um 1100. Diplomatische Textausgabe der Wiener Notker Psalmen, Cantica, Wessobrunner Predigten und katechetischen Denkmäler. Mit Konkordanzen und Wortlisten auf einer CD, herausgegeben von Evelyn Scherabon Firchow unter Mitarbeit von Richard Louis Hotchkiss. - Olms-Weidmann, Hildesheim-Zürich-New York 2009 (Arend Quak) ... 289

Quellen zur Alltagsgeschichte im Früh- und Hochmittelalter. Zweiter Teil. Ausgewählt und übersetzt von Ulrich Nonn (Ausgewählte Quellen zur deutschen Geschichte des Mittelalters. Freiherr-vom-Stein-Gedächtnisaus-

gabe. Bd. XLb). - Wissenschaftliche Buchgesellschaft, Darmstadt 2007
(Arend Quak) 290
Die Weltchronik Heinrichs von München Neue Ee. Herausgegeben von Frank
Shaw, Johannes Fournier und Kurt Gärtner (Deutsche Texte des Mittelalters, hg. v.d. Berlin-Brandenburgischen Akademie der Wissenschaften.
Band LXXXVIII). - Akademie Verlag, Berlin 2008 (Arend Quak) 292
Wörterbuch der mittelhochdeutschen Urkundensprache (WMU) auf der
Grundlage des *Corpus der altdeutschen Originalurkunden bis zum Jahr
1300.* Unter Leitung von Bettina Kirschstein und Ursula Schulze erarbeitet
von Sibylle Ohly und Daniela Schmidt. 23.+ 24 Lieferung: **verswîgen -
vorder** + **vorder - wagen** (Veröffentlichungen der Kommission für
deutsche Literatur des Mittelalters der Bayerischen Akademie der Wissenschaften). - Erich Schmidt Verlag, Berlin 2007, 2008 (Arend Quak) 293
Claudine Moulin & Michel Pauly (Hrsg.), *Die Rechnungsbücher der Stadt Luxemburg.* Erstes Heft 1388-1399 (Schriftenreihe des Stadtarchivs Luxemburg. Band 1). - Luxemburg 2007 (Arend Quak) 294
Per Vikstrand, *Bebyggelsenamnen i Mörbylånga kommun. Ortnamnen i Kalmar län 7* (Skrifter utgivna av Institut för Språk och Folkminnen, Namnavdelningen. Serie A: Sveriges ortnamn). - Institut för Språk och Folkminnen, Uppsala 2007 (Arend Quak) 295
Klaus von See & Julia Zernack (Hgg.), *þú ert vísust kvenna.* Beatrice La Farge
zum 60. Geburtstag (Skandinavistsische Arbeiten B d. 22). - Universitätsverlag Winter, Heidelberg 2007 (Arend Quak) 296
Proceedings of the 21st International Congress of Onomastic Sciences. Uppsala 19-24 August 2002, 4. Ed. Eva Brylla & Mats Wahlberg in collaboration with Dieter Kremer & Botolv Helleland, Uppsala 2008 (Rob
Rentenaar) 296
Thomas Neukirchen, *Die ganze aventiure und ihre lere. Der „Jüngere Titurel" Albrechts als Kritik und Vervollkommung des „Parzival" Wolframs
von Eschenbach.* – Universitätsverlag Winter, Heidelberg 2006 (Gary C.
Shockey) 298
Claudia Lauer, *Ästhetik der Identität. Sänger-Rollen in der Spruchdichtung
des 13. Jahrhunderts.* - Universitätsverlag Winter, Heidelberg 2008 (A. H.
Touber) 302
Bernhard Anton Schmitz, *Gauvain, Gawein, Walewein. Die Emanzipation des
ewig Verspäteten.* - Tübingen, Max Niemeyer Verlag, 2008 (Veerle Uyttersprot) 310
Cordula Kropik, *Reflexionen des Geschichtlichen. Zur literarischen Konstituierung mittelhochdeutscher Heldenepik.* (Jenaer germanistische Forschungen, Neue Folge, Band 24). - Universitätsverlag Winter, Heidelberg 2008
(Norbert Voorwinden) 314
Mai und Beaflor. Herausgegeben, übersetzt, kommentiert und mit einer Einleitung von Albrecht Classen (Beihefte zur Mediaevistik, Bd. 6). - Peter
Lang, Frankfurt am Main, Berlin, Bern, Bruxelles, New York, Oxford,
Wien 2006 (Fritz Wagner) 318
Jörg Schwarz, *Stadtluft macht frei. Leben in der mittelalterlichen Stadt* (Geschichte erzählt Bd. 15). - Primus Verlag, Darmstadt 2008 (Job Weststrate) 318

A. D. KYLSTRA 1920–2009

von Tette Hofstra – Roden

Andries Dirk Kylstra wurde am 8. Oktober 1920 in Zwaagwesteinde, einem Dorf in Friesland, geboren. Seine Jugend verbrachte er aber in der Stadt Utrecht, und hier absolvierte er die höhere Handelsschule, obwohl der Begabung des Knaben, der bereits vor der Grundschule lesen konnte, das leider unerschwingliche Gymnasium wohl eher entsprochen hätte. Im Zweiten Weltkrieg versuchte Kylstra sich dem Griff der deutschen Machthaber zu entziehen, indem er untertauchte. Er wurde jedoch gefasst und zur Zwangsarbeit nach Deutschland abtransportiert. Dort begegnete er in Freiburg im Breisgau Margrit Irene Linder. Liebe entflammte, und zusammen zogen die zwei im September 1945 in die Niederlande.

Der sprachbegabte Kylstra erwarb sich – in unermüdlichem Einsatz – in kürzester Zeit die Lehrbefugnis an höheren Schulen („M.O.-A") für Englisch (1946) und Deutsch (1948). Er bestand das Examen (Latein, Griechisch), das ein Universitätsstudium ermöglichte. Ab 1951 studierte er Germanistik an der Universität Utrecht; Nebenfächer waren Altgermanisch und Russisch. Sowohl die Zwischenprüfung (1954) wie die Abschlussprüfung (1956, sog. „doctoraal examen") brachte ihm die höchste Anerkennung (*cum laude*). Seit der Rückkehr 1945 verband Kylstra das Studium immer mit gleichzeitiger beruflicher Tätigkeit.

Dank einem Stipendium der Niederländischen Forschungsgemeinschaft (Z.W.O.) konnte Kylstra 1956 mit seiner Familie nach Finnland ziehen und sich an der Universität Helsinki zwei Jahre lang dem Finnischen und der Finnougristik widmen. Im Herbst 1958 wurde er Gymnasiallehrer in der Kleinstadt Steenwijk. Trotz der Vollzeitbeschäftigung als Lehrer konnte er bereits am 12. Mai 1961 seine Dissertation *Geschichte der germanisch-finnischen Lehnwortforschung* an der Universität Utrecht verteidigen, wiederum *cum laude*. Die Dissertation fand ein sehr positives Echo und löste in Finnland die Neubelebung der Lehnwortforschung aus. Ab 1. September 1962 war

Kylstra Ordinarius für „Oud-Germanistiek" an der Universität Groningen. Die Antrittsvorlesung am 23. Oktober 1962 galt einer Frage, die Kylstra auch später noch beschäftigen sollte und die immer noch aktuell ist: *Substraatinvloed in het Oudnoors*?

Im Dezember 1966 kam grünes Licht für einen akademischen Studiengang Altgermanisch in Amsterdam, Utrecht und Groningen. Studenten konnten jetzt – nach bestandener Zwischenprüfung Niederländisch, Englisch, Deutsch oder Skandinavisch – Altgermanisch im Hauptfach studieren. Bereits in den achtziger Jahren wurde dieser Studiengang schrittweise ausgehöhlt, überdauerte aber in Groningen noch einige Jahre Kylstras Emeritierung im November 1985.

Kylstra machte in seinen Vorlesungen gelegentlich Abstecher in den Bereich der Finnougristik, z. B. des Finnischen. Durch diese Exkurse angeregt, bat ein Dutzend Studenten um eine Einführung in die Finnougristik. Kylstra, für den Studenten immer an erster Stelle kamen, gab bereits 1963/64 der Bitte nach und legte so den Grundstein für die Groninger Finnougristik. Der Lehrauftrag wurde 1966 um die Finnougristik erweitert; dadurch wurden Finnisch, Ungarisch und Finnougristik als Nebenfächer möglich. Als selbständiges akademisches Studium wurde die Finnougristik 1972 vom Unterrichtsministerium anerkannt; ab 1973 konnte ein vollwertiges akademisches Studium sowohl der finnischen wie der ungarischen Sprache und Literatur angeboten werden und war außerdem ein Studienabschluss im Bereich der finnougrischen Sprachwissenschaft möglich. Kylstra besetzte die Stellen, die ihm für den Ausbau des Finnischen und des Ungarischen zur Verfügung gestellt wurden, mit glücklicher Hand. Die Finnougristik gedieh und überflügelte bald die „Oud-Germanistiek". Auf den alljährlich im Sommer unternommenen Reisen nach Ungarn, Finnland oder Lappland erweiterte Kylstra seine Kenntnisse von Land und Leuten und ihrer Sprache und pflegte er für die Groninger Finnougristik nützliche Kontakte.

Kylstra hatte einen festen Tagesrhythmus. Am Vormittag war er zu Hause und bereitete sich auf seine vielen und vielseitigen Lehrveranstaltungen vor. Sein Haus zählte auf die Dauer drei Studierzimmer, alle mit eigener Bibliothek: ein altgermanisches, ein finnisches und ein ungarisches Zimmer. Die Vorlesungen und Seminare waren am Nachmittag. Abends fanden im altgermanischen Studierzimmer die mündlichen Prüfungen auf dem Gebiet sowohl des Altgermanischen wie auch des Finnougrischen statt.

Kylstra erwies sich als guter Organisator. Er war 1970 Mitbegründer und 1970–1978 Vorsitzender des Arktischen Zentrums, das immer noch wesentlich zur Namensbekanntheit der Universität Groningen beiträgt. Seit 1970 leitete Kylstra die viel Zeit und Energie kostenden staatlichen Prüfungskommissionen für die Lehrbefugnis für Deutsch an höheren Schulen oder eine sonstige auf dem zweiten Bildungsweg zu erwerbende, staatlich anerkannte Fähigkeit im Deutschen (bis etwa 1990); später kamen die Kommissionen für Dolmetscher und Übersetzer Finnisch und Ungarisch noch hinzu.

Obwohl der vielseitige Unterricht und die Organisationsarbeit nur wenig Zeit für Forschung ließen, hat Kylstra zu unterschiedlichsten Themen aus seinen Wissensgebieten wesentliche Beiträge veröffentlicht. Die Themen der von ihm begleiteten Promotionen spiegeln die Breite seines Blickes nur teilweise wider: Das Werk von Rasmus Rask (Gryte Piebenga, 1971), germanisch-finnische Lehnwortforschung (Tette Hofstra, 1985), alte finnische Schriftsprache (Osmo Nikkilä, 1985), moderne ungarische Literatur (Jolanta Jastrzębska, 1989). Die germanischen Lehnwörter des Ostseefinnischen behielten immer Kylstras Interesse. Der erste Band des von ihm begonnenen *Lexikons der älteren germanischen Lehnwörter in den ostseefinnischen Sprachen* erschien 1991. Die Weiterführung des Werks hat er danach seinen ehemaligen Mitarbeitern anvertraut.

1985, das Jahr der Emeritierung, war ein Erntejahr. Im Mai 1985 verlieh ihm die Universität Tampere die Ehrendoktorwürde. Sowohl die finnische wie die ungarische Regierung zeichnete ihn mit einem hohen Orden aus. Kylstra lehrte noch einige Jahre in der Finnougristik, bis zur Ernennung seines Nachfolgers.

Nach 1985 fand Kylstra Zeit für Türkisch, Arabisch und die Lektüre des Korans. Als Altgermanist empfand er bald eine besondere Herausforderung: Jan de Vries (1890–1964). Er wollte das Verhalten dieses Leidener Altgermanisten während des Zweiten Weltkriegs verstehen. Dazu zog er Briefe, Amtsberichte, sonstige historische Dokumentation und Veröffentlichungen von De Vries heran. Drei 1998–2001 im Selbstverlag erschienene Bücher waren das Ergebnis. Es handelt sich nicht um einen Beschönigungsversuch oder gar um eine Ehrenrettung. Dennoch stieß der Versuch, das Handeln des international angesehenen, vielseitigen Gelehrten zu verstehen, bei manchem auf Skepsis, ja Ablehnung.

Im großen Haus an der De Savornin Lohmanlaan in Groningen war ein blühendes Familienleben, in dem Musik und Kunst eine wichtige Rolle spielten. In- und ausländische Gäste kamen gern. Kylstra war ein guter Erzähler, und wer zu Kaffee und Kuchen oder zum Abendessen eingeladen war, konnte leicht die Zeit vergessen.

Als die drei Söhne längst das elterliche Haus verlassen hatten und an eine Wohnung ohne Treppen gedacht werden musste, zogen die Kylstras im Jahre 2000 in einen Bungalow im Seniorenkomplex am Rande von Roden; dazu musste allerdings ein Großteil der umfangreichen Büchersammlung aufgegeben werden. Andries und Margrit Kylstra genossen, oft im Volvo, die Reize der ländlichen Umgebung von Roden. Margrits Tod im Mai 2008 nach einer glücklichen Ehe von 63 Jahren war ein schwerer Schlag. Bald danach traten mit dem Alter verbundene Beschwerden ein; Kylstras Geist blieb aber hellwach, sein Wille ungebrochen, die Mobilität gesichert, wenn auch zuletzt auf 45 km/h beschränkt. Seinem Lebensende sah Kylstra gefasst entgegen. Er starb am 10. Dezember 2009 im eigenen Haus und wurde am 15. Dezember auf dem Rodener Kommunalfriedhof mit seiner Frau vereint.

Einige herangezogene Quellen

Anonymus 1986: „*A.D. Kylstra zum 65. Geburtstag*", in: Károly Gerstner et al. (Hrsg.), *Lyökämme käsi kätehen. Beiträge zur Sprachkontaktforschung im Bereich des Finnougrischen und des Germanischen A.D. Kylstra zum 65. Geburtstag*, Amsterdam, XV–XIX.

Hahmo 1995: Sirkka-Liisa Hahmo, „*A.D. Kylstra 75-vuotias*", in: Ago Künnap (Hrsg.), *Minor Uralic Languages: Grammar and Lexis*, Tartu / Groningen, 31–37.

Jaarboek der Rijksuniversiteit te Groningen 1963, 99.

Kylstra 1978: A.D. Kylstra, "*Tien jaar Finoegristiek in Groningen*", in: *Tien jaar Finoegristiek in Groningen 1966 – 1976*, Groningen, 7–20.

Virtaranta 1995: Pertti Virtaranta, "*A. D. Kylstra: Groningenin yliopiston fennougristiikan perustaja*", in: Idem, *Suomeen suostuneita. Kielimiehiä ja kulttuuripersoonia*, Helsinki 1995, 163–195.

GOTHIC RELATIVE CLAUSES INTRODUCED BY *IZEI* AND *SEI* REVISITED

by Elena Afros – University of Waterloo, Canada

Abstract

The Gothic invariant relativizers *izei* and *sei* have been analyzed in different ways. Von der Gabelentz and Loebe (1836/1846), Harbert (1992), Klinghardt (1877), and Streitberg (1910) treated *izei* and *sei* as indeclinable relative particles. Musić (1929) and Wright (1954), on the other hand, regarded them as relative pronouns. The present study shows that in the attested Gothic, *izei* and *sei* do not form a symmetric system with the opposition of gender. In addition, *izei* and *sei* appear to lack the grammatical categories of number and case applicable to the pronominal relativizers in Gothic and therefore cannot be classified as pronouns. Significantly, the elements *izei* and *sei* are reserved for certain types of antecedents and constructions, which might indicate that diachronically, they might have been in complementary distribution with relative pronouns, as suggested by Delbrück (1909). Synchronically, however, it is impossible to account for overlapping distribution of the relativizers *izei* and *sei*, the relative pronoun based on the demonstrative, and the complementizers *ei* and *þei*.

The issue of the Gothic relative clauses introduced by the elements *izei* and *sei* remained controversial throughout the nineteenth and twentieth centuries. Von der Gabelentz and Loebe (1836/1846), Harbert (1992), Klinghardt (1877), and Streitberg (1910) considered *izei* and *sei* indeclinable relative particles, whereas Musić (1929) and Wright (1954) treated these elements as relative pronouns. The present discussion of *izei*- and *sei*-clauses begins with the detailed examination of the Gothic data. It then offers a brief overview of the debate on the syntactic function of *izei* and *sei* and concludes with a summary of the findings.

Since the comparison between the Gothic *izei*- and *sei*-clauses with the Greek and Latin constructions they render has shown no systematic correspondence between the *Vorlage* and the choice of the relativizer in Gothic, reference to the Greek and Latin versions in this paper is limited to a few instances, while the examination focuses on the Gothic translation.[1]

---

[1] Though relative clauses introduced by *sei* sometimes render ἥτις- relative clauses,

1. Relative clauses introduced by *izei*

Relative clauses introduced by *izei* and *sei* can be classified according to the antecedent they modify. Thus, fifteen *izei*-clauses have a masculine singular nominal (John 8:40, John 15:26, 1 Cor 15:57, 2 Cor 1:9-10, 2 Cor 3:5-6, 2 Cor 8:16, Eph 1:3, Eph 1:13-14B, Gal 1:1, Gal 1:3-4) or pronominal (John 11:37, 1 Cor 15:27, 2 Cor 5:21, Eph 4:15) antecedent denoting deity (Jesus, Father, God, Holy Spirit) or a biblical character (John 12:4):

> (**1**) *iþ **guda** awiliuþ ize gaf unsis sigis þairh fraujan unsarana Iesu Xristau* 'But thanks be to God, who gave us the victory through our Lord Jesus Christ' (1 Cor 15:57)[2]
>
> (**2**) *qaþ þan ains þize siponje is, **Judas Seimonis sa Iskariotes**, izei skaftida sik du galewjan ina* 'But one of His disciples, Judas Iscariot, Simon's [son], who betrayed Him, said' (John 12:4)

None of the nominal antecedents of the clauses introduced by *izei* is premodified by a demonstrative.

In addition, *izei* is found in seven relative clauses modifying plural animate nominal (Mt 7:15) and pronominal (Lk 8:13, Lk 8:15, Mk 9:1, Gal 6:13A, Eph 2:17A, 1 Tim 1:16) antecedents:

> (**3**) *atsaihviþ sweþauh faura **liugnapraufetum þaim** izei qimand at izwis in wastjom lambe...* 'Beware of false prophets, those who come to you in sheep's clothing' (Mt 7:15)
>
> (**4**) *iþ þata ana þizai godon airþai þai sind **þai** ize in hairtin godamma jah seljamma gahausjandans þata waurd gahaband jah akran bairand in þulainai* 'But the ones that fell on the

---

no additional adverbial nuance in Gothic can be detected. Scholars of the New Testament Greek (Black 1967; Turner 1993; Zerwick 1963) warn not to read too much consecutive or concessive meaning into the relative pronouns of general and indeterminate reference. Zerwick (1963, §216) states that, for instance, in Lk 2:4 (example 18 below) "the sense is clearly simply the determinate '(the one) which is called Bethlehem' ..."

[2] The Gothic Bible is quoted from Snædal (1998) and Streitberg (1950). *Skeireins* is quoted from Bennett (1960). The English translation of the examples draws on *Holy Bible: New King James Version*. Greek is quoted from Nestle et al. (1988); Latin from Fischer et al. (2007) and Jülicher (1938-1963).

good ground are those who, having heard the word with a noble and good heart, keep it and bear fruit with patience' (Lk 8:15)

In this group, the demonstrative also appears after the head in the nominal antecedent.

Finally, *izei* introduces three generalizing relative clauses in combination with the demonstrative *sa* (Mt 5:32) and indefinite *sahvazuh* (John 16:2, John 19:12) pronouns of masculine gender denoting human beings:

> (5) ...*sa ize afsatida liugaiþ, horinoþ* '...whoever marries a woman who is divorced commits adultery' (Mt 5:32)
> (6) ...*sahvazuh izei þiudan sik silban taujiþ, andstandiþ kaisara* '...Whoever makes himself a king speaks against Caesar' (John 19:12)

In definite relative clauses, *izei* is, on the one hand, in overlapping distribution with the relative pronoun based on the demonstrative, which, like *izei*, is employed in relative clauses modifying antecedents denoting deity, e.g. (7), and biblical characters, e.g. (8), with or without a demonstrative:

> (7) *þatuþ-þan ist god jah andanem in andwairþja **nasjandis unsaris gudis**, saei allans mans wili ganisan jah in ufkunþja sunjos qiman* 'For this *is* good and acceptable in the sight of God our Savior, who desires all men to be saved and to come to the knowledge of the truth' (1 Tim 2:3-4)
> (8) *Iudan Iakobaus jah **Iudan Iskarioten**, saei jah warþ galewjands ina* 'Judas *the son* of James, and Judas Iscariot who also became a traitor' (Lk 6:16)

On the other hand, *izei* is in overlapping distribution with the enclitic complementizer *ei*, which, like *izei*, can introduce relative clauses modifying singular and plural pronominal antecedents, e.g.:

> (9) ...*þat-ist waurstw gudis, ei galaubjaiþ **þamm-** [DAT SG MASC] -**ei** insandida jains* 'This is the work of God, that you believe in Him whom He sent' (John 6:29)
> (10) *ibai þairh hvana **þize-** [GEN PL MASC] -**ei** insandida du izwis bifaihoda izwis?* 'Did I take advantage of you by any of those whom I sent to you?' (2 Cor 12:17)

But the relative pronoun based on the demonstrative has a wider distribution than *izei*: it can also refer to inanimate antecedents of all genders as well as introduce the clauses relativized on oblique NPs:

> (11) *ni manna izwis uslu[s]to **lausaim waurdam**, þairh þoei qimiþ hatis gudis ana sunum ungalaubeinais* 'Let no one deceive you with empty words, through which the wrath of God comes upon the sons of disbelief' (Eph 5:6)

The enclitic complementizer *ei*, like the relative pronoun based on the demonstrative, can introduce the clauses modifying inanimate antecedents and the clauses relativized on oblique NPs, e.g.:

> (12) *...nu fagino in **þaim- ei** winna faur izwis...* 'I now rejoice in those *things* which I suffer for you' (Col 1:24A)

In generalizing relative clauses, *izei* is in overlapping distribution with the relative pronoun based on the demonstrative and the complementizers *ei* and *þei*, e.g.:

> (13) *...**hvazuh saei** saihviþ þana sunu jah galaubeiþ du imma, aigi libain aiweinon...* '...whoever sees the Son and believes in Him may have everlasting life...' (John 6:40)
>
> (14) *...**þishvazuh ei** qiþai du þamma fairgunja ... wairþiþ imma...* '...whoever says to this mountain ... it will happen to him' (Mk 11:23)
>
> (15) *...**þishvammeh þei** wiljau, giba þata* '...I give it to whomever I wish' (Lk 4:6)

However, the relative pronoun based on the demonstrative and the complementizer *þei*, in contrast with *izei*, are not restricted to the antecedents of masculine gender, e.g.:[3]

> (16) *...qiþa izwis **þatei þishvah** [ACC SG NEUT] **þei** bidjiþ attan in namin meinamma, gibiþ izwis* '...I say to you, whatever you ask the Father in My name He will give you' (John 16:23)

In addition, the relative pronoun based on the demonstrative can introduce sentential relative clauses, whereas *izei* cannot.

---

[3] Stolzenburg (1905, 379) attributes the difference between *hvazuh saei - sa izei* and *izei - þaiei* to "Wechsel im ausdruck."

As can be seen, *izei* is found in both definite and generalizing relative clauses. *izei*-clauses invariably modify antecedents of masculine gender, most of which refer to a biblical character, deity or a supernatural entity related to the religious cult. Since *izei* is used both with singular and plural antecedents, the category of number seems inapplicable to it. Moreover, it is impossible to determine whether *izei* has a category of case because it is restricted to the clauses relativized on the nominative NPs. These properties of *izei* indicate that it cannot be analyzed as a pronoun.

2. Relative clauses introduced by *sei*

Like relative clauses introduced by *izei*, *sei*-clauses can be grouped according to the antecedent they modify. An antecedent of six *sei*-clauses is a singular noun of feminine gender with or without a demonstrative or an anaphoric pronoun referring to a biblical character (Lk 1:36, Lk 2:5, and Lk 8:2), or a geographic name (Lk 1:26, Lk 2:4, and Gal 4:26), e.g.:

> **(17)** *iþ **so iupa Iairusalem** frija ist, sei ist aiþei unsara* 'but the Jerusalem above is free, which is our mother...' (Gal 4:26)

The demonstrative precedes the head in all nominal antecedents in this group. In four of these relative clauses (Lk 1:26, Lk 1:36, Lk 2:4, and Lk 8:2), the main verb is *haitan* 'call':

> **(18)** *...in **baurg Daweidis** sei haitada Beþla<i>haim...* '...to the city of David, which is called Bethlehem...' (Lk 2:4)

Three *sei*-clauses refer to an animate feminine noun with (Lk 7:39) or without (Lk 7:37 and 1 Tim 5:9) a demonstrative:

> **(19)** ***widuwo** gawaljaidau ni mins saihs tigum jere, sei wesi ainis abins qens* 'Let a widow be chosen not under sixty years old who has been the wife of one man' (1 Tim 5:9)

Yet most of the *sei*-clauses (31) modify an abstract noun with (John 12:17, Phil 3:6, Col 3:14, 1 Tim 1:10-11, 1 Tim 4:14, 2 Tim 1:5 (2 *sei*-clauses), Skeir 1a:20-1b:2) or without (Lk 2:10, Lk 15:12, John 6:22, John 12:12, John 12:29, Rom 7:10, Rom 7:20, Rom 12:3, 2 Cor 9:11, Gal 4:24, Eph 1:22-23, Eph 3:2, Phil 3:9B, Col 1:23, Col 1:25-26, Col

1:29, Col 3:5A, 2 Tim 1:1, 2 Tim 1:6, 2 Tim 1:9, 2 Tim 2:10, Titus 1:1, Titus 1:3) a demonstrative:[4]

> **(20)** *weitwodida ... **so managei**, sei was miþ imma...* '...the multitude that was with Him ... bore witness' (John 12:17)
> **(21)** *...jah ni afwagidai af **wenai** aiwaggeljons, þoei hausidedup, sei merida ist in alla gaskaft þo uf himina...* '...and [you] are not moved away from the hope of the gospel which you heard, which was preached to every creature under heaven...' (Col 1:23)

The demonstrative precedes the head in all but one (Phil 3:6) instances in this group. Of eight *sei*-clauses modifying an abstract noun with a demonstrative determiner, two intervene between the demonstrative and the head noun:

> **(22)** *gamaudein andnimands **þizos** sei ist in þus unliutons galaubeinais...* - ὑπόμνησιν λαβὼν τῆς ἐν σοὶ ἀνυποκρίτου πίστεως... - *recordationem accipiens eius fidei quae est in te non ficta...* 'when I call to remembrance that which is in you genuine faith...' (2 Tim 1:5)
> **(23)** *þata nu gasaihvands iohannes þo sei ustauhana habaida wairþan fram fin **garehsn*** 'Now John perceiving this, the plan that was to be fulfilled by the Lord' (Skeir 1a:20-1b:2)

Of 23 *sei*-clauses modifying an abstract noun without a determiner, two – Col 1:29 and Titus 1:3 – refer to the antecedent of neuter gender:

> **(24)** *iþ ataugida ... **waurd** sein in mereinai, sei gatrauaida ist mis bi anabusnai nasjandis unsaris gudis* - ἐφανέρωσεν δὲ ... τὸν λόγον αὐτοῦ ἐν κηρύγματι, ὃ ἐπιστεύθην ἐγὼ κατ' ἐπιταγὴν τοῦ σωτῆρος ἡμῶν Θεοῦ - *manifestavit autem ... **verbum** suum in praedicatione quae credita est mihi secundum praeceptum salvatoris nostri Dei* 'but has ... manifested His word through preaching, which was entrusted to me according to the commandment of God our Savior' (Titus 1:3)

---

[4] Gal 4:24 is included in this group even though the feminine noun *triggwa* 'covenant' is ellipted in the main clause.

(25) *du þammei arbaidja usdaudjands bi **waurstwa** sei inna uswaurkeiþ in mis in mahtai -* εἰς ὃ καὶ κοπιῶ ἀγωνιζόμενος κατὰ **τὴν ἐνέργειαν** αὐτοῦ τὴν ἐνεργουμένην ἐν ἐμοὶ ἐν δυνάμει *- in quo et laboro certando secundum **operationem** eius quam operator in me in virtute* 'To this end I also labor, striving according to the deed which works in me mightily' (Col 1:29)

Whereas the Greek strongly suggests that the *sei*-clause in (24) modifies the neuter noun *waurd* 'word', Streitberg (1950, 445), probably in order to supply a feminine antecedent to the *sei*-clause, relates this sentence to Latin, where the relative clause modifies the feminine noun *praedicatio* (corresponding to the Gothic feminine noun *mereins*).

On the form *sei* in (25) Streitberg (1950) comments: "...sei] A: worauf bezüglich? Wenn die EB. §346 Anm. gegebene Erklärung richtig ist, so könnte das ursprüngl. nicht *fem.* sei auf *waurstwa* bezogen werden (vgl. relat. 'so' im ältern Nhd.). Freilich gestattet der vereinzelte Fall keine sichere Entscheidung." The apparatus in Stamm's (1878) edition reads: "usdaujans *Cod. B. - mit* bi *bricht Cod. B ab. -* bi vaurstva þatei inna vaurkeiþ] *so Uppstr.*; *die Buchstaben* ei inna *im Cod. ganz erloschen*; bi vaurstva sei inna usvaurkeiþ *las Castiglione*." Snædal (1998, xxiii) chooses *þatei* following Uppström; he remarks that this form "makes more sense," and is "slightly more likely, while it is far from certain. It is also possible that the manuscript reading is the same as Wrede's conjecture, *is ei*..." Curme (1911), on the other hand, asserts that in (25), the relative *sei*-clause precedes its antecedent: "*sei* does not go back to *waurstwa*, but points to its [feminine] antecedent *mahtai*, which stands at the end" (359); therefore, he translates this verse as "Whereunto I labor, striving with energy by the aid of that power which works within me" (358). Harbert (1978, 380) suggests that an alternative explanation "is perhaps to be found in the fact that the neuter *waurstw* has a near synonym in the feminine *waurstwei*." In the absence of decisive manuscript evidence, however, it has to be admitted that *sei*-clauses can modify neuter antecedents.

In the following three instances, the *sei*-clause precedes an abstract noun it modifies:

(26) *jah bigitaidau in imma ni habands meina garaihtein, þo us witoda, akei þo þairh galaubein Xristaus Iesuis,* **sei** *us guda ist* **garaihtei** *ana galaubeinai* - καὶ εὑρεθῶ ἐν αὐτῷ, μὴ ἔχων ἐμὴν δικαιοσύνην τὴν ἐκ νόμου ἀλλὰ τὴν διὰ πίστεως Χριστοῦ, **τὴν** ἐκ Θεοῦ **δικαιοσύνην** ἐπὶ τῇ πίστει - *et inveniar in illo non habens meam iustitiam quae ex lege est sed illam quae ex fide est Christi (c: iesu)* **quae** *ex Deo est* **iustitia** *in fide* 'and I am found in Him, not having my own righteousness, which *is* from the law, but that which *is* through faith in Christ, *the righteousness* which is from God by faith' (Phil 3:9B)

(27) *...gif mis,* **sei** *undrinnai mik* **dail** *aiginis...* - ...δός μοι **τὸ** ἐπιβάλλον **μέρος** τῆς οὐσίας... - *...da mihi* **quod** *me tanget partem substantiae...* (*d*) '...give me the portion of goods that falls to me...' (Lk 15:12)

(28) *...ju ni ik waurkja ita, ak* **sei** *bauiþ in mis* **frawaurhts** - ...οὐκέτι ἐγὼ κατεργάζομαι αὐτὸ ἀλλὰ **ἡ** οἰκοῦσα ἐν ἐμοὶ **ἁμαρτία** - *...non ego operor illud sed* **quod** *habitat in me* **peccatum** '...it is no longer I who do it, but sin that dwells in me' (Rom 7:20)

Streitberg (1910, 230) suggests that the influence of the Greek can account for placement of the *sei*-clause in (26), (27), and (28). Curme (1911) and Moerkerken (1888), on the other hand, consider these instances representative of Gothic since, they argue, Gothic relative clauses can both precede and follow their antecedents. Moerkerken (1888, 29) treats the *sei*-clause in (22) as preceding its antecedent as well even though the *sei*-clause in this verse intervenes between the demonstrative determiner and the head of the antecedent. Curme (1911, 356-357), in contrast, cites (22) and (26) as the examples of two distinct patterns: the former illustrating the relative clause following its antecedent; the latter the relative clause preceding its antecedent. Curme (1911, 357) dismisses Streitberg's (1910) analysis: "A glance at the two constructions, Gothic and Latin, will make it plain that the two constructions are entirely different. In Latin the *quod* clause is a substantive clause, in Gothic the corresponding clause is a relative clause." Despite Curme's (1911) severe criticism of Streitberg (1950), the Greek and Latin versions seem to account both for the structure of (26), (27), and (28) and for the difference between these three sentences and (22).

On the whole, *sei* is in overlapping distribution with the relative pronoun based on the demonstrative, on the one hand, and with the complementizer *ei*, on the other. Both *sei* and the relative pronoun based on the demonstrative can refer to abstract and concrete (both animate and inanimate) nouns of feminine and neuter genders with or without a demonstrative:

> (**29**) *wasuh þan **Marja**, soei salboda fraujan balsana jah biswarb fotuns is skufta seinamma...* 'It was *that* Mary who anointed the Lord with fragrant oil and wiped His feet with her hair...' (John 11:2)
>
> (**30**) *gasaihvandans þan gakannidedun bi **þata waurd** þatei rodiþ was du im bi þata barn* 'Now when they had seen *Him*, they made known the word which was told them concerning this child' (Lk 2:17)

But the use of *sei* is confined to the clauses relativized on the nominative NPs modifying singular antecedents, whereas the relative pronoun based on the demonstrative can be coreferential with the antecedents of all genders and numbers and can introduce clauses relativized on both nominative and oblique NPs. The relative pronoun based on the demonstrative is also employed in generalizing relative clauses and sentential relatives, whereas *sei* is not.[5]

In addition, *sei* is in overlapping distribution with the complementizer *ei*, which, like *sei*, can introduce relative clauses intervening between the demonstrative determiner and its head, e.g.:

> (**31**) *...þanuh þan salida in **þamm**-ei was **stada** twans dagans* '...then He stayed two days in the place in which He was' (John 11:6)

However, relative *ei*-clauses, in contrast to *sei*-clauses, do not modify anaphoric pronouns.

Morphological properties of *sei* clearly indicate that it cannot be classified as a pronoun. Since, like *izei*, *sei* is restricted to the clauses relativized on the nominative NPs, the category of case seems irrelevant to it. As the *sei* relative clauses modify feminine and neuter

---

[5] Interestingly, the form *soei* (nominative singular feminine of the relative pronoun based on the demonstrative) is used less frequently than *sei*.

nouns, the category of gender seems inapplicable to it either. *sei* is found exclusively in definite relative clauses modifying both abstract and concrete (animate and inanimate) nouns as well as anaphoric pronouns.

3. Discussion

Scholars differ on etymology and syntactic function of *izei* and *sei*. Streitberg (1910) connects *sei* with the Latin *sī* (from the I-E *sei), the original 'so' (compare *sī-c* from *sei-ke), to which, he claims, it corresponds in form and meaning. The form *izei* Streitberg (1910) derives from *e-sei. He proposes the following proportion: "*sei*: *izei* = ion. *κεῖ*. *ἐ-κεῖ*, *κεῖνος*. *ἐ-κεῖνος*, *χθές*. *ἐ-χθές*, aind. *á-sau*: aw. *hāu*, pälign. *eco-* 'hic': lat. *ce-do*" (229). Streitberg (1910) dismisses the etymology suggested by Grimm (Gr. 3,14), who derives *izei* from *is* and *ei* and *sei* from *si* and *ei*. This false (in Streitberg's (1910) view) association of *izei* and *sei* with *is* and *si* Streitberg (1910, 229) attributes to the fact that *izei* is confined to the masculine and *sei* to feminine.

Streitberg (1910, 228-229) outlines three major analytical problems with Grimm's etymology: first, *izei* and *sei* do not have an oblique case; second, *izei* is used for both plural and singular. The third objection Streitberg (1910, 229) raises is syntactic:

> wären Konstruktionen wie M 7,15 [example (3) above] undenkbar, wenn es sich um die Verbindung des Pronomens der 3. Person mit *-ei* handelte ... denn wie Neckel S. 68 mit Recht hervorhebt, müsste das Demonstrativ *þaim* alsdann unter allen Umständen vor dem Nomen stehn. Ebenso unmöglich wäre L 8,15 [example (4) above].[6]

---

[6] Neckel's (1900) observation that nominal phrases postmodified by the demonstrative pronouns are relativized exclusively by *izei* and *sei* holds unless 2 Cor 13:10 is taken into account: *duþþe þata aljaþro melja, ei andwairþs harduba ni taujau bi **waldufnja þamm- -ei** frauja fragaf mis du gatimreinai jah ni du gataurþai* 'Therefore I write these things being absent, lest being present I should use sharpness, according to that authority which the Lord has given me for edification and not for destruction' (2 Cor 13:10). In this verse, the relative clause can be analyzed as introduced by the complementizer *ei* cliticized to the demonstrative postmodifier of the noun *waldufnja* since the demonstrative *þamm-* is assigned case by the governor in the main clause.

For these reasons, Streitberg (1910, 229) agrees with von der Gabelentz and Loebe's (1836/1846) analysis of *izei* and *sei* as indeclinable relative particles.

Delbrück (1909), on the other hand, interprets the three factors – absence of the special form coreferential with the neuter antecedent; absence of the oblique case forms; and use of *izei* in relativizing a clause on the plural NPs – as the evidence that *izei* and *sei* emerged as relative pronouns. Delbrück (1909) points out that absence of the form **itei* can be easily explained if one admits that *izei* and *sei* originally referred to persons and thus were distinguished from the relative *saei soei patei*. Absence of the oblique forms of *izei* and *sei* he relates in the following way: if one speculates that the nominative case in Germanic relative clauses is, in general, the most frequent case, and probably because of the fact that the genitive *is* coincides with the nominative, then *izei izei* is less practical than *saei þizei*.[7]

As far as emergence of *izei* in the plural context is concerned, Delbrück (1909, 687) develops the following scenario:

> Ein Satz wie Joh. 12.4 [example (2) above] hieß ursprünglich: *Iudas Seimonis sa Iskariotes ei skaftida sik,* dann trat *is* vor das *ei*: 'er der'. Nun wuchs *izei* zusammen und wurde dann als maskulinisches Relativum empfunden, welches das Subjekt des Nebensatzes ausdrückt. Bei dieser Auffassung konnte es sich auch an ein vorhergehendes *sa* anlehnen, und die Häufung der Pronomina war in *sa izei,* eben weil *izei* leidiglich als Relativum gefühlt wurde, ebensowenig anstößig, wie etwa ein *se se-þe* im Ags. z. B. *se se þe leohtra is* Oros. 248,11 und sonst (Wülfing 1, 402). Hieraus erklärt sich nun auch, warum *izei* auch unmittelbar auf ein pluralisches *þai, þaim* folgen kann. Es ist in diese Verbindung weder singularisch noch pluralisch, sondern einfach relativisch (wie das nordische *es, er, das,* wie ich annehme, mit *izei* identisch ist).

Thus, Delbrück (1909) suggests that *izei* and *sei* originated as relative

---

Neckel (1900) and Streitberg (1910), however, disregard this (counter)example because, like von der Gabelentz and Loebe (1836/1846), they treat it as an instance of attraction of the relative pronoun into the main clause.

[7] This argument, however, seems to be less applicable to *sei* since the genitive of *si* is *izos* (*soei þizozei*).

pronouns, but were later reanalyzed as relativizers. It is also noteworthy that according to this interpretation, *izei* and *sei* were initially in complementary distribution with the relative pronouns based on the demonstrative so that *izei* and *sei* were used only with human antecedents.

In Musić's view (1929, 244), there are no grounds for treating *izei* and *sei* as indeclinable particles. Unlike Delbrück (1909), Streitberg (1910), and von der Gabelentz and Loebe (1836/1846), he maintains that these forms retain their etymological value, i.e. they are synchronically analyzable as an anaphoric pronoun with the enclitic particle *ei*: "und er = der er." Since Musić (1929, 244) assigns *ei* a copulative function and argues that in Gothic paratactic and hypotactic relative clauses are attested synchronically, he considers the forms *izei* and *sei* "parathetisches geschaffen und scheint auch allein immer so gebraucht zu werden, obgleich man (insbesondere wenn der relativsatz ein griech. mit dem artikel versehenes particip übersetzt) geneigt sein könnte es als hypothetisches anzusehen, wobei das correlative demonstrativum zu ergänzen ware." At the same time, he adds, these forms can be used hypotactically "wenn es sich auf ein substantivum in verbindung mit einem demonstrativum (*sa*) oder auf dieses allein bezieht" (244). He explains that in (32) "die hypothetische bedeutung kommt eben von der beziehung auf das demonstrativum (*so qino*), das *izei* bestimmt ..., diese beziehung setzt aber die relativische bedeutung von *izei* voraus, wie wir sie in parathetischen relativsätzen gefunden haben (*sa izei = sa ei*)" (244), as in Mt 5:32 (example (5) above):

> (**32**) ...*sa iþ wesi praufetus, ufkunþedi þau, hvo jah hvileika so qino sei tekiþ imma, þatei frawaurhta ist* '...This man, if He were a prophet, would know who and what manner of woman *this is* who is touching Him, that she is sinner' (Lk 7:39)

The most recent discussion of *izei*- and *sei*-clauses is found in Harbert (1978) and Harbert (1992). On the basis of morphological, phonetic, and orthographic evidence, Harbert (1978, 1992), like von der Gabelentz and Loebe (1836/1846), Klinghardt (1877), and Streitberg (1910), classifies *izei* and *sei* as non-pronominal relativizers. In his dissertation, Harbert (1978) attempts to account for the distribution of *izei* and *sei* along restrictive/nonrestrictive lines. He points out that *izei*-clauses modifying nominal antecedents tend to be nonrestrictive.

This tendency does not, however, hold for the *izei*-clauses referring to pronominal antecedents; what is more, *sei* can introduce restrictive clauses on nominal heads as well. Therefore Harbert (1978, 331) states that synchronically it is not demonstrable that *izei* and *sei* are used exclusively as nonrestrictive relativizers, yet diachronically "statistical evidence tends to support the view that this was their function at an earlier stage in the language."

What is demonstrable synchronically is that *izei* and *sei* are a special kind of complementizer selected only for relative clauses with subject traces (Harbert 1992). The evidence drawn from French, Flemish, and Arabic suggests that Gothic is not unique in restricting a certain complementizer to co-occurrence with subject traces created by movement of a null relative operator (Harbert 1992). Harbert (1992, 137) states that "the claim that *izei* is dependent on the head for licensing of its agreement features might also provide a basis for accounting for two other properties of its distribution. First, unlike true relative pronouns of the *sa-ei* paradigm, it [*izei/sei*] never introduces free relatives," i.e. the clauses of the type represented by (33):

> (33) *þaimei iupa sind fraþjaiþ...* 'Set your mind on those which are above...' (Col 3:2)

Second, *izei*- and *sei*-clauses are "characteristically not extraposed" in contrast with the clauses introduced by the relative pronouns based on the demonstrative. Harbert (1978, 330) suggests that "[t]his fact could be interpreted as a reflection of the general reluctance of nonrestrictive clauses to extrapose." Whereas it is true that all *izei*- and *sei*-clauses are bound, the claim that *izei*- and *sei*-clauses are "characteristically not extraposed" contradicts the data (see, for instance, examples (1), (17), and (19) above as well as Lk 7:37, Eph 4:15, 2 Cor 3:5-6, and 1 Tim 1:10-11; (26), (27), and (28), where the relative clause precedes its antecedent, should probably be added to this list as well).[8] Moreover, among these "exceptions" are both restrictive and nonrestrictive clauses. Finally, placement of all *izei*- and *sei*-clauses with regard to their antecedents in Gothic is the same as in the Greek and Latin versions and therefore does not reconfirm Harbert's (1978, 1992) obser-

---

[8] Whether Gothic has free relative clauses is also a matter of debate. For instance, the relative clause in (33) can also be treated as bound with the demonstrative *þaim-* as antecedent and *ei* as relativizer.

vation.

On the other hand, support for Harbert's (1992) claim that syntactically Gothic relativizers *izei* and *sei* are not unique can be found in Old English. Like *izei* and *sei*, the Old English construction *þara þe* is limited to the clauses relativized on the nominative NPs (see, for instance, Delbrück 1909; Johansen 1935; Mitchell 1987). In addition, *þara þe*-clauses, like *izei*-clauses, modify both singular and plural antecedents.

Another parallel can be drawn between the semantic characteristic feature of the antecedents of *izei*- and *sei*- relative clauses and the similar property of the antecedents of the relative clauses introduced by the compound relative pronoun in Old English. Kivimaa (1966, 45) observes that in the Old English prose the compound relative pronoun was generally employed to refer to persons of high rank and deity. Johansen (1935) also cites Anklam (30) who notes that a compound relative pronoun *se þe* has a tendency to refer to personal antecedents: in Ælfric Homilies I, for example, he counts 167 occurrences of *se þe* with a person as antecedent and only 25 with non-personal antecedents.

4. Summary

The present study has shown that in the attested Gothic, *izei* and *sei* do not form a symmetric system with the opposition of gender. Synchronically, *izei* and *sei* can be analyzed as non-pronominal relativizers since the grammatical categories of gender, number, and case applicable to the pronominal relativizers in Gothic, seem to be irrelevant to them. The relativizers *izei* and *sei* are reserved for certain types of antecedents and constructions. While *izei* occurs in relative clauses modifying masculine singular and plural nominal and pronominal antecedents, *sei* appears in relative clauses referring to singular feminine nominal and pronominal as well as neuter nominal antecedents. Most of the antecedents of the *izei*-clauses are animate nouns of a generally known Biblical reference (Moerkerken 1888); the antecedents of the *sei*-clauses are more semantically diverse: besides animate and inanimate nouns denoting Biblical characters and geographic locations, they also include abstract and animate nouns with more general reference. Both *izei* and *sei* can introduce definite relative clauses; however, only *izei* is found in generalizing relative clauses.

Synchronically, it is impossible to account for overlapping distribution of the relative pronoun based on the demonstrative, the complementizers *ei* and *þei*, and the relativizers *izei* and *sei*. But the fact that the forms *izei* and *sei* do not have a neuter counterpart, that they are used exclusively in the clauses relativized on the nominative NPs, and that *izei* can refer to singular and plural antecedents indicates that diachronically, *izei* and *sei* might have been in complementary distribution with relative pronouns, as suggested by Delbrück (1909). The latter are likely to have intruded into the field of the forms *izei* and *sei*.

On comparative grounds, *izei* and *sei* resemble the Old English compound relative pronoun and the combination *þara þe*. While the Old English and Gothic relativizers share a number of syntactic properties, they appear not to be etymologically connected.

Bibliography

Bennett 1960: *The Gothic commentary on the Gospel of John*, ed. William H. Bennett, New York.
Black 1967: *An Aramaic approach to the Gospels and Acts*, ed. Matthew Black, 3rd edn., Oxford.
Curme 1911: George O. Curme, "Is the Gothic Bible Gothic?" in: *Journal of English and Germanic Philology* 10: 151-190, 335-377.
Delbrück 1909: Berthold Delbrück, *Zu den germanischen Relativsätzen*, Leipzig.
Fischer et al. 2007: *Biblia sacra: iuxta Vulgatam versionem*, eds. Bonifatius Fischer, I. Gribomont, H. F. D. Sparks, W. Thiele, Robert Weber & Roger Gryson, 5th edn., Stuttgart.
von der Gabelentz and Loebe 1843-1846: Hans Conon von der Gabelentz and Johann Loebe, *Grammatik der gotischen Sprache*, vol. 2, Leipzig. (Original work published 1836).
Harbert 1978: Wayne E. Harbert, *Gothic syntax: A relational grammar* (Doctoral dissertation, University of Illinois at Urbana-Champaign).
– 1992: "Gothic relative clauses and syntactic theory," in: *On Germanic linguistics*, eds. Irmengard Rauch, Gerald F. Carr & Robert L. Kyes, Berlin, 109-146.
Holy Bible: New King James Version, 1982, Nashville.
Johansen 1935: Holger Johansen, *Zur Entwicklungsgeschichte der altgermanischen Relativsatzkonstruktionen*, Kopenhagen.
Jülicher 1938-1963: *Itala, Das Neue Testament in altlateinischer Überlieferung*, ed. Adolf Jülicher, Berlin.
Kivimaa 1966: Kirsti Kivimaa, "*þe* and *þat* as clause connectives in Early Middle English with special consideration of the emergence of the pleonastic *þat*," in: *Comentationes Humanarum Litterarum* 39: 1-271.

Klinghardt 1877: Hermann Klinghardt, "Die Syntax der gotischen Partikel *ei*," in: *Zeitschrift für deutsche Philologie* 8: 127-180, 289-329.
Mitchell 1987: Bruce Mitchell, *Old English syntax*, 2 vols., Oxford.
Moerkerken 1888: Pieter Hendrik van Moerkerken, *Over de Verbinding der Volzinnen in 't Gotisch*, Gent.
Musić 1929: A. Musić, "Die gotischen Partikeln *ei* und *þei*," in: *Beiträge zur Geschichte der deutschen Sprache und Literatur* 53: 228-262.
Neckel 1900: Gustav Neckel, *Über die altgermanischen relativsätze* (Palaestra V), Berlin.
Nestle et al. 1988: *Novum Testamentum Graece*, eds. Eberhard Nestle, Erwin Nestle, Kurt Aland, M. Black, C. M. Martini, Manning B. Metzger & A. Wikgren, 26th edn., Stuttgart. (Original work published 1979).
Snædal 1998: *A concordance to biblical Gothic*, ed. Magnús Snædal, 2 vols., Reykjavík.
Stamm 1878: *Ulfilas oder die uns erhaltenen Denkmäler der gothischen Sprache*, ed. Ludwig F. Stamm, Paderborn.
Stolzenburg 1905: H. Stolzenburg, "Die Übersetzungstechnik des Wulfila," in: *Zeitschrift für deutsche Philologie* 37: 145-193, 352-392.
Streitberg 1910: Wilhelm Streitberg, *Gotisches Elementarbuch*, 5th edn., Heidelberg.
– 1950: *Die gotische Bibel*, 3rd edn., 2 vols., Heidelberg.
Turner 1993: Nigle Turner, *A grammar of New Testament Greek*, vol. 3, Edinburgh.
Wright 1954: Joseph Wright, *Grammar of the Gothic language*, 2nd edn., Oxford.
Zerwick 1963: Maximilian S. J. Zerwick, *Biblical Greek*, Rome.

FAROESE *TA* AND ITS RELEVANCE TO THE GERMANIC *AUSLAUTSGESETZE*

by Guus Kroonen — Leiden

Abstract

In Germanic, the Proto-Indo-European accusative of the feminine demonstrative, i.e. *teh_2-m*, emerges in two different forms: Gothic *þo* versus Old Norse and Old English *þá*. Since PIE *eh_2 regularly gives *$ō$ in Germanic, it is usually assumed that the reflex *þá* developed out of *$þō$ through an unstressed stage. But this view was recently questioned by Peter Schrijver. He argued that the merger of *$ā$ and *$ō$ was forestalled in North West Germanic by a tautosyllabic nasal, and that *þá* therefore must be regular. This solution seems to be contradicted by Faroese, however, where the demonstrative form is *ta*. This *ta* may continue an Old Norse variant *þa* with a short vowel, and thus seems to indicate that PNWGm. *þá* indeed developed out of *$þō$ through an unstressed form, viz. *$þa$.

In Germanic historical linguistics, the development of the final syllables is a lingering and at the same time ever-acute problem. The problem basically revolves around the fact that certain Proto-Indo-European endings appear to have dissimilar sets of reflexes in the Germanic dialects. For instance, what is often reconstructed as Pre-Germanic *-$ōn$, becomes ON -ø, OE -e, OHG -a in the accusative of the strong feminines (PIE *-eh_2-m), but ON -a, OE -a, OHG -o in the genitive plural of the strong masculines (PIE *-$ōm$ < *-o-om). The debate on the issue is symptomatic of the Proto-Germanic stress being confined to the beginning of the word, which resulted in an innate tendency of the final syllables to wear off at various stages.

Several approaches to the *Auslautgesetze* are at hand. Within the traditional Quantitative Theory, the dialectal differences are resolved by postulating a triple opposition of short, long (acute) and overlong (circumflex) vowels in the Proto-Germanic endings. Thus the feminine accusative is reconstructed as -$ón$ versus the masculine genitive plural as *-$\tilde{o}n$. The tailor made distinction between long and overlong vowels in the final syllables was systematically avoided as a way to explain the linguistic changes by Kortlandt and Boutkan. In a number of smaller publications and particularly in Boutkan's monograph 'The Germanic *Auslautgesetze*', they developed an alternative model. This model basically differs from the Quantative Model in that a relatively large role is assigned to analogy, i.e. the leveling of endings. In the above case, they argued that the masculine genitive plural was supplanted by the feminine form *-ōan < *-eh$_2$-om in North West Germanic (Kortlandt 1978; Boutkan 1995, 194).

Both models were criticized by Schrijver at the 1999 Eichstätt conference on 'Languages in Prehistoric Europe'. Schrijver instead advocated reviving the generally abandoned Qualitative Theory as modeled by e.g. Möller (1880) and Jellinek (1891), which revolved around the idea that Pre-Germanic *ō and *ā did not always merge syllable-finally. Following these Neogrammarians, Schrijver claimed that in North West Germanic *ā and *ō remained distinct before a word final nasal, assuming that the different outcomes of the feminine accusative singular and the masculine genitive plural endings would be regular from Pre-Germanic *-ām and *-ōm.[1]

Schrijver's discussion of the evidence was largely centered around the feminine accusative singular of the demonstrative. A survey of this form across the Germanic dialects reveals a fundamental difference between North West Germanic on the one hand, and East Germanic on the other: whereas Gothic *þo* can only have developed out of PGm. *þō(n) with *ō, ON, Icel. as well as Old English *þá* seem to point to a proto-form *þā(n). The problem is that both forms must somehow continue PIE *teh$_2$m. Within the traditional Quantitative Theory of the Germanic *Auslautgesetze*, the difference between the two forms has been explained by assuming that Go. *þo* is the regular outcome of PIE *teh$_2$m and that ON and OE *þá* continue a form that arose in unstressed position (cf. Streitberg 1896, 271). Schrijver (2003) argued that the Qualitative Theory had been improperly dismissed, because it would be more economical to regard ON and OE *þá* as regular developments of PNWGm. *þān and PIE *teh$_2$m without an intermediate form *þōn. He further adduced the feminine accusative plural ON *þær*,[2] OSw. *þār* as additional evidence, because the underlying form

---

[1] For a response by Kortlandt see his 2005 article on the *ā*-stems.
[2] With *ǣ* from *ā by *z*-fronting.

*þā(n)z can similarly be regarded as the direct continuation of PIE *teh₂ns.

Schrijver's resuscitation of the Qualitative Theory has its advantages at first sight. Regarding the Auslautgesetze, "one is immediately struck by the large number of forms that the qualitative theory is capable of explaining straightforwardly" (Schrijver 2003, 197). Attractive is, too, the possibility that the PIE masculine and feminine dative endings *-o-ei and *-eh₂-i remained distinct as PGm. *-ōi and *-āi (cf. Go. *daga* vs *gibai*), since a similar retention is found in Slavic (OCS -*u* vs -*ě*), where *ā and *ō otherwise merged as well. Regarding the demonstrative forms, however, I do not think that Schrijver's analysis can be maintained. Compare the outcome of the PIE demonstratives in Gothic and Old Norse:

Proto-Indo-European			**Gothic**			**Old Norse**		
*so	*seh₂	*tod	sa	so	þata	sá	sú	þat
*tom	*teh₂m	*tod	þana	þo	þata	þann	þá	þat
*toi	*teh₂es	*teh₂	þai	þos	þo	þeir	þær	þau
*tons	*teh₂ns	*teh₂	þans	þos	þo	þá	þær	þau

An important objection to the direct derivation of ON *þær* from PGm. *þāz is that, unlike the Gothic plural demonstratives, the Old Norse forms are highly innovative, and leave little room for far-reaching conclusions on their original vocalism. The nominatives *þeir*, *þær* and *þau* seem to have arisen through the generalization of the masculine plural form *þai and the addition of the usual *a*- and *ō*-stem endings. The Proto-Norse forms can thus be reconstructed as *þajiz, *þajaz and *þaju from PGm. *þai+iz, *þai+ōz and *þai+ō,³ i.e. PIE *toi+es, *toi+eh₂es and *toi+eh₂. Since the derivation of the feminine plural *þær* from *þajaz is confirmed by the corresponding Runic Istaby form *þaiaz* (Kock 1891, 254), there is no evidence for a primary form *þāz that can justify Schrijver's application of the Qualitative Theory.

---

³ Cf. ON *tveir* m., *tvær* f., *tvau* n. 'two' < *twajiz, *twajōz, *twajō vs Go. *twai, twos, twa*. The masculine form *twai as well as *bai 'both' (Go. *bai*) spread to the genitive before Holtzmann's Law, cf. Go. *twaddje, baddje*, ON *tveggja, beggja*. Further note that Go. *twa* < quasi-PIE *dueh₂* and *ba* < *bʰ-eh₂ have an ending that must, too, have arisen in unstressed position.

As a result, the feminine accusative singular *þá* from alleged PNWGm. **þā(n)* becomes the only remaining piece of evidence. The evidential value of this form, however, is challenged by material that is offered by Modern Faroese, as I shall try to demonstrate.

In Faroese, the paradigms of the demonstratives have been simplified to some extent, though not nearly as much as in the other Scandinavian languages. The nominatives with initial *s* were supplanted by the masculine accusative form as on the mainland, but the case and gender distinctions largely remained intact as in Icelandic. As such, the Faroese system constitutes an intermediate stage between conservative Icelandic on the one hand and innovative Norwegian, Danish and Swedish on the other:

Icelandic			**Faroese**[4]			**Norwegian/Danish**		
sá	sú	það	tann	tann	tað	den	den	det
þann	þá	það	tann	ta	tað	den	den	det
þeir	þær	þau	teir	tær	tey	de	de	de
þá	þær	þau	teir/tá	tær	tey	de	de	de

Most relevant in this context is that the Faroese form of the feminine accusative is *ta* [tʰæa].[5] Since [æa] is the default outcome of stressed short *a* in open syllables, cf. *fara* [fæaɹa] 'to go' < ON *fara*, this *ta* points to ON *þă* with a short vowel. It is fundamentally different from the Icelandic form *þá* [θau], which, with its diphthong presupposes ON *þá* with a long *a*. The question now arises whether **þa* developed out of **þá* or – conversely – that **þá* arose from **þa*. For obvious reasons, the answer to this question is pertinent to the debate on the Qualitative Theory: if *þá* has a secondarily lengthened vowel, it can no longer straightforwardly be derived from **þā(n)* < **teh₂m*.

Indeed, it appears that the difference between Icelandic and Faroese cannot be resolved by assuming that the originally short vowel of *ta* arose from ON *þá* due to shortening in unstressed position. The analysis is contradicted by the Faroese masculine accusative plural form *tá*

---

[4] The Faroese data are taken from Lockwood (1977, 71) and Þráinsson *et al.* (2004, 124).

[5] Pronunciation as given by Hammershaimb (1891 II, 344). Þráinsson *et al.* use [ɛa] for the same diphthong.

[tʰɔa], which in the ballads occurs beside the intrusive nominative form *teir*. The vowel length of ON *þá* is ascertained by its PGm. derivation from **þans* (cf. Go. *þans*), and resulted from the nasalization of the **a* by the following **n*.[6] Now since Faroese *tá* with its diphthong reflects this old length, it would be inconsistent with the assumption that it was lost in the feminine accusative singular *ta*.

Moreover, the lengthening of final **a* in monosyllables has an excellent parallel. This is the Old Norse and Icelandic masculine nominative form *sá*, which continues PGm. **sa* from PIE **so*. Since the original shortness of this vowel is ascertained by its etymology, the best way to account for the originally long *a* of Icel. *sá* (pronounced [sau] with [au] from ON *ā*) is again to assume that the vowel was lengthened in stressed position. As a result, it is possible to assume that the same development changed *þa* into *þá*. As a matter of fact, should it be pointed out that Far. *ta* developed out of ON *þá* after all, for reasons of which I am unaware, it still remains possible that this *þá* first had developed out of **þa*. Meantime, it seems safe to assume that the long vowel implied by the Icelandic diphthong is not necessarily representative for all the Old West Norse dialects; it may well be the case that the standard Old Norse form *þá* developed from **þa* in stressed position, and that the Proto-Faroese sub-dialect somehow escaped this process, perhaps because (some of) its speakers had already isolated themselves from the Old Norse continuum when they colonized the Faroe Islands in the early 9th century.

The seniority of **þă* as opposed to **þā* is not contradicted by the Old English feminine accusative *þá*, as one might contend. Notwithstanding e.g. Wright (1925, 244), Campbell (1959, 290) or Algeo & Pyles (2009, 96), who cite the form with a long *a*, there does not seem to be any direct evidence for vowel length in this form, vowel length usually not being indicated in the Old English manuscripts. But even if the form was *þā* with a long vowel, it must still have developed from *þă* in stressed position. This is in fact what Wright explicitly assumes in his discussion of the demonstrative (1925 §465). The logic behind this is that if the Proto-North West Germanic form was **þā*, as

---

[6] It can be surmised that the *á* of *þá* was still "í nef kveðit", i.e. nasalized at the time of the *First Grammatical Treatise*.

one could perhaps conclude on the basis of the parallelism with Nordic *þá*, the outcome would have simply been different in Old English. This has to do with the historical development of PGm. *$\bar{e}_1$ in Anglo-Frisian. If it is true that PGm. *$\bar{æ}$ was lowered to *$\bar{a}$ in Proto-North West Germanic only to be raised again by the Anglo-Frisian brightening, the outcome of *þā should have been **þǣ. This is not the case. And if PGm. *$\bar{æ}$ was not lowered to *$\bar{a}$ in Proto-North West Germanic, but only later in the individual non-Anglo-Frisian dialects, there could not have been a *þā in the first place, because the required vowel did not yet exist. Both scenarios therefore seem to require a protoform *þa rather than *þā.

The issue that is at stake here bears resemblance to the complicated evolution of PGm. adverb *swa 'so, thus' (cf. Go. swa) in the Old English dialects, where it emerges as both swā̆ and swæ̆. It was claimed by Hogg (1980) that the former variant arose through late lengthening of *swa, which had not been brightened to *swæ̆ because it was in unstressed position (cf. Campbell 1959 §§125, 335). It would thus run fully parallel to the here supposed evolution of OE þā̆ from *þa. Hogg further claimed that the Old English variant swæ̆ developed from PNWGm. *swā, and that as such it demonstrated the hotly debated PNWGm. lowering of *$\bar{æ}$ to *$\bar{a}$.[7] His argument is destroyed, however, by the possible interference of PGm. *swē, cf. Go. swe 'as, like',[8] which would regularly give OE swǣ.[9] This counter-argument, which was later acknowledged by Hogg himself (Stiles 2004: 390 ff), is especially plausible in view of the fact that the lexically more isolated interrogative pronoun hwā̆ < *hwa < PGm. *hwaz < PIE *k^wos does not have a variant with ǣ̆ (cf. Campbell 1959 §125). Now, the lack of a form **þǣ can probably be added here.

---

[7] For a recent treatment of the issue see Patrick Stiles's 2004 article on the developments of the place-adverbs.

[8] The origin of ON svá is ambiguous, because it, too, can have developed from both *swa and *swē.

[9] I suppose that OE swǣ could also have developed from *swæ̆, the expected stressed and brightened variant of *swā̆, by secondary lengthening. This process can probably also account for the "difficult" (Campbell, Hogg l.c.) form swē in Northumbrian, where the expected outcome of Proto-Anglo-Frisian *swǣ is **swē.

All the evidence taken together, it seems evident that the Proto-North West Germanic feminine accusative of the demonstrative was *þa, not *þā, and that this form was preserved Proto-Anglo-Frisian as well as the Proto-Faroese sub-dialect of the Old Norse vernacular. As a consequence, this demonstrative form offers no compelling evidence in favor of Schrijver's view that word-final Pre-Gm. *ā and *ō remained distinct before a nasal in Proto-North West Germanic. The material rather seems to confirm the traditional view that the regular outcome of PIE *teh₂m in Proto-Germanic was *þō(n), and that the vowel of this form was unrounded in unstressed position.

References

Algeo & Pyles 2009: J. Algeo & T. Pyles, *The origins and development of the English language*, 6th ed., Boston.
Boutkan 1995: D. Boutkan, *The Germanic 'Auslautgesetze'*, Amsterdam – Atlanta.
Campbell 1959: A. Campbell, *Old English grammar*, Oxford.
Hammershaimb 1891: V. U. Hammershaimb, *Færøsk anthologi : I Tekst samt historisk og grammatisk indledning; II Ordsamling og register*, udarb. af Jakob Jakobsen, København.
Hogg 1980: R. M. Hogg, "Æ₁", in: *York papers in linguistics* 8: 49-54.
Jellinek 1891: M. H. Jellinek, *Beiträge zur Erklärung der germanischen Flexion*, Berlin.
Kock 1891: A. Kock, "Zur Laut- und Formenlehre der altnordischen Sprachen", in: *Beiträge zur Geschichte der deutschen Sprache und Literatur* 15: 244-267.
Kortlandt 1978: F. Kortlandt, "On the history of the genitive plural in Slavic, Baltic, Germanic, and Indo-European", in: *Lingua* 45: 281-300.
Kortlandt 2005: F. Kortlandt, "The inflexion of the Indo-European ā-stems in Germanic", in: *Amsterdamer Beiträge zur älteren Germanistik* 60: 1-4.
Lockwood 1977: W. B. Lockwood, *An introduction to Modern Faroese*, Tórshavn.
Möller 1880: H. Möller, "Zur Declination; germanisches AEO in den Endungen des Nomens und die Entstehung des o (a₂)", in: *Beiträge zur Geschichte der deutschen Sprache und Literatur* 7: 482-547.
Schrijver 2003: P. Schrijver, "Early developments of the vowel systems of North-West Germanic and Saami", in: *Languages in Prehistoric Europe*, ed. Alfred Bammesberger & Theo Vennemann, Heidelberg, 195-226.
Streitberg 1896: W. A. Streitberg, *Urgermanische Grammatik*, Heidelberg.
Stiles 2004: P. V. Stiles, "Place-adverbs and the development of Proto-Germanic long *ē₁ in early West Germanic", in: *Etymologie, Entlehnungen und Entwicklungen, Festschrift für Jorma Koivulehto zum 70. Geburtstag* (= Mémoires de la Société

Néophilologique de Helsinki LXIII), ed. Irma Hyvärinen, Petri Kallio & Jarmo Korhonen, Helsinki, 385-396.

Þráinsson *et al.* 2004: H. Þráinsson, Hj. P. Petersen, J. í Lon Jacobsen & Z. S. Hansen, *Faroese, an overview and reference grammar*, Tórshavn.

Wright 1925: J. Wright & E. M. Wright, *Old English grammar*, 3rd. ed., Oxford.

VESTJYSK STØD AGAIN

by Frederik Kortlandt — Leiden

Abstract
While I claim that preglottalization is ancient and that non-initial aspiration is recent, Perridon maintains the contrary. Both the alleged reinforcement of unaspirated stops and the following suppression of aspiration in recent centuries are quite unmotivated and unnatural. In my view, the whole development of obstruents from Proto-Germanic times up to the modern dialects can be viewed as a continuous process of lenition.

My recent article about the origin of the vestjysk stød (2009) evoked an immediate reaction from Harry Perridon (2009), which may stimulate further discussion of the subject. It is therefore important to specify the nature and origin of our disagreement.

First of all I would like to emphasize that my analysis of the Germanic consonant system is in no way dependent on any theories about the Indo-European proto-language. My view that the vestjysk stød is ancient is based on its correspondence with preglottalization, preaspiration, gemination and affrication in other Germanic languages (cf. Kortlandt 2003a, 2003b, 2007). The hypothesis that the vestjysk stød is a spontaneous dialectal innovation (thus Kock 1891: 368fn., Jespersen 1913: 23, Ringgaard 1960: 108) implies the equally spontaneous independent development of preglottalization in English, preaspiration in western Scandinavia, gemination in eastern Scandinavia (and elsewhere), and affrication in High German (and elsewhere), while nothing comparable is found in the surrounding Celtic, Romance, Slavic and Finnic languages except for the development of preaspiration in Scottish Gaelic under the influence of a Scandinavian substratum (cf. Marstrander 1932: 298) and independently in Saami (cf. Sammallahti 1998: 54f.). My theory that the vestjysk stød and its English counterpart are of Proto-Germanic origin and developed into preaspiration, gemination and affrication elsewhere offers a principled explanation of these phenomena. Moreover, it accounts for the curious observation that Proto-Germanic *b, *d, *g allegedly became devoiced independently in High German, Danish (and neighboring dialects of Swedish, Norwegian, Low German and Frisian) and Icelandic (and Faroese), and then word-initially in Swedish, Norwegian, English and Low German (thus Goblirsch 2005: 17). In a strict comparative analysis one would rather assume an archaism in High German, Danish and Icelandic and substratum influence from Celtic, Romance, Slavic and Finnish in northern English, Low and Central Franconian, northern Middle German and eastern Swedish, in spite of Goblirsch's statement to the contrary (2005: 79). In my reconstruction, the absence of voicedness in Icelandic, Danish and Upper German obstruents represents the original state of affairs (cf. Kortlandt 2000), which also explains the rise of the younger futhark in Scandinavia (cf. Kortlandt 2003b).

I have claimed that the vestjysk stød in *kjøvʔd* 'bought' and *bruwʔd* 'used' (Danish *købte, brugte*) continues the glottal closure of the unreleased stops in the original clusters **pt* [ʔpt] and **kt* [ʔkt], cf. German *kaufen* < **-p-* [ʔp], *brauchen* < **-k-* [ʔk], just as the vestjysk stød in *fæmʔd* 'fifth', *oʔd* 'eight', *næʔdə* 'nights' (Danish *femte, otte, nætter*) reflects the preserved glottal closure of the Proto-Germanic geminate **tt*. Perridon objects that the verb *bruge* "is a loanword from Middle Low German (*brûken*) which entered the language/ dialects in the course of the 13th or 14th century, i.e. one or two centuries after an alleged change from non-geminated [ʔk] to [k] which Kortlandt (2009) suggests took place in the 12th century" (2009: 6). The objection is mistaken because the glottalization was preserved in the geminate and became a concomitant feature of the unlenited stop, yielding the vestjysk stød (cf. Kortlandt 2009: 3f.). As a result, *kjøvʔd* < *køʔftæ* < *keyʔpta* with preservation of the glottal closure after the voiced segment is the expected development. When the glide *v* was devoiced to *f* in southern Jutland (cf. Perridon 2009: 6fn.), the glottal stop was lost because it was no longer preceded by a voiced segment: *kjøft* < *kjøvʔt*. The vestjysk stød in the preterit *bløʔd* 'bled' (Ringgaard 1960: 25) < **-dd-* is evidently of morphological origin.

Perridon argues that the loss of final shwa preceded the lenition of postvocalic *p, t, k*, e.g. in the preterit *døpt* 'baptized' < *døptæ* (2009: 8). It follows that the vestjysk stød which distinguishes the preterite *døvʔt* < *døptæ* from the participle *døvt* < *døpt* is not only older than the apocope (thus already Ringgaard) but also older than the lenition. Perridon's presupposition that this cannot be the case (2009: 5) forces him to asssume an early rise and later loss of aspiration in final stops (stages 1 and 6 of Perridon 2009: 9) before and after the apocope (stage 3) and the spontaneous rise of the vestjysk stød (stage 5) in order to keep the two forms apart. This scenario is quite unmotivated. Moreover, it is at variance with the fact that the vestjysk stød is also found in the northeastern part of the vestfynsk dialects, where the Jutland apocope never took place (cf. also Ejskjær 1990). Hansson has drawn attention to the fact that the vestjysk stød is found on original monosyllables and polysyllables alike in the most remote and isolated villages on the island of Als, where it coexists with true pitch accents representing the original accents 1 and 2 from which the Common Danish stød opposition developed (2001: 166). It follows that outside these archaic dialects the vestjysk stød was lost in original monosyllables, as was the case with preglottalization in Newcastle English (cf. Kortlandt 2003a: 6). Thus, I conclude that preglottalization was inherited from Proto-Germanic, generally lost word-finally before the apocope, and preserved as vestjysk stød elsewhere.

References

Ejskjær 1990: Inger Ejskjær, "Stød and pitch accents in the Danish dialects", in: *Acta Linguistica Hafniensia* 22: 49-75.
Goblirsch 1005: Kurt Gustav Goblirsch, *Lautverschiebungen in den germanischen Sprachen*. Heidelberg.
Hansson 2001: Gunnar Ólafur Hansson, "Remains of a submerged continent: Preaspiration in the languages of northwest Europe", in: *Historical Linguistics 1999*: 157-173. Amsterdam.
Jespersen 1913: Otto Jespersen, "Det danske stød og urnordisk synkope", in: *Arkiv för Nordisk Filologi* 29: 1-32.
Kock 1891, Axel Kock, "Fornnordiska kvantitets- och akcentfrågor", in: *Arkiv för Nordisk Filologi* 7: 334-377.
Kortlandt 2000: Frederik Kortlandt, "Preaspiration or preglottalization?", in: *Amsterdamer Beiträge zur älteren Germanistik* 53: 7-10.
— 2003a: Frederik Kortlandt, "Glottalization, preaspiration and gemination in English and Scandinavian", in: *Amsterdamer Beiträge zur älteren Germanistik* 58: 5-10.
— 2003b: Frederik Kortlandt, "Early Runic consonants and the origin of the younger futhark", in: *North-Western European Language Evolution* 43: 71-76.
— 2007: Frederik Kortlandt, "Proto-Germanic obstruents and the comparative method", in: *North-Western European Language Evolution* 52: 3-7.
— 2009: Frederik Kortlandt, "The origin of the vestjysk stød", in: *Amsterdamer Beiträge zur älteren Germanistik* 65: 1-4.

Marstrander 1932: Carl J.S. Marstrander, "Okklusiver og substrater", in: *Norsk Tidsskrift for Sprogvidenskap* 5: 258-314.
Perridon 2009: Harry Perridon, "How old is the vestjysk stød?", in" *Amsterdamer Beiträge zur älteren Germanistik* 65: 5-10.
Ringgaard 1960: Kristian Ringgaard, *Vestjysk stød*, Aarhus.
Sammallahti 1998: Pekka Sammallahti, *The Saami languages: An introduction*, Kárášjohka.

On Morphological Restructuring in the Old English and Old Saxon Nominal Paradigms [1]

Elżbieta Adamczyk — Adam Mickiewicz University, Poland

One of the prominent features of the early Germanic nominal inflection was the presence of extensive restructuring processes, affecting the *minor* (i.e. unproductive) paradigm. The development was manifested in the gradual expansion and permeation of the productive inflection (notably *a*- and *ō*-stems) into the paradigm of the unproductive types. The present paper investigates the process of morphological restructuring in one of the minor inflectional types, namely the *i*-stem declension, as attested in the two representatives of the Ingvaeonic subbranch of Germanic: Old English and Old Saxon. The material offered by both languages evinces a striking instability of the original *i*-stem type which inclines towards the productive inflection. The fluctuation between the inflectional paradigms in both languages attests to the process of ongoing reanalysis, resulting in the eventual demise of the etymological stem type distinctions. The present study will attempt to determine the pattern of dissemination of the productive inflection in the original *i*-stems. It is assumed that the two investigated languages display some discrepant behaviour with respect to the process of paradigmatic restructuring. Accordingly, the analysis seeks to trace down and compare the peculiarities and tendencies characteristic of both languages, including those with respect to which the two do not pattern alike.

1. Introductory remarks

The present paper addresses the issue of morphological constitution of the early Germanic nominal system, focusing on the developments

---

[1] An earlier version of this paper was presented at the *22nd Scandinavian Conference of Linguistics*, Aalborg 2006. I am very grateful to the participants of the conference for their valuable comments. I would also like to thank Professor Piotr Gąsiorowski and Professor Marcin Krygier for their insightful remarks on earlier versions of the paper.

which resulted in its later restructuring in individual Germanic dialects.[2] One of the salient features of the early Germanic substantival inflection was an evident predilection, revealed by nouns traditionally classified as *minor*, i.e. synchronically unproductive, to appropriate the inflectional endings of the *major*, productive declensional types, such as *a*-stems, *ō*-stems and *n*-stems.[3] The ensuing fluctuation of nouns between the inherited and innovative paradigms obscured the once stable and neatly organised system and, consequently, shattered the stability of certain declensional paradigms. The phenomenon has been briefly referred to, among others, by Ramat (1981, 61) who observes:

> (...) Es kann daher nicht erstaunen, daß im Germ. einige Flexionstypen zu Gunsten anderer, häufigerer Typen durch Analogie aufgegeben wurden. So wurde nicht nur der heteroklitische Typus (der schon in der idg. Epoche nicht mehr produktiv war) wie in allen anderen Sprachen derselben Familie aufgegeben (...), sondern auch die Deklination der *i*-Stämme nimmt viele Formen der *a*-Stämme auf, die *u*-Deklination weist zahlreiche Formen der *i*- bzw. *a*-Deklination. auf, usw.

The marked inclination of some nouns is attested in all minor declensional patterns, including the formations containing the original *i*-stems, known in the standard historical grammars of particular Germanic languages as the *i*-declension.[4] This very numerous (well attested primarily in the masculine and feminine gender), yet unstable group of nouns constitutes the focus of the present study. The investigation, comparative in nature, takes into account the data provided by

---

[2] The term "early Germanic inflection" refers here to the inflection of early Germanic languages rather than of the early Germanic language, understood as some stage of Proto-Germanic.

[3] The terms "productive" and "unproductive" are employed here in line with the definition of productivity provided by Wurzel (1989, 149), whereby a productive inflectional class needs to fulfill the following criteria: (a) ability to acquire new words (borrowings and neologisms), (b) ability to attract words from other inflectional classes, and (c) resistance to losing words to other inflectional classes. An unproductive inflectional class, in contrast, is one which does not meet any of the abovementioned requirements.

[4] See, for example, the grammars by Campbell (1959), Brunner (1965), Lass (1994) for Old English, and Gallée (1993), Holthausen (1921) for Old Saxon.

two representatives of West Germanic: Old English and Old Saxon. The available textual material evinces an apparent instability of the original *i*-declension, whose members tend to lean towards the productive masculine and neuter *a*-stem type and feminine *ō*-stem type.[5] The evident and frequent fluctuation within the minor inflectional paradigm may testify to an early presence of some disintegrative tendencies which, having subsequently spread, led eventually to a demise of the etymological stem type distinctions in individual Germanic languages.

The aim of the present study is to determine the extent and pattern of dissemination of the productive inflectional endings among nouns whose stems originally terminated in *-*i*-. The analysis seeks to trace down and compare the peculiarities and tendencies displayed by the two investigated languages, including those with respect to which the two evince a discrepant pattern, with a view to capturing even minor and seemingly insignificant differences. It must be noticed, at the same time, that the present study does not aim to be exhaustive and hence the quantitative investigation as well as its results will have a limited scope.[6]

2. The descent of the *i*-stem inflection and its constitution in Old English

The *i*-declension, which constituted one of the most numerous declensional types in Germanic, was comprised of all nouns containing the original thematic *-*i*- vowel, and encompassed originally both short- and long-stemmed nouns of the masculine, feminine and neuter gender.[7] Old English retained essentially such a state of affairs, yet the

---

[5] The terms "*a*-stem" and "*ō*-stem" refer here to the regular Proto-Germanic development of Proto-Indo-European **o*- and **ā*-stems, respectively.

[6] The present investigation was intended as a pilot study to a comprehensive analysis of the restructuring process in the Germanic minor paradigm which will cover all the minor declensional types in the earliest stage of West Germanic.

[7] From a purely derivational point of view, nouns belonging to the *i*-declension were originally subdivided into two subgroups: *i*-stems and *ti*-stems, the latter encompassing feminine nouns of the type **ris-ti* (OE —*ǣrist*). From the perspective of the present investigation, the subdivision is of no special relevance and no distinction will further be made between these two subtypes.

declension tended to be less stable gender-wise. Evident transitions between gender classes involved particularly neuter formations which inclined to opt for masculine inflection (e.g. OE *mere* 'lake', *mene* 'mind', *ele* 'oil', *bere* 'barley', *eġe* 'ache', *hete* 'hate'), as well as feminine nouns, drawn, in turn, by the scarcely attested neuter type (e.g. *gehygd* 'thought', *gemynd* 'memory') (Brunner 1965, 220, 222). Although the declension is still very well represented in Old English, particular gender classes evince discrepant patterns of attestation. While the group of masculine nouns, both short- and long-stemmed, is the largest of the three and well attested, the neuter subtype seems to be least stable and rather poorly represented, probably due to the mentioned persistent migrations of its members between gender types. The same holds true for the meagerly attested short-stemmed feminine nouns, identifiable as *i*-stems solely by the presence of a mutated vowel in the root. Their low incidence can be partly accounted for by their early transfer to the *ō*-stem paradigm, dated to prehistoric times (Brunner 1965, 226; Campbell 1959, 242; Wright & Wright 1908, 188).[8]

The Proto-Germanic *i*-stem paradigm can be reconstructed as follows (long-stemmed masculine **gast-* 'guest, stranger') (after Bammesberger 1990, 125; cf. Krahe 1969, 26f; Ringe 2006, 272):

singular	*plural*
N. *gastiz	N. *gastijiz (> *gastīz)
G. *gastiza	G. *gastiô^n
D. *gastai, (-ī)	D. *gastimiz
A. *gasti^n	A. *gastinz
I. *gastī	--

Table 1. A reconstructed Proto-Germanic *i*-stem paradigm

The Old English (and Old Saxon for that matter) endings of the genitive and dative singular, which had not developed regularly from the

---

[8] The motivation behind the early assimilation of the short-stemmed feminine nouns to the productive *ō*-stem inflection may have been the need to avoid confusion with the short-stemmed masculine paradigm; otherwise the two paradigms would have been indistinguishable (Keyser & O'Neil 1985, 104).

original Proto-Indo-European endings, are assumed to have extended from the productive *a*-inflection already in prehistoric times.⁹ The genitive pl. *-a* ending, found in heavy syllable stems, is believed to represent a Germanic formation, however, in light syllable stems it can be traced back to the combined influence of the long-stem paradigm and other declensional types (i.e. *a*- and consonantal stems) (Campbell 1959, 241). Among the Old English residues of the original pattern there are endingless short-stemmed masculine forms (i.e. preserving the inherited final *-e*) in the nominative and accusative pl. (*mere* 'sea, lake', *dene* 'dale'), the genitive pl. *-iġa*, which survives exclusively in poetic texts (*winiġ(e)a*, *Deniġa*), and the feminine endingless accusative sg. (*bēn* 'pray, request').¹⁰ Early textual material testifies to the presence of *-i*, later *-e*, as a marker of nominative and accusative pl. (frequent primarily in onomastic material, e.g. *Ediluini, Osuini, Hedeshamstedi*) as well as nominative and accusative sg. (attested mainly in early Mercian texts, e.g. *cyri* 'choice', *caeli* 'keel', *meri* 'lake').¹¹

The Old English paradigm retained essentially two reflexes of the original thematic vowel *-i-: (a) the presence of an *i*-umlauted vowel in the root – a major feature which renders this group of nouns distinct from *a*- and *ō*-stems (not from *-ja-* and *-jō-* stems though), and (b) the contrast between the nominative sg. *-e* ending in short-stemmed nouns and zero inflectional marker in long-stemmed formations, as in: *wine* (< *weni-z*) 'friend', *byre* (< *beri-z*) 'son' vs. *ġiest, gast* (<

---

⁹ Not so in Old High German however; according to Krahe (1969) the neuter dative sg. marker was an original *i*-stem ending: "Dat. Sg. Ahd. *meri* „dem Meer" hat gegenüber dem Masc. *gaste* (…) die echte Dat.-Endung der *i*-Stämme (alter Lok. *-ēi*) bewahrt." (Krahe 1969, 29; cf. Braune 2004, 193).

¹⁰ The archaic genitive formations in *-iġa* can be found in the following poetic contexts (culled from the *Dictionary of Old English Electronic Corpus* (Healey 2000)):
   a). ac me geuðe ylda waldend þæt ic on wage geseah wlitig hangian eald sweord eacen oftost wisode *winigea* leasum…[*Beowulf*].
   b). ðu on ofeste, hat in gan seon sibbegedriht samod ætgædere; gesaga him eac wordum þæt hie sint wilcuman *Deniga* leodum. [*Beowulf*]

¹¹ Some of the examples to be found in the texts of Mercian provenance include: (1) stagnum staeg uel *meri* [*ErGl*], (2) Rostrum neb uel scipes *caeli* [*ErGl*], (3) Anetum dili [*CorpGl 1*], (4) Delectum *cyri* [*CorpGl 1*], (5) Passus faeðm uel tuegen *stridi* [*CorpGl*]. For some more details on the presence of the influence of the productive inflection in the Anglian *i*-stems, see Adamczyk (2008).

gasti-z) 'ghost', *wyrm* (< *wurmi-z*) 'worm'.¹²

An important feature of the Old English *i*-declension, which may have some bearing on the pattern of restructuring within this declensional type, is the remarkable nonuniformity of its etymological constitution. A number of nouns classified as *i*-stems from the synchronic (Old English) perspective originated in some other declensional types and their descent can be easily traced by external comparison. Accordingly, the light masculine stems, such as *bere* 'barley', *eġe* 'terror', *hete* 'hate', *sele* 'hall' and *seġe* 'victory' originated as *-es/-os* stems, as indicated by cognate forms in Gothic (*barizeins* (adj.) 'made of barley', *agis* (cf. OE *egesa* 'terror' and the verb *egsian* 'terrify', both testifying to an original *s*-stem (Bammesberger 1990, 134, 211)), *hatis* 'hatred', *sigis* 'victory'.¹³ The *-es/-os* descent can also be detected in nouns of the type of *ġecynd* 'race', which evince an alternation between the mutated and unmutated root vowel, e.g. *ġefēġ* ~ *ġefōg* 'joint', *ġeheald* ~ *ġehyld* 'guard', *ġewealc* ~ *ġewylċ* 'rolling' (Campbell 1959, 244f). The testified etymological heterogeneity of the *i*-declension may be indicative of the fact that this declensional pattern, capable of appropriating a considerable number of nouns deriving from other declensional types, could have been, to some extent, productive at its incipient stage of development.¹⁴ Assuming that the internal stability of a paradigm may be dependent, to a degree at least, on its etymological uniformity in that the latter functions potentially as

---

¹² Anomalous here is a group of nouns which, though formally classified as *i*-stems, exhibit no traces of *i*-mutation. These include the masculine tribe name *Seaxe* 'Saxons', feminine *ġesceaft* (*ġescæft*) 'creature', *ġeðeaht* 'idea, thought' (whose *i*-stem membership can be established on the basis of the endingless accusative singular), *meaht* 'might, power' (alongside mutated *mieht*) and *sliht* 'blow' (alongside mutated *slæht*). The relative chronology of the operation of *i*-mutation and the transference of *i*-stems to productive inflectional types has been adduced to account for such a state of affairs, and accordingly, the substitution of inflectional endings is viewed as prior to the operation of *i*-mutation (Brunner 1965, 220; Campbell 1959, 84, 244).

¹³ Interestingly, all of these forms are traditionally classified as strong neuter nouns (*a*-stems) in Gothic (Wright 1957, 87). The *-es/-os* origin of *sele* can be confirmed, in its turn, by the OE variant *salor* 'hall, palace'.

¹⁴ Such a presumption has been adopted, for instance, by Bammesberger (1990) who, invoking the quantitative profile of *i*-declension, stated: "Wegen der hohen Zahl der Mitglieder bei dieser Klasse ist anzunehmen, dass die Bildungsweise im Urgermanischen produktiv war" (Bammesberger 1990, 128).

a factor encouraging stability in the paradigm, the attested lack of etymological homogeneity can be perceived as a factor motivating the morphological reorganisation in this declensional type.

2.1. *Paradigmatic restructuring in the Old English i-stem paradigm*

The analogical transference of *i*-stems to other inflectional paradigms seems to have been a salient feature of this declensional type, evinced possibly in all dialects of Old English. As has already been mentioned, the available material allows a premise, not uncontroversial though, that the spread of the synchronically productive *a*-stem inflection across other declensional types may have begun as early as in prehistoric times. Such a claim seems to find support in the genitive and dative endings (both singular and plural) which cannot be a Germanic continuation of the original PIE forms, but rather can be viewed as an analogical development on the pattern furnished by the expanding *a*-stem paradigm.[15] In fact, the *a*-stem declension, comprising by Old English times roughly 60% of all nouns (Hogg 1992, 127, Kastovsky 1995, 232), is assumed to have constituted a template for the reorganisation of other paradigms even earlier than the East/North-West Germanic split. Such a postulate seems to be corroborated by the fact that the Gothic material evinces the presence of *a*-stem inflection in the singular of nouns formally classified as *i*-stems.[16]

---

[15] The forms of genitive and dative sg. are not unanimously viewed as having developed by analogy. According to some opinions (notably Fulk (1992, 421)), such a conclusion can be drawn only on the basis of the material offered by North and East Germanic, not West Germanic dialects though. Accordingly, the dative sg. -*e* ending is assumed to have developed from -*i* which "happens to be the short-stem ending in Old Saxon (cf. long-stemmed -*e*)". Likewise, the short-stemmed dative sg. ending -*i*, attested in the earliest Old High German glossaries alongside -*e*, is viewed as original rather than analogical to the nominative/accusative sg. of *a*-stems.

[16] The category which retains a transparent *i*-stem identity in Germanic is the Gothic plural of masculine and neuter nouns (Hogg 1980, 132). All the other cases, to a greater or lesser degree, bear witness to the presence of the productive declensional types as observed by Bammesberger (1990, 124): "Im Gotischen folgt der langsilbige *i*-Stamm urg. **gasti-* im Singular der Flexionsweise der *a*-Stämme (*gast* ~ *dags*, *gastis* ~ *dagis*, *gasta* ~ *daga*, *gast* ~ *dag*), während der Plural (*gasteis* etc.) seine Eigenständigkeit bewahrt hat. Nachdem **-i-* ebenso wie **-a-* beim Nominativ geschwunden war (urg. **gastiz*, **dagaz* > got. *gasts*, *dags*), lag hier sicherlich eine Übergangsstelle vor. Aber damit allein ist die Tatsache, daß die maskulinen *i*-Stämme

The gradual morphological restructuring within the Old English *i*-stem paradigm involved essentially two parallel developments whereby the masculine and neuter *i*-stems had been reorganised on the pattern of the largest masculine and neuter class – the *a*-stems, whereas the feminine *i*-stems followed the most numerous feminine noun class, namely the productive *ō*-stem declension. The impact of the masculine inflection is best attested in the forms of the nominative and accusative plural which testify to a synchronic alternation between the inherited *-i* (light stems) or zero ending (heavy stems) and the innovative *-as* ending. The influence of the feminine inflection can be seen, for instance, in forms of the accusative sg. of heavy stems, where the innovative *-e* marker tends to appear sporadically, e.g. *tīde, cwēne*, alongside the expected *tīd* and *cwēn*.

Although the two major vocalic declensional patterns were certainly most influential, they were not the exclusive types ready to absorb *i*-stems, as the presence of weak inflectional endings, indicative of the expansion of the weak declensional type, is well attested. The weak inflectional pattern seems to have been especially appealing to long-stemmed masculine nouns denoting peoples or tribes, which began to exhibit the weak variants in Early West Saxon (i.e. by the 10th century); hence frequently attested are forms such as *lēodan, Seaxan, waran* 'inhabitants', *Wihtwaran* 'inhabitants of the Isle of Wight', etc. which survive in the Southern and West Midland dialects of Middle English. The impact of weak inflection is most evident in forms of the genitive pl., found in West-Saxon prose texts, where nouns denoting tribal names are regularly attested either with the non-syncopated ending *-ena* (*-ana, -ona*) or the syncopated *-na*, as in: *Gotena, Iudena* (*-ana*), *-seaxna, Francna, Longbeardna, Miercna, Sumursætna* (Brunner 1965, 231) (cf. etymologically weak *gumena, heortena, namena*). The following sentences, culled from the *Dictionary of Old English* corpus (Healey 2000), may serve to illustrate the tendency:

(1) þær mihton geseon Winceastre *leodan* rancne here. & unearhne. þæt hi be hyra gate to sæ eodon. [*ChronE* (Plummer)]

---

im Singular die Flexionsweise der *a*-Stämme annahmen, nicht erklärbar. Möglicherweise war die Zahl der maskulinen *i*-Stämme im urgermanischen nicht hoch". For some more detail, see Braune 1981, 74f, Wright 1957, 91f.

(2) mid arfæstum geyppaþ lofum *cæstergewaran* rodorlice singaþ caflice ece geyppað mid lofum. [*HyGl 3* (Gneuss)]

(3) & on Wiht gehergade Wulfhere Pending, & gesalde *Wihtwaran* æþelwalde Suþ *Seaxna* cyninge. forþon Wulfhere hine onfeng æt fulwihte. [*ChronA* (Plummer)]

(4) Ond ic wæs mid Eormanrice ealle þrage, þær me *Gotena* cyning gode dohte. [*Widsith*]

(5) ðurh Albinus swiðost ic geðristlæhte þæt ic dorste þis weorc ongynnan, & eac mid Danieles þæs arwurðan *Westseaxna* biscopes, se nu gyt lifigende is. [*BedePref*]

It must be emphasised that the short- and long-stemmed nouns display a disparate behaviour with respect to morphological restructuring, which can be well illustrated by the masculine type. While the vestiges of the original structure of the i-stem paradigm can still be found in the short syllable stems, which fluctuate between the archaic and innovative patterns, the long stem nouns appear to be less stable and, in effect, lose their identity, displaying the progressive *-as* (nominative/accusative) plural ending throughout (e.g. *wyrmas* 'dragons', *wrenceas* 'turns', *strengeas* 'threads'). In the light of the fact that even the earliest Old English texts bear witness to the presence of an expansive *-as* marker in the nominative and accusative pl. of heavy base i-stems, the beginning of the restructuring process in this subtype can be dated before the literary period. Consequently, when seen from a purely synchronic perspective, the heavy syllable stems can well be classified among the a- or $ō$-stems, since they exhibit endings identical to the endings of the productive patterns.

As regards the chronological setting (both relative and absolute) of the disintegration process within the i-stem paradigm, the merger of the i-stem feminine nouns with the $ō$-stems is believed to have been the first class merger which "happened after i-mutation, but before the time of the earliest texts", i.e. in the seventh century, and was followed by a fusion of the remaining i-stems with their a-stem equivalents in the eighth century. The available Late West Saxon material indicates that the restructuring process must have been a significant feature of the ninth and tenth century (Hogg 1992, 132) (cf. footnote 18 below).

Exceptional with respect to the preservation of the inherited nominative/accusative pl. *-e* ending were the masculine *i*-stems denoting names of peoples and tribes (e.g. *Myrce* 'Mercians', *Seaxe* 'Saxons', *Norþymbre* 'Northumbrians'), the collectives denoting people: *lēode*, *ylde* (Anglian *ælde*) 'men', as well as the suffixes denoting dwellers *-sæte*, *-ware* (*Cantware*, *Wihtware*) and the noun *ælf* 'elf'.[17] The pattern was apparently followed by loanwords such as *Egypte* 'Egyptians', *Beornice* 'Bernicians', *Dēre* 'Deirans', which, quite unexpectedly, testify to some restricted productivity of the otherwise unproductive long-stemmed masculine type, confined however to nouns denoting people or peoples.[18] The pattern can be illustrated by the following sentences (6) - (8):[19]

(6) Swyðe fela hi me sædon fram gehwylcum biscopum, & hwylcum cyninga tidum *Eastseaxe* & *Westseaxe* & *Eastengle* & *Norðanhumbre* þære gife onfengon Cristes geleafan. [*BedePref*]

(7) þanon untydras ealle onwocon, eotenas ond *ylfe* ond orcneas, swylce (CORR gigantas, þa wið gode wunnon lange þrage; he him ðæs lean forgeald [*Beo*]

---

[17] Hogg (1980) mentions in this context also a single occurrence of the long-stemmed *dǣle* 'part', attested in early *Corpus Glossary* in the phrase *gelimplice dǣle* 'suitable parts' (Hogg 1980, 283).

[18] It is believed that the morphology of the long syllable masculine *i*-stems was reorganised after the separation of Old English from the Continental West Germanic dialect continuum, as these (continental) dialects retained (at least partly) the long *i*-stem masculine type, e.g. OHG *gast – gesti* (pl.) (Braune 2004, 198f), OS *wurm – wurmi* (Gallée 1993, 209f), and after the advent of front mutation, since the etymological *i*-stems which migrated to *a*-stem declension frequently contain a mutated vowel. The restructuring process within the long-stemmed masculine paradigm (just as in the long-stemmed feminine paradigm) must have ended prior to the first written attestations, i.e. by the second half of the 7th century. It must be noticed however that such relative chronology of paradigmatic restructuring and mutation becomes questionable given the attested presence of such unmutated forms as *stapes*, *stapum* (vs. *stepe*), or *gasta* (vs. *giest*), which apparently prove that the substitution of the productive inflection must have occurred prior to the operation of *i*-mutation (Campbell 1959, 244).

[19] Given that many ancient tribal names seem to have followed the *i*-stem declension (e.g. many Latin names inflect according to the second declension with the nominative sg. *-us* and the nominative pl. *-i*), the unexpected preservation of the final *-i* in tribal names may have possibly been a part of a broader tendency present in non-Germanic languages, too.

(8) Swelce eac mid þisses cyninges geornisse þa twa mægða Norðhymbra, *Dere & Beornice*, þa ðe oð þæt him betweoh ungeþwære & ungesibbe wæron, in ane sibbe... [*Bede 3*]

3. The Old Saxon *i*-stem declension: General characteristics

In keeping with the Old English state of affairs, the Old Saxon *i*-declension comprised nouns of masculine, feminine and neuter gender, which have traditionally been divided into short and long syllable stems. While the masculine and feminine formations are well attested in the Old Saxon material, constituting one of the most numerous declensional types, the neuter category is limited to no more than a handful of nouns.[20] As regards their descent, the Old Saxon *i*-stems, just like their Old English cognates, form a rather heterogeneous group and, consequently, nouns deriving from various declensional types may be expected to belong here. Such is the case with the OS *segg* 'man' (nominative pl. *seggi*) or *locc* 'hair, curl' (nominative pl. *loc[k]i*, cf. OE *loccas*, OHG *lochā*), which originated as a *ja*-stem and *a*-stem respectively, but followed, at least to a degree, the pattern of the *i*-declension. Likewise, the origin of the OS *hugi* 'mind' is to be sought in the *u*-stems, whereas *heti* 'hate' and *seli* 'hall', classified formally as short masculine stems, are etymological neuter *-es-/-os*-stems (cf. Gothic forms, section 2).

A significant characteristic of the Old Saxon *i*-stem paradigm is the pattern of preservation of *i*-umlaut. In stark contrast to Old English, mutated vowels do not permeate the whole paradigm as the process of mutation took place later here, and was indicated in spelling merely in the case of /a/. Accordingly, while the plural of masculine long-stemmed nouns testifies to an earlier mutation, the singular is left unaffected by the process, the reason being an early loss of the stem formative in the latter category, which meant essentially the disappearance of the environment conducive to the operation of *i*-umlaut. In this way, the process can be viewed as a device serving to differentiate be-

---

[20] Some attested nouns tend to oscillate between the neuter and feminine or masculine gender. The most familiar examples include: OS *wiht* (Go. *waíhts* feminine) attested as masculine in the nominative/accusative pl. in the sense 'ghost, demon', but as neuter when denoting 'thing, something'; likewise OS *thionost* 'service' appears as feminine in manuscript C of *Hêliand* (line 2905: *an thia godes thionost*), yet it is neuter in manuscript M (line 2905: *an that godes thionost*).

tween the singular and the plural in these stems, as in *gast* (sg.) – *gesti* (pl.) (Prokosch 1939, 247).[21] Conversely, short stemmed nouns, in which the *-i* marker is preserved, irrespective of gender, consistently display mutated vowels throughout the whole paradigm, e.g. *seli* 'hall' (masculine), *stedi* 'stead' (feminine). In the case of long feminine stems the reflex of mutation surfaces not only in the plural, but also (occasionally) in the genitive and dative singular, e.g. *fard* 'journey', but *ferdi* (genitive, dative).[22]

3.1. *Paradigmatic restructuring in the Old Saxon i-stem paradigm*

The innovative forms which may be expected to appear as a result of morphological restructuring in the Old Saxon *i*-stem paradigm are much like the Old English ones in that they owe their existence to the influence of the strong masculine (and neuter) *a*-stems on the one hand, and feminine *ō*-stems on the other. The light masculine and the scarcely attested neuter nouns pattern alike, displaying considerable archaism in the singular, where the original stem formative *-i* functions as the inflectional exponent on all cases save for the genitive which testifies to the early influence of the *a*-declension (*-es* ending) or *ja*-declension (*-ies/-ias* ending). Traces of the process of morpho-

---

[21] Needless to say, the present-day German state of affairs, with a differentiation of singular and plural by means of the *i*-umlauted vowel, owes its existence to the relatively late appearance of mutation in Continental Germanic.

[22] This extensive spread of umlaut as a marker of plurality in German is a major feature which makes the later restructuring process of the declensional system in the two languages so divergent. The eminent function of umlaut in the subsequent development of German has been described by Iverson & Salmons (2004) who, contrasting it with its rather modest function in the other West Germanic languages, state: "Across West Germanic, umlaut morphologized as a plural marker even where there was no historical phonetic motivation for the process (…). Growing from an old generalization made about *i*-stem nouns (OHG *lamb ~ lembir*…), this pattern spread across many or even most nominal classes in the apocopating modern German dialects, even to the far larger *a*-stem classes, apparently in order to maintain plural forms distinct from the singulars (…). In short, independent phonological developments promoted the spread of umlaut qua apophonic plural marker in dialects where umlaut had reached a full flowering. By contrast, in Dutch and English, where umlaut matured to a much lesser extent, the process tended to recede over time, leaving only a few marginal traces in the plural systems (such as *mouse ~ mice*)" (Iverson & Salmons 2004, 84; cf. Kastovsky 1994, 153).

logical restructuring can be expected in the nominative plural, with a competition between the inflectional *-i* and *-ios*, the former a hallmark of the *i*-declension identity, the latter a plural marker of the influential and expansive *a*-stem inflection.[23] Long-stemmed masculine nouns, in turn, exhibit innovative features in the singular, adopting the desinences of *a*-stems (*ja-*), whereas the plural remains relatively archaic (e.g. with the inherited nominative/accusative pl. *-i* marker, e.g. *wurmi* 'worms'). As far as the feminine paradigm is concerned, the syncretic singular of light stems, with a common inflectional ending *-i*, testifies to a relative stability of this category. The sporadic signs of innovation can be seen in the dative sg. which is occasionally attested with the *-iu* marker in later texts (c. 11th century) by analogy to *jō*-stems (Holthausen 1921, 103). The occasional presence of *-es/-ies/-eas* endings in the genitive sg. can be certainly attributed to the extension of the masculine inflection (Gallée 1993, 210). A similar situation obtains for the plural, where only forms of the nominative and accusative are well attested with the original *i*-stem inflection (e.g. *ensti* 'favour'). Traces of innovation can be detected in heavy feminine stems where the inherited nominative/ accusative pl. *-i* marker tends to alternate with the progressive endings of the strong feminine *ō*-stems (the nominative pl. *-a* ending on the pattern of *gaba* 'gift'). According to Holthausen (1921, 103f), some innovative inflectional endings in the paradigm of heavy stem feminines, including *-es/-as* and zero ending in the genitive sg., and *-e/-a* or zero ending in the dative sg., can be ascribed to the impact of consonantal stems (of the type *burg*, *-es*). It is assumed that this particular development may be partly responsible for the instability of the paradigm and the gradual gender shift to the masculine type.[24]

---

[23] In consonance with the Old Saxon phonological developments, the marker of the nominative/accusative singular and plural, i.e. the unaccented *-i*, was commonly weakened to *-e*, e.g. *ferde, liude, Egypte, hôhe* (Gallée 1993, 90).

[24] This general tendency, i.e. the advance of the restructuring process in the *i*-stem paradigm, can also be observed in masculine stems in Old High German, which, however, in contrast to Ingvaeonic dialects, does not show a further subdivision into light and heavy stems: "Im Ahd. jedoch haben die masc. *i*-Stämme im Sg. völlig die *a*-Deklination angenommen. Das ist auch die Ursache dafür, dass später ein und dasselbe Wort im Pl. sowohl nach der *i*- als auch nach der *a*-Deklination flektieren kann" (Schmidt 2004, 225).

4. Analysis

4.1. *The corpora*

The present investigation is based on two representative samples of Old English and Old Saxon: the data for the Old English section come from a selection of texts as edited in the *Dictionary of Old English Electronic Corpus* (Healey 2000), whereas the analysis of the Old Saxon part has been conducted on the two most representative Old Saxon texts, namely the *Hêliand* (manuscripts Cottonianus (C) and Monacensis (M)) (Sievers 1878) and *Genesis* (Taeger 1996). In order to keep (approximately) accurate proportions in the size of the two analysed corpora, the substantial corpus of Old English has been confined to a sample of texts. Another factor determining the shape of the Old English material to be investigated was the age of the manuscripts. Consequently, given that the Old English corpus spans the period of 600 - 1150 and that the two manuscripts of the *Hêliand* date to the 9th (M) and 10th c. (C),[25] and the *Genesis* to mid 9th c., the Old English sample was compiled in such a way so as to include texts of approximately the same date. These comprise mostly texts of Late West Saxon provenance: the Parker manuscript of the *Anglo-Saxon Chronicle* (c. 1000), *Orosius* (Lauderdale MS) (early 10th century), a translation of Gregory's *Cura Pastoralis* (c. 1000), a gloss on the *Junius Psalter* (early 10th century) and *West Saxon Gospels* (dated to c. 1000).

Due to the impressive size of the investigated declensional type, the scope of the quantitative analysis has been limited for the purpose of the present study to one subgroup within the *i*-declension, namely the light masculine stems, which in both dialects evince a synchronic fluc-

---

[25] The Monacensis manuscript is the most complete of the extant *Hêliand* manuscripts, albeit it still misses some fragments. It was purportedly written in one hand since the language appears to be relatively consistent. The Cotton Caligula A.VII manuscript, on the other hand, displays less consistency with regard to its forms, and the evident influence of Franconian features can be detected (e.g. diphthongisation of Old Saxon /e:/ <ê> to /ie/, spelled <ie> and of /o:/ to /uo/, spelled <uo>, as well as the third person plural indicative ending *-ent* (Cathey 2002, 23). It is assumed that the composition of the manuscript was completed in Winchester, England.

tuation between the archaic and the innovative paradigms, testifying thus to the process of morphological restructuring in the making.

4.2. *The Old English material*

The list of *i*-stems which were included in the quantitative analysis was compiled on the basis of the information found in standard historical grammars: Campbell (1959) and Brunner (1965), the *Anglo-Saxon dictionary* by Bosworth & Toller (1898), and was subsequently checked against a list of Proto-Germanic stems provided by Bammesberger (1990, 128f). Only words unambiguous etymologically, i.e. those which can be traced back to Proto-Germanic *i*-declension, were included in the study and their etymology was verified by recourse to the information found in the *Oxford English Dictionary* (*OED*). The analysis comprised the following nouns, not all of which, however, were attested in the analysed corpus: *bere* 'barley', *bite* 'bite', *blice* 'glance', *bryce* 'use, service', *bryne* 'flame', *byge* 'turning', *byre* 'youth, son',[26] *cwide* 'speech', *cyme* 'coming, approach', *cyre* 'choice', *dene* 'valley',[27] *Dene* 'Dane', *dile* 'dill', *drepe* (*drype*) 'blow', *dryre* 'decline', *dyne* 'noise', *ece* 'ache', *ege* 'fear', *ele* 'oil',[28] *flyge* 'flight', *forenyme* 'presumption', *gryre* 'terror', *gyte* 'flood', *hefe* 'weight', *hege* 'hedge', *hete* 'hate', *hryre* 'decay, ruin', *hyge* 'mind', *hype* 'hip', *hyse* 'youth', *gripe* 'grip', (*æt-*, *on-*) *hrine* 'contact', *ile* 'sole', *lyġe* 'lie', *lyre* 'damage', *mene* 'necklace', *mere* 'lake', *mete* 'food', *myne* 'mind', *oftige* 'withholding', *pyle* 'pillow', *ryge* 'rye', *ryne* 'course', *scride* (*scriðe*) 'step', *scyfe* 'instigation', *scyte*

---

[26] Bammesberger (1990) points to at least three other meanings of OE *byre* (Go. *baúr* 'son'); these are: (a) 'time, occasion', (b) 'hill, mound', (c) 'gale', and attributes this multiplicity of meanings to the polysemic development of the PGmc **bur-i* (Bammesberger 1990, 132).

[27] The form *dene* has been attested alongside a parallel short-stemmed feminine formation *denu* 'valley' (Campbell 1959, 242).

[28] Since the history of the word is rather obscure, the preservation of the final *-e* in *oele* has been attributed to the trisyllabic character of this Romance word (**ol-i-um* instead of **ol-jum*, attested by Italian *olio*, Old French *uile*, Spanish *olio*, etc.) (Ross 1937, 77). Alternatively, the form can be viewed as an old neuter in **-ija* (having a tendency to move to the masculine paradigm) rather than an original masculine **i-*stem.

'shooting', *sele* 'room',[29] *sice* 'sigh', *sige* 'victory', *slege* 'blow, beat', *slide* 'fall', *snide* 'slice', *spiwe* 'vomit', *stæpe* 'step', *stede* (*styde*) 'place', *stice* 'puncture', *stige* 'going up or down', *stride* 'stride', *swice* 'smell', *swile* (*swyle*) 'swelling', *sype* 'suction', *ðyle* 'orator, narrator', *wlite* 'countenance, beauty', and compounds in -*scipe*, e.g. *bēorscipe* 'feast', *frēondscipe* 'friendship', *wærscipe* 'prudence', etc. The quantitative analysis investigated the incidence of the original *i*-stem inflectional endings in relation to the innovative *a*- (*ja*-) stem endings in the paradigm.

The two competing paradigms of short-stemmed masculine nouns in Old English are presented in Table 2. It must be noticed that the term *innovative* in the present investigation refers not only to traces of the masculine *a*-stem inflection, but also of the *ja*- inflection. The influence of the latter may have brought about an occasional loss of ending in the nominative/accusative sg. and pl. The forms containing a geminate consonant, frequently attested in the Old English material, can be attributed precisely to the influence of the *ja*-stems, in which the stem formative triggered doubling of the root final consonant in accordance with the process of West Germanic Gemination (Campbell 1959, 167), e.g. *mettas* 'food', *hyssas* 'youths', *illas* 'soles of foot'.[30] Traces of innovation which seem to be deep-rooted in the paradigm by Old English times, namely the forms of the genitive and dative, both singular and plural, acquired the productive endings in the prehistoric stage and thus do not bear witness to any synchronic alternation, indicative of the disintegrating processes underway, but can merely testify to an alternation between forms appearing due to the influence of the *a*-stems on the one hand, and *ja*-stems on the other (e.g. *metas* vs. *mettas*, *mete* vs. *mette*).

---

[29] Cf. related forms: *a*-stem *sæl*, pl. *salu* and *ja*-stem *sel*.

[30] When given a closer look, the relation between the *i*-stems and *ja*-stems turns out to be quite complex, granted their early (pre-)history. The early Germanic data testify to the presence of related, parallel forms, deriving from original -*i* and -*a* stem extensions: e.g. **gard-i/gard-a-* > Go. *gards* 'house, family' (*i*-stem with dative pl. *gardim*) vs. OE *geard*, ON *garðr* (*a*-stems); **sangw-i-/sangw-a-* > Go. *saggws* 'song' (*i*-stem with dative pl. *saggwim*) vs. OE *sang* (*a*-stem) (Bjorvand 1995, 3; Bammesberger 1990, 128). Bammesberger (1990) goes so far as to postulate their common origin in the PIE **s*-stems, whereby the *a*-stems are based on the original (PIE) nominative **-os* (> PGmc. **-az*), whereas *i*-stems on the original oblique **-es-* (> PGmc. **-ez-* > *-iz-*) (Bammesberger 1990, 138f).

	archaic		innovative	
	singular	*plural*	*singular*	*plural*
nominative	mete	mete	met(t)	met(t)**as**, met(t)
genitive	metes	meta	metes	met(t)a
dative	mete	metum	met(t)e	met(t)um
accusative	mete	mete	met(t)	met(t)**as**, met(t)

Table 2. The competing paradigms of the Old English short masculine *i*-stems [31]

The tabulated results of the quantitative analysis of the Old English data are presented in Table 3. The square brackets have been used to present the results for those cases in which no synchronic alternation is present, either due to the early transition to the productive inflectional class (genitive and dative sg. and pl.), or due to the impossibility to manifest the influence in an unambiguous way (nominative and accusative sg., cf. masculine -*ja*-stem *here* 'army'). These forms thus could not be included in the overall percentage distribution of archaic vs. innovative inflection.

	archaic		innovative	
	singular	*plural*	*singular*	*plural*
nominative	[85] 100 %	(3) 37.5%	-	(5) 62.5%
genitive	-	-	[36] 100%	[3] 100%
dative	-	-	[205] 100%	[25] 100%
accusative	[240] 100%	(7) 26.9%	-	(19) 73.1%
overall	**29.4%**		**70.6%**	

Table 3. The distribution of the *i*-stem vs. *a*-stem inflection in the Old English short-stemmed masculine paradigm

---

[31] In fact, the expected developments of the original genitive and dative forms would have resulted in: genitive sg. *mete*, genitive pl. *metija* (*metiġa*) and dative pl. *metim* (cf. Hogg 1992, 131). None of these forms is attested in the Old English corpus.

The investigated material indicates that the Old English *i*-stems lend themselves relatively easily to the growing influence of the productive masculine type, manifested primarily in the expansion of the nominative and accusative plural *-as* ending. In the former category the incidence of forms displaying innovation amounts to over 60%, whereas in the latter slightly above 70% of all attested forms. An interesting feature of the pattern of distribution of the innovative forms in the investigated material, is an apparent lack of gradualness of the process. There seems to be no synchronic alternation between the competing forms (e.g. *mete* and *mettas*, or *hete* and *hetas*), and thus the competition can not be captured as a progressing development (in the analysed material), which points to the fact that certain words/forms must have yielded to the influence of the productive inflection more radically than others. Such a state of affairs may owe its existence, at least to a degree, to the fact that the extensive Old English corpus has been limited to a sample of texts, which certainly cannot be fully representative.

A set of forms indicative of the aforementioned tendencies is presented in context in sentences (9) through (25) below:[32]

(9) & ure Alisend geðolode mid ðam ilcan mannum ðe he self gesceop, & hu fela edwites & unnyttra worda he forbær, & hu manige **hleorslægeas** he underfeng æt ðæm ðe hine bismredon. [Gregory, Pastoral Care]

(10) & forbeodað monnum ðæt hie hiwien, & ða **mettas** ðe God self gesceop to etanne geleaffullum monnum, ðæm ðe ongietað soðfæsðnisse, & Gode ðonciað mid goodum weorcum his giefa. [Gregory, Pastoral Care]

(11) ðu somod mid me swete name **mettas** on huse dryhtnes wit eodon mid geðafunge (*qui simul mecum dulces capiebas cybos in domo domini ambulavimus cum consensus*) [PsGlB]

(12) ða cwæð he to him: se þe hæfð twa tunecan sylle þam þe næfð, & þam gelice do se þe **mettas** hæfþ. [Lk (WSCp)]

(13) & agildeð him dryhten unryhtwisnessa hira & on **hetas** hira tostrigdeð hie dryhten god ure (*Et reddet illis dominus iniquitates ipsorum et in malitias eorum disperdet illos dominus deus noster*) [PsGlB]

---

[32] The present set of quotations does not include a complete list of innovative occurrences found in the analysed material, but represents just a sample. The same holds true for the Old Saxon illustration found in section 4.3.

(14) & þær sint swiðe micle **meras** fersce geond þa moras, & berað þa Cwenas hyra scypu ofer land on ða **meras** & þanon hergiað on ða Norðmen; hy habbað swyðe lytle scypa & swyðe leohte. [Orosius, Book1]

(15) Demi on cneorisse gefylleð **hryras** gescæneð heafdu monige on eorðan genyhtsumre (*Judicabit in nationibus implevit ruinas conquassavit capita multa in terra copiosa*) [PsGlB]

(16) & weard swa micel eorþbeofung þæt on Caria & on Roþum þæm iglondum wurdon micle **hryras**, ond Colosus gehreas. [Orosius, Book 4]

(17) On ðæm gefeohte wæron þa mæstan **blodgytas** on ægþere healfe þara folca. [Orosius, Book3]

(18) ... se simle bið cnyssende ðæt scip ðære heortan mid ðara geðohta ystum, & bið drifen hider & ðider on swiðe nearwe **bygeas** worda & weorca, [Gregory, Pastoral Care]

(19) From dryhtne **stapas** monnes beoð gerehte & weg his gewilnað swiðe (*A domino gressus hominis dirigentur et viam eius cupiet*) [PsGlB]

(20) Mine **stapas** gerece æfter ðinum gesprece þætte ne walde min æghwylc unryhtwisnes (*Gressus meos dirige secundum eloquium tuum ut non dominetur mei omnis iniustitia*). [PsGlB]

(21) ða recceras sceolon bion beforan ðæm folce sua sua monnes eage beforan his lichoman, his weg & his **stæpas** to sceawianne. [Gregory, Pastoral Care]

(22) ðonne sint eac ðæm ilcan monnum suiðe ðearllice to recceanne ða godcundan **cwidas**, ðæt hie bi ðam oncnawæn, ðonne hie geðencen ðone ecean dom, to hwæm hiera agen wise wirð. [Orosius, Book3]

(23) ðonne we ongietað inweardlice ða æ, & onwreoð ða dieglan **cwidas**, swelce we nimen ðone clænan hwæte, & weorpen ðæt ceaf onweg. [Gregory, Pastoral Care]

(24) ða cwæð se hlaford þa gyt to þam þeowan, Gageond þas wegas & **hegas**, & nyd hig þæt hig gan in, þæt min hus si gefylled. [Lk (WSCp)]

(25) ða cwæþ he to his leorningcnihtun, Doþ þæt hig sitton þurh **gebeorscypas** fiftegum. [Lk (WSCp)]

4.3. *The Old Saxon material*

The procedure applied in the investigation was parallel to that employed for the Old English material and accordingly the quantitative analysis investigated the incidence of the original *i*-stem inflectional endings relative to the innovative *a*-stem endings in the paradigm. The list of nouns for the analysis was compiled on the basis of the information found in the standard historical grammars of Old Saxon (Gallée (1993) and Holthausen (1921)), which, just as in the case of Old English, were in turn checked against a list of Proto-Germanic stems provided by Bammesberger (1990, 128-149), and was supplemented by the data from the two comprehensive Old Saxon dictionaries: *Altsächsisches Wörterbuch* by Holthausen (1967) and *Altsächsisches Wörterbuch* by Köbler (2000). The following nouns were examined in the analysis of the Old Saxon corpus: *biti* 'bite', *bruki* 'breach', *cumi* 'coming, approach', *flugi* 'flight', *fluti* 'flow', *gruri* 'terror', *hardburi* 'authority', *heti* 'hatred', *hugi, -hugi* 'mind', *nîthhugi* 'hate' *morthhugi* 'thought of murder', *strîdhugi* 'fighting spirit', *meti* 'food', *hardburi* 'authority', *halsmeni* 'necklace', *missiburi* 'misfortune', *quidi, -quidi* 'speech', *gelpquidi* 'mockery', *firinquidi* 'wicked speech', *harmquidi* 'abuse', *wordquidi* 'speech', *seli, -seli* 'hall, room', *gastseli* 'hall, hostel', *hornseli* 'gable house', *wînseli, (uuînseli)* 'tavern', *segi* 'victory', *slegi, ôrslegi* 'blow, beat', *stiki* 'stitch', *selfkuri* 'discretion', *-scepi* '-ship', *thili* 'orator, narrator', *wini* 'friend', *wliti* 'countenance, beauty'.[33] The results of the quantitative analysis of the masculine short *i*-stems are presented in Table 5.

The Old Saxon data appear to be somewhat confusing, for they bear witness to the presence of advanced synchronic alternations, not all of which, however, can be viewed as "innovations" in the sense adopted for the purpose of the present paper. Truly innovative are certainly the new inflectional endings in the nominative and accusative pl., where the rivalry between an etymological *i*-stem ending (*-i*) and the encroaching ending of the expansive *a*-declension (*-ios*) takes place. The

---

[33] The nouns **wrisi* 'giant' and **muni* 'love' were excluded from the quantitative analysis as they appear only in compounds in the function of adjectives: *wrisi-lîk* and *muni-lîk* (Holthausen 1921, 101). Interestingly, *halsmeni*, declining as masculine in Old English, is classified as neuter in Old Saxon.

alternations attested in the dative singular may exhibit, in fact, a competition between two productive endings: one extended from the productive *a*-stem type in prehistoric times (*-e*), the other more recent, extended from the *ja*-stem type (*-ie*). An identical situation obtains for the genitive sg., with competition between two productive endings (*-es* vs. *-ies*). As such, they cannot provide information about the influence of the productive paradigm on the original *i*-stem declension in Old Saxon, instead they testify to a complete, two-stage submission of these stems to the *a*-stem pattern. The productive endings extended in prehistoric times could be viewed then as "archaic" only in the sense that they are earlier than the other endings resulting from the influence of *ja*-stems.

Finally, due to the impossibility of unambiguous identification of the productive influence in the nominative and accusative sg., (cf. masculine *-ja*-stem *heri* 'army'), these forms could not be included in the overall percentage distribution of archaic vs. innovative inflection.

The reason why they were included into the quantitative part of the analysis is that the two investigated manuscripts turned out to behave disparately with respect to these alternations. Table 4 presents the two alternative paradigms of short masculine *i*-stems, resulting from the (synchronic) competition between archaic and innovative forms.

	archaic		innovative	
	singular	plural	singular	plural
nominative	hugi	hugi	hugi	hugios
genitive	huges	hugio	hugies, -ias	hugio
dative	hugi	hugiun, -ion	hugie, -ia, -e	hugiun, -ion
accusative	hugi	hugi	hugi	hugios
instrumental	hugi	-	hugiu	-

Table 4. The competing paradigms of the Old Saxon short masculine *i*-stems

Table 5 presents the incidence of the innovative and archaic light masculine *i*-stem formations in Old Saxon, as found in the analysed corpus. As has already been mentioned, since the two manuscripts did not originate at the same time, and could thus be expected to display discrepant features, they were analysed separately. Square brackets have been used to present the results for the genitive, which, as has already been mentioned, due to the early transition of the inflectional endings to the productive paradigm, show mere synchronic alternation between the two productive types, rather than a factual alternation between the *i*-stem and *a*-stem ending.

	archaic		innovative	
	singular	plural	singular	plural
nominative	[104] 100%	(9) 90%	-	(1) 10%
[genitive]	[2] 25%	-	[6] 75%	-
dative	(24) 27.9%	-	(62) 72.1%	[1] 100%
accusative	[133] 100%	(14) 93.3%	-	(1) 6.7%
instrumental	(1) 5.9%	-	(16) 94.1%	-

Table 5. The distribution of the *i*-stem vs. *a*-stem inflection in the Old Saxon *Hêliand* (Manuscript C)

	archaic		innovative	
	singular	plural	singular	plural
nominative	[80] 100%	(7) 87.5%	-	(1) 12.5%
[genitive]	[1] 12.5%	-	[7] 87.5%	-
dative	(60) 85.7%	-	(10) 14.3%	[2] 100%
accusative	[113] 100%	(10) 100%	-	-
instrumental	(18) 90%	-	(2) 10%	-

Table 6. The distribution of the *i*-stem vs. *a*-stem inflection in the Old Saxon *Hêliand* (Manuscript M)

The data from *Genesis* make contribution almost exclusively to the singular (not counting one single instance of the dative pl. *quidium*). No traces of innovative inflection have been found in the text of the Old Saxon *Genesis*. The overall distribution of the archaic and innovative forms in the investigated Old Saxon corpus is presented in Tables 7 and 8, independently for the two manuscripts of *Hêliand* (the genitive singular, as well as dative plural were discarded from the total count for reasons discussed in the foregoing section).

	archaic		innovative	
	singular	plural	singular	plural
nominative	(109) 100%	(9) 90%	-	(1) 10%
[genitive]	[2] 25%	-	[6] 75%	-
dative [34]	(29) 31.9%	-	(62) 68.1%	[2] 100%
accusative	[139] 100%	(14) 93.3%	-	(1) 6.7%
instrumental	(4) 19%	-	(17) 81%	-
overall	**40.9%**		**59.1%**	

Table 7. The overall distribution of the *i*-stem vs. *a*-stem inflection in the Old Saxon *Genesis* and *Hêliand* (Manuscript C)

	archaic		innovative	
	singular	plural	singular	plural
nominative	(85) 100%	(7) 87.5%	-	(1) 12.5%
[genitive]	(1) 12.5%	-	(7) 87.5%	-
dative	(65) 86.7%	-	(10) 13.3%	(3) 100%
accusative	(119) 100%	(10) 100%	-	-
instrumental	(21) 91.3%	-	(2) 8.7%	-
overall	**88.8%**		**11.2%**	

Table 8. The overall distribution of the *i*-stem vs. *a*-stem inflection in the Old Saxon *Genesis* and *Hêliand* (Manuscript M)

A cursory look at the data suffices to notice that the Old Saxon *i*-stem paradigm was only to a very limited extent prone to the influence of the productive *a*-declension. No synchronic alternation is attested in the nominative or accusative singular where the original *i*-stem ending is retained with remarkable regularity.[35] Scant traces of alternation appear in the nominative and accusative plural and are better attested in

---

[34] The interpretation of the data for the dative sg. is quite problematic. The total count for the dative sg. includes 5 instances with the inflectional *-e*, treated as innovative in the present investigation. Given that the original *-i* ending could have potentially undergone a regular phonological development, whereby /i/ > /e/, the rare *-e* marker of the dative sg. can possibly be viewed as a relic of the archaic pattern.

[35] The sole exception found in the investigated corpus appears to be the single occurrence of *segg* 'man' (5460 Thie **segg** uuarð thuo an sîðe, | antat hie sittian fand (C, M)), attested without the *i*-stem marker by virtue of its descent. As the noun formally belongs to the group of heavy stems, it could not be included in the final count.

manuscript C, yet their value, due to the scarce attestation, is, to a large extent, limited. Quite unexpected is the extremely high incidence of the innovative endings on the instrumental sg., found in manuscript C, reaching close to 100% of all the attested forms (vs. 10% in manuscript M). As far as the disparity between the two analysed manuscripts is concerned, it is evident that MS M tends to showcase more archaic characteristics when compared to the more innovative MS C, with the overall percentage of innovation amounting to 11.2% in the former and 59.1% in the latter. Such discrepancy, however, is only to be expected given the age of the two manuscripts. Examples (26) through (34) below demonstrate both the rare innovative forms as well as some prevalent archaic ones attested in both manuscripts:

(26) 112 georno fulgangan --, | **grurios** quâmun im,
113 egison an them alahe: | (C, M)

(27) 3683 Thuo gisah uualdand Crist
3684 thie gôdo to Hierusalm, | gumono besta,
3685 blîcan thena berges uual | endi bû Iudeono,
3686 hôha **hornselios** | (C)

(28) 3683 Thô gesah uualdand Krist
3684 the gôdo te Hierusalem, | gumono bezta,
3685 blîcan thene burges uual | endi bû Iudeono,
3686 hôha **hornseli** | (M)

(29) 1967 Thesa **quidi** uuerðad uuâra,
1968 that eo ne bilîbid, | ne hi thes lôn sculi, (C, M)

(30) 68 that im uuârun sô gihôriga | hildiscalcos,
69 aβaron Israheles | elleanruoβa:
70 suîðo unuuanda **uuini**, | than lang hie giuuald êhta, (C,M)

(31) 5959 Thuo bigunnun im **quidi** managa
5960 under them uueron uuahsan, | thar sia after them uuege fuorun, (C)

(32) 1375 that hi ne uuillea mid hluttro **hugi** | te heβenrîkea
1376 spanen mid is sprâcu | endi seggean spel godes, (M)

(33) 1375 that hi ni uuillie mid hluttru **hugiu** | te heβanrîkie
1376 spanan mid is sprâcu | endi seggian spel godes, (C)

(34) 5845 ne mahtun an thia engilos godes
5846 bi themo **uulite** scauuon: | uuas im thiu uuânami te strang,
5847 te suîði te sehanne. (C)

5. Concluding remarks

The comparison of the Old English and Old Saxon material reveals that the two closely related dialects do display a discrepant pattern of development with respect to the restructuring process in the light masculine *i*-stems. While the Old English data give substantial evidence for the process of restructuring of the *i*-stem paradigm towards the *a*- (*-ja-*) declensional type, the traces of this tendency are evident only to a limited extent in the Old Saxon material.

Although the Old English paradigm turned out to have been relatively conducive to the influence of the innovation, and the innovative forms are an evident sign of the system undergoing a change, the process certainly cannot be viewed as a wholesale, rapid development, permeating the lexicon in its totality. Instead, the vacillation of forms between the archaic *i*-stem paradigm and the innovative pattern of the productive declension evinces a slow, soon systematic expansion of the latter, resulting in a gradual loss of the earlier stability of the *i*-declension. The process conforms to the mechanism of restructuring described in detail by Wurzel (1989), whereby inflectional classes which lack stability are inevitably eliminated as their members are transferred to more stable inflectional patterns. Accordingly, the *i*-declension, though not much reduced quantitatively, became gradually unstable, which opened the way to the subsequent transformation of this declensional type in Old English and, to some extent, also in Old Saxon.

What seems striking about the restructuring process in the Germanic *i*-declension is the fact that it constituted one of the most numerous declensional types in Germanic, and nevertheless did not resist the pervasive influence of the *a*-stem inflection. Of some significance for such a state of affairs may be the fact that the declension did not contain nouns of high frequency of occurrence, which tended essentially to be less vulnerable to analogical pressure.

With reference to the chronology of the process of morphological restructuring, it has been claimed that the expansion of the plural marker *-as* in Old English was initiated by the loss of the characteristic nominative sg. morpheme *-i-* (alongside *-u-*) in long syllable masculine *i*- and *u*-stems, whereupon these nouns could no longer be distinguished from the *a*-stems (with nominative/accusative pl. *wyrm-as*, *feld-as*). The group of long-stemmed nouns was soon to be followed by short stems of *i-* and *u-* inflectional classes (*win-as*, *sun-as*) (Wurzel 1989, 102f). This chronology of events, however, is rather implausible for the Old Saxon state of affairs, where, despite the formal similarity of the nominative sg. of *i-* and *a-*stems, the *-i* marker on the nominative/accusative pl. is well attested (e.g. *gesti*, *-e*, cf. OE *gast*), resisting apparently the influence of the productive *a-*stem paradigm. This very fact may be partly responsible for the attested greater archaism of the Old Saxon nominal morphology, where the productive masculine *-os* marker is not the sole expanding inflectional ending (which seems to be the case in Old English). In fact, equally, if not more productive, is the *ja-* masculine type which also preserved the original *-i* signal on the category of nominative/accusative pl. (*-ios*) and as such may have appeared to be more familiar in terms of its acquisition. In a broader perspective, the productivity of types other than the *a-*stem declension, characteristic of Old (Low) German inflection, rendered the Old Saxon *-os* marker less distinct and hence far less expansive than the Old English inflectional *-as*, guaranteeing it, at the same time, no privileged status in the process of morphological restructuring.

Another circumstance which may, to some extent, account for the outcome of the analysis is the heterogeneous nature of the investigated corpora, in particular the fact that texts of a poetic character are more likely to reveal considerable archaism when compared to non-poetic material. Accordingly, the Old Saxon sample, represented by poetic texts, including an epic poem written in alliterative verse, must have turned out to be more archaic when compared to much more variegated Old English material, comprising glosses and larger fragments of prose writing. In order to get a clear, comprehensive picture of the developments and draw detailed conclusions about the process of morphological restructuring within the *i-*declension, a thorough analysis involving the complete corpora of Old English and Old Saxon needs to be performed.

The transference of lexical items from the minor to major declensional patterns testifies to the marked activity of analogical processes, aimed essentially at levelling the irregularity within the paradigm. The working of analogy, though certainly responsible for the gradual migrations between paradigms, is itself, in fact, more a part of the mechanism of the process of disintegration than a trigger or the major disintegrative factor. With a view to explaining the motivation behind the transition in Old English nouns, Hogg (1980: 283) invokes functional considerations, drawing attention to the functional strength of various inflectional endings. Accordingly, the substitution of the productive *-as* ending for the original, inherited *-i* in Old English is viewed as a factor permitting to keep the distinction between the singular and plural in the nominative and accusative cases. This way of reasoning could be extended to the interpretation of the Old Saxon data, where the competition takes place between the inherited *-i* and innovative *-(i)os* endings (otherwise the endings of the singular and plural, i.e. OE *-e* and OS *-i*, would have been identical). The existence of a group of *pluralia tantum* in Old English, which comprises primarily the nouns of tribes and nationalities, preserving the final *-e* in the nominative/accusative pl. (as in *Myrċe, Dene, Seaxe*), is adduced to demonstrate the postulated functional pressure. The operation of the analogical process is thus induced by the need to mark the functional distinction between the singular and plural.

At the same time, the role of the extra-morphological processes (such as phonological reduction and deletion, so characteristic of the Germanic languages) in the spread of the *a*-stem plurals cannot be underestimated. Their intense activity in the paradigm of *i*-stems led to a generalization of one common *-e* ending, whereby this declensional type lost its communicative function very early and was ready to appropriate endings from the stronger, more influential and more distinct paradigms, i.e. *a*-stems and *ō*-stems. In fact, the phonological developments which affected the minor paradigm (as well as other paradigms), namely the progressive weakening of the unaccented back vowels to *schwa*, have been commonly perceived as the primary trigger for the relatively early restructuring of the Old English nominal system.

Another determinant which may be crucial to the gradual obliteration of the morphological structure of nominal inflection, as observed by Kastovsky (1995) with regard to Old English, is the change in the status of stem formative, which, unless it was lost, was reinterpreted as a case-number exponent. Accordingly, the reflex of the original *i*-stem formative, the final vowel *-e* (as in OE *cyre*), was reanalysed as part of the stem (*cyre#*) on the pattern furnished by *-a, -ja* stems (*here*), which had no ending in the nominative and accusative singular (referred to as unmarked base form) (Kastovsky 1995, 228; Keyser & O'Neil 1985, 101). Such restructuring led to a situation where class affiliation "…was therefore no longer marked explicitly by a morphological segment, but became an implicit morphological property of the stem, i.e. was largely unpredictable" (Kastovsky 1995, 228) (cf. Hogg 1980, 282).

The attested predominance and productivity of the paradigmatic pattern of the *a*-declension, so well attested in the Old English material, can be attributed to several interrelated factors. Of prime importance here is the quantitative prominence of the *a*-declension, comprising a majority of Old English lexical stock, as well as the presence of distinct inflectional markers in the nominative/accusative pl. and other cases, which prevented potential ambiguity and the blurring of the opposition between singular and plural (which could not be averted e.g. in short syllable *i*-stems, where the -*e* ending served as an inflectional marker for the nominative, accusative and dative sg. as well as the nominative and accusative pl.). Worth mentioning in this context is also the typological status of the Old English morphological system which can be viewed as heterogeneous (Kastovsky 1990, 262; 1994, 149), given that stem inflection, serving as the basic inflectional type, coexisted with word inflection, characterising part of the Old English nominal system. It has been assumed, accordingly, that the *a*-declension (but for a few exceptions) must have had word rather than stem based inflection and as such was morphosemantically and morphotactically more transparent (Kastovsky 1994, 147; 1997, 67).

Finally, the pattern of preservation of the archaic features of *i*-declension as attested in the analysed material, may be viewed, in a sense, as a forerunner of the tendencies present in the later stages of this exceedingly divergent development of English and Low German. While the former may be perceived as a monoparadigmatic type (Kastovsky 1995, 236) with one declensional pattern (*a*-stems) creating a template for other types,[36] the latter is characterised by poly-

---

[36] The special position of English with respect to morphological restructuring of the nominal system has been emphasised (among others) by Ramat (1981) who states explicitly: "Die Vermeidung der Zahl von Flexionsparadigmen ist also im Germ. ein allgemeines Phänomen des morphologischen Ausgleich (und ist auch anderen Sprachen des Idg. eignen) und stellt die erste Phase einer Krise des auf Flexion beruhenden

paradigmatic noun morphology where more than one declensional type turns out to be productive and none seems to have a special, privileged status.

References

Adamczyk 2008: Elżbieta Adamczyk, "The disintegration of the nominal inflection in Anglian: The case of *i*-stems", in: *Studia Anglica Posnaniensia* 44: 101-120.
Bammesberger 1990: Alfred Bammesberger, *Morphologie des urgermanischen Nomens*, Heidelberg.
Bjorvand 1995: Harald Bjorvand, "Nominale Stammbildung des Germanischen: maskuline Verbalnomina: *a*-Stämme oder *i*-Stämme? ", in: *NOWELE Supplement* 13: 1-69.
Bosworth & Toller 1898: Joseph Bosworth & T. Northcote Toller, eds. *An Anglo-Saxon Dictionary. Supplement* (1921) by T. N. Toller, Oxford.
Braune 2004: Wilhelm Braune, *Althochdeutsche Grammatik*, 15th ed., Tübingen.
Braune 1981: Wilhelm Braune, *Gotische Grammatik mit Lesestücke und Wörterverzeichnis*, 19th ed., Tübingen.
Brunner 1965: Karl Brunner, *Altenglische Grammatik. Nach der angelsächsischen Grammatik von Eduard Sievers*, 3rd ed., Tübingen.
Campbell 1959: Alistair Campbell, *Old English grammar*, Oxford.
  Cathey 2002: James E. Cathey, ed. *Hêliand. Text and commentary* (Medieval European Studies II), Morgantown.
Fulk 1992: Robert D. Fulk, *A history of Old English meter*, Philadelphia.
Gallée 1993: Johan H. Gallée, *Altsächsische Grammatik*, 3rd ed., Tübingen.
Healey 2000: Antoinette di Paolo Healey, ed. *The Dictionary of Old English Corpus in Electronic Form*, Toronto.
Hogg 1980: Richard M. Hogg, "Analogy as a source of morphological complexity", in: *Folia Linguistica Historica* 1/2: 277-284.
— 1992: Richard M. Hogg, "Phonology and morphology", in: *The Cambridge history of the English language. Vol. 1. The beginnings to 1066*, ed. Richard M. Hogg, Cambridge, 67-167.
Holthausen 1921: Ferdinand Holthausen, *Altsächsisches Elementarbuch*, Heidelberg.
Holthausen 1967: Ferdinand Holthausen, *Altsächsisches Wörterbuch*, 2nd ed., Köln.
Iverson & Salmons 2004: Gregory K. Iverson & Joseph C. Salmons, "The conundrum of Old Norse umlaut: Sound change versus crisis analogy", in: *Journal of Germanic Linguistics* 16/1: 77- 110.
Kastovsky 1990: Dieter Kastovsky, "Whatever happened to the ablaut nouns in English and why did it not happen in German?", in: *Historical Linguistics 1987. Papers from the 8th International Conference on Historical Linguistics, Lille, August 30-September 4, 1987*, (Current Issues in Linguistic Theory 66), eds. Henning Andersen & E.F.K. Koerner, Amsterdam, 253- 264.

Sprachtyps dar, der Krise die im English der Gegenwart am weitesten ihr fortgestrittenes Studium erreicht hat..." (Ramat 1981, 63; cf. also Kastovsky 1994).

— 1994: Dieter Kastovsky, "Typological differences between English and German morphology and their causes", in: *Language change and language structure: older Germanic languages in a comparative perspective*, eds. Toril Swan, Endre Mørck, Olaf Jansen Westvik, Berlin, 135-157.

— 1995: Dieter Kastovsky, "Morphological reanalysis and typology: The case of the German *r*-plural and why English did not develop it", in: *Historical linguistics: Selected papers from the Eleventh International Conference on Historical linguistics, Los Angeles, 16-20 August 1993*. (Current Issues in Linguistic Theory 124), ed. Henning Andersen, Amsterdam, 227-238.

— 1997: Dieter Kastovsky, "Morphological classification in English historical linguistics: The interplay of diachrony, synchrony and morphological theory", in: *To explain the present: Studies in the changing English language in honour of Matti Rissanen*. (Mémoires de la Société Néophilologique de Helsinki 52), eds. Terttu Nevalainen & Leena Kahlas-Tarkka, Helsinki, 63-75.

Keyser & Wayne 1985: Samuel Jay Keyser & O'Neil Wayne, "The simplification of the Old English strong nominal paradigms", in: *Papers from the 4th International Conference on English Historical Linguistics, Amsterdam, April 10–13, 1985*. (Current Issues in Linguistic Theory 41), eds. Roger Eaton, Olga Fischer, Willem F. Koopman, Frederike van der Leek, Amsterdam, 85-107.

Krahe 1969: Hans Krahe, *Germanische Sprachwissenschaft II. Formenlehre*, Berlin.

Lass 1994: Roger Lass, *Old English: A historical linguistic companion*, Cambridge.

Prokosch 1939: Eduard Prokosch, *A comparative Germanic grammar*, Baltimore.

Ramat 1981: Paolo Ramat, *Einführung in das Germanische*, Tübingen.

Ringe 2006: Donald Ringe, *A History of English: Volume I: From Proto-Indo-European to Proto-Germanic*, Oxford.

Ross 1937: Ross, Alan S. C., *Studies in the accidence of the Lindisfarne Gospels*, Leeds.

Schmidt 2004: Wilhelm Schmidt, *Geschichte der deutschen Sprache. Ein Lehrbuch für das germanistische Studium*, 9th ed., Stuttgart.

Sievers 1878: Eduard Sievers, *Hêliand*, Halle, Verlag der Buchhandlung des Waisenhauses.

Taeger 1996: Burkhard Taeger, *Genesis*, 10th ed., Tübingen.

Wright & Wright 1908: Joseph Wright & Elisabeth Wright, *Old English grammar*, London, Oxford University Press.

Wright 1957: Joseph Wright, *Grammar of the Gothic language*, Oxford.

Wurzel 1989: Wolfgang Ulrich Wurzel, *Inflectional morphology and naturalness*, Berlin.

Internet sources

Köbler 2000: Gerhard Köbler, *Altsächsisches Wörterbuch*, 3rd ed. available at: http://homepage.uibk.ac.at/~c30310/aswbhinw.html

Sievers 1878: Eduard Sievers, *Hêliand*. An electronic facsimile edition of Sievers' authoritative edition available at: http://www.wulfila.be/lib/sievers/1878/

Simpson & Weiner 1989: John A. Simpson & Edmund S. C. Weiner, eds. *Oxford English dictionary (OED)*, available at: http://www.oed.com/

HINTERGRÜNDE EINES ALTNIEDERLÄNDISCHEN TEXTES

von Arend Quak — Amsterdam

Zusammenfassung

Die fragmentarischen Wachtendonckschen Psalmen aus dem 10. Jahrhundert weisen auch innerhalb der Fragmente Lücken auf. Dazu kommt die unterschiedliche Übersetzungstechnik: manchmal gut, manchmal mangelhaft. Das deutet darauf hin, dass an der Übersetzung mehrere Personen beteiligt waren und dass der volkssprachige Text möglicherweise auf eine Gebrauchshandschrift zurückgeht, an der verschiedene Glossatoren gearbeitet haben. Der altniederländische Bearbeiter hat vielleicht den Text an manchen Stellen in seiner eigenen Sprache ergänzen müssen.

1. Einleitung

Seit 2000 wird am Institut für niederländische Lexikologie (INL) in Leiden an einem altniederländischen Wörterbuch gearbeitet. Darin soll der älteste Wortschatz des Niederländischen in weitestem Sinne festgelegt werden. Zur Zeit sind etwa 4.500 bis 5.000 Lemmata bearbeitet worden, was kein schlechtes Resultat ist, wenn man bedenkt, dass in einem Lehrbuch vom Jahre 1973 das Altniederländische überhaupt nicht existierte (van den Toorn 1973: 20). Nur der bekannte Schreibervers *Hebban olla uogala* ... (vgl. u.a. Louwen 2009) sei als altniederländischer Text da. Inzwischen verfügt man über drei größere Quellen, die mit gewissen Einschränkungen als altniederländisch gelten können: die 'Wachtendonckschen Psalmenfragmente', den 'Leidener Williram' und die 'Mittelfränkische Reimbibel'. Auf die erstgenannte Quelle wird hier noch etwas näher eingegangen.

2. Wachtendoncksche Psalmen

Es handelt sich hier bekanntlich um eine fragmentarische interlineare Übersetzung der Psalmen und Cantica, die nach dem letztbekannten Besitzer, dem Kanoniker Arnold Wachtendonck, benannt wurde. Der ursprüngliche Text, der vermutlich aus dem 10. Jahrhundert stammte, ist allerdings seit dem Ende des 16. Jahrhunderts verschollen. Vermutlich ist die mittelalterliche Handschrift, wie so viele andere Handschriften, um diese Zeit im Leimtopf oder im günstigsten Fall im Umschlag eines gebundenen Buches verschwunden.[1] Was wir besitzen, sind fragmentarische Abschriften des Originals. Es handelt sich dabei um folgende Fragmente:

1. eine Abschrift aus dem 17. Jahrhundert von Ps. 1,1-3,6, vermutlich nach einer Vorlage aus der Zeit um 1600 - somit ein Kopie einer Kopie! - (= Ms. 149, Provinciale en BUMA-Bibliotheek, Leeuwarden);
2. eine Abschrift von Ps. 53,7- 73,9, vermutlich hergestellt um 1600 im Auftrag des Humanisten Justus Lipsius (= hs. Diez C quart 90, Deutsche Staatsbibliothek, Berlin;
3. eine gedruckte Fassung von Psalm 18 in Abraham van de Myles *Lingva Belgica*, Leiden 1612;
4. eine Handschrift mit einer Wörterliste und mit Notizen von Justus Lipsius selbst (= Ms. Lips. 53, UB Leiden);
5. ein Brief von Justus Lipsius mit einer Wörterliste, die möglicherweise auf Nr. 4 zurückgeht (*Iusti Lipsii epistolarum selectarum centuria tertia ad Belgas*, Antwerpen 1602);
6. sieben Wörter aus Ps. 55 in einer jetzt verschollenen Handschrift, die sich vermutlich in irgendeiner amerikanischen Bibliothek befindet (Elias Steinmeyer & Eduard Sievers, *Die althochdeutschen Glossen*, Bd. IV, Berlin 1898, S. 685-86).

Insgesamt besitzen wir also 21 Psalmen komplett und 3 nur teilweise und weiter zwei Listen mit Wörtern aus der ganzen Handschrift, die sich allerdings zum größten Teil decken. Die Datierung der ursprünglichen Handschrift beruht auf sprachlichen Argumenten, den Bemerkungen von Lipsius und den Bemerkungen des Herausgebers der sieben Wörter aus Ps. 55, der sich übrigens nicht dessen bewusst war, dass es Wörter aus den 'Wachtendonckschen Psalmen' betraf. Das wurde erst sehr viel später entdeckt (Götz 1959).

Bei diesem altniederländischen Text handelt es sich, wie gesagt, um die interlineare Übertragung der Psalmen und Cantica. Wegen der un-

---

[1] Vgl. die Studie nach dem Schicksal der Handschrift bei Van Hal 2006.

günstigen Überlieferung weiß man nicht, ob der Text von einem Schreiber geschrieben wurd oder ob mehrere Hände am Text gearbeitet haben. Wohl scheint ziemlich sicher, dass es sich um die altniederländische Bearbeitung eines ursprünglich hochdeutschen, vermutlich mittelfränkischen, Textes handelt. Das kann man aus der Tatsache schließen, dass am Anfang des Textes sehr viele hochdeutsche Formen auftreten - z.B. *saz* 'saß', *holz* 'Holz', *fluzze* 'Fluss', *uuassere* 'Wasser', *anlucce* 'Antlitz' alle aus Ps. 1 -, aber ab Ps. 10 diese Formen seltener werden und im Berliner Fragment ein fast rein altniederländischer Text erscheint, in dem höchstens ab und zu noch eine hochdeutsche Form auftritt (Smith 1976; Quak 2005). Weiter scheinen Zusammenhänge mit anderen hoch- und niederdeutschen Psalmenübersetzungen zu bestehen, die vielleicht auch auf ein mittelfränkisches Original zurückgehen (Rooth 1924 u.a.). Über die Entstehung des Textes lässt sich somit weiter sehr wenig sagen. Man kann nur durch Vergleich mit ähnlichen Texten und unter Heranziehung der wenigen Hinweise im Text selbst etwas darüber sagen.

In einer bekannte Studie hat Stefan Sonderegger 1965 die frühen Übersetzungsmethoden im Althochdeutschen behandelt. Er weist darauf hin, dass zwischen den einzelnen überlieferten Interlinearversionen große Unterschiede bestehen und unterscheidet dabei vier Typen:

1. unvollständige Interlinearübersetzungen ohne die Absicht, einen zusammenhängenden Text zu schaffen; [2]
2. den Normalfall, wobei eine vollständige Interlinearübersetzung angefertigt wurde;
3. den Sonderfall, wobei ein gelegentlich sogar poetischer Text entsteht, mit als einzigem Beispiel im Althochdeutschen die 'Murbacher Hymnen' (ca. 800); und
4. die scheinbar interlineare Übersetzung (Sonderegger 1965: 102).

Sonderegger betont weiter, dass eine Interlinearversion als Ganzes eher ein Versuch zur Erklärung als eine echte Übertragung sei (1965: 103). Nicht ganz zu Unrecht vergleicht er ein solches Verfahren mit

---

[2] Die dabei genannten St. Pauler Lukasglosse dürften eher der Rest einer vollständigen Übertragung in die Volkssprache sein, vgl. Voetz 1985.

der Rohübersetzung einer Übersetzungsmaschine. Es gibt also einen Unterschied zwischen der formellen Übersetzung und dem Zweck der Übersetzung ("Übersetzungssinn"). In der Gruppe 1 bleibe die Identität zwischen dem lateinischen Text und dem volkssprachigen Text völlig erhalten, während man in den Gruppen 2 und 3 öfters Abweichungen vom lateinischen Text antreffen könne. Letzteres hänge mit dem Versuch zusammen, die Absichten des lateinischen Textes wiederzugeben, während in der ersten Gruppe das Verständnis der lateinischen Konstruktionen zentral stehe.

Trotz der Probleme bei der Überlieferung des Textes soll hier doch der Versuch gemacht werden, den Text der Wachtendonckschen Psalmen (WPs.)[3] genauer zu betrachten um zu sehen, ob sich in Bezug auf die Übersetzer und die Absichten des Textes und auf die Frage, zu welchem Typ der Interlinearversion die WPs. gehören, Näheres sagen lässt.

3. Charakter des Textes

Bei einer näheren Betrachtung der überlieferten Fragmente fallen zwei Dinge auf:
1. der Text ist auch innerhalb der Fragmente nicht vollständig;
2. es gibt manchmal große Unterschiede in der Art der Übersetzung.

3.1. *Lücken im Text*
In den WPs. fehlen die folgenden zwei Stellen, wo auch die Handschrift - in diesem Fall Handschrift B - das ausdrücklich erwähnt: Ps. 59,5 'potasti nos vino conpunctionis' *drencodos unsig ... bereunissi*, wo die Übersetzung von *vino* fehlt mit der Bemerkung: "deest una dictio" (Bl. 10r),[4] und Ps. 71,4 'et humiliabit calumniatorem' mit *in genitheron sal* gefolgt von einer Leerzeile, wo die Übertragung von *calumniatorem* hätte stehen sollen. Am Schluss der Leerzeile steht die Mitteilung "deest huius vocis interpretatio" (Bl. 28v). Weiter fehlen,

---

[3] Zitiert nach der Ausgabe von Quak (1981) unter Vergleich mit dem Text bei de Grauwe 1979-82.

[4] De Grauwe (1991: 91) möchte annehmen, dass ein mittelfränkisches *bit uuîne reuuon* der Vorlage als Ganzes mit *bereuunissi* wiedergegeben wurde. Das scheint im Hinblick auf die Bemerkung in der Handschrift weniger wahrscheinlich. Offenbar fehlte über dem lateinischen Wort *uino* die altniederländische Vokabel.

ohne dass dies ausdrücklich in der Handschrift vermerkt wird: *et emundabor* in Ps. 18,14, *vocem meam* in Ps. 54,18, *in (terra)* in Ps. 57,12, *te* in Ps. 55,10, *Deo* in Ps. 61,6, *pauperi* in Ps. 67,11, *(adiutor) meus* in Ps. 69,6, *(adiutorium) meum* in Ps. 70,12, *semper* in Ps. 70,14 und *tota die* in Ps. 70,24, das allerdings auch im 'Psalterium Romanum' fehlt, sodass eventuell eine Variante im lateinischen Psalmentext vorliegen könnte. Dasselbe gilt vielleicht auch für die fehlenden Possessivpronomina in den Versen 69,6 en 70,12 und das Fehlen der Konjunktion *et* in Ps. 54,22 und 54,23. Sonst fehlt noch einige Male das Hilfsverb in zusammengesetzten Zeitformen: *uuerthunt* in Ps. 62,12 (*laudabuntur*) und 72,10 (*invenientur*) und *salt* in Ps. 64,4 (*propitiaberis*). In den letzten Fällen kann eventuell eine Unsorgfältigkeit seitens des altniederländischen Bearbeiters oder des Kopisten des späten 16. Jahrhunderts vorliegen. Außer Betracht bleiben hier die Auslassungen, die Entsprechungen im 'Psalterium Gallicanum' in der Redaktion des Alkuin haben, da der lateinische Text der WPs. vermutlich zu dieser Redaktion gehörte (Quak 1973: 3-36).

Wenn man sich die Frage stellt, wie sich diese Lücken erklären lassen, liegt es nahe anzunehmen, dass dies mit der Entstehung des Textes zu tun hat. Es scheint nicht ausgeschlossen, dass die ursprüngliche Vorlage dadurch entstanden ist, dass ein lateinischer Text der Psalmen und Cantica von einem Benutzer - oder von mehreren Benutzern - hier und da mit interlinearen Glossierungen versehen wurde. Beispiele solcher Psalmenglossierungen kennen wir aus der althochdeutschen Literatur (vgl. u.a. Quak 1987) und auch die althochdeutsche 'Benediktinerregel' von etwa 800 beginnt mit einer ziemlich vollständigen interlinearen Übertragung, fängt dann an, Lücken aufzuweisen und hört schließlich ganz auf. Wenn das auch bei der Vorlage der WPs. der Fall war, würde das bedeuten, dass der Text somit zum Typ 1 von Sonderegger gehört, und auch dass sich größere oder kleinere Lücken im Text befunden haben dürften. Als der spätere Bearbeiter die Aufgabe übernahm, diesen hochdeutschen Text ins Altniederländische umzusetzen, hat er möglicherweise auf der einen Seite hochdeutsche Formen in altniederländische umgesetzt und anderseits offene Stellen in der Vorlage mit Übersetzungen in der eigenen Mundart ergänzt. Dies könnte eventuell erklären, warum altniederländische Formen in einer sonst hochdeutschen Umgebung stehen, wie etwa *foruuirpet* 'proicit' mit einem altniederländischen /p/ in Ps. 1,4, das sich dadurch deutlich von *ueruuerfon uuir* 'proiciamus' in Ps. 2,3 mit hochdeutschem /f/ unterscheidet.[5] Bisher hat man angenommen, dass der Bearbeiter nicht ganz konsequent verfuhr bei der Umsetzung der hochdeutschen Formen und ab und zu eine solche Form stehen ließ.

3.2 *Übersetzungsfähigkeit*
In einigen Fällen weicht die überlieferte altniederländischer Übersetzung vom üblichen Text der lateinischen Vulgata ab. Das kann bedeuten, dass der Übersetzer einen Fehler gemacht hat oder dass er in seiner Vorlage eine andere Variante des lateinischen Textes vorfand, als in der Vulgata steht. Es sieht nämlich danach aus, dass der lateinische Text der WPs. Abweichungen aufwies, die dem 'Psalterium Gallicanum' in der Fassung Alkuins entsprechen. Es handelt sich dabei um eine Fassung, die vor allem in Handschriften aus Nordfrankreich überliefert ist, das dem Entstehungsgebiet der eventuell mittelfränkischen Vorlage bzw. des altniederländischen Textes nahe liegt. So findet man etwa in Ps. 1,5 der Vulgata *resurgent* 'sie werden aufstehen', während der altniederländische Text *upstandunt* 'sie stehen auf' bietet, was lat. *resurgunt* entspricht, welche Variante gerade in der Fassung des Alkuin erscheint (Quak 1973: 15).

In manchen Fällen dürfte es sich um einfache Lesefehler handeln, etwa in Ps. 104,24: *et auxit populum eius vehementer* 'und er hat sein Volk stark vermehrt', wo lat. *auxit* offenbar als *anxit* gelesen wurde, das zum Verb *angere* 'in die Enge treiben, ängstigen' gehört: Hs. Ld: *kestegoda. Anxit 104*, Sch: "Kestegoda, *Anxit: an à castigando*". Die Wiedergabe mit anl. *kestigon* 'kasteien, strafen' und die Form des lateinischen Lemmas in den beiden Fragmenten deuten darauf hin. Ein Fehler findet sich vielleicht auch in Ps. 2,6, wo lat. *praeceptum eius* 'sein Gebot' im Altniederländischen mit *gebot sina* wiedergegeben wird, das im Hinblick auf die Endung des Possesivpronomens eine Mehrzahl 'seine Gebote' sein muss. Eine Variante *praecepta* scheint in den lateinischen Fassungen des Textes nicht vorzukommen.[6]

Manchmal stehen im Text jedoch auch sehr gelungene Wiedergaben lateinischer Wörter und Satzkonstruktionen. So findet sich in Ps. 54,13 der Satz *so mohti geburran* 'wenn es geschehen könnte' für lat.

---
[5] Auch die Form des Personalpronomens *wir* ist hier hochdeutsch.
[6] De Grauwe (1982: 406) nennt nur das 'Psalterium Mozarabicum'.

forsitan 'vielleicht' und in Ps. 65,20 wird die lateinische Passivkonstruktion *sicut examinatur argentum* 'wie Silber erprobt wird' mit *also man irsuokit siluer* übersetzt, also mit einer Konstruktion mit 'man' in der Volkssprache (Quak 1987). Auch hat der oder irgendein Übersetzer den Psalmenkommentar des Augustinus benutzt. Am deutlichsten ist das in Ps. 118,19 der Fall: *incola ego sum in terra,* wo lat. *incola* 'Bewohner' mit *elelendig* 'Verbannter, Fremder' übersetzt wird. Hier hat Augustinus: "*Incola,* vel *advena* vel *inquilinus sum in terra*", vgl. Quak 1973: 34.

Auf der anderen Seite finden sich manchmal sehr mangelhafte Übersetzungen, aus denen deutlich hervorgeht, dass der Übersetzer seine lateinische Vorlage kaum verstand und manchmal automatisch übersetzte, was er zu lesen glaubte. Ein für dieses Verfahren charakteristische Stelle im Text lautet auf Latein: *in terra deserta et invia et inaquosa* 'auf der verlassenen und unwegsamen und wasserlosen Erde' (Ps. 62,3). Dies wird im Altniederländischen mit *An erthon uustera in an uuega in an uuaterfollora* wiedergegeben, was buchstäblich 'auf der verlassenen Erde, auf dem Wege und auf dem Wasserreichen' bedeutet, was für den letzten Teil im Grunde also das Umgekehrte von dem ist, was im Lateinischen da steht. Der Übersetzer hat das lateinische Präfix *in-* offenbar als die Präposition *in* aufgefasst und dementsprechend übertragen. Etwas Ähnliches findet man in Ps. 15,7. Dort ist in der Stelle *qui tribuit mihi intellectum* 'der mir Verstand gegeben hat' das letzte Wort mit *anuarnunst,* buchstäblich 'in Vernunft' übersetzt. Auch hier scheint der Übersetzer das Präfix *in-* als Präposition aufgefasst zu haben.[7] Auch die Stelle in Ps. 54,24, wo in der lateinischen Stelle *in puteum interitus* 'im Brunnen des Untergangs' lat. *interîtus* 'das Verschwinden, der Untergang' mit etwas wie lat. *terri-* in *terribilis* 'schrecklich', *terror* 'Schrecken' assoziert worden scheint, denn die Übersetzung lautet: *an pute an freson* 'im Brunnen in Furcht'' In Ps. 67,8 ist die lateinische Konjunktion *cum* 'als' zweimal übersetzt worden: zunächst mit anl. *mit* 'mit' und dann mit anl. *so* 'als'. Es sieht aus, ob ein Übersetzer das lateinische Wort anfangs als die Präposition *cum* aufgefasst und dementsprechend übersetzt hat, worauf er, oder ein anderer Übersetzer, den Fehler erkannt

---

[7] Übrigens dürfte das darauf hinweisen, dass im Original die Worttrennungen undeutlich waren oder ganz fehlten.

und die richtige Form eingefügt hat, ohne die falsche Form zu streichen.[8] Allerdings besteht hier auch die Möglichkeit, dass *mit so* hier die temporale Bedeutung der lateinischen Konjunktion *cum* entspricht und sich so die abweichende Übersetzung — lat. *cum* als Konjunktion wird sonst immer mit 'so' übertragen — erklären lässt (de Grauwe 1979-82: §338). In dem Falle müsste man gerade von einer gelungenen Übersetzung sprechen.

In anderen Fällen ist ein lateinisches Wort mit einem anderen Wort verwechselt und so falsch wiedergegeben worden. So steht in Ps. 53,7 *an uuarheide thinro te spreide sia* 'zerstreue sie im Namen deiner Wahrheit" während im lateinischen Text *in veritate tua disperde illos* staat. Möglicherweise steht hier die falsche Übersetzung, weil der Bearbeiter/Übersetzer *disperge* 'zerstreue' statt *disperde* 'zerstöre' gelesen hat. In Ps. 108,11 steht: *scrutetur fenerator omnem substantiam eius* 'der Wucherer strebe nach seinem ganzen Besitz'; lat. *fenerator* wird aber mit *Iagere* 'Jäger' wiedergegeben, das zu lat. *venator* passt. Auffällig ist dabei, dass sowohl in der Handschrift L wie im Text von Lipsius' Brief ausdrücklich *fenerator* als lateinisches Lemma angegeben wird. Man kann also davon ausgehen, dass das auch in der ursprünglichen Handschrift stand. Etwas Ähnliches findet sich auch im Canticum I Reg. 2,8: *ut sedeat cum principibus et solium gloriae teneat* 'damit er sitze mit den Fürsten und den Thron der Glorie besitzen möge'. Lat. *solium* 'Thron' wurde fälschlich mit *solre* 'Dachboden, Söller' (lat. *solarium*) übersetzt, worauf auch Lipsius in seinem Brief an Schottius beiläufig hinweist: "*Solre, Solium. an Solarium*" (vgl. lat. *an* 'oder vielleicht?'). In Ps. 105,38 *et interfecta est terra sanguinibus* ist der Fehler so offensichtlich, dass Lipsius ihn auch bemerkte und in der Handschrift L verbesserte. Die Glosse lautet dort: *beuuollan/ duart. Interfecta 105*. Lipsius notierte dazu: *quid liber habuit. Infecta, qua magis huic interpretatione consonat*, wonach er im Brief an Schottius einfach die richtige Form *Infecta* als lateinisches Lemma aufnahm. Offenbar basierte Lipsius seine Meinung auf der Tatsache, dass das starke Verb *biwellan* an anderen Stellen im Text als Wiedergabe von lat. *profanare* 'entheiligen, entweihen', *contaminare* 'verderben, beflecken, entweihen', *polluere* 'verunreinigen, besudeln'

---

[8] Oder ist hier vielleicht die Rede von einer "Schulmeisterglosse", wobei die beiden Möglichkeiten der Übersetzung angegeben wurden?

und *inquinare* 'besudeln, beschmutzen' benutzt wird, während *interficere* 'verzehren, zugrunderichten' bedeutet.

4. Schlussfolgerung

Die hier und da fehlenden Stellen im überlieferten Text können darauf hindeuten, dass dieser ursprünglich nur teilweise übersetzt worden war und erst von dem Bearbeiter/den Bearbeitern ergänzt wurde. Eine Parallele dazu findet man in den altsächsischen 'Lubliner Psalmen', in der auch Wörter und Satzteile fehlen: Ps. 28,8 *condensa*, 32,14 *praeparato*, 32,15 *finxit sigillatim*, 111,5 *disponit*, 111,6 *auditione mala* und 115,3 *retribuam*. Im letzten Fall könnte es so sein, dass das Verb nicht übersetzt wurde, weil es auch in der nächsten Zeile erscheint, wo es mit *forgiuið* übertragen wird.

Die oben erwähnten Unterschiede in der Übersetzungsfertigkeit können weiter darauf hindeuten, dass am Text mehrere Übersetzer/Bearbeiter gearbeitet haben. Es lässt sich ja nicht verstehen, dass ein und derselbe Mann das eine Mal die lateinischen Wörter schlecht verstand und das andere Mal eine ausgezeichnete Wiedergabe einer lateinischen Vokabel produzierte. Man darf ihm oder ihnen auf jeden Fall dankbar dafür sein, dass sie ihre althochdeutsche Vorlage nicht ohne weiteres übernahmen, sondern diese ziemlich stark ihrer eigenen Sprache anpassten, viel stärker etwa als der/die Bearbeiter des 'Leidener Williram' um 1100 tat(en).

Der Zweck des Textes ist weniger deutlich. Man bedenke aber, dass in der *Admonitio generalis* von 789 festgelegt worden war, dass die Psalmen und die Cantica zur verpflichteten Lektüre der Geistlichkeit gehörten. Da nicht jeder Mönch das Latein gut beherrscht haben dürfte, braucht es nicht zu wundern, dass gerade aus dem 9. und 10. Jahrhundert aus dem nieder- und hochdeutschen Gebiet mindestens fünf fragmentarische interlineare Psalmenübersetzungen überliefert sind.[9] Es werden sicherlich noch weitere gegeben haben. Für das niederländische Gebiet kann man auf ein "psalterium teutonice glosatum" in der Bibliothek des Klosters Egmond hinweisen, das möglicherweise

---

[9] Neben den 'Wachtendonckschen Psalmen' sind dies die altsächsischen 'Lubliner Psalmen', das Paderborner Fragment einer weiteren altsächsischen Übersetzung, die 'Rheinfränkischen Cantica' und die 'Altalemannischen Psalmen'.

durch Egbert von Trier nach Nordholland gekommen ist (Gumbert 1997: 154).

Es gibt ziemlich viele Hinweise, dass die ursprüngliche Handschrift der WPs. aus Münsterbilzen stammt. So schreibt Lipsius am 3. September 1591 an seinen Freund Jan van Hout in Leiden, dass er die Handschrift von der Äbtissin von St. Amor bekommen habe. In den Niederlanden gab es damals nur ein Kloster, das diesen Namen trug und das war Munsterbilzen (Wijnen 1999). Die Tatsache, dass dies ein Nonnenkloster war, erklärt vielleicht das Bedürfnis nach einer interlinearen Übersetzung. Unter den Nonnen dürften die Lateinkenntnisse noch etwas weniger gut gewesen sein als unter den Mönchen. Hier in diesem Kloster konnte eine Interlinearversion also sehr nützlich sein.

Man kann sich vorstellen, dass die ursprüngliche Handschrift ein Gebrauchstext aus einem anderen Kloster war, die dort von den unterschiedlichen Benutzern schon mit einer unvollständigen Glossierung versehen worden war.[10] Diese lateinische Handschrift wurde dann in einem niederländischsprachigen Kloster - vielleicht in Munsterbilzen - kopiert. Das geschah zusammen mit dem dort vielleicht schon anwesenden volksprachigen interlinearen Wörtern, wobei der Abschreiber/die Abschreiber anfangs den hochdeutschen Text mehr oder weniger genau übernahm(en), aber allmählich eine gewisse Unabhängigkeit seiner Vorlage gegenüber gewann(en) und immer mehr die eigene Sprache benutzte(n) oder, wenn seine Vorlage Lücken enthielt, diese Lücken mit Vokabeln aus der eigenen Mundart ausfüllte(n). Dass er seine althochdeutsche Vorlage tatsächlich ins Altniederländische umgesetzt hat, geht aus einer Anzahl hyperkorrekten Formen hervor, wie etwa *uuitton* 'wissen' (Ps. 59,14) en *suottera* 'süßer' (Ps. 18,11) beide mit doppeltem <t> nach dem Vorbild von ahd. *wizzan* und *suozzira*.

Es scheint jedoch nicht ausgeschlossen, dass die Abschrift, ebenso wie die Vorlage, Lücken aufwies, die von den niederländischen Benutzer(inne)n mit mehr oder weniger Erfolg in der eigenen Sprache ergänzt wurden. Das Resultat, wie es in den Fragmenten erscheint, bil-

---

[10] Ein Hinweis dafür ist die Tatsache, dass neben dem Mittelfränkischen offenbar noch eine weitere Mundart eine wichtige Rolle spielte. Es scheinen nämlich auch altsächsische (oder altenglische?) Formen vorzukommen wie etwa *hlothu* 'Beute' in Ps. 16,12. Diese Formen erscheinen vor allem in den ersten 20 Psalmen und dürften somit aus der Vorlage stammen. Eine solche Mischung von Mittelfränkisch und Altsächsisch scheint möglich in Nordfrankreich (vgl. Blech) und in Werden an der Ruhr.

det dann eine kuriose Mischung altniederländischer, mittelfränkischer und sogar altsächsischer Formen. Für die Zusammensetzer des altniederländischen Wörterbuchs bedeutet, dass man immer wieder bei sich überlegen soll, ob man mit einer "echt" altniederländischen Form zu tun hat oder nicht.

Literatur

Blech 1997: Ulrike Blech, *Germanistische Glossenstudien zu Handschriften in französischen Bibliotheken* (Monographien zur Sprachwissenschaft 4), Heidelberg.

Grauwe 1979-82: Luc de Grauwe, *De Wachtendonckse psalmen en glossen. Een lexicologisch-woordgeografische studie met proeve van kritische leestekst en glossaria. I-II.* Gent.

Gumbert 1997: J.P. Gumbert, "De Egmondse boekenlijst", in: G. N. M. Vis (red.), *In het spoor van Egbert. Aarstbisschop Egbert van Trier, de bibliotheek en de geschiedschrijving van het klooster Egmond* (Egmondse Studiën 3), Hilversum, 151-179.

Hal 2006: Toon van Hal, "Een 'geurtje' rond de Wachtendonckse Psalmen?", in: *De Gulden Passer* jg. 84: 27-44.

Lasch 1979: Agathe Lasch, *Ausgewählte Schriften zur niederdeutschen Philologie.* Hg. v. Robert Peters und Timothy Sodmann, Neumünster.

Quak 1973: Arend Quak, *Studien zu den altmittel- und altniederfränkischen Psalmen und Glossen* (Amsterdamer Publikationen zur Sprache und Literatur 12), Amsterdam.

— 1981: Arend Quak, *Die altmittel- und altniederfränkischen Psalmen und Glossen. Nach den Handschriften und Erstdrucken neu herausgegeben.* (Amsterdamer Publikationen zur Sprache und Literatur 47), Amsterdam.

— 1983: Arend Quak, "Zur Übersetzungstechnik in den altniederfränkischen Psalmenfragmenten", in: *Ars et Ingenium. Studien zum Übersetzen. Festgabe für Frans Stoks zum 60. Geburtstag.* Amsterdam, 99-111.

— 1987: Arend Quak, "Zu den Psalmenglossen des Clm. 22201", in: *Althochdeutsch.* In Verbindung mit Herbert Kolb, Klaus Matzel, Karl Stackmann herausgegeben von Rolf Bergmann, Heinrich Tiefenbach, Lothar Voetz. Rudolf Schützeichel zum 60. Geburtstag am 20. Mai 1987 gewidmet. Heidelberg, 576-585.

— 2005: Arend Quak, "Altmittelfränkisches in den 'Wachtendonckschen Psalmen'", in: Arend Quak & Tanneke Schoonheim (red.): *Gehugdic sis samnungun thinro. Liber amicorum W. J. J. Pijnenburg*, Groningen, 277-291.

Rooth 1924: Erik Rooth, *Studien zu den altniederfränkischen und altwestfälischen Psalterversionen* (Uppsala universitets årsskrift), Uppsala.

Smith 1976: Jim Smith, "Mittel- und Niederfränkisches in den Wachtendonckschen Psalmen", in: *Niederdeutsches Wort* 16: 63-74.

Sonderegger 1965: Stefan Sonderegger, "Übersetzungsschichten im Althochdeutschen. Ein methodischer Beitrag", in: *Philologia Deutsch. Festschrift für W. Henzen.* Hg. v. W. Kohlschmidt und P. Zinsli, Bern, 101-114.

Toorn 1973: M.C. van der Toorn, Nederlandse taalkunde (AULA 499), Utrecht.
Voetz 1985: Lothar Voetz, *Die St. Pauler Lukasglossen* (Studien zum Althochdeutschen 7), Göttingen.
Wijnen 1999: Mathieu Wijnen, "Arnold Wachtendonck en de Wachtendonckse Psalmen", in: Patrick Slechten (red.) tesi samanunga. *Symposium Bilzen en de oudste bronnen van het Nederlands. Lezingen gehouden te Bilzen op 11 december 1999*, Bilzen.

Bergþór's Voice:
Orality in the Homicide Laws of the Old Icelandic *Grágás*

by Michael P. McGlynn — Wichita

Abstract

This article considers what has traditionally been called 'orality' in the oldest section of the oldest Icelandic law code, the *Grágás*, revising outdated, romantic notions of a universal, poetic, pan-Germanic origin for the *Grágás*. This article begins to describe a poetics of oral law which takes into account performance, pragmatics, syntax and a cross-cultural study of law without abandoning the philological tradition of literary studies. The most recent theories of orality break down the hard distinction between orality and literacy, revise the notion of oral formula, and challenge the distinction between verse and prose. Having redefined basic concepts such as orality and law, we conclude that the *Grágás* certainly shows a relationship to oral uses of law even as we affirm that the *Grágás* is a modern law code born of a written tradition.

1. Introduction

Can we detect traces of orality in the oldest portion of the oldest laws of Iceland? Can we hear echoes of the voices of those who spoke the law before it was written? The earliest Icelandic law known collectively as the *Grágás* survives in two manuscripts and a host of fragmentary ones. The *Kónungsbók Grágás* (or *Codex Regius*) contains a section called *Vígslóði*, or 'homicide laws'.[1] According to eleventh-century Icelandic history and modern Icelandic historiography, this section was one of the first to be written in the winter of 1117-1118, when Icelandic law was first transformed from an oral tradition into a written tradition.[2] The writing of the laws of Iceland formed part of a bureaucratization in Europe that came in with Church and Roman bureaucracy. The first laws of any kind to be written in Iceland were

---

[1] All *Kónungsbók Grágás* quotations, unless otherwise specified, are from Vilhjálmur Finsen's edition. K refers to *Kónungsbók*, the page reference refers to the pagination of Finsen's edition.

[2] *Íslendingabók*, chapter ten, pp.23-4 in *Íslendingabók*.

probably the tithe laws of 1097, which were likely written as they were promulgated. Since manuscript practices in Iceland were borrowed from England, Germany and France at this time, it is not surprising that the impulse to write in Iceland was for the purpose of recording property holdings, not unlike the *Doomsday Book* in England. It is well known that there was some collaboration between the Roman Church and secular powers as the latter consolidated power in medieval Europe. Of course secular authority in Iceland has no relations with monarchy until the *Jónsbók* was issued. The writing of law codes accompanies the establishment of ecclesial and secular authority in many of the countries of Western Europe. Charlemagne issued laws to each ethnicity he conquered: Frisians, Saxons, Bavarians, etc. The Visigothic monarchy in Spain issued a massive code of laws which is at once a document of the monarchy and of the Church.

That the first law to be written in Iceland was personal injury law is not surprising in light of the history of legal codification. Personal injury law is one of the prime constituents of ancient law codes from Hammurabi onward. In European legal history, *Lex Frisionum, Lex Saxonum, Lex Salica, Codex Euricanus* and other first codifications of ethnic laws include injury tables.

To study the history of the *Grágás* we must first look internally--at language and content. For example, some laws, such as those regulating the *Alþingi*, clearly belong to a later phase of Icelandic law; laws on slavery to an earlier (oral) phase. The *Grágás* offers plenty of evidence of laws from the twelfth century and less direct evidence from earlier centuries.

According to Ári Fróði, author of the *Íslendingabók*, the last lawspeaker of the oral period was made to recite the law to scribes at the farm of Hafliði Másson:

> Et fyrsta sumar, es Bergþórr sagði lög upp, vas nýmæli þat gört, at lög ór skyldi skrifa á bók at Halfliða Mássonar of vetrinn eptir at sögu ok umbráði þeira Bergþórs ok annarra spakra manna, þeira es til þess váru teknir. Skyldu þeir görva nýmæli þau öll í lögum, es þeim litisk þau betri en en fornu lög. Skyldi þau segja upp et næstu sumar eptir í lögréttu ok þau öll halda, es en meiri hlutr manna mælti þá eigi gegn. En þat varð at framfara, at þá vas skrifaðr Vígslóði ok margt annat í lögum ok sagt upp í

lögréttu af kennimönnum of sumarit eptir. (23-4)
("And the first summer during which Bergthor recited the law [as lawspeaker] a new law was enacted, namely, that our law should be written as a book at Halfliði Másson's the following winter, according to the recitation and counsel of Bergthor and other experts assigned to this task. They were to make new laws out of the law wherever they thought they could improve the old law. These laws would be recited the following summer at the law council. Those accepted by the majority would be enacted. And so it happened that the homicide laws were written and much else in the law. These were recited by clerics in the law council the following summer").

What happened that winter or whenever this rich body of oral law was first set to parchment is the only way to explain what survives as the *Kónungsbók Grágás*. The operative phrases *Skyldu þeir görva nýmæli þau öll í lögum* ("They were to make new laws out of the old laws"), *es þeim litisk þau betri en en fornu lög* ("whenever it seemed to them that they could improve the old law") and *sagt upp í lögréttu af kennimönnum* ("recited in the law council by clerics") indicate clearly that the text was transformed. The great Icelandic *Grágás* scholar Ólafur Lárusson held this to be the precise moment when the *Grágás* became a literary text. It was this "law commission which revised the law".[3] It could be this very moment when whatever features made Icelandic law coherent as an oral text were traded for the features that make the *Grágás* coherent as a literate text. There are still oral features discernible in the *Kónungsbók Grágás*, which become visible if we move out of old distinctions and definitions. Redefinition of basic concepts and the discernment of oral features is the task I undertake here.[4]

---

[3] Lárusson 88.

[4] The choice of the *Kónungsbók* requires a methodological discussion which I am hesitant to undertake in this essay. Much has been written on the differences between the *Kónungsbók* and the *Staðarhólsbók Grágás*. They have been assumed to be part of a coherent corpus of laws, which have combined into a single edition of the *Grágás* (*Grágás: Lagsafn Íslenska Þjóðveldsins*), though now it is generally assumed among legal historians that these two exemplars were private collections of the law which may reflect idiosyncratic views of actual legal practice. The extant *Grágás* manuscripts may contain laws that were outdated already by the first writing of the *Grágás* in 1117, which raises the question of why anyone was writing outdated laws,

2. The Concept of Oral Law

According to Icelandic historiography, Icelandic law began when Ulfljótr brought the *Gulaþingslög* from Norway.[5] We know from studying other cultures that it is unlikely that the development of law was so simple. It is more likely that certain customary practices were brought by each ethnic group which emigrated to Iceland and that these customary practices might have had some relationship to legal texts. However, it is not unreasonable to take the *Gulaþingslög*, still preserved in a later, thirteenth-century reflex, as one of the ingredients in what eventually became the *Grágás*. In other words, some kind of Norwegian oral law was brought to Iceland in the mind of one of its settlers. The question of what sort of oral law this was has not been and cannot be answered on the basis of extant sources. Searching for sources through comparisons with other, contemporaneous legal traditions risk comparative fallacies; comparisons with later Scandinavian laws risk other fallacies, such as falsely-imposed teleologies or simply unfounded speculation about what oral law 'must' look like (or sound like). One such teleology informing the historiography of the *Grágás* is the debate about Icelandic texts in general, which centers around arguments whether Icelandic sagas are autochthonous insular texts of the middle ages or whether they belong to an older Scandinavian tradition (for a summary see Mitchell, 2001, 169-170). Though this scholarly debate has been superseded by other perspectives, some of the written history of the *Grágás* falls within the Freeprose-Bookprose debate, sometimes assuming the *Grágás* to be a unique Icelandic cultural form. *Comparanda* are useful, but only if we refrain from positing genetic relationships or direct lines of influence where there is no evidence for genetic relationships. Useful *comparanda* can be found in ethnographic studies of modern oral texts which naturally say nothing directly about the *Grágás*, but do guide us in imagining what is humanly possible.

---

namely the extant copies of the *Grágás*, at all. The reason I restrict myself in this essay to the *Kónungsbók Grágás* is that the particularities of each manuscript are sufficiently important to merit such a restricted study. Generalizing about homicide laws assumes that there was a uniform legal culture and practice that can be traced in extant manuscripts.

[5] See chapter two of the *Íslendingabók*.

For the *Grágás* we have mostly literary evidence, but, as with so many of the most interesting issues of literary scholarship, the closed system of literary hypothesis and literary evidence might not answer the question about the orality and performance of the *Grágás*. Outside evidence can shed light on the *Grágás*. We may make an ethnographic reading of the *Grágás* to attempt a poetics of oral law. To begin, we may assume that the speaking of the law is a performance. The nature of the performance (recitation) of law can also be considered in light of pragmatics. The recitation of the law required a special kind of pragmatic competence: law in action depends essentially on what Roman Jakobson termed the conative function of language, or the attempt to elicit some behavior from the addressee. The recitation of law at the *Alþingi* would be of a different sort since the purpose was a kind of display and confirmation of the authority of law. What was the nature of this performance? Would the lawspeaker explicate each point? The notion that the *Grágás* represents indexical information, memory supports for something never written in the extant manuscripts, is supported by Gunnar Karlsson (more below).

We do not necessarily find definitive answers in the autochthonous sense of poetic performance. Stephen Mitchell describes the association of poetry with mead and hospitality (2001, 181) in which poetry is a kind of regurgitation (177). Lawspeaking is figured as a more sober activity in the Icelandic literary and historical traditions, but there is a relationship between poetry and law in that both activities require similar mental skills. We have several instances of young men learning the law through fosterage, including the famous Njál (*Njáls saga* 27). The story surrounding Gunnlaug Ormstunga's learning of the law provides more cultural information about tenth-century oral law. Gunnlaug learns the law from Þorstein (*nam lögspeki af Þorsteini*), who has taken in the runaway (*Gunnlaugs saga ormstungu* 4). Gunnlaug apparently tries to trick his mentor into betrothing his daughter, but Þorstein issues a caveat dissolving the validity of the betrothal procedure. Gunnlaug is adept at law, poetry and fighting because he is bold and clever. Njál was likewise known for his great mental capacity, and his actions indicate courage and boldness. It seems reasonable to assume that the kind of facility to form a "mental text" (Honko's term, more below) that made Gunnlaug a good poet is not unlike skill in making mental texts that made him a good practitioner of law.

Their respective narrators show Gunnlaug and Njál to be quick-witted and able to apply their knowledge to situations as they arose. As we shall see, the latest field work in oral theory and legal anthropology support the idea that early Icelandic law was not a memorized text.[6] 'Law' in medieval Iceland does not correspond exactly to a modern, Western concept of statutory law (see Bourdieu, McGlynn, 2008, and Wormald). As William Ian Miller points out, there was no state enforcement mechanism and many rules were not absolute (1990, 228). Medieval Icelandic law codified customary behavior (1990, 229). Saga narrative likely provided illustrations of the working of the law, and details about wounds and other legal damages were part of the stored memory of the workings of law.[7] The law itself was no more a fixed verbalization than is an oral epic until it is codified as writing. Could the recitation of the law have been as unique as the varying performances of a given epic by the same singer? Could the recitation of the law have been as unique to each speaker as is the repertoire of each singer?

As we imagine what was codified in the winter of 1117, we must first clarify our notion of orality. The notion of orality as a polar opposite of literacy has been challenged and nuanced. Mark Amodio rightly points out the orality and literacy as exclusive states are theoretical constructs not found in the real world (2004, 4, 93); Amodio also argues for a persistence of oral poetics as a kind of stylistic database for poets who can thus engage the deep, affective associations for an audience that no longer really understands the oral system as such (2004, 130, 137). Lauri Honko and others also write about the existence of the "epic register" in written texts (Honko, 2000b, 19). The *Grágás* possesses "anterior speech" (Honko's term, see 2000b, 7), which means that the scribes have internalized something of the oral register. We might go further, viewing orality and literacy as complementary ways of preserving and using a living knowledge, which seems to be the case with the *Grágás*. Honko's notion of a "mental text" provides us a more nuanced sense of oral law as it existed in the mind of Ulfljótr. Honko defines mental text as that which precedes the performance of an oral text, as "an organized collection of relevant con-

---

[6] Private conversation with Professor Gísli Sigurðsson, July 2005.
[7] Private conversation with Professor Gísli Sigurðsson, July 2005.

scious and unconscious material present in the singer's mind" consisting of textual elements and generic rules for reproduction (2000b, 4). According to Honko, mental texts are not fixed verbalizations but comprise mental images and units of meaning (5). By "image", Honko means something that can give rise to many fixed verbalizations (5). What would be the mental image for legal dispositions?

As each generation of scholars updates previous work, Honko revises Foley's notion of formula and type-scene with the notion of 'multiforms', or "repeatable, artistic descriptions and expressions that are constitutive for the oral epic and function as its generic markers" (20004, 9). To apply the concept of multiform to law, we must substitute some concept for "artistic". Whereas nineteenth- and twentieth-century notions of law might view early law as a matter of formal accuracy, pragmatic competence is more likely the 'artistry' of early law. Honko's notion of multiforms is meant as a replacement of the notion of oral formulae. Rather than knitting together fixed verbalizations, the singer responds to a given context. Storyline and performance strategy will influence the creation of multiforms. This notion is useful for the recitation or performance of law, especially because we know from the *Grágás* that the performance time was up to six weeks spread over three years (K 116, p.209), and we have no evidence to make any assumption about performance strategy. The assumption that the performance mode was linear monovoiced 'narration' in a single register might seem logical to moderns only because it is consonant with our experience of 'lawspeaking' (court).

We find a complementary model of orality in Lars Lönnroth's 1980 "model for saga communication in thirteenth-century Iceland," in which the following nine components interact in complex ways to produce saga as they are recorded in extant manuscripts: oral performance 1, traditional narrative grammar, formulaic oral *þættir*, literary patterns, saga writer, saga text, oral performance 2 (reading aloud), and aristocratic sponsor plus audience. Some of these components could be said to participate in the production of the *Kónunksbók Grágás*. Given that the law was read at the *Alþing*, what Lönnroth calls "oral performance 2" is especially interesting for our attempted description of the oral features of the *Grágás*, which we are not taking to be an uncomplicated picture of the past, or of a pristine oral culture. We would also have to add features to Lönnroth's saga model, for law will intersect with international culture in ways that Icelandic or Scandinavian narrative does not.

To describe a poetics of oral law, not only our concept of orality but our concept of law must be expanded per cross-cultural study of empirical data on language and law. There are other traditions of the recitation of law. One of the most interesting is Albania's *Kanuni i Lekë Dukagjinit*, a corpus of oral law that circulated from the fifteenth century until 1913, when it was written by a the Franciscan priest Gjeçov (Hasluck, 13). The fifteenth-century Albanian prince Lek Dukagjinit learned and codified the customary law of his region and issued his version at a General Assembly, the traditional forum for making changes to the customary law (Hasluck, 148, Tarifa, 4). The repository before and after Lek Dukagjinit was the memory of the elders. The corpus of law was not preserved without variation, but varied from village to village and changed over time (Kastrati, 124). Legal historians have for the most part assumed, with foundational English legal historian Henry Sumner Maine, "It is impossible to suppose that the customs of any race or tribe remained unaltered during the whole of the long — in some cases immense —interval between their declaration ... and writing" (1986, 20). The connection between narrative and law has been posited in Albania as we are positing the connection between the sagas and the *Grágás*. According to Fatos Tarifa, citing others, epic served as a repository for, among other things, legal norms and institutions (2008, 6). In some ways, the connection between epic and law should not be surprising. We would hardly suppose language, for example, to exist without a community of speakers and a narrative tradition. They are interdependent. They are aspects or registers of community discourse.

As we search for orality in the *Kóngungsbók Grágás*, the *Kanuni* provides us a portrait of the preservation of oral law. The known oral circulation of this body of law in Albania provides one way in which oral law is preserved. In her portrait of oral law in Albania, Margaret Hasluck shows that customary law continued to change and evolve as it survived as the knowledge of the elders and other officials who acted as advocates, judges, and law-givers (1954, 133). Their knowledge was activated by the arising needs of the community. Insofar as they remembered more than others, no one could correct their recall. Even so, strict rules bound litigants and attendees of general assemblies from interrupting their dictations (150). In the *Grágás*, a similar rule holds for the council of legal experts which the lawspeaker can call if his knowledge falters (K 116, p.209). Presumably, the Icelandic lawspeaker would be at his weakest and most susceptible to influence and corruption during his open admission of ignorance and lack of authority.

The key to understanding the nature of the orality of the *Grágás* is in this clause about the lawspeaker not having knowledge as complete as other men. The fact that the lawspeaker sometimes had to bolster his understanding or memory with the help of other legal experts shows that the *Grágás* corresponds to a stage where oral law was something understood, not something memorized. Law is an occasional social form, even if it might eventually become a monument (a moralizing, idealizing code intended for a kind of social deduction rather than induction). Oral law in Albania was stored as knowledge in the minds of the elders. The *Grágás* clause does not require accuracy of the lawspeaker but thoroughness. The text stipulates that the lawspeaker is to recite the law so completely (*sva gerla*) that no one knows the law so completely (*at engi vite eina miclogi ger*). The extent of the lawspeaker's knowledge is a relative value. There is no absolute original. Reciting the law is interactive, provoking a response from any audience who might know more. Thus, as a performance, lawspeaking differs radically from modern sense of performance, in which performers stand aloof from the audience, as if in another discursive world.

The verb used for lawspeaking, *segja upp*, implies a kind of exhausting of the theme. The semantic field of Icelandic *upp* overlaps in many ways with Modern English 'up', as in 'eat it all up.' In any job, more experienced staff can offer more exhaustive knowledge, but this knowledge is never versified or memorized. Law is a knowledge acquired primarily through experience and secondarily through being clever enough to deploy and use law. In this context we might think of law as 'social strategy'. Lawspeaking, which was not the ordinary use of 'social strategy', might have been more like a discussion than a lyric performance, which of course is the *Deutsche Rechtsschule* notion of lawspeaking. Indeed, what alliteration and other features associated with the poetics of lyric that can be found in the *Grágás* more likely date from late Latin influences. (See McGlynn, 2009, for bibliography on this topic).

Like Gunnlaug the Serpent-Tongued, the famous Albanian lawgiver was also known for his cleverness (Hasluck, 15). The artistry of singer of tales corresponds to the cleverness of law-reciters. This cleverness would naturally be a species of practical intelligence, for lawspeakers were drawn from the ranks of men learned in law, and men learned in law were adepts at using the law. Knowledge of some kind of mental text was a prerequisite for deploying law in set circumstances to achieve specific aims, whether that was keeping the peace, beating an opponent, etc. Not only the exploits of Njál and other legal experts of the Icelandic literary tradition but also the practice of law in modern times as 'beating the system' make it clear that law was a living knowledge whose application varied according to the man applying it and the purpose of the application. The ethnographic record supports this view of men learned in law (see Hasluck's portrait of Albanian canon elders and *voivode*, or legal experts, 130-138, 139).

To understand the *Grágás*, moderns should probably resist our notion of law as an objective, externalized body of knowledge and view it rather as a living, potential body of knowledge that took shape as need arose, in response to context. This is what Honko and other theorists call performative context and what oral historians called 'shared authority', or a merging of the subject and object (Shuman 2003, 130-131). For the *Grágás*, this would be a merging of the litigant and lawspeaker, of custom and immediate need, of speaker and oral text.

3. Preservation and Performance

Perhaps one promising line of future investigation is law's intertextual connections with stories. Oral law was preserved in part in illustrative stories, constituting a kind of oral case law, whether these cases were real or hypothetical. This might have been one of the functions of the *Íslendingasögur*, especially the *þáttr*, or smaller prose narratives. The argument could be extended further to medieval European epic in general. Texts such as *Þorsteins þáttr stangarhöggs* or *Ölkofra þáttr* are famous for the legal knots they propose to solve; legal actions constitute the narrative. Havelock's dated dictum, "a language of action rather than of reflection is a pre-requisite for oral memorization" (1986, 76) might be tenable insofar as a non-marked language could be tied to narrative. It is doubtful that oral law was memorized as such. Helgi Kjartansson came to the conclusion that no evidence exists that the lawspeaker ever recited the law in its entirety before it was written (10).

An oral law would have to have self-preservation encoded into itself or in its community of users. For as much as his theories have proven too simple or have been superseded for other reasons, Walter Ong rightly points out that narrative might have served the purpose of preserving information, that "primary oral culture is little concerned with preserving knowledge of skills as an abstract, self-sufficient corpus" (1988, 43, 137). Models for oral law were based by Germanists on literature, on alliterative poetry. There are better discursive models for oral law. The same limited view is common among literary scholars in general. Rather than thinking of law as text, perhaps we might do better to think of law as an activity. Fencing, like law, was a practical body of knowledge. There survive manuscripts from a German fencing school. In the martial arts of Asia and Europe, knowledge was sometimes encoded in verse. The late medieval fencing master Liechtenauer encoded his practical knowledge in verses, which a later disciple copied and glossed.[8] Both the verses and the glosses are useless without some knowledge of fencing. In his 'muscle memory' (his kinesthetic knowledge), a human being preserved the information about fencing; the verses served not as storage but rather as 'search engine,' or organizing principle. The verses served more as indices than as containers of knowledge. The difference, in other words, between the *Rechtschule*'s idea of the *Grágás* or Havelock's vision of "authority in primary orality" and what is here suggested is that 'storage language,' in whatever form, would only be an index to the fuller understanding of law.

Thus we move away from the idea of a fixed form of law. As Honko writes of epic, "Oral performance cannot be captured in letters and words" (Honko 2000a, vii). Honko writes that scholars were mistaken in cobbling together "composite texts" from different versions (vii). Her notion that there is no totalized version has very interesting implications for the notion of an oral law: "The whole epic is available only as non-transferrable mental texts in the minds of individual singers"

---

[8]See Tobler.

(viii). This is also apparently the case with the *Grágás*. The lawspeaker was charged with having the most complete mental text, but it was not always the case that the lawspeaker knew more than others, which suggests a lack of an original, totalized text existing in memory or between memories in some kind of Platonic realm of idealized forms. The *Kónungsbók Grágás* is not the text that was spoken before 1117 because a performed text is a situation. Scholars attempting to encode performances of oral epics as writing create extended texts, verbal texts with notations that record paralinguistic expressions such as gesture, pitch, stop, intonation. Even so, this written performance does not totalize the law, for "any performance is a compromise" (Honko 2000b, 13).

4. Not a Memorized Text, Not a Prose Text

According to Dell Hymes, who has elaborated ethnographies of speaking and communication, texts such as the *Grágás* might have lines, which is to say that it has patterning, or intrinsic form. As with the distinction between orality and literacy, so, too, must verse and prose be redefined, especially in relation to practice and performance. The *Grágás* has patterning, and we must search beyond metrical verse patterns, which Hymes calls "overdetermined" (1998, 478). Indeed, the notion that quotidian speech is prose betrays a post-Gutenberg prejudice. That the *Kónungsbók Grágás* is arranged in titles has to do with the manuscript practice of medieval Europe. We need not assume that the law was spoken exactly as written. That which was written when writing was an expensive technology was not necessarily the most important information, which was already memorized. Writing as account keeping testifies to a special relationship of writing and non-memorized texts. (The earliest cuneiform tablets from Mesopotamia were accounts and ledgers). Perhaps the *Kónungsbók Grágás* was a kind of ledger, reference notes for the lawspeaker, who knew stories or perhaps even aphorisms to illustrate the law. Hymes' fascinating hypothesis (though not a major point in his article) that most narratives have some kind of verse and that this form might be acquired through repetition (495) suggests that performance itself induces rhyme, not the opposite. Verse is rehearsed language; rehearsal and repetition allow for the speaker/expert to draw out main points by arranging syntagms in a meaningful way. Lyric poets have always struggled with lines. Ritual contexts for law would be a natural place for verse to develop. But that does not mean that these verses are poetry. Ethnographers usually make use of intonation and other dynamics of voice from live performances or sound recordings to determine the nature of the basic unit of an oral text. Determining this pattern in the written text is possible according to Hymes (478). Hymes points up equivalence as a unit-marker. In traditional prosody, equivalence corresponds to parallelism, including repetition of any kind such as rhyme, anaphora, etc. The *Grágás* certainly has this kind of intrinsic structuring: *það er mælt*, for example, what Hymes calls "quotative element" (478). Hymes points out that when twentieth-century folklorists and ethnographers transcribed oral texts, they did not record all repetitions, and they assumed that they were transcribing prose (479). Could the early *Grágás* transcribers have done the same thing, recording only summary information as a kind of receipt, suppressing repetition, rhyme, personalization, etc.?

Having concluded that the *Grágás* was not a memorized text, it is still valid to ask whether the extant manuscript text offers any clues about whether the language was marked in any way to aid memory or whether it still bears markings of performance. Even as a written document, it is a kind performance, or particular instantiation of a potential text made in response to certain environmental conditions. We have seen Hymes' suggestion about patterns existing in texts recorded in writing as if they were prose. Could there have been certain key phrases and sentences that experienced legal officials could expand and explicate with examples, lists and definitions? This might be the case of phrases like *heilundar sár, holundar sár, mergundar sár*. This indexical phrase, if memorized, could prompt the lawspeaker to define each of the terms of the list. This is the way it is presented in the *Kónungsbók Grágás* (K 86, p.145). Presumably, the phrase *heilundar sár, holundar sár, mergundar sár* would be easy to remember, since it consists of three syllables *–undar sár* repeated twice, tacked onto the monosyllabic series *heil-*, *hol-*, and *merg-*. The assumption that the lawspeaker actually memorized the entirety of the law has been questioned before the present article.⁹ Also questioned is the idea that the only manner of memorizing long portions of text was by making speech rhythmical or poetry.¹⁰

Either way, the *Grágás* is an aural text — a written document used in conjunction with oral delivery. The audience generally experienced law in Iceland during the Free States period through exclusively oral media, whereas those who actually preserved, selected and edited what is left of this period of Icelandic law would have experienced the law both orally (listening to lawspeakers) and as a written text. Over one hundred years had passed between the first writing of the law and the writing of the copy we have, so it would seem that the text had long been free from the need for memorization, yet the office of the lawspeaker continued to exist until 1271, when the king of Norway abolished the office by sending the Icelanders a new book of law and, in effect, a new legal system.

5. The Manuscript [11]

The *Kónungsbók Grágás Vígslóði* contains twenty-two titles spread over nine folios (corresponding to the manuscript page numbers 59-75) written in one, thirteenth-century hand. Titles are marked with a colored capital which hangs in the margin of the page. Subtopics within the title are marked by a smaller capital hanging the margin of the

---

⁹ Helgi Skúli Kjartansson 5. Gísli Sigurðsson reconsiders the arrival of literacy in *The Medieval Icelandic Saga and Oral Tradition: A Discourse on Method.* See chapter one for a presenation of the arrival of literacy as a "power struggle." On page 79, Sigurðsson writes that evidence in the *Grágás* "suggests that the lawspeaker's oral ruling was taken to complement the existing written version of the law [in the twelfth century]."

¹⁰ In his often-cited book *The Muse Learns to Write,* Havelock writes that poetry was the "solution" to the problem of the need to memorize large amounts of language. If we assume this is true universally, however, we are stuck with the notion of a Germanic lawspeaker essentially "singing" a poetic legal text consisting of alliterative half-lines separated by a caesura and held together by three lifts. Of course, there is no evidence for any of this.

¹¹ See the 1932 facsimile and the introduction to it by Páll Eggert Ólasson.. There is general agreement about the rough date of 1250 for the *Kónungsbók Grágás.* When I discuss the *Vígslóði* I include title 112, which some editors do not include in the *Vígslóði.*

page. From this we can see that the law known as the *Grágás*, whatever else it was, was organized and conceived as a law book. What bears further consideration and what is the topic at hand is the extent to which its existence as a book allowed for oral features to exist or reflected patterning of oral performance.

The *Vígslóði* and the *Kónungsbók* seem to have the textual, literate qualities of being both additive and what Ong calls "conceptual" and "categorical" (as opposed to "operational" and "situational") (1988, 49-51). The *Vígslóði* seems additive in that it seems that scribes added on new bits of information about the law as they were going. Oliver offers a similar notion when she writes that the Laws of Æthelberht of Kent are collected by accretion and change (2002, 57). The *Grágás* is categorical insofar as the material is organized in subordinating, schematic fashion. If we focus on the pragmatalinguistic context of the winter of 1117, it would be natural to assume a scene in which the copyists ask Bergþór, who knew more law than anyone else, "What comes next?" or "What else do you know about this topic?" If this were the case, then it is relatively easy to see how what Ólasson calls "the law commission" completely transformed an oral law into a written law. By subjecting a different ordering principle (that of the scribe) upon Bergþór's materials, they would have altered the nature of the law. The accuracy of the law would have also been changed. The office of the lawspeaker must have been instituted partly in order to insure the preservation of the law. Writing does this, but it also introduces the notion of accuracy. Public recitation would have given other legal experts a chance to opine about the law and add to or check the contents of the lawspeaker's memory. Perhaps this was the point of the recitation of the law: to allow everyone to prompt the lawspeaker's memory or to draw out the knowledge by means of question and answer. The answers could have taken the form of definitions, lists of examples, or brief narratives.

The *Vígslóði* is not an oral text, even by outdated, overstated standards of orality, such as Ong's notion that oral expression is situational and not abstract (1988, 49). In the *Vígslóði*, terms are routinely defined, such as *þingför* (eligible for assembly attendance), *morð* (murder), or *lögfostr* (foster parent). Roman law often presents definitions in its titles, whereas the earliest English law, usually taken to be less influenced by Roman law than other vernacular medieval law codes, does not. The most common sentence pattern in Æthelberht's laws follow this pattern: If a man slays a freeman, he shall pay fifty shillings to the king.... (6: *Gif man fringe mannan ofsleahþ, cyninge L scill'*....) (Attenborough, 4). In Hlothere's laws, Rothair's laws, *Lex Saxonum* and other early medieval law codes, similar syntactical patterns without definitions of terms predominate. (We shall look at syntax more closely in the next section).

The *Grágás* is formulaic if we define formulae as linguistic resources that limit the speaker's options in response to the pressure of performing (Kuiper, 296). There is indeed a kind of formulaic quality in the *Grágás*, which is evident in that most of the *Vígslóði* section can be analyzed as one of six sentence types, which, far from being artistic oral formulae or the prosody of lyric, does reduce the burden of the lawspeakers' linguistic choices to a manageable set of choices, and we can imagine him droning on, "It is said a ... if a man a..., it is said b... if a man b." This formulaic style is embedded, however, in definitions and other indicators of the presence of writing.

6. Sentence Types and Syntax in the *Vígslóði*

Syntax is one way to enquire after the oral history of the *Grágás*. Some scholars believe that the injury table, or price-list, is the most basic form of law.[12] That the *Vígslóði* would be one of the first parts of the law to be written accords with the generally accepted notion of primitive law as a more evolved alternative to violent self-redress.[13] It is more likely that the price-list is the most primitive form of written law. As Oliver points out in *The Beginnings of Old English Law*, we do not necessarily write what is of primary importance (2002, 101). The price-list might have been written because it was precisely that portion of law which was least memorable and, in a way, the least substantial. Writing very likely changed the law and even the price-list. In an oral culture, would it be surprising if the table of values for

---

[12] William Ian Miller "Eye for an Eye," public lecture at the University of Iceland, Reykjavík, Iceland, Tuesday, May 23, 2006. This assertion is part of Dr. Miller's thesis that law as expressed in the *lex talionis* is essentially an economic exchange and not a punitive system (see the book of the same name: *Eye for an Eye*).

[13] The *Kónungsbók Grágás* price-list itself, the *Baugatal*, has been called the oldest section of the *Grágás*: see, for example Helgi Skúli Kjartansson 4.

injury compensation were more symbolic and less detailed, i.e. something to the effect that the king's compensation be double the nobleman's, etc.? The closest thing to a price-list in the *Grágás* is the *Kónungsbók Baugatal*, which opens with a simple statement that there are four degrees of personal compensation and then a list of who pays and receives each degree (K 113). This is the sort of information we might expect to find in a primary oral culture. Even though much has been made of our modern misconceptions of memory and memorization,[14] we can be sure that the kind of asymmetrical, overwhelmingly detailed lists that are characteristic of our written documents and even some medieval documents would not be found in an oral culture.

It is not an uncommon procedure for scholars to try to date the earliest English law by syntactical or linguistic analysis. When analyzing Æthelberht's laws, Patrick Wormald repeats a common assumption which must be considered carefully before being applied to the *Grágás*, namely that simple syntax is an index of the antiquity of a law code (Wormald 1996, 25) If homicide laws belong to the most basic kind of law and one of the first written in Iceland, what syntactical shape would oral law take?[15] Would it be simple wergild lists in the style of early Anglo-Saxon, Saxon, Lombard and other laws (If a man does x, then he shall pay y)? Though injury tables, as part of rules of dispute settlement, logically characterize the first impulses of written law in many traditions, 'primitive' wergild lists nowhere characterize the *Kónungsbók Grágás*, despite the *Baugatal*, which could be translated as 'wergild list' or even 'injuries price-list'.[16] The *Baugatal* resembles the *Vígslóði* in its syntax, which cannot be called primitive, and which shows demonstrable evidence of literate culture. The syntax of the *Vígslóði* provides some information about what sort of text the *Grágás* is.

The syntax is neither highly literate nor highly oral. It is the product

---

[14] See, for example Carruthers.

[15] Church laws, in particular the tithe laws, were probably the first laws written in Iceland. See Patricia Pires Boulhosa, 45-86, for a general and up-to-date discussion early Icelandic law and of the ideological suppositions that motivate widely-held assumptions about early Icelandic legal history.

[16] Cleasby explains in his entry for *baugr* that snippets from gold spun into a spiral was used for payments in general and that the word came to mean, in the proper context, wergild.

of both orality and literacy. Much of the *Vígslóði* is built of coordinated clauses (parataxis), using the conjunction 'og' in a wide semantic field. There are also instances of subordination (hypotaxis) and other more literate ways of organizing the legal material. It is right to resist overly simplified analyses. Writing about Old English poetry, Donoghue and Mitchell argue that "the authors and original audience of OE poems very likely perceived more of an equivalence between coordinate and subordinate clauses than we do" (1992, 168). The authors rightly note that grammatical categories created for Latin (or any language) when applied to OE (or any other language) must be modified (163). The authors are working within the OE poetic tradition, clarifying literary and linguistic uses of grammatical terms. For the present analysis of the *Grágás*, we may note that the absence of the perception of subordination among OE writers and audiences supports the notion that modern literary texts (texts composed under the notion of writing) can be noted as such due to the presence of parataxis.

There are six recurrent sentence types in the *Vígslóði*, after which sentences in the section can be characterized: hypotheticals, stipulations, lists, definitions, legal formulae, and procedural instructions.

	Sentence Structure	Function	Syntax
1	*ef maðr*	hypothesizes a problem	hypotaxis with conjunction
2	*það er mælt / það er rétt*	stipulates; positive law	hypotaxis
3	lists	enumerates aspects of a thing	parataxis
4	definitions	positive law	simple finite sentence
5	legal formulae	procedural law	often imperative
6	*maðr skal*	procedural instructions or positive law	imperative

Table 1: Six Sentence Types in *Kónungsbók Vígslóði*

Two of these usually involve hypotaxis and the others are finite sentences without hypotaxis. We can neither say that the syntax of the *Grágás* is that of a primitive stage of writing nor can we say that it is anything like a transcript of oral law. The sentences beginning with *ef maðr* are closest to what appears to be the primitive character of ancient law codes that are chiefly price lists, if we can generalize the character of *Lex Salica*, Æþelstan's laws, and other early Germanic law codes as being primitive. The oral marker *það er mælt* is common in the *Vígslóði*, though we cannot say that this phrase is not an artificially archaizing formula. Would Bergþór or Úlfljótr have said this phrase as a way of referring to the oral tradition which they were reciting and as a way of legitimizing their memory to their audience? Even if this were so, even if *það er mælt* is a kind of formulaic expression of oral law, there is no guarantee that sentences in the *Vígslóði* that begin with this tag proceed or date from oral law. It could be the legal equivalent of 'epic register.'

Það er rétt could easily be a calque on the Latin *ius est*, i.e. a marker for literacy and literate influence among the *Grágás* (Hauksson and Óskarsson 1994, 232). Another apparently oral feature of syntax in the *Vígslóði* is that many sentences in the *Vígslóði* are long strings of finite clauses strung together paratactically (with *og*). As mentioned, it is generally believed that parataxis indicates some degree of orality and hypotaxis is more typical of literacy. Regarding Icelandic, Haraldur Matthíasson opens his study of syntax thus: "Menn vita þannig, að undirskipunn (hypotaxis) er mjög gömul" ("It is known that hypotaxis is very old") (1959, 5). He builds his book-length argument on the notion that compound sentences grew from two related but unconnected finite sentences, that parataxis precedes hypotaxis. At least since the generation of oral theorists that included Eric Havelock, coordination, 'parataxis,' was part of the theory of how language was preserved orally. Havelock writes that to be memorized, language is a language of action, a series of agents doing things connected not "in any thoughtful way" but simply strung together by coordination (Havelock 1986: 76). In the history of Spanish or of the Slavic languages, for example, it is generally true that the earliest prose writing is paratactic almost to the exclusion of hypotaxis. There is linguistic research supporting the notion that oral texts will tend toward parataxis given that hypotaxis (embedded linguistic structures) places a greater burden on working memory (Kuiper, 290). Working memory is that part of memory that would hold items retrieved from long term memory (oral formulae, for example) while they are assembled into a syntagm according to discourse structure rules (Kuiper, 280-281). The tendency toward parataxis is not a medieval phenomenon, then, but rather a function of the brain. Modern auctioneers and sports commentators also tend toward "flat" discourse (Kuiper, 291). The notion that early, oral literatures are typically paratactic may or may not apply to Icelandic law. After all, the *Kónungsbók Grágás* is the product of a mixculture both oral and literate, and what parataxis there is in this manuscript could be a false positive. A study of patterning in the *Grágás* might answer this question more definitively. Line breaks might constitute a natural patterning akin to verse that does not suppose the need for externally-imposed metrical regularity.

The *Vígslóði* shows literate organization in the sentences which summarize preceding information, which is more characteristic of literate culture in general. We may consider the opening of each title. Of the twenty-six opening sentences of the twenty-six titles, 35% (nine title-opening sentences) begin with *það er mælt*. 15% (4 sentences) begin with the presentation of some hypothetical with *ef*. 35% begin with a statement followed close on by either *það er mælt* or *ef*. 15% begin with a summary of preceding information, something like *allir er hér eru talaðir* ("all of the above-mentioned"). Titles 87, 89, 98, 104 and 106 begin with one of these seemingly literate summary sentences. In conclusion, the vast majority of titles begin with some kind of formulaic phrase previously associated with orality. Only 15% of *Vígslóði* titles begin with and are organized around a statement that seems to grow only out of the technology of writing.

Of course it is very difficult to characterize a given sentence in a given manuscript as oral or literate. As noted, these polar terms have been re-defined as mere hypothetical extremes. Nor can we verify the provenance of particular textual features. Nonetheless, we can speak about probabilities. The summary sentences in the *Vígslóði* would seem to be more literate than oral, especially in light of the resemblance they bear to Roman law. The titles of the *Institutes of Justinian* often begin with definition of the matter at hand. Also, titles of both the *Institutes* and the *Grágás* often begin with an enumeration. The division of the *Grágás* reflects both its Latin and its Nordic inheritance (see Sveinbjörn Rafnsson 1977: 720-732).

If we consider the nature of legal discourse as it was in Iceland during the Free States period, then we might draw certain conclusions about the nature of syntax we can expect of an oral text. The *lögsögumaðr* recited the law orally from 927 until 1117. If we exchange the notion of thoroughness for the notion of accuracy, then the survival of the law orally is easy to understand. It survived in the memory of everyone who used it. Oral tradition is flux. Would the *lögsögumaðr*'s oral text have hypotaxis? Mathíasson in his study of Icelandic syntax draws no conclusions about the rise of hypotaxis, relying on the theory that dialogue tends to favor short periods whereas narration tends to favor longer periods with a lot of hypotaxis, or subordinated clauses which serve to explain what was just mentioned (1959, 221-227, 289). Presumably, oral law would be like a narration, a kind of oral performance which may or may not have been punctuated by affirmations or challenges, illustrations, or questions.

Concluding our brief survey of syntax in the *Vígslóði*, we note that the register and style of the language of the *Grágás* varies by section (Christian laws, Assembly Procedures Section, Homicide Laws, etc.). The language of the *Kónungsbók Vígslóði* is clear, objective, and plain with few adjectives (Hauksson and Óskarsson 1994, 226). The language is neither an everyday language nor a technical jargon, but something in between. The syntax shows some particularities, such as the use of the conjunction *og* when *þá* would normally be used (Hauksson and Óskarsson 1994: 233). This and other "syntactical inconsistencies" could be an indication of the relation that the extant texts bear to oral tradition (Hauksson and Óskarsson 1994, 234). As we have seen, the syntax of the text does relate to oral performance, though not of the kind previously imagined.

7. Church Influence and Roman Law

Our analysis of orality in the *Vígslóði* must take into account the Church's influence on the *Grágás*, which is obvious from the very existence of the Christian Laws section. Besides that, however, we might suspect ecclesiastic influence in certain concepts. In the *Kónungsbók Grágás*, certain moral provisions make one suspect the presence of the Church. If the Church were present, then Roman law was present, and the presence of Roman law will condition everything about our understanding of the *Grágás*, including the very language of the text. For example, in title 90 there appears the words *misræða*, here meaning 'illicit intercourse', literally meaning 'mis-application, misdeed, ill-advised.' OI (Old Icelandic) *ræða* is a verb meaning 'to care for' related to the productive OI *ráð*, 'counsel, care' which has cognates in most Germanic languages. *Misræða* appears only in the *Grágás*. It does not appear in the saga literature or in *Norges Gamle Lov*. Besides the four appearances of the word in title 90, it appears only in the marriage and betrothals laws of the *Grágás* (in K 155), where it merely states the punishment for illicit intercourse. Cleasby lists the etymology as deriving from Latin *nefandus* 'heinous, wicked.' *Nefandus* of course is merely the negative of *fandus*, 'lawful.' None of the other common medieval dictionaries or etymological dictionaries list *misræða*.[17] *Fornicatio* is probably an idea that came with the Church. *Gulaþingslov* 25 stipulates that a man shall have but one woman. This law explains that if a man has a wife, he should not keep a concubine as well. If prohibitions arise when social practices create a need for them, then we may assume that concubinage was practiced among the residents of the area governed by the *Gulaþingslov*, and probably also in Iceland. There is also ample saga evidence and comparative Germanic evidence to suggest that monogamy was an idea that came with the Church, which is probably the logic that led Cleasby to conclude that *misræða* was a calque on a Latin term.

If *Kónungsbók Grágás* belongs to Church culture, then we have more evidence of an aural culture; we have reason to consider pre-lection as a possible mode of lawspeaking in the age when the manuscript was copied. Rafnsson believes that documents were used in court procedures during the Icelandic Commonwealth and that this was due to the influence of Roman law (1977, 726).

---

[17] I refer to De Vries, Fischer, Fritzner, and Alexander Jóhannesson.

8. A Look at the Text

The titles of the Vígslóði are well organized. Consider title 89 in outline:

> **Outline of K 89: Calling**
> I) On preparing cases (calling)
>   A) Nine neighbors
>   B) Summoning case—twelve neighbors
>   C) First blow debate
>   D) Who can serve on a jury
>   1) Kinship qualifications
>   2) Disqualifying someone
>   3) Property owners
>   4) *Þingför*
>   E) Procedure for calling
>   1) Time and order
>   2) Both parties call the same people
>   3) Disputes about calling
>   4) Calling too may neighbors
>   5) Lying
>   6) Stalling

Ideas are subordinated in a way that is consonant with written law, in a way that suggests the presence of written documents.

Title 90 begins, as do titles 87 and 89, with what would seem to be a literate feature. The first sentence of title 90 states that there are six women for whom a man may kill with impunity. *Prima facie* this seems to be an abstract organizational principle, an index of reading. There are two cognate object constructions: *Sækja sök* (p.165: "to prosecute a case") and *vigit hefir vegit* (p.165: "did the killing") and one legal formula to witness a calling. This entire section shares the same features—a few cognate object constructions, a possible alliteration, rational principles of organization, as do *Vígslóði* titles 86-90. These titles have a common, four-part structure: they begin with a summary and introductory sentence about the nature of the topic at hand; second, mitigating circumstances and borderline cases are considered; third, procedure is explained; fourth, necessary legal formulae are presented. An outline of title 90 shows that it, too, follows this four-part pattern:

Outline of K 90: Killing justified by a woman
 I) Women for whom a man may kill (summary sentence)
 II) Wrongful intercourse (mitigating circumstances)
   A) Intended
   B) Transpired
 III) Procedure
   1) Neighbors decide on killing and intentions
   2) Who prosecutes—procedural details
   3) Defense of five neighbours
 IV) Summoning formula for the avenger

From title 94 onwards, the *Vígslóði* titles vary in structure from the four-part structure cited above, although the titles continue to present general information first followed by specific and explanatory information. Title 94, for example, opens with a statement that when a man is killed, a man's son or heir should be the one to bring a complaint. The title then states more particularly who can be his heir, goes into even more detail about who can bring the complaint and ends with special cases such as mental retardation, non-family members, and foreigners.

In title 94 there are five rubrics that have no text that follows. What seem to be section headings without a section are not uncommon in the *Kónungsbók Grágás*. In his edition, Finsen filled out the section with another manuscript testimony when he was able. The empty rubrics in title 94 are:

> *Eckia asialf eða mær xx* (p.168: "a widow or a virgin of twenty"), *ef utlendr maðr nórøn verðr vegin* (p.169: "if a foreign man from Norway is killed"), *ef víg geraz a alþingi* (p.169: "If a fight happens at the Althing"), *þriðia brøðra eða nanare menn* (p.170: "fourth cousins or nearer relatives"), *ef maðr verðr begin eða omale* (p.170: "if a man is killed or rendered mute").

The scribe was using these rubrics as place-holders, but perhaps not because he did not know any more on the subject but rather that he knew the subject well. The *Kónungsbók Grágás* leaves no space on the lines following but does leave the rest of the line blank and does begin these lines with a majuscule, signalling that it is a subtopic. Was the scribe copying from an incomplete manuscript? Were these issues that a scribe thought important but could not settle himself? These empty section headers can give us clues about the nature of the manuscript.

Gunnar Karlsson (2004, 53) writes:

> Líklegra finnst mér að styttu klausurnar séu leif af eins konar millistigi munnlega og skriflega varðveitta laga.
> ("It seems likely to me that the short clauses are due to some kind of middle phase between the oral and literate preservation of law").

Karlsson's theory concords with the most logical and obvious conclusions we can draw about the nature of orality in the *Vígslóði* and about the way the lawspeaker learned his text. In this middle phase between orality and literacy documents were use as mnemonic schema for legal experts, just as we have noticed in the development of compensation-lists in personal injury laws in Germanic laws in general. As time went on, these mnemonic indices became more and more fleshed out until the whole of the law was copied down. This gradual fleshing out is what Karlsson sees in the *Grágás*, and it is how he explains the difference between the *Kónungsbók Vígslóði* and the more complete *Staðarhólsbók Vígslóði*: the latter is the next step in the development from oral to literate (54-5).

9. Conclusion

The *Grágás* can only be disappointing for anyone looking for an oral text or pre-literate law, but the *Grágás* is promising for anyone who would undertake a pragmatic analysis or search for speech patterning, free of any attachment to orality or literacy. Memory is not the only vector through which the *Vígslóði*-tradition projects its content. The spirit of this law is modern, syncretistic, and imitative of Roman models. The strength of this law is precisely in this modernity.

In conclusion, we cannot hear Bergþór's voice, but, given an updated notion of orality and law, we can perceive performative features in the *Kóngungsbók Grágás* even as we distance this parchment artifact from the recitation of the law.

Primary Literature

Ári 1986: Ári Fróði. *Íslendingabók, Landnámabók. Íslenzk Fornrit* I, Reykjavík.
Attenborough 1963: F.L. Attenborough. *The Laws of the Earliest English Kings*, New York.
Brennu-Njáls saga. Íslensk fornrit XII. Ed. Einar Ól. Sveinsson. Reykjavík, 1954.
Grágás: Lagsafn Íslenska Þjóðveldsins, Reykjavík, 1992.
The Codex Regius of Grágás. ed. Páll Eggert Ólasson: Copenhagen, 1932.
Grágás: Islændernes Lovboog i fristatens tid, ed. Vilhjálmur Finsen Copenhagen: 1852.
Gulaþingslov: Den Eldre Gulatingslova, eds. Bjørn Eithun, Magnus Rindal and Tor Ulset, Oslo, 1994.
Gunnlaugs saga ormstungu, in *Borgfirðinga sögur,* eds. Sigurður Nordal and Guðni Jónsson, Reykjavík, 2001.

Secondary Literature

Amodio 2004: Mark C. Amodio. *Writing the Oral Tradition: Oral Poetics and Literatre Culture in Medieval England*, Notre Dame, Indiana.
Bauman 1986: Richard Bauman, "Performance and Honor in 13th-Century Iceland," in: *The Journal of American Folklore* 99.392: 131-150.
Boehm 1984: Christopher Boehm, *Blood Revenge: The Anthropology of Feuding in Montenegro and Other Tribal Societies,* Lawrence, Kansas.
Boulhosa 2005: Patricia Pires Boulhosa, *Icelanders and the Kings of Norway: Medieval Sagas and Legal Texts*, Leiden.
Bourdieu 1990: Pierre Bourdieu, "Codification,"in: *In Other Words*, Oxford.
Carruthers 1994: Mary Carruthers, *The Book of Memory: A Study of Memory in Medieval Culture*, Cambridge, 1994.
Cleasby and Vigfusson 1874: Richard Cleasby & Guðbrand Vigfusson, *An Icelandic-English Dictionary*, Oxford.
De Vries 1962: Jan De Vries. *Altnordisches etymologisches Wörterbuch*, 2nd ed, Leiden.
Donoghue and Mitchell 1992: Daniel Donoghue and Bruce Mitchell, "Parataxis and Hypotaxis: A Review of Some Terms Used for Old English Syntax," in: *Neophilologische Mitteilungen* 93: 163-183.
Fischer 1909: Frank Fischer, *Die Lehnwörter des Altwestnordischen*, Berlin.
Fritzner 1886: Johan Fritzner. *Ordbog over det gamle norske Sprog*, Kristiania.
Karlsson 2004: Gunnar Karlsson, *Goðamenning: Staða og áhrif goðorðsmanna í þjóðveldi íslendinga*, Reykjavík.
Hasluck 1954: Margaret Hasluck, *The Unwritten Law in Albania*, Cambridge.
Hauksson and Óskarsson 1994: Þorleifur Hauksson & Þórir Óskarsson, *Íslensk Stílfræði*, Reykjavík.
Havelock 1986: Eric A. Havelock, *The Muse Learns to Write: Reflections on Orality and Literacy from Antiquity to the Present*, New Haven, CT.

Kjartansson 1986: Helgi Skúli Kjartansson, "Lagauppsaga lögsögumanns," in: *Erindi og greinar, Félag áhugamanna um réttarsögu* 23.
Honko 1996: Lauri Honko, "Epics Along the Silk Roads: Mental Text, Performance, and Written Codification," in: *Oral Tradition* 11.1: 1-17.
— 2000a: Lauri Honko, "Preface," in *Textualization of Oral Epics*, New York, vii-viii.
— 2000b: Lauri Honko, "Text as Process and Practice: The Textualization of Oral Epics," in: *Textualization of Oral Epics.* New York, 1-54.
Hymes 1998: Dell Hymes, "When is Oral Narrative Poetry? Generative Form and Its Pragmatic Conditions," in: *Pragmatics* 8.4: 475-500.
Jóhannesson 1956: Alexander Jóhannesson, *Isländisches etymologisches Wörterbuch*, Berlin.
Kastrati 1955: Qazim Kastrati, "Some Sources of Unwritten Law in Albania," in: *Man* 134: 124-127.
Kuiper 2000: Koenraad Kuiper, "On the Linguistic Properities of Formulaic Speech," in: *Oral Tradition* 15.2 (2000): 279-305.
Lárusson 1958: Ólafur Lárusson, "On *Grágás* – the Oldest Icelandic Code of Law" in: *Þriðji Víkingafundur*, Third Viking Congress, Reykjavík.
Lönnroth 1980: Lars Lönnroth, "New Dimensions and Old Directions in Saga Research" in: *Scandinavica* 19.1: 357-361.
Maine 1986: Henry Sumner Maine, *Ancient Law*,Tuscon, Arizona.
Matthíasson 1959: Haraldur Matthíasson, *Setningaform og Stíll*, Reykjavík.
McGlynn 2008: Michael P. McGlynn, "Feuding in the *Siete Infantes de Lara*," in: *Colorado Review of Hispanic Studies* 6: 3-22.
— 2009: Michael P. McGlynn, "Legal Formulae in the Assembly Procedures Section of the Old Icelandic *Grágás*," in: *Neophilologus* 93: 521-536.
Miller 1990: William Ian Miller, *Bloodtaking and Peacemaking: Feud, Law, and Society in Saga Iceland*, Chicago, 1990.
— 2006a: William Ian Miller, "Eye for an Eye," public lecture at the University of Iceland, Reykjavík, Iceland, Tuesday, May 23, 2006.
— 2006b: William Ian Miller, *Eye for an Eye*, Cambridge.
Mitchell 2001: Stephen A.Mitchell, "Performance and Norse Poetry: the Hydromel of Praise and the Effluvia of Scorn," in: *Oral Tradition* 16.1: 168-202.
Mitchell 2003: Stephen A.Mitchell, "Reconstructing Old Norse Oral Tradition," in: *Oral Tradition* 18.2: 203-206.
Moore 1978: Sally Falk Moore, *Law as Process: An Anthropological Approach*, London, 1978.
Ólasson 1932, Páll Eggert Ólasson, *The Codex Regius of Grágás*, Copenhagen.
Oliver 2002:Lisi Oliver, *The Beginnings of Old English Law*, Toronto.
Ong 1988, Walter Ong, *Orality and Literacy: The Technologizing of the Word*, London.
Rafnsson 1977: Sveinbjörn Rafnsson, "Grágás og Digesta Iustiniani," in: *Sjötíu Ritgerðir*, ed. Jakobi Benediktsyni, Reykjavík, 720-732.
Sigurðsson 2004: Gísli Sigurðsson, *The Medieval Icelandic Saga and Oral Tradition: A Discourse on Method,* trans. Nicholas Jones, Cambridge, Massachusetts.

Shuman 2003: Amy Shuman, "Oral History," in: *Oral Tradition* 18.1: 130-131.

Tarifa 2008: Fatos Tarifa. "Of Time, Honor, and Memory: Oral Law in Albania," in: *Oral Tradition* 23.1: 3-14.

Tobler 2001: Christian Henry Tobler, trans,n*Secrets of Medieval German Swordsmanship: Sigmund Ringeck's Commentaries on Liechtenauer's Verse*, Texas.

Wormald 1996: Patrick Wormald. "Exemplum Romanorum," in: *Rome in the North*, eds. Ellegård and Åkerström-Hougen, 15-27.

HEINRICH VON VELDEKE'S *ENEAS* AND THE TRADITION OF THE ALLITERATING WORD-PAIR

John M. Jeep — Oxford (Ohio)

Abstract

Building on recent findings from Early Middle High German literature, this study compiles and analyses for the first time completely the circa eighty alliterating word-pairs from Heinrich's *Eneas*, a work dated just after the evasive temporal boundary between Early Middle High and Middle High German (circa 1170). Comparisons are established to pairs from Heinrich's somewhat earlier *Minnesang* texts and comprehensive data available on Old High and Early Middle High German. Methodology considers speculation on the figurative nature of some of the expressions and formal issues related to idiomatic usage.

1. Introduction

Heinrich probably completed his German version of the Old French *Roman d'Eneas* during the 1180s.[1] This temporally locates his courtly verse romance at the beginning of the Middle High German period, where dates of composition and surviving manuscript transmissions seldom coincide.[2] This study consists of a complete set of data and considers earlier research on various aspects of the pairings.[3]

2. Data

2.1. *Heinrich von Veldeke*, Eneas-Roman
80 Alliterating Word-pairs (81 including one variant, from h) Sequentially as they Appear in the Text

der gesunden noch der siechen,	17,27	27
sîne mâge und sîne man,	19,11	71
ir rûder und ôuh ir rahen:	22,13	193

---

[1] Kartschoke 1986, 853; Kasten 1993, 76f.; Diemer et al. 1992, 755. Citations follow Kartschoke; Diemer et al. and Schieb et al. 1970 were also consulted.

[2] See Jeep 2006, 19, with relevant secondary literature.

[3] On definition of and earlier treatment of medieval German alliterating word-pairs see Jeep 2006 (11f., with literature). See Wolff et al. (1981, 283) for abbreviations of manuscript variants included below: G = Gotha, LB, cod. chart A 584; h = Heidelberg, UB, cpg 403; H = Heidelberg, UB, cpg 368; M = Munich, cgm 57).

Ir diende lût unde lant,	26,9	349
uns hat weter unde wint	29,24	486
umbe ellende und umb unheil	30,26	528
ich teile im lûte unde lant	31,4	546
ûzen unde innen.	35,5	707
ze storme und ze strîte	40,35	937
obene unde under	41,30	972
von sige unde von sâlden,	45,3	1135
si brâchen die borch unde branden,	47,15	1201
diu naht zegleit und zergienk	52,26	1411
mit worden und mit werken,	55,37	1543
ungemach und arbeit.	58,9	1635
mit berlen unde borden,	60,3	1711
der zobel brûn unde breit.	60,15	1723
wunne unde wîstûm,	76,33	2379
mîn schade und mîn schande.	77,31	2417
arbeit / lîden unde ungemach."	83,2f.	2628f.
grôz und grâ was ir daz hâr	85,2	2708
arbeit unde ungemach,	103,11	3437
an hûte unde an hâre	108,31	3661
von siten und von sinnen,	108,33	3663
alse fleisch unde vische	110,4	3714
ir fleisch unde ir vische.	111,23	3773
beidiu lûte unde lant,	116,38	3988
ez sî uns lieb oder leit.	117,3	3993
si worhten unde wachten,	119,7	4077
si hiewen unde hûben,	119,15	4087
dem minnern und dem mêren.	120,21	4133
manne unde mâge,	129,13	4487
sîne mâge und sîne man,	130,3	4515
die schande / und den schaden	136,8f.	4760f.
getrîben unde getragen	137,33	4825
im unde û hât getän	141,14	4260
der zobel was brûn unde breit,	147,12	5198
und ein bein rôt und ein bûch,	148,28	5254
mîne mâge und mîne man	150,30	5336
habe unde behalde.	152,7	5393
den schaden und die schande,	152,26	5412

Erwarp her und gewan. [G]	155,35	5541
oben unde under,	156,24	5570
swaz her gebôt unde bat.	157,3	5589
ir gebot und ir bete.	163,11	5837
der eine und ouch der ander.	163,31	5857
mit gewâfen unde mit gewande.	174,27	6293
si spilden unde sprungen	180,18	6528
mit willen und mit werken.	181,21	6571
der wîn und diu wâfen	181,30	6580
beidiu gebôt unde bat,	189,9	6881
her gebôt unde bat	191,34	6986
hern was in storm noch in strît	206,30	7580
sîn tugent und sîn trouwe.	211,5	7755
in stormen und in strîten.	218,17	8051
mit werken joch mit worden	222,12	8208
vil wol erkande man unde erkôs	238,40	8884
Turnûses helfe und sîn here,	246,31	9195
Turnus hulfe und her [G]		
knehte unde koufman.	248,7	9251
in stormen und in strîten,	257,21	9625
vermerren und vermiden [h]	263,15	9867
von ûzen unde von innen	266,26	9998
wiste ich weme oder wâ.	273,33	10281
als umben lewen und umbez lamp.	299,40	11330
sin schade und sîn schande.	303,1	11451
gewaldich unde wol geboren	308,32	11682
slege grimme unde grôz.	325,39	12367
ez wâre im lieb oder leit,	334,20	12708
von sange und von seitspile.	339,31	12919
offenlîche und unverholen	340,31	12959
ze werken und ze worden.	341,3	12971
ûf samit unde ûf sîde.	341,9	12977
ûwer lob und ûwern lîb.	343,31	13079
wunne unde wirtschaft,	346,34	13202
wand er unmahtich was und alt.	349,1	13289
an [dem B,M,h] *hâre und an der hûte.*	350,19	13349
an worten unde an werken	350,24	13354
witewen unde weisen	351,37	13407

dorch sîn gebot und dorch sîn bete.	353,31	13481
gewalt unde wunne	354,14	13503

2.2. Heinrich von Veldeke, Eneas, 80 Word-pairs
(81 including one variant, from h)
Listed Alphabetically by First Alliterating Phoneme

arbeit / lîden unde ungemach."	83,2f.	2628f.
arbeit unde ungemach,	103,11	3437
und ein bein rôt und ein bûch,	148,28	5254
mit berlen unde borden,	60,3	1711
swaz her gebôt unde bat.	157,3	5589
ir gebot und ir bete.	163,11	5837
beidiu gebôt unde bat,	189,9	6881
her gebôt unde bat	191,34	6986
dorch sîn gebot und dorch sîn bete.	353,31	13481
si brâchen die borch unde branden,	47,15	1201
der zobel brûn unde breit.	60,15	1723
der zobel was brûn unde breit,	147,12	5198
der eine und ouch der ander.	163,31	5857
umbe ellende und umb unheil	30,26	528
alse fleisch unde vische	110,4	3714
ir fleisch unde ir vische.	111,23	3773
diu naht zegleit und zergienk	52,26	1411
slege grimme unde grôz.	325,39	12367
grôz und grâ was ir daz hâr	85,2	2708
habe unde behalde.	152,7	5393
an [dem B,M,h] hâre und an der hûte.	350,19	13349
an hûte unde an hâre	108,3	13661
Turnûses helfe und sîn here,	246,31	9195
Turnus hulfe und her [G]		
si hiewen unde hûben,	119,15	4087
im unde û hât getân	141,14	4260
vil wol erkande man unde erkôs	238,40	8884
knehte unde koufman.	248,7	9251
als umben lewen und umbez lamp.	299,40	11330
ez sî uns lieb oder leit.	117,3	3993
ez wâre im lieb oder leit,	334,20	12708

ûwer lob und ûwern lîb.	343,31	13079
Ir diende lût unde lant,	26,9	349
ich teile im lûte unde lant	31,4	546
beidiu lûte unde lant,	116,38	3988
sîne mâge und sîne man,	19,11	71
manne unde mâge,	129,13	4487
sîne mâge und sîne man,	130,3	4515
mîne mâge und mîne man	150,30	5336
vermerren und vermiden [h]	263,15	9867
dem minnern und dem mêren.	120,21	4133
obene unde under	41,30	972
oben unde under,	156,24	5570
offenlîche und unverholen	340,31	12959
ir rûder und ôuh ir rahen:	22,13	193
ûf samit unde ûf sîde.	341,9	12977
von sange und von seitspile.	339,31	12919
mîn schade und mîn schande.	77,31	2417
den schaden und die schande,	152,26	5412
sin schade und sîn schande.	303,1	11451
die schande / und den schaden	136,8f.	4760f.
von sige unde von sâlden,	45,31	1135
von siten und von sinnen,	108,33	3663
si spilden unde sprungen	180,18	6528
hern was in storm noch in strît	206,30	7580
ze storme und ze strîte	40,35	937
in stormen und in strîten.	218,17	8051
in stormen und in strîten,	257,21	9625
der gesunden noch der siechen,	17,27	27
getrîben unde getragen	137,33	4825
sîn tugent und sîn trouwe.	211,5	7755
ungemach und arbeit.	58,9	1635
wand er unmahtich was und alt.	349,1	13289
ûzen unde innen.	35,5	707
von ûzen unde von innen,	266,26	9998
mit gewâfen unde mit gewande.	174,27	6293
gewaldich unde wol geboren	308,32	11682
gewalt unde wunne	354,14	13503
Erwarp her und gewan. [G]	155,35	5541

wiste ich weme oder wâ.	273,33	10281
mit werken joch mit worden	222,12	8208
ze werken und ze worden.	341,3	12971
uns hat weter unde wint	29,24	486
mit willen und mit werken.	181,21	6571
der wîn und diu wâfen	181,30	6580
witewen unde weisen	351,37	13407
si worhten unde wachten,	119,7	4077
mit worden und mit werken,	55,37	1543
an worten unde an werken	350,24	13354
wunne unde wirtschaft,	346,34	13202
wunne unde wîstûm,	76,33	2379

2.3. *Multiple Pairs by Frequency*
(variants not included; also see below)

mâge : man		*eine : ander*	1
(manne : mâge)	4	*ellende : unheil*	1
schade : schande		*zegleit : zergieng*	1
(schande : schade)	4	*grimme : grôz*	1
storm(-): strît(-)	4	*grôz : grâ*	1
werken : worden		*habe : behalde*	1
(word/ten : werken 2)	4	*helfe : here*	1
arbeit : ungemach		*hiewen : hûben*	1
(arbeit : ungemach)	3	*im : û*	1
gebôt : bat	3	*erkande : erkôs*	1
lût(e) : lant	3	*knehte : koufman*	1
gebot : bete	2	*lewen : lamp*	1
brûn : breit	2	*lob : lïb*	1
fleisch : fische	2	*vermerren : vermiden*	1
hare : hûte	2	*minnern : mêren*	1
lieb : leit	2	*offenlîche : unverholen*	1
oben(e) : under	2	*rûder : rahen*	1
ûzen : innen	2	*samit : sîde*	1
bein : bûch	1	*sange : seitspile*	1
berlen : borden	1	*sige : sâlden*	1
brâchen : branden	1	*siten : sinnen*	1

spilden : sprungen	1	*weme : wâ*	1
gesunden : siechen	1	*weter : wint*	1
getrîben : getragen	1	*willen ; werken*	1
tugent : trouwe	1	*wîn : wâfen*	1
unmahtich : alt	1	*witewen : weisen*	1
gewâfen : gewande	1	*worhten : wachten*	1
gewaldich : wol geboren	1	*wunne : wirtschaft*	1
gewalt : wunne	1	*wunne : wîstûm*	1
Erwarp : gewan	1		

Results of this frequency analysis: 4 word-pairs recorded 4x + 4 pairs recorded 3x + 7 pairs recorded 2x + 42 pairs recorded 1x = 55 different pairs (of 80 total). An analysis of the data sorted by alliterating morpheme reveals a somewhat higher frequency of morphemes, as these appear in different words (as compounds or as other parts of speech).

2.4. *Alliterating Morphemes by Frequency*
Multiple Usages (also see above)

un-	6
beten	5
gebot	5
werk	5
grôz	2
mer(r)	2
wâf	2
gewalt	2
wunne	2

2.5. *Conjunctions Alphabetical: Distribution*

joch	1
-n...noh	1
noh	1
oder	3
und(e)	73
und ouch	1

Heinrich's use of conjunctions in alliterating word-pairs reveals relatively low variation.

2.6. Alliterating Old High German and Early Middle High German Word-Pairs (see Jeep 2006, 99-119, with common abbreviations of OHG and EMHG works.) Also Recorded in Eneas *(earlier attestation cited; noteworthy variations in Heinrich von Veldeke listed in parentheses)*

ált neíst . noh únmáre (unmahtich)	Notker, *Dec.*
arbêit . unde únreht	Notker, *Ps.*
arbeit : un-	(3 other examples)
bat ande gebot	*Mfr. Reimibel*
zebrechen und verbrennen (brâchen, branden)	*Kaiserchronik*
ir eines leben noch des andern	Heinr. v. Melk, *Priesterleben*
(beide) fleisc unde viske	*Vom Himmelreich;* Hartman, *Rede*
habet min bibot inti heltit thiu (behalde)	*Tatian*
hût unt hâr; in hute juoch in hare	*Kaiserchronik; Von der Siebenzahl*
lieb : leit	(12 examples)
liut : lant	(6 examples)
min : mer	(7 examples; 15 more reversed)
obene : undene	Hartman, *Rede* (2x; 3 more in other texts reversed)
mit singendo unde mit seîtspile (sang)	Notker, *Ps.* Gloss
scaden unde scante	*Genesis*
stúrme : strît	Notker, *Ps;* Lamprecht, *Alexanderlied*
sieh : gesunt	(12 examples, some reversed)
ûz : in	(26 examples, some reversed)
úmbe geuuált . únde úmbe uuúnna	Notker, *Dec.*
werk : wort	(23 examples, some reversed)
mit weter joch mit winde	*Wahrheit*
willen : werken	(7 examples, some reversed)
witewen : weisen	(15 examples, some reversed)

This comparison allows for assessment of relative continuity and innovation with respect to Heinrich's use of the alliterating word-pair within the traditions of the earliest stages of recorded German. Of the fifty-five different pairs in *Eneas*, twenty-three pairs (or circa 42%) were previously recorded in Old and/or Early Middle High German texts. Seen from another perspective, nearly 60% of Heinrich's pairs are first recorded in German in his version of *Eneas*. Further studies may help to reveal how many of these pairs appear in later stages of German, and how many are recorded as Heinrich's formulation alone.

As a rule, the use of the word-pairs in Old High/Early Middle High German and in Heinrich's *Eneas* is similar in semantic nature, if not identical. Morphological and syntactic variation seems to be the dominant mode, and thus a constant characteristic.

3. Analyses

Fairly unusual among the known medieval German authors is the fact that Heinrich produced works that fall both before and after the accepted demarcation of Early Middle High German and Early Middle High German, around 1170. In Heinrich's case, *Minnesang* (courtly love poetry), it is agreed, makes up his earlier works, and the courtly verse romance *Eneas* follows. For this reason, a comparison of his use of alliterating word-pairs in various works and genres seems particularly interesting. As is common among medieval poets, biographical and many other related details are largely based on conjecture (see Wolff 1981, 278, on the dating of Heinrich's songs). In any case, the differing genres offer interesting points for comparison. A total of five alliterating word-pairs occur, each only once, in his forty song texts (some nearly 500 lines total). This results in a frequency of approximately one pair per 100 lines. In the *Eneas,* 80 pairs occur in 13,528 lines, or one per circa 170 lines.

3.1. *Alliterating Word-Pairs in Heinrich's Minnesang* [4]

arme und eine	XVIII,5
Dest mê noch dest min	XIII,2,1
minne und meine	XXXIX,4,7
von tumbheit und von trouwe	I,2,5
sunder wîc und wân	V,3,9

---

[4] See Jeep 2006, 60-61 and 134; citations from Schweikle 1997.

The pair *mê : min* represents a reversal of the alliterating morphemes in *Eneas: dem minnern und dem mêren,* one of the most common of the alliterating word-pairs in both Old High and Early Middle High German. Examples of the latter are recorded in *Vom Himmelreich,* Heinrich von Melk's *Priesterleben, Kaiserchronik,* Hartman's *Rede vom heiligen Glauben,* and Frau Ava's *Leben Jesu*.[5] Friedrich (2006, 297f.) only lists examples of the pair in the sequence *min- : mêr,* including the one from *Eneas.* Earlier texts provide at least twenty-three examples of the pair in the same sequence as in Heinrich's song (Jeep 2006, 108). Indeed, from the same time period, only seven *min- : mêr* pairs are recorded.[6] The sequence may have been influenced in this song by the desire to rhyme with *bin;* in fact, only the pair *minne and meine* occurs out of the end of line context, and thus outside of the rhyming environment. Hence, the pairs from Heinrich's songs tend to fill a line or occur at the end.

In addition to an earlier attestation in a religious context – *St. Trudperter Hoheslied*[7] - with Heinrich, then, for the first time *minne und meine* appears (in reverse order) in a secular setting. Here the object of the narrator's affection is *ir êre* 'her honor' and *si* 'her', i.e. the woman about whom (and presumably also for whom) the love song is composed. Friedrich (297) lists this passage, albeit, due to uncertainty with respect to the authorship, under Ulrich von Liechtenstein's name.[8] Of further interest is the fact that the *Minnesang* poet makes reference to Tristan and Isolde in the following strophe (see XXXIX,5,3f.). Gottfried von Straßburg, who in his own version of *Tristan and Isolde* famously lauds Heinrich's narrative skills (4723-4750), employs the same pair *minnen und meinen* twice and as a noun pair once.[9] It is no accident that Gottfried closes his passage on Heinrich and the *Minnesänger* with an alliterating word-pair: *an worten und an wisen* 'in texts and in songs', clearly a reference to the combination of lyrics and melody in *Minnesang*,[10] maybe even a nod to Heinrich's very own song. A second reference to *Tristan* occurs in another of Heinrich's

---

[5] See Jeep 2006, 37 and 125f.
[6] Jeep 2006, 109.
[7] See Jeep 2006, 72f. and 125.
[8] See Schweikle 1997, 448.
[9] See Friedrich 2006, 297 and 291
[10] See Krohn 1980, 66f.

songs, *Tristra*nt *muose sunder sînen danc* (IV).[11] If indeed Gottfried was familiar with Heinrich's *Mîn sendes denken,* Heinrich may have influenced him in his decision to use the pair *minnen* and *meinen.*

Heinrich's five alliterating word-pairs represent just over half of those recorded for the Early Middle High German *Minnesänger*. The four remaining examples,[12] and their authors are:

lieb únde léide	Der von Kürenberg
ûf und ouch abe	Kaiser Heinrich
under oder obe	Ulrich von Gutenberg
beide ûzerhalp und inne	Graf Rudolf von Fenis.

With the exception of *ûf : ab*, all four are previously recorded in Old High and/or Early Middle High German, and in Heinrich's *Eneas* (*ober : under* in reverse order). Each pair describes opposites with a contextualized meaning of 'everything' or 'everywhere,' respectively. Peter Czerwinski (1898, 306) sees in those passages – such as *ûz : in* – where the abstract notions of external and internal are evoked, evidence of a heightened form of abstract thinking. Such word-pairs serve both religious and secular contexts.[13]

4. Previous Research

Hitherto, despite many studies on Heinrich von Veldeke and his contemporaries,[14] no complete listing of the alliterating word-pairs in *Eneas* has emerged; hence the need for the present study, that supercedes earlier work through its completeness of data and by building on recent new surveys of the earlier stages of German both in methodology and, subsequently, in presentation. The challenges of approaching completeness in studying large bodies of texts are obvious; even most recent research reaffirms this conclusion. In working with a clearly defined entity, studies such as the present one help point to the areas where such challenges may be greatest, while suggesting a methodolo-

---

[11] See Kasten 2005, 619f.
[12] See Jeep 2006, 60-62 and 134.
[13] See Jeep 2006, 32; Czerwinski 1898, 300; Jackson 1994, 220, 224.
[14] See Jeep 2006, 11f., on the state of research on Middle High German alliterating word-pairs; for the current state of research on phraseology, see Filatkina (2007) and HiFoS.

gy worth considering for other expressions. In the following, some select publications will be assessed with respect to their findings and the new data for Heinrich's *Eneas*.

An essay by Zingerle (1864) explicitly follows the lead of Jacob Grimm's monumental collection of legal terms published in *Deutsche Rechtsaltertümer* (1828), listing Middle High German pairs by part of speech (123-151). Grimm (1816) had very early on championed the study of alliterating word-pairs – among other rhetorical devices – in an effort to link what he thought to be relics of old (Germanic) oral legal parlance with literary remnants of oral poetry, examples of which he and others sought to find in medieval German texts.[15] Grimm's extensive list (1828, 8-17) from a range of Germanic languages impresses still today in its breadth, but his findings were not an attempt to be comprehensive. Schulze (1871-72) expanded upon Grimm's list, but like Grimm only includes a handful of Heinrich's pairings. Of Heinrich's eighty-plus pairs, Zingerle catalogues approximately 45, with at least one (*brûn und niht breit,* p. 141) not included in the data set here above, as it does not follow the conventional word-pair definition, according to which alliterating elements must share any modifiers. While providing numerous welcome literary parallels, Zingerle nowhere indicates how complete his lists intend to be.

Roetteken (1887, 93) later provided 44 examples of alliterating word-pairs from Heinrich's *Eneas,* five of which do not appear above. Twice he included examples with /sch-/ that do not, however, alliterate with other phonemes, in another case, a supposed Low German form /t/ is cited in *tinnen* 'tin', whereby the manuscripts show High German /z/; a fourth case incorrectly cites *enwolde* alliterating with *wolde,* and the final entry rejected in my compilation is one where an adverb probably only modifies the first of two adjectives: *gnûch grôz unde gût.* These thirty-nine valid citations represent less than half of the total of the alliterating word-pairs in *Eneas*. Roetteken acknowledges only listing one example, as he returns to discuss some, but by no means all of the multiple examples that appear later on in his study. In a rare example of restraint among philologists in the field, Roetteken refuses to make a ruling on the level of formulaic idiomacity (106), and focuses instead on semantic relationships between the paired elements (106-115).

---

[15] See Jeep 1995, 10f.

Frustratingly, then, Roetteken only provides some one third of the total material (113f.).

Later, Ehrismann (1927, 93), drawing on Roetteken's and others' studies, outlined a contrast between certain ornamental rhetorical elements and stiff, formulaic usage. In a similar vein, Minis (1974, 33, 36, 40), after comparing examples of paired formulas with Heinrich's Old French source text, attested to Heinrich particular skill in employing word-pairs to reflect the rhymes of his Romance predecessor. Minis outlines three possible sources for Heinrich's word-pairs: German tradition, French influence, and new coinages (40). His encouraging statement that careful consideration of Heinrich's – and other authors' – formulaic language can lead to surprising findings (35, n. 6) informs the present line of research. It is worth noting that a study on the use of alliteration in Virgil's *Aeneid* came to a similar conclusion, namely that the use of alliteration in the Latin poem is intentional (Clark 1976). Given the evidence that Heinrich not only used his Old French source, but also Virgil's Latin text (Minis 1959, 80), one could imagine Heinrich using his native alliterating rhetorical tools to enhance the poetics of his German poem. Luster (1970) adds solid evidence to support this notion.

Jungbluth collected a good number of the word-pairs – both alliterating and non-alliterating – in an attempt to compare Heinrich's *Eneas* with the Straßburg *Alexanderlied* and the *Servatius* fragments, two other Early Middle High German works. Jungbluth had hoped to link Heinrich with the supposed later texts, but was ultimately unsuccessful.[16] Jungbluth (1937, 111, 133) rightfully complains about incomplete earlier listings of word-pairs. Before and after Jungbluth, two scholars (van Dam 1923 and Teusink 1946) came to a similar evaluation of Heinrich's use of word-pairs in general, declaring *Eneas* the leader among the six pre-courtly (or early courtly) epic works (*Kaiserchronik, Rolandslied, König Rothar, Tristran, Alexanderlied,* and *Eneas*), measured by use of word-pairs. Schröder finds van Dam's thesis plausible, that Heinrich knew, and probably was influenced by, the Straßburg *Alexander*. Teusink's compilation and comparison of frequency of usage of word-pairs suggests affinity between the two works (113).

Schieb and Frings, finally, in their monumental edition (Schieb et al.

---

[16] See Schröder, in Wolff et al. 1981, 286.

1970), make mention of Heinrich's predelection for pairings (2, cii), and attribute over one hundred such collocations to him,[17] while citing only two alliterating ones.

Studies on most, if not all of the known Middle High German authors of courtly romance contain examples of alliterating word-pairs, with practically no cases of complete listings. Hans Dieter Lutz (1974, 439f.) rightfully cautions against the use of statistics in literary analysis without a well-constructed methodological framework. Of equal importance is a clear definition of terms.

Archer Taylor summarized his findings concerning the history of legal word-pairs, "We cannot easily distinguish the old from the new in such formulae" (1931, 89). In a similar vein, Jesko Friedrich concedes that the figurative ("phraseologische") nature of passages in historical texts is difficult to ascertain (2006, V, 10, and *passim*).

As a result of considerations cited above, this study collects and analyzes all alliterating word-pairs from a given text to enable reliable comparison with other similar sets of data. Progressing chronologically, this line of research is telling the story of the development of the German alliterating word-pair in its earliest stages.

5. A New Dictionary of Middle High German Idioms

The appearance in 2006 of a new dictionary of Middle High German idioms (Friedrich) provides an opportunity to compare the data drawn from Heinrich's *Eneas* with Friedrich's findings. The following lists (in alphabetical order of the alliterating element) those alliterating word-pairs from Heinrich's *Eneas* also recorded by Friedrich (citations are from my listing above), with discussion where warranted. Repetition of pairs and passages already discussed above is avoided. The analysis may provide – beyond an assessment of the data relevant Heinrich's *Eneas* – insights into the overall value of Friedrich's lexicon and the current state of phraseological lexicology. Where relevant, observations on listings from some other Early Middle High German pairs are included. After this section, the remaining word-pairs recorded in Heinrich's *Eneas,* but missing in Friedrich, will be presented and analyzed.

---

[17] 2,388; see Roetteken 1887, 115.

For one alliterating word-pair, Friedrich (157) includes two citations,

swaz her gebôt unde bat	157,3	5589
her gebôt unde bat	191,34	6986,

but three further passages with the pair are lacking:

ir gebot und ir bete	163,11	5837
beidiu gebôt unde bat,	189,9	6881
dorch sîn gebot und dorch sîn bete	353,31	13481.

For these pairings, one verb example is not included, and the two noun pairs are omitted.

Friedrich lists the following pair only under *hût*, but not under *hâr:*

an hûte unde an hâre	108,31	3661;

this choice may correlate to the fact that a passage with the pair in reversed order is also omitted:

an hâre und an der hûte	350,19	13349,

although the semantic usage[18] in the second passage, too, is metaphorical. The reversal of the elements at this juncture[19] is due to rhyme. Friedrich fails to list one example each of this pair from the *Kaiserchronik* and the poem *Von der Siebenzahl*.[20] These two particular passages in Heinrich refer to the same object, Eneas's son, in the context of a genealogical summary provided by the narrator.[21] In the second instance, the word pair *an worten unde an werken* (350,24; see below) occurs as the last pair in a triad spanning six verses. The use of the same pair, even in reversed order, serves to remind the reader of the earlier passage, one in its own right supported by a further alliterating pair: *von siten und von sinnen* (108,33; see below).

For another pair,

---

[18] See Friedrich, 232.
[19] See Friedrich, 232, with some seventeen examples, many in prose, of the reverse sequence *hut : har*.
[20] See Jeep 2006, 30f., 66, 105.
[21] See Kartschoke 1986, 783.

> *ez wâre im lieb oder leit,*   334,20   12708,

this one example is listed (272), but

> *ez sî uns lieb oder leit*   117,3   3993

is not.

In still another case, only one of two passages appears (279),

> *Ir diende lût unde lant,*   26,9   349;

missing is:

> *beidiu lûte unde lant,*   116,38   3988.

For a further pair, only two of four relevant citations are included (283, 285):

> *sîne mâge und sîne man,*   19,11   71
> *manne unde mâge,*   129,13   4487

Friedrich lists parallel citations from Middle High German works, some of which (285: *man, / und ouch ein teil ihr mâge*) differ significantly in syntax from the idiom heading *man unde mâge*. As mentioned above, an imprecise definition of the word-pair leads to uneven data. The two missing citations from *Eneas* are:

> *sîne mâge und sîne man,*   130,3   4515
> *mîne mâge und mîne man*   150,30   5336.

Luster (1970, 77) provides the Old French source for the first example (19,11), 'all his people,' thus suggesting metaphorical usage of the pair. In fact, it follows the noun *frunt* 'friends' in the previous line, thus serving as a kind of a definition, 'relatives and vassals.'

The following pair is included, with instructive (but incomplete, see above) parallel citations from other works (297):

> *dem minnern und dem mêren*   120,21   4133.

Friedrich describes the pair

ûf samit unde ûf sîde	341,91	2977

as 'but probably still literal here' ("hier aber wohl noch wörtl[ich]," 343).

Three of four listings for one pair,

den schaden und die schande,	152,26	5412
sin schade und sîn schande	303,11	1451
die schande / und den schaden	136,8f.	4760f.

are all accounted for (344, 348), but not

mîn schade und mîn schande	77,31	2417.

Similarly, while

ze storme und ze strîte	40,35	937

is included (385), three other examples of the pairing are not:

hern was in storm noch in strît	206,30	7580
in stormen und in strîten.	218,17	8051
in stormen und in strîten,	257,21	9625.

Schieb (1965, 2,18, also see the other passages) lists all four occurrences and identified the pair as a common one in Middle High German. Four examples from the *Alexanderlied*,[22] only one of which is listed in Friedrich, support this assertion.

Friedrich (454) lists

mit werken joch mit worden	222,12	8208

but not

ze werken und ze worden	341,3	12971;

similarly, only one of the two reversed citations is included

---

[22] 42, 120, 3276; also 4372, in reverse order.

mit worden und mit werken,	55,37	1543,

whereby a second one,

an worten unde an werken	350,24	13354

is listed following citations with the preposition *in* (479, with typo in heading *wort under* [recte *unde*] *wërc*). An entry for *Ezzolied* ("28") is not substantiated by the text. While the sources considered for the *St. Trudperter Hohelied* include the confessional triad "in thought, word, and deed," Biblical sources for other early German pairings consist of paired Latin expressions,[23] and thus represent at least equally possible models for the formulation.

Minis (1974, 32) provides some documentation, and notes that the word sequence reversals in pairings allow for rhyme in each case. In Friedrich's dictionary, as is common elsewhere, listings of the wording of this pair reduce it to a uniformity that is not borne out by the textual evidence. An extreme example is from Spalding's generally laudable *Historical Dictionary of German Figurative Usage* (this lexicon does not attempt to cover the earlier periods of German), where the modern word-pair *mit Wort und Tat* is cited together with a reference to the *Old Saxon Heliand,* "first as *mit [Wort] und Werk"* (2000, 2686*).* In fact, the *Heliand* contains a total of nineteen examples that vary considerably.[24] The Old High and Early Middle High German examples of this pair are equally diverse, with some examples in singular and many in plural, two different prepositions (*in, mit*), once with elision of the second *mit,* and one pair including possessives.[25] These examples are all from religious texts, but the pair also appears (later) in legal contexts.[26] In the passage *ze werken und ze worden,* Lavinia's ladies in waiting are praised for their education and manners. Later in the same passage, their splendid clothing is depicted, including the pair *ûf samît unde ûf side* (see below). Obviously with the later switch from *Werk* to *Tat,* the alliteration is lost. Spalding's notes the appearance of *Tat* for *Werk* in this word-pair since Early New High German times, but in fact

---

[23] See Jeep 2006, 47-49, 57, 73f.
[24] See Jeep 2002, 111f.
[25] See listings in Jeep 2006, 118.
[26] See Schmidt-Wiegand 2002, 352.

in Worten und Werken is still listed today as a current idiom, as a variant to *mit Wort und Tat* (*Redewendungen*, 715, 800, 818). The currency – recognized as such or not – of Luther's Bible translation may be largely responsible for this otherwise outdated usage.[27] Of course, religious language often displays markedly traditional stylistic aspects. In this example, an older lexical item is combined in an alliterating word-pair, resulting in a rhetorically enhanced collocation.

Looking temporally in the other direction, backwards towards Old High German, Friedrich (480) lists one example (of three) in the Old High German Otfrid, but omits examples from the *Monsee Fragments*, *Tatian*, Notker, and from glosses to Notker.[28]

Friedrich (456, 470) lists correctly and completely these final two pairs:

uns hat weter unde wint	29,24	486
witewen unde weisen	351,37	13407.

According to Luster (1970, 76, following Minis 1959, 19), Heinrich expanded the source term 'wind' from the Old French in using the pair *weter unde wint*, suggesting metaphorical meaning.

In total, Friedrich records some twelve different pairs (in seventeen citations) from the *Eneas*. More often than not, multiple listings are incomplete. While admitting the difficulties of establishing whether a given medieval German passage is idiomatic, Friedrich seems, in the case of alliterating word-pairs, to err on the side of caution (see 36), thus omitting pairs that may indeed have been idiomatic. Friedrich is willing to consult later periods of German (New High German) to support the case of idiomatic currency for a given expression (17). It proves equally worthwhile, however, to also cast a glance backwards in time to identify phrases perhaps once idiomatic that may not have survived down to the modern period. Examples of pairs from *Eneas* (frequency greater than one) that appear in at least one earlier text but are not listed in Friedrich include *ein- : ander, fleisch : fische* (twice), *habe : behalde, oben : unden* (twice), *sieh : gesunt, storm : strît* (four times), *ûz : in* (twice). These pairs thus represent some overlooked but arguably common pairings in medieval German texts.

---

[27] See Jeep 1995, 60.
[28] See Jeep 2006, 116, 118.

Beyond the question of idiomatic usage, one might consider the overall use of alliteration as a poetic/rhetorical device by Heinrich von Veldeke. As Friedrich rightfully notes (60, although the reference to Haymes 1970 is lacking in the bibliography), there is a relationship between the alliterating word-pair and Germanic verse forms. The results provided above, however, reveal a distribution of various and varying structures within many of the pairings that go beyond easy morphological classification. Nouns, verbs, and adjective/adverbs appear in alliterating pairs with or without prepositions and/or articles or possessives. More complete listings of alliterating word-pairs in early German texts have resulted in similar findings. Some listings, as mentioned above, reveal a priori decisions on the idiomatic nature of some examples, resulting in incomplete data and, as a result, leading to insufficient analysis.

Schieb (1965, 2,1) noted the idiomatic/formulaic nature of the pair *der gesunden noch der siechen* (17,27) 'none of the healthy ones nor of the ailing' to describe 'everyone' (see 17,26: *nieman,* "no one") in Troy killed by Menalelaus's Greek troops.

Thus, Friedrich's own description of his data as incomplete (16) is verified here with respect to Heinrich's use of alliterating word-pairs in his *Eneas*. While Friedrich's collection of Middle High German idiomatic expressions is indeed impressive, as a reference work it must be used with caution, specifically with the knowledge that listings contained therein are not comprehensive. In addition, some of Friedrich's listings suggest a more uniform and simplified record of the form of the alliterating word-pairs than the texts themelves document.[29] This practice reflects much of what has gone on before in published research. On pairs not recorded before Heinrich von Veldeke, see the discussion in the following section, below. Further study must ascertain whether these characterizations apply to Friedrich's findings on expressions other than the alliterating word-pair.

6. Alliterating Word-pairs First Appearing in *Eneas*

Especially for the earlier periods of German, complete coverage of rhetorical expressions should be the goal. Apparently this objective does

---

[29] See also Jesko 2006, 587.

not extend to the end of the Middle High German period,[30] at least as far as the monumental new *Middle High German Dictionary* (*MHW*) project is concerned. Thus, projects of a more limited perspective than one attempting to list all idiomatic expressions will be needed to approach, over time, a comprehensive description of the history of given pairs, and of other related idiomatic phrases. For certain phrase types, a large data base will provide a better basis for further research than one limited by pre-determined factors. In fact, extensive findings enrich our understanding of earlier as well as of later periods of German. An example of the latter is the somewhat sparingly listed pairing of *eine* and *andere* – see *weder das eine noch das andere* or *der eine oder der andere* (*Stilwörterbuch,* 38) – that appears in Early Middle High German and in Heinrich von Veldeke. Thus, future research is needed to clarify the idiomatic currency status of less frequently recorded pairs.

A second example of an overlooked pair, *haben : halten,* provides evidence of idiomatic usage over time. Minis (1974, 33, based largely on Minnis, 1959) commends Heinrich von Veldeke on his creative use of *habe unde behalde* to imitate, in a sense, the combination of both semantic and rhymed elements in the Old French source text. Alliteration, of course, occurs between the root morphems *haben* and *halten,* so that the unstressed prefix *be-* can be set aside, so to speak, when looking for parallel pairings. The existence of an Old High German example and many later ones,[31] including a Protestant decree in Prussia (1874) proscribing the formula twice as part of the wedding vows (*Provinzial-Correspondenz*, 2), attest to the longevity of the pair. Heinrich's medieval usage with respect to the wedding tradition reveals the transfer of bride and property as legal practice, at least in the context of the *Eneas* story. Minis – although he devotes a part of his study to rhyming pairs (1974, 37f.) – fails to mention Heinrich's switch from rhyme to alliteration, even though Heinrich, by employing alliteration, emphasizes phonetically the connection between the elements forged by the word-pair. As a matter of fact, assonance and homoeoteleuton further associate the terms acoustically with each other in this passage. The *Deutsches Wörterbuch* acknowledges the long and

---

[30] See Friedrich, 16.
[31] See Jeep 1995, 98-100.

widely spread tradition of this alliterating pairing, citing Old English, Frisian, and other German examples (*DWB* 10, col. 50). The *Deutsches Rechtswörterbuch* lists the pair as a legal formula, with examples from the fourteenth century onward (*DRW* 4, 1370; 1507-1524, examples under *halten,* with no explicit mention of the idiomatic nature of the pairing), in either order. As is usually the case, the sequence chosen by Heinrich reflects rhyme needs. Thus, Heinrich's writing represents another link in a long chain of recorded usages of the pairing *haben* and *halten.* When a single passage cannot provide enough linguistic context to allow for a clear semantic determination, diachronic views may supply data helpful in ascertaining the potential idiomatic nature of the phrasing in question.

In alphabetical order, here below follows discussion of the other alliterating word-pairs first recorded by Heinrich von Veldeke in *Eneas.*

und ein bein rôt und ein bûch,   148,28   5254

With this pair Heinrich describes the clothing covering legs and stomach, whereby elision of the adjective *rôt* occurs with respect to the second noun. The expressions for clothing are derived from the body parts covered.

mit berlen unde borden,   60,3   1711

forms part of the description of Dido's extravagant hunting outfit, one that includes a fur dress embellished with gold and jewels (*mit golde und mit gesteine,* 59,27; employing, it may be noted, a form of alliteration not reflecting the Germanic practice limited to stressed syllables), and, later, *der zobel brûn unde breit,* 60,15 (see below). This pair is the object of two alliterating verbs (*wol gezieret / und vil wohl gezieret,* 60,1-2). A passage such as this one reveals use of alliteration beyond the word-pairs that form the narower subject of this study, and suggests potential gains to be won through further research of related rhetorical phenomena. The distinction between Germanic (stressed) and non-Germanic alliteration is not always observed in research.

si brâchen die borch unde branden,   47,15   1201

is from Eneas's description of the destruction of Troy by the Greeks, with effective alliteration between the verbs and the word for the city (*borch*).

der zobel brûn unde breit.	60,15	1723
der zobel was brûn unde breit,	147,12	5198

The first of these was mentioned above (see *berlen*); it describes the marten fur, and is repeated in a similar description of the decorative clothing of the Volsker queen Camilla.

umbe ellende und umb unheil	30,26	528

is used by Dido to describe her understanding of what it is to be exiled and unfortunate. Luster (1970, 78) attributes the use of alliteration here to an attempt by Heinrich to emulate the homeoteleuton conjoining two verbs in the Old French version.

diu naht zegleit und zergienk	52,26	1411

describes the night turning into dawn, as it fades and goes away following the cock's crow. While Kartschoke's translation (1986) suggests the second verb only refers to the breaking morning, Fromm reduces the pair to one verb ("verging"), implying the verb pair is synonymous.

slege grimme unde grôz.	325,39	12367

forms part of the depiction of blows traded in the duel between Eneas and Turnus, here 'viscous and hefty.'

grôz und grâ was ir daz hâr	85,2	2708

depicts Sibylle's unsightly hair, 'long and grey.' Schieb (1965, 2,83) identifies this pair as a formulaic expression.

Turnûses helfe und sîn here,	246,31	9195
Turnus hulfe und her [G]		

is transmitted in two manuscripts (G and h) as a pair ('supporting troops and army'), whereby the critical editions opt for a variant that, because the modifiers vary, would not qualify as a pair.

> *si hiewen unde hûben,*   119,15   4087

describes the construction of the castle Montalbane, following the pair *worhten unde wachten* (see below).

> *im unde û hât getän*   141,14   4260

employs two dative pronouns, 'him and you [the queen, second person plural].' While conjoined pronoun usage is relatively rare, they do occur as alliterating word-pairs.

> *vil wol erkande man unde erkôs*   238,40   8884

is used with a paired direct object: *ir stiche unde ire slege* (239,1); the verbs denote sensual and intellectual recognition, and in the collocation suggest an intensifying connotation appropriate to the situation at hand, where Trojan troops are being besieged.

> *knehte unde koufman.*   248,7   9251

represents the second of two pairings, following *ritâre und gebûre* in the preceding line, together describing various societal positions: knights and peasants, servants and merchants.

> *als umben lewen und umbez lamp.*   299,40   11330

The lion and the lamb, symbols of ferocity and peace, are conjoined in this pair. Here Eneas is dismissing the threat of Turnus, comparing himself with the lion and his opponent with a helpless victim.

> *ûwer lob und ûwern lîb.*   343,31   13079

is spoken by Lavina's daughter, warning her mother that if the queen were to die she would lose both her prestige and her life.

> *ermerren und vermiden* [h]   263,15   9867

only appears as a variant reading in manuscript "h"; Schieb (1965, 2,288) speculates this variant could represent an old alliterating word-pair, without providing any parallel pairings. The variant represents a alternative formulation for *verren und vermîden,* with alliteration of a non-stressed syllable.

offenlîche und unverholen 340,31 12959

Eneas commands Lavina's teacher, openly and publicly, to watch over her. These adverbs here are used as intensifying synonyms.

ir rûder und ôuh ir rahen: 22,13 193

forms part of a series of four pairs over six lines – *beide storm unde wint, / mit regene und mit hagele [...] ir segele unde ir maste* (22,8-12), reflecting structurally the wind and waves in the midst of a storm caused by Juno to punish Eneas and his men. Here, in the final pairing, oars and yards, technical terms from shipping are combined.

ûf samit unde ûf sîde. 341,9 12977

Here is recorded the first occurrence of a pair that still is used today, with another preposition, *mit Samt und Seide.* Lavinia's ladies in waiting wear lovely clothing, this collocation highlighting the expensive material. In this same description, their education is praised, using *ze wereken und ze worden* (see above).

von sange und von seitspile. 339,31 12919

is employed to describe part of the festivities at Laurentum. Other pairs using the etymon *sing-* 'to sing' are recorded in a gloss to Notker's Psalms translation and in Early Middle High German (see Jeep 2006, 40-42). Other terms that alliterate with 'to sing' include *seite* ('string), *salm* ('Psalm'), and *sagen* ('to say,' 'to compose poetry').

von sige unde von sâlden, 45,31 1135

Eneas uses this pair to describe the fame of the Trojan horse, achieved 'through victory and fate.' Luster (1970, 78), following Minis (1959, 49), attributes this alliterating formulation to Heinrich's attempt to imitate the rhyme in the French version.

von siten und von sinnen,   108,33   3663

Here Anchises is prophesizing to Eneas about his son, who will resemble his father physically (*an hûte unde an hâre,* 108,31; see above) and in his behavior and thoughts. The pairs, separated in the text by an authorial interpolation *(daz sage ich dir zewâre)* (108,32; parenthesis part of citation), would occur sequentially in a dramatic reading of the monologue. Thus the structure and the acoustics of the pairs reinforce each other.

si spilden unde sprungen   180,18   6528

forms part of a triad of pairs describing the festivities of Ascanius's army: *si bliesen unde sungen, / si spilden unde sprungen / und wachten und riefen,* perhaps in imitation of the movement of dancing, back and forth, until they finally fall asleep: *sine hôrden noch ensâgen* (180,22), and are overcome by their enemies. As part of an explanation for their submission Heinrich employs yet another pair: *der wîn und diu wâfen* (181,30; see below). This pair also appears in the nearly contemporary *Alexanderlied* (Straßbourg version): *di spileten unde sprungen* (5215).

getrîben unde getragen   137,33   4825

describes the removal of the spoils of war by the Trojan army, perhaps referring to animals *(getrîben)* and other property that was mobile. Filling the verse line, it appears to define what is named in the preceding line as *gefûren,* 'remove, take away,' and is followed by another verb + object, *leiten manegen wagen.* According to Schieb (1965, 2, 152), this pair is an old legal formula.

sîn tugent und sîn trouwe.   211,5   7755

forms the second part of a sequence of two pairs used by Eneas to bemoan Pallas's death: *sîn jugent und sîn êre* 'his youth and his honor,' 'his virtue and his steadfastness.'

mit gewâfen unde mit gewande.   174,27   6293

'with weapons and with clothing' describes Pallas as he is prepared for his investiture. His father provided these items. A similar pair is found in the earlier Vorau version of the *Alexanderlied: beidu wâfen unde gewât* (581).

gewaldich unde wol geboren   308,32   11682

is used by Eneas to describe his ancestor Dardanus, 'powerful and nobly born.' Manuscript B (Berlin) shows *wolgeboren*. I follow the *Deutsches Wörterbuch* (30, 1120f.) in interpreting the second element as a compound adjective (also see Michels 1921, 338, and discussion above), not as an adverb followed by a participial adjective. Even though deemed old-fashioned by the end of the nineteenth century, a 1968 Swiss film contains the word, *Eugen heißt wohlgeboren.*

Erwarp her und gewan. [G]   155,35   5541

appears only in a variant reading, where the main manuscript has the singleton verb *erwarb*. We interpret the variant as a word-pair with idiomatic, perhaps intesifying connotation, expanding the meaining from 'obtained' to 'obtained and acquired.' Quite skillfully, the variant *gewan* rhymes as did the main manuscript reading *Troiân*, which could be omitted due to contextual clarity.

wiste ich weme oder wâ.   273,33   10281

here two interrogatives are conjoined, also sharing alliteration with the verb *wiste* 'if I knew,' that in turn alliterates with *wâne* 'I believe' from the previous line. Lavina is holding a monologue, addressing the deity Amor, and knows not 'to whom or where' she could register her complaints.

der wîn und diu wâfen   181,30   6580

is used, as mentioned above, to describe the weakened state of Ascanius's army. After a long day's battle and evening festivities, they fall asleep and become victims of their oppressors.

si worhten unde wachten,   119,7   4077

is employed to describe the Trojans working hard on the construction of the castle at Montalbane, 'working and watching.' This is an appropriate combination of the duties necessary for the project to move forward.

>   *wunne unde wirtschaft,*   346,34   13202

defines *hêrschaft* 'pomp' from the preceding line as 'festive joy and hospitality' in the context of the festivities surrounding the coronation of Eneas and Lavinia.

>   *wunne unde wîstûm,*   76,33   2379

forms the middle part of a triad, *ouwî êre unde gût, / wunne unde wîstûm, / gewalt unde rîchtûm,* 'honor and possessions, happiness and wisdom, power and wealth,' all named by Dido as part of her fortune, the greater it being, the worse she feels about her fall. While each term is used in alliterating word-pairs previously, Heinrich's combination is new. It represents an expansion on the Old French source text (Luster 1970, 77). The Berlin manuscript replaced *wunne* with *minne* 'courtly love,' thus eliminating the alliteration.

7. Looking Forward

For some pairs, especially those that have apparently not yet been investigated in depth, Internet sources provide useful and handy input with respect to an assessment of their currency in medieval and post-medieval German. In what follows, I have selected alliterating pairs occurring in Heinrich von Veldeke that may, according to recent spot searches, have "descendents" in later medieval and/or in modern German usage.

Martin Luther uses *Arbeit und Ungemach* (*viel arbeit und ungemach treiben und leiden; DWB*) in combination with a non-alliterating verb pair. More recently (2001), a Swiss author using the penname "baerwurz" employed the pair in a description of potential dangers while traveling to a new destination (Zurich). A textual variant uses *angest* for *arbeit,* with obvious consequences for evaluation of Heinrich's use of his source.[32] As for more modern examples of this formulation, the seventeenth-century poet Buchholz uses *Angst und Ungemach*; a prose

---

[32] See Minis, 1974, 31.

citation exists from another seventeenth-century source, a letter by Engelbert Kämpfer to his brother (Kämpfer 1688). For Luster (1970, 77), following Minis (1974, 31), Heinrich's choice of alliteration was based on an attempt to imitate the rhyme conjoining two corresponding French terms in the source text, *peor : dolor.*

The adjectives *braun und breit* appear in a radio broadcast about silk from 1999 (Lorenz), describing a fur sash. As it turns out, this is a direct translation of the same passage listed above from Heinrich's *Eneas*. However, in an earlier, unrelated prose text, hands are so characterized (Löns, d. 1914).

Stricker uses *brechen und brennen ir bethus* (cited in *DRW*) in his *Karl* (circa or after 1220 [33]). The use of the pair and the alliterating direct object is much like Heinrich's example: *si brâchen die borch unde branden* (47,15). In each case, the phrase 'tear down and burn up' suggests total destruction. Heinrich's variation in word order could be explained by the rhyme with *sanden* in the following line. Modern translations suggest elision of the object following the second verb.[34]

eine and *ander* (163,31) is now a common pairing in modern German.[35]

The pair *Elend und Unheil* occurs, for example, in a parish bulletin (Fronhausen 2007) as *gegen Elend und Unheil*, in Hannes Stein, *Enzyklopädie der Alltagsqualen* (2006,9), and as *aus Elend und Unheil* in a review of a film from 2004 (Müller-Lobeck).

Fleische und Fische appears in numerous culinary contexts, restaurants, cookbooks, etc. The idiomatic expression *weder Fisch noch Fleisch sein (Redewendungen,* 208f.) has a long history. Heinrich's use describes highly valued food, and may, in a comparable vein, encompass non-related entities (synecdoche).

These examples should suffice to inspire further searches for later examples of alliterating word-pairs recorded in earlier stages of German, with the aim of establishing or arguing against their idiomacy. Equally important, they remind the researcher that native proficiency checks are limited to live subjects.

---

[33] Bumke 1990, 257.
[34] Kartschoke 1986; Fromm 1992.
[35] *KStW* 1, 128; *Stilwörterbuch,* q.v.; Peyerl 2008, 36f.

8. Phonological Aspects

The alliterating pair *mit berlen unde borden* (60,3) is only possible in those dialects which employ /b-/ for initial /p-/ in *Perle* "pearl". According to Grimm (*DWB*), both forms appear into the Early New High German period.

Due to Schieb's and Frings's edition of the text (Schieb et al. 1970), an attempt to recast the text in its supposedly Limburgish original (Lienert 2001, 77), their reconstructed forms of some pairs have left a trail of so-called *Karteileichen* (bogus citations) in the secondary literature. One example is *bûten ende binnen* (707, e.g. Minis 1959, 28), dealt with here in the discussion of *ûzen unde innen.* Similarly, *turne* (or *torne*) *ende tinnen* (Roetteken 1887, 93; Minis 1959, 37) is not considered in this study due to its manuscript transmission as *ir torne unde ir zinne* (6342), thus not as an alliterating word-pair.

9. Orthographic Issues

Medieval spelling of German was often unclear with respect to the separation (or connection) of prefixes to their root elements (see Nerius 2003, 2463-2466). The case of <*wol geboren*> (308,32) gives rise to the question of determining whether *wol* is an adverb or the prefix of an adjective. In the passage in question, a prefixed *wol-* could alliterate with another adjective (here *gewaldich*) in a word-pair. Grimms' *DWB* cites examples of the use of *wol-* starting 1200, but it seems reasonable to include this term among the prefixes formed with *wol.* This interpretation is supported indirectly via the translations into New High German with the adjective *edel* (Kartschoke 1986; Fromm 1992; for Middle High German see Michels 1921, 338; also see discussion above). In the *Alexanderlied,* the pair *sîn fleisch und sine vische* (75) reveal alliteration not reflected in the spelling. A forthcoming study deals with the alliterating word-pairs in the *Alexanderlied.*

10. Issues for Future Consideration

Norden (1957, 416f. and *passim*) discusses the use of alliteration in Virgil's Latin *Aeneid* and in the broader context of classical literature. In one example, however, C. Day Lewis's English translation better reveals the word-pairings ("Their destinies and fortunes, their characters and their deeds," 136) than Norden's German rendering ("an der lieben Enkel Schicksal dachte, / An ihren Edelsinn und Heldenmut," 91) for "fataque fortunasque virum, Moresque manusque" (Norden, l. 683). The many examples cited by Norden suggest a frequency that may have had an effect on a poetically sensitive reader such as Heinrich, who also drew on Virgil's Latin text (Lienert 2001, 78). A deeper appreciation of Heinrich's rhetorical usage of alliteration would include even more detailed comparisons with his source texts in the context of their respective poetic inventories.[36] The present study is intended to provide an example of the methodology of how such a study might be undertaken. At the same time it advances the state of knowledge regarding medieval German alliterating word-pairs.

Literature

Alexanderlied: *Das Alexanderlied des Pfaffen Lamprecht (Straßburger Alexander): Text Nacherzählung Worterklärungen,* ed. Irene Ruttmann, Darmstadt, 1974.
  baerwurz 2001: http://www.ciao.de/Zurich_und_Zentralschweiz_Polyglott_ Reisefuhrer__Test_1887907 (June 7, 2001; accessed Dec. 9, 2009).
Buchholz 1642: A.H. Buchholz, "Schauenburgische Trauerklage und Grabelied" http://www.geschichtsforum.de/f7/gedichte-zur-geschichte-3464/index9.html (accessed Dec. 9, 2009).
Bumke 1990: Joachim Bumke, *Geschichte der deutschen Literatur im hohen Mittelalter, Geschichte der deutschen Literatur im Mittelalter* 2, dtv 4552, Munich.
Clark 1976: W. M. Clark, "Intentional Alliteration in Vergil and Ovid," in: *Latomus* 35: 276-300.
Czerwinski 1898: Peter Czerwinski, *Der Glanz der Abstraktion: Frühe Formen von Reflexivität im Mittelater: Exempel einer Geschichte der Wahrnehmeung,* Frankfurt am Main-New York.
van Dam 1923: Jan van Dam, *Zur Vorgeschichte des höfischen Epos: Lamprecht, Eilhart, Veldeke* (Rheinische Beiträge und Hülfsbücher zur germanischen Philologie und Volkskunde 8), Bonn-Leipzig.
Diemer et al. 1992: Dorothea Diemer and Peter Diemer, eds. *Heinrich von Veldeke. Eneasroman. Die Berliner Bilderhandschrift mit Übersetzung und Kommentar. Mit den Miniaturen der Handschrift und einem Aufsatz* (Bibliothek des Mittelalters 4), Frankfurt am Main.
DRW = *Deutsches Rechtswörterbuch.* Weimar: Böhlau, 1914ff.
  http://drw-www.adw.uni-heidelberg.de/drw/.
DWB = *Deutsches Wörterbuch von Jacob and Wilhelm Grimm.* 1852-1971.
  http://germazope.uni-trier.de/Projects/WBB/woerterbuecher/dwb/.

---

[36] See Minis 1974; Clark 1976.

Ehrismann 1927: Gustav Ehrismann, *Die mittelhochdeutsche Literatur II. Blütezeit Erste Hälfte,* Geschichte der deutschen Literatur bis zum Ausgang des Mittelalters, Handbuch des deutschen Unterrichts an höheren Schulen 6,2,2,1, Reprint Munich 1954.

Filatkina 2007: Natalia Filatikina, "Formelhafte Sprache und Traditionen des Formulierens (HiFoS): Vorstellung eines Projekts zur historischern formelhaften Sprache," in: *Sprachwissenschaft* 32: 217-242.

Friedrich 2006: Jesko Friedrich, *Phraseologisches Wörterbuch des Mittelhochdeutschen: Redensarten, Sprichwörter und andere feste Wortverbindungen in Texten von 1050-1350* (Reihe Germanistische Linguistik 264), Dissertation Göttingen, Tübingen.

Fromm 1992. Hans Fromm, ed. *Heinrich von Veldeke, Eneasroman: Die Berliner Bilderhandschrift mit Übersetzung und Kommentar* (Bibliothek des Mittelalters 4), Frankfurt am Main.

Fronhausen 2007: www.katholische-kirche-fronhausen.de/pfarrbote/TIP_2007_18.pdf (accessed Dec. 9, 2009).

Gottfried von Straßburg, *Tristan und Isold,* ed. Friedrich Ranke, Dublin/Zurich, 15th ed. 1978

Grimm 1899: Jacob Grimm, *Deutsche Rechtsaltertümer,* 2 vols. 1828, 4th, rev. ed., ed. Andreas Heusler, Reprint Leipzig 1922.

- 1816: Jacob Grimm, "Von der Poesie in Recht," in: *Zeitschrift für geschichtliche Rechtswissenschaft* 2, rept. Darmstadt 1957, 25-99.

Haymes 1970: Edward R. Haymes, *Mündliches Epos in mittelhochdeutscher Zeit*, reissued Göppingen, 1975.

HiFoS: Historische formelhafte Sprache und Traditionen des Formulierens. http://www.hifos.uni-trier.de/Forschungsstand.htm (accessed Dec. 9, 2009).

Jackson, 1994: Timothy R. Jackson, "Außen und Innen bei Konrad von Würzburg: Die Achill-Deidamia-Episode im *Trojanischen Krieg*," in *Personenbeziehungen in der mittelalterlichen Literatur,* ed. Helmut Brall, Barbara Haupt, Urban Küsters (Studia humanoiora 25), Düsseldorf, 219-249.

Jeep 1995. John M. Jeep, *Alliterating Word-Pairs in Old High German* (Studien zur Phraseologie und Parömiologie 3), Bochum.

- 2002: John M. Jeep, "The rhetorical significance of the alliterative tradition in the *Heliand,*" in: *New Insights in Germanic Linguistics III,* eds. Rauch Irmengard and Gerald F. Carr (Berkeley Insights in Linguistics and Semiotics 52), New York, 107-130

- 2006: John M. Jeep, *Alliterating Word-pairs in Early Middle High German* (Phraseologie und Parömiologie 21), Baltmannsweiler.

Jesko 2006: Friedrich Jesko, review of Friedrich 2006, in: *Germanistik* 47: 587.

Jungbluth 1937: Günther Jungbluth, *Untersuchungen zu Heinrich von Veldeke* (Deutsche Forschungen 31), Frankfurt am Main.

Kämpfer 1688: Engelbert Kämpfer, ed. Michel, Wolfgang. http://www.flc.kyushu-u.ac.jp/~michel/serv/ek/gbj/1-00text.html (accessed Dec. 9, 2009).

Kartschoke 1986: Dieter Kartschoke, ed., *Heinrich von Veldeke. Eneasroman: Mittel-*

hochdeutsch/Neuhochdeutsch. Nach dem Text von Ludwig Ettmüller ins Neuhochdeutsche übersetzt, mit einem Stellenkommentar und einem Nachwort (UB 8303), Stuttgart.

Kasten 1995: Ingrid Kasten, ed., *Deutsche Lyrik des frühen und hohen Mittelalters: Edition der Texte und Kommentar*. Kuhn, Margherita, transl. (Bibliothek des Mittelalters 3), reprint Deutscher Klassiker Verlag im Taschenbuch 6, Frankfurt am Main, 2005.

Kasten 1993: Ingrid Kasten, "Heinrich von Veldeke: *Eneasroman*," in: *Interpretationen: Mittelhochdeutsche Romane und Heldenepen*, ed. Horst Brunner (UB 8914) Stuttgart, 75-96.

Krohn 1980: Rüdiger Krohn, ed., *Gottfried von Straßburg. Tristan. Band 3: Kommentar, Nachwort und Register* (UB 4473) Stuttgart.

KStW: Ruth Klappenbach and Wolfgang Steinitz, *Wörterbuch der deutschen Gegenwartssprache*, 6 vols., Berlin, 1964-1977.

Lewis, C. Day. See Virgil.

Lienert 2001: Elisabeth Lienert, *Deutsche Antikenromane des Mittelalters,* Grundlagen der Germanistik 39, Berlin.

Löns 1917: Hermann Löns, *Die Häuser von Ohlenhof.*
http://gutenberg.spiegel.de/?id=12&xid=1678&Kapitel=4&cHash=efadbba0082 (Chapter "Der Dieshof", accessed Dec. 9, 2009).

Lorenz 1999: Dagmar Lorenz, "Seide". http://74.125.47.132/search?q=cache:tilEsezfoRwJ:db.swr.de/upload/manuskriptdienst/wissen/wi0620021494.rtf+dagmar+lorenz+seide&hl=en&ct=clnk&cd=6&gl=us&client=firefox-a (first broadcast January 22, 1999; accessed Dec. 9, 2009).

Luster 1970: Gawaina D. Luster, *Untersuchungen zum Stabreimstil in der Eneide Heinrichs von Veldeke,* Europäische Hochschulschriften I, 13. Bern.

Lutz 1974: Hans Dieter Lutz, "Zur Formelhaftigkeit mittelhochdeutscher Texte und zur 'theory of oral-formulaic compostition'," *Deutsche Vierteljahresschrift für Literaturwissenschaft und Geistesgeschichte* 48: 432-447.

MHW: *Mittelhochdeutsches Wörterbuch*, Kurt Gärtner, Klaus Grubmüller, Karl Stackmann, eds., Stuttgart, 2006ff.

Michels 1921: Victor Michels, *Mittelhochdeutsche Grammatik,* 4th ed. 1921, reprint as 5th ed., Hugo Stopp ed. (Germanische Bibliothek, I. Reihe: Grammatiken), Heidelberg, 1979.

Minis 1974: Cola Minis, "Zur Formelsprache im *Roman d'Eneas* und in Veldekes *Eneide,*" in: *Studien zur deutschen Literatur und Sprache des Mittelalters: Festschrift für Hugo Moser zum 65. Geburtstag,* ed. Werner Besch et al., Berlin, 31-40.

- 1959: Cola Minis, *Textkritische Studien über den Roman d'Eneas und die Eneide von Henric van Veldeke* (Studia Litteraria Rheno-Traiectina 5), Groningen.

Müller Lobeck 2004: Christiane Müller Lobeck, "Astreines Purimspiel," in: http://www.filmtext.com/start.jsp?mode=1&key=595 (review of film "El abrazo partido" 2004, accessed Dec. 9, 2009).

Nerius 2003: Dieter Nerius, "Graphematische Entwicklungstendenzen in der Geschichte des Deutschen," in: *Sprachgeschichte: Ein Handbuch [...],* ed. Werner Besch et al. (Handbücher zur Sprach- und Kommunikationswissenschaft 2.3), 2nd

ed. Berlin/New York, 2461-2472.
Norden 1957: Eduard Norden, ed., *P. Vergilius Maro Aeneis Buch VI*. 8th ed. Strassburg, reprint Darmstadt, 1984.
Peyerl 2008. Elke Peyerl, *Zwillingsformeln in der österreichischen Alltagssprache, Schriftenreihe "tribüne"* 1, Wien.
Provinzial-Correspondenz 1874: vol. 12/38, Sept. 23, 1874, in: http://amtspresse.staatsbibliothek-berlin.de/vollanzeige.php?file=9838247/1874/1874-09-23.xml&s=1 (accessed Dec. 9, 2009).
Redewendungen: Redewendungen und sprichwörtliche Redensarten: Wörterbuch der deutschen Idiomatik, ed. Günther Drosdowski and Werner Scholze-Stubenrecht (Duden 11), Mannheim, 1994.
Roetteken 1887: Hubert Roetteken, *Die epische Kunst Heinrichs von Veldeke und Hartmans von Aue: Ein Beitrag zur mittelhochdeutschen Literaturgeschichte*, Halle.
Schieb et al. 1970: Gabriele Schieb and Theodor Frings, eds., *Henric van Veldeken, Eneide* (Deutsche Texte des Mittelalters 58, 59, 62), 3 vols. Berlin, 1964, 1965, 1970.
Schmidt-Wiegand 2002: Ruth Schmidt-Wiegand, ed., *Deutsche Rechtsregeln und Rechtssprichwörter: Ein Lexikon,* Beck'sche Reihe 1470, 2nd., rev. ed., Munich.
Schulze 1873: Carl Schulze, "Die sprichwörtlichen Formeln der deutschen Sprache," in: *Archiv für das Studium der neueren Sprachen und Literaturen* 48 (1871): 435-450; 49 (1872): 139-162; 50 (1872): 83-122; 51 (1873): 195-212.
Schweikle 1977: Günther Schweikle, *Die Mittelhochdeutsche Minnelyrik I: Die Frühe Minnelyrik. Texte und Übertragungen. Einführung und Kommentar*, Darmstadt.
Spalding 2000: Keith Spalding, *An Historical Dictionary of German Figurative Usage*, Oxford, 1952-2000.
Stein 2006: Hannes Stein, *Enzyklopädie der Alltagsqualen: Ein Trostbuch für den geplagten Zeitgenossen*, Berlin, Vorbemerkung , 9f.
Stilwörterbuch: Stilwörterbuch der deutschen Sprache, 6th ed. Günther Drosdowski, ed., (Der große Duden 2), Mannheim, 1970.
Taylor, 1931: Archer Taylor, *The Proverb and an Index to "The Proverb,"* Cambridge, reprint Hatbore-Copenhangen, 1962.
Teusink 1946: Derk Teusink, *Das Verhältnis zwischen Veldekes Eneide und dem Alexanderlied*, Dissertation Amsterdam, Amsterdam.
Virgil: Virgil, *The Aeneid*, transl. C. Day Lewis, London, 1952.
Wolff et al. 1981: Ludwig Wolff and W. Schröder, "Heinrich von Veldeke," *Die deutsche Literatur des Mittelalters: Verfasserlexikon*, 2nd ed. Vol. 3, col. 899-918, reprint in: *Deutschsprachige Literatur des Mittelalters: Studienauswahl [...]*, ed. Burghart Wachinger, Berlin-New York, 2001, 274-293.
Zingerle 1864: Ignaz von Zingerle, "Die Alliteration bei mittelhochdeutschen Dichtern," in: *Stizungsberichte der philosophisch-historischen Classe der Kaiserlichen Akademie der Wissenschaften Wien* 47: 103-174.

WIRNTS VON GRAVENBERC *WIGALOIS*
EIN ARTUSROMAN KONZIPIERT ALS DICHTERISCHE
AUSEINANDERSETZUNG MIT DEN POLITISCHEN WIRREN SEINER ZEIT

von Helmut Beifuss - Leipzig

Zusammenfassung

Der nachfolgende Beitrag weist dem *Wigalois* von Wirnt von Gravenberc eine auf dem Werk in seiner Gesamtheit beruhende Interpretation zu, die gleichzeitig eine Datierung erlaubt bzw. diese als überaus plausibel erscheinen lässt. Sie bezieht dementsprechend den Aufbau und in besonderer Weise das so genannte Achtergewicht als notwendigen, aus der Intention des Autors sich in konsequenter Weise ergebenden, Bestandteil der Dichtung mit ein. Aufbau und Intention hängen, wie gezeigt werden wird, sehr eng zusammen, sie bedingen sich. Der Aufbau des *Wigalois* muss in dessen Interpretation mit einbezogen werden, nur so kann man dem Werk und seinem Verfasser gerecht werden. Mit diesen Aussagen soll keineswegs einer Art von Modellhaftigkeit das Wort geredet werden, eher im Gegenteil, es handelt sich um den individuellen Versuch eines Autors, sich möglicherweise im Sinne seines Mäzens - mit den ihn umgebenden politischen Verhältnissen auseinander zu setzen. Gerade darin ist einer der Gründe dafür zu sehen, dass Werk und Autor lange Zeit und eigentlich immer noch nicht entsprechend gewürdigt wurden bzw. werden.

1. Ein kurzer Exkurs in die Wirkungs- und jüngere Forschungsgeschichte

Der *Wigalois* Wirnts von Gravenberc war nach Ausweis der Überlieferung ein überaus geschätztes, beliebtes Werk. Aus dem Kreis der Artusromane ist nur Wolframs „arthurischer Gralroman" *Parzival* reicher bezeugt. Nur Wolframs *Willehalm* ist noch reicher bezeugt als der *Parzival*, er gehört aber nicht zur hier angesprochenen Gattung. Das anhaltende Interesse dokumentieren nicht nur die Handschriften, sondern auch die intensive und vielgestaltige Rezeption, die das Werk erfuhr. Diese reicht auf literarischer Seite bis zur *Wigoleis*-Version in Ulrich Fuetrers *Buch der Abenteuer*, oder der Umformulierung der gesamten Romanhandlung in Prosa in der *History von Wigoleis vom Rade*,[1] die als 'Volksbuch' mehrere Drucke erlebte, bis schließlich

---

[1] Die Abhängigkeitsverhältnisse und die Datierung der beiden Texte sind umstritten.

zum jiddischen *Widuwilt*. Damit gehört der *Wigalois* zu den mittelalterlichen Versromanen, die über die Prosabearbeitung in das Zeitalter des Buchdrucks gelangten und durch diesen rasche Verbreitung fanden. Zu der offenkundigen Wertschätzung von Autor und Werk stehen die negativen Werturteile in krassem Widerspruch, die in der Forschung bis in die jüngste Vergangenheit immer wieder zum Tragen kommen. Als Ergänzung ließe sich in diesem Zusammenhang darauf hinweisen, dass Wirnt in Konrads von Würzburg *Der Welt Lohn* selbst zur literarischen Gestalt wurde. Auf die zahlreichen Beurteilungen, die das Werk erfuhr, und den Wandel in der Einschätzung, der in den letzten Jahrzehnten stattgefunden hat, wird im Folgenden nur in soweit eingegangen, als es für die Argumentation der nachfolgenden Ausführungen wichtig erscheint. Eine Sonderstellung nimmt der isoliert stehende Versuch Schröders (1986, 235-277) ein, der versucht, die alten Negativurteile aufleben zu lassen. Symptomatisch für den gesamten Beitrag ist der fast verzweifelt zu nennende Versuch, Wirnt die Kenntnis des *Willehalm* nachzuweisen, und ungeachtet der Tatsache, dass dies nicht recht gelingen will, daran festzuhalten, dass Wirnt den *Willehalm* gekannt haben muss. Auf weitere Werturteile, die der Fundierung entbehren, soll an dieser Stelle nicht eingegangen werden. Es ließe sich allerdings allgemein die Frage stellen, ob sich nicht auch hinter dem Aufbrechen, Verlassen von Strukturen, deren Bedeutung ohnedies von den Literarhistorikern möglicherweise höher veranschlagt wird als von den zeitgenössischen Autoren, oder auch der Kombination von Strukturen unterschiedlicher Herkunft eine Manifestation von 'Sinn', ein absichtsvolles, gezieltes Vorgehen seitens des Autors verbergen kann. Einen kurzen Überblick zu verschiedenen Deutungsansätzen bieten z.B.: Fuchs (1997, 100-112), Wennerhold (2005, 74-127),[2] Jaeger (2000, 92-116), der auch auf andere Zusammenfassungen von Deutungsansätzen hinweist. Zu Wennerhold wäre anzumerken, dass die Behandlung des *Lanzelet* in einer Arbeit, die sich auf die späten Artusromane konzentriert, zumindest befremdlich erscheint. Neben die stetigen Versuche, Quellen und Vorlagen ausfindig zu machen und die Anleihen Wirnts bei anderen Autoren respektive deren Werken aufzuspüren, traten in jüngerer Zeit vor allem Bemühungen, die verschiedene Einzelaspekte des Werkes beleuchteten. Zu den

---

[2] Zu unterschiedlichen Werturteilen siehe besonders die Bemerkungen S. 126f.

im Folgenden angesprochenen Gesichtspunkten, die nur eine Auswahl darstellen, sollen jeweils nur wenige Hinweise auf die Sekundärliteratur angeführt werden. Bei den Arbeiten standen mehrfach der Titelheld (z.B.: Daiber 1999; Fuchs 1997, 100-112), seine besondere Befähigung zum Ritter und Herrscher sowie sein Werdegang im Vordergrund, aber auch die 'bezeichenunge', die sich mit den Gegenständen und der Tierwelt im *Wigalois* verbinden lässt (Lohbeck 1999), wurde untersucht. Des Weiteren wurde der Versuch unternommen, die Funktion des Wunderbaren zu analysieren (Eming 1999; Dietl 2003) oder die Bedeutung der „dark figures" zu interpretieren (Henderson 1986). Außerdem wurde die Wirkabsicht des Korntinteils des Werkes untersucht (Brinker 1995), auch die Frage nach dem Stellenwert des *Wigalois* innerhalb der Gattung Artusepik fand Interesse (z. B. Cormeau 1977; Ringeler 2000), um eine Analyse dessen, was das Werk insgesamt bezweckt, also eine Untersuchung dessen, was Wirnt mit seinem Epos leisten will, hat sich die Forschung jedoch nur selten bemüht (Gottzmann 1979; Heinzle 1973; Hahn 1994; Grubmüller 1985). Hahn sieht das Werk vor dem Hintergrund der Minne und des triuwe-Pathos bzw. der Minnetriuwe, wobei Wirnt ihrer Meinung nach das Thema im Vergleich zu seinen Vorgängern stärker instrumentalisiert. Allerdings übersieht Hahn dabei, dass Wigalois selbst seine Beziehung zu Gott über seine Minnebeziehung stellt V. 8981-8984.

Auf Grubmüller (1985) sei kurz eingegangen, denn sein Beitrag zeigt, dass selbst diejenigen, die anerkennen, dass Wirnts Werk nicht dem - heute ohnedies als gattungsrelevant bzw. gattungsbestimmend nicht mehr allgemein anerkannten - 'Strukturmodell' des so genannten 'klassischen' Artusromans folgt, Schwierigkeiten haben, sich bei ihrer Argumentation davon zu lösen, dieses als Vergleichsfolie heranzuziehen: „(…), in der Anlage des Romans sichtbar zu machen, und die Konsequenz, mit der er seine neuen Akzente setzt, läßt den Verdacht aufkommen, nicht mangelnde Einsicht in die Strukturgesetze des Artusromans sei ihre Ursache, sondern bewußte Umwertung." (Grubmüller 1985, 224). Immerhin kommt Grubmüller dann in seinem Fazit unter anderem doch zu dem Schluss: „Literarische Schemata sollten nicht zu normativer Gültigkeit hypostasiert werden. Es wird notwendig sein, die Gattungsgeschichte des Artusromans wieder vor der Vielfalt der Einzelfälle zu diskutieren." (Grubmüller 1985, 239). Der Gedanke der bewussten Umwertung könnte als Grundlage für die Interpretation der gestalterischen Möglichkeiten Wirnts neue Dimensionen eröffnen. Dies aber nur dann, wenn die Interpreten bereit sind, sich von altbekannten Bedenken zu lösen und es zulassen, dass es neben den 'Klassikern' weitere, gute, vielleicht sogar sehr gute, ebenbürtige Autoren gab. Wirnts Vorgehen wäre dann nicht Schwäche oder eine Folge von verpassten Chancen den Roman aufzuwerten, eine Ansicht die selbstverständlich wieder nur die Abhängigkeit vom 'klassischen Strukturmodell' zeigt, sondern ein Spiel mit Motiven, die aufgegriffen werden, um mit den Erwartungshaltungen der Rezipienten zu spielen, ihre Neugier zu wecken bzw. zu erhalten, damit die eigentliche Botschaft nicht durch mangelndes Interesse ins Leere geht. Dies gilt trotz der Riesen, Drachen und ähnlicher Gestalten, die wohl eher für den heutigen Leser etwas Außergewöhnliches darstellen als für den mittelalterlichen Rezipienten. Eher am Rande zu erwähnen wäre Wild, der vor dem Hintergrund des Doppelwegmodells versucht, die Entwicklung zum Roman der Frühen Neuzeit zu analysieren bzw. die Form der Adaptation des Modells zu charakterisieren (Wild 1999).

Nach der Intention, die der Autor mit seinem Werk verbindet, zu fragen, sollte aber selbst dann ein zentrales Anliegen der Forschung sein, wenn diese möglicherweise nicht den Erfolg seiner Dichtung begründete.[3] Das Ziel des nachfolgenden Beitrages wird es deshalb sein, die Wirkungsabsicht, die Wirnt mit seinem *Wigalois* verband, herauszuarbeiten. Dabei werden vor allem auch Fragen nach der Datierung, zu der es bisher nur widersprüchliche und keinesfalls befriedigende Aussagen gibt, sowie dem Mäzen eine Rolle spielen. Ihre Beantwortung eröffnet die Möglichkeit, den zeitgeschichtlich-politischen Hintergrund, also die allgemeinen Lebensumstände des Dichters sowie seines Umfeldes, zu konkretisieren und dadurch dem Ziel des Aufsatzes näher zu kommen.

2. Inhaltsskizze

König Joram erscheint am Hof von Artus und bittet dessen Frau, Ginover, einen Gürtel als Geschenk anzunehmen. Sollte sein Geschenk nicht akzeptiert werden, wolle er mit den Artusrittern kämpfen und gegebenenfalls sein Leben verlieren. Die Königin bittet Gawein

---

[3] Der Aspekt des Deutungsangebots wird im weiteren Verlauf aufzugreifen sein.

um Rat. Dieser rät der Königin von der Annahme des Geschenkes ab, woraufhin die Artusritter - zuletzt auch Gawein - zum Kampf antreten und unterliegen. Gawein muss Joram in dessen Reich folgen. Während des Rittes erfährt Gawein von Joram, dass einzig sein Gürtel die Siege möglich machte. Diesen Gürtel schenkt Joram Gawein, der sich, in Jorams Reich angekommen, in dessen Nichte verliebt und diese heiratet. Gawein verlässt seine schwangere Frau, um an den Artushof zurückzukehren. Er lässt den Gürtel bei seiner Frau, was zur Folge hat, dass er nicht in Jorams Reich zurückkehren kann. Wigalois, Gaweins Sohn, wächst ohne seinen Vater bei seiner Mutter auf. Er erhält in Jorams Reich auch eine Ausbildung. Herangewachsen begehrt er, Artusritter zu werden. Ausgestattet - auch mit dem Gürtel - verlässt er seine Mutter, um an den Artushof zu ziehen. Dort angelangt setzt er sich auf den Tugendstein. Dies ist eine Probe, die selbst Gawein (wegen des Vergehens gegen eine Frau) nicht bestehen konnte. Bisher war - so der Text - es einzig Artus selbst vorbehalten, sich auf den Stein setzen zu können. Wigalois wird, ohne dass sich Vater und Sohn erkennen, Gawein zur ritterlichen Erziehung anvertraut. Diese ist gerade abgeschlossen, als Nereja, eine Botin der Königin Amena, am Artushof eintrifft, um Artus zu bitten, ihr seinen besten Ritter zur Verfügung zu stellen, um eine *âventiure* auf Leben und Tod zu bestehen. Sie denkt dabei an Gawein, Wigalois erbittet allerdings von Artus das Vorrecht, die *âventiure* bestehen zu dürfen. Diesem Wunsch gibt Artus zur Verärgerung von Nereja nach. Nereja und Wigalois brechen zusammen auf. Das Ziel ihres Weges ist Korntin.

Mit dem Verlassen des Artushofes beginnt eine erste *âventiure*-Sequenz[4], die aus fünf âventiuren besteht:

1. Kampf gegen einen Burgherren, der nur demjenigen Unterkunft gewährt, der ihn besiegt; damit ist zwar kein Kampf auf Leben und Tod gemeint, dennoch tötet Wigalois seinen Gegner.
2. Wigalois befreit eine Jungfrau, die von zwei Riesen bedrängt wird, wobei er den einen tötet, den anderen mit der Jungfrau an den Artushof schickt.
3. Wigalois und Nereja begegnet eine Bracke, die Wigalois Nereja zu deren Freude schenkt. Als der Besitzer des Hundes diesen zurück-

---

[4] Mit dieser Formulierung soll keinesfalls auf das so genannte "Doppelwegmodell" angespielt werden.

fordert, kommt es zum Kampf, bei dem Wigalois den Besitzer des Hundes tötet.
4. Wigalois hilft Êlamîe, den ihr zuerkannten, jedoch von Hojir von Mannesvelt für seine *amîe* geraubten Schönheitspreis zurückzugewinnen, indem er Hojir im Zweikampf tötet.
5. Wigalois wird von Schaffilun, der seit Jahren darauf wartet, die nun von Wigalois angestrebte *âventiure* bestehen zu dürfen, zum Kampf herausgefordert. Wigalois tötet auch Schaffilun.

Durch die bestandenen Kämpfe ist Nereja endlich davon überzeugt, dass Wigalois hinreichend Kampferfahrung und Tapferkeit besitzt, um die ihn erwartende *âventiure* bestehen zu können. In Roimunt, der Burg Amenas, begegnet Wigalois schließlich Lârîe, der Tochter Amenas, und verliebt sich in sie. Um ihre Hand gewinnen zu können, muss Wigalois das Reich Korntin befreien, das König Lar, der Vater Lârîes, durch argloses Verhalten an den mit dem Teufel im Bund stehenden Roaz verloren hat. Vor dem Aufbruch wird sehr deutlich, was vorher schon eher unterschwellig angesprochen wurde, Wigalois ist bei seinem Tun darauf bedacht, sich der Hilfe und Unterstützung Gottes zu vergewissern, worauf auch seine Umgebung in Roimunt Wert legt. Am Abend vor dem Aufbruch vertraut sich Wigalois der Gnade und des Beistandes Gottes an. Es werden Wigalois am nächsten Morgen, zusätzlich zu seinem Wunsch, vor dem Aufbruch eine Messe abzuhalten, apotropäische Hilfsmittel überreicht. Wigalois erhält einen *brief, der gap im vesten muot: / vür älliu zouber was er guot.* (V. 4428-4429)[5], dieser wird ihm von einem Priester an sein Schwert geheftet; und:

    ein brôt daz was geleit dar în
    geworht mit grôzer meisterschaft:
    von wurzen hêt ez solhe kraft
    daz in lie diu hungers nôt

---

[5] Zitiert wird nach: *Wigalois der Ritter mit dem Rade* von Wirnt von Gravenberc, hrsg. v. J. M. N. Kapteyn. Erster Band: Text, Bonn 1926 (Rheinische Beiträge und Hülfsbücher zur germanischen Philologie und Volkskunde, Bd. 9). Hinzuweisen ist dennoch auf die neue Ausgabe: Wirnt von Grafenberg *Wigalois*. Text - Übersetzung - Stellenkommentar. Text der Ausgabe von J. M. N. Kapteyn übersetzt, erläutert und mit einem Nachwort versehen von Sabine Seelbach und Ulrich Seelbach, Berlin-New York 2005.

als erz engegen dem munde bôt;
ez gap im muot und solhe maht: (V. 4470-4475).

Dieses, sich in einer kostbaren Tasche befindende Brot wird Wigalois von Lârîe gesandt, die Wigalois - zeitgemäß - nur heimlich liebt, während die Liebe bei Wigalois offenkundig ist. Solchermaßen ausgestattet begibt sich Wigalois auf seine Mission. Es handelt sich dabei um einen Befreiungs- besser einen Erlösungsweg mit mehreren Stationen. Der Zugang zum Reich Korntin ist nur möglich in Begleitung eines wundersamen Tieres, das sich als eine Art verwunschene Gestalt des ehemaligen Königs des Reiches, Lar, entpuppt. Wigalois begegnet zunächst den Rittern König Lars, die im Fegefeuer immerzu turnieren müssen. Ein Versuch von Wigalois, an diesen Wettkämpfen teilzunehmen, scheitert kläglich, woraufhin dieser zu der Erkenntnis gelangt, dass die nicht endenden Kämpfe der Ritter eine Strafe Gottes darstellen. Das 'Tier' geleitet Wigalois zu einem Anger, auf dem sich dessen, bereits erwähnte, wahre Gestalt offenbart. König Lar darf sich von den Mühsalen seines ehemaligen Reiches auf Grund einer guten Handlung während seiner Regentschaft hier eine Stunde am Tag erholen. Durch Lar erfährt Wigalois seine Abkunft, und er erhält - als drittes schützendes Attribut - eine Blüte vom Baum des Angers. Diese soll ihn vor dem Atem des Drachen, den Wigalois besiegen muss, schützen. Dieser Kampf kostet Wigalois dennoch fast das Leben, denn das sterbende Untier trifft Wigalois mit seinem Schwanz und schleudert ihn unter einen Baum, unter dem er ohnmächtig liegen bleibt.

Ein armes Fischerehepaar, das vorüberzieht, beraubt ihn. Es bleiben dem nun nackten Wigalois nur die Blüte und die Tasche mit dem Brot. Als er erwacht, denkt er zunächst, dass sein bisheriges Leben nur ein Traum war. Erst als er Lârîes Geschenk, die kostbare Seidentasche, entdeckt, beginnt die Erinnerung zurückzukehren, jedenfalls empfindet Wigalois es als tröstlich, dass ihm die Tasche geblieben war. Die Selbstzweifel sind für Wigalois jedoch keine existenziell bedrohliche Situation. Er wird von Bêlêare, deren Mann Wigalois vor dem Untier gerettet hatte, gesund gepflegt und erhält bei seinen Aufbruch Waffen, ein Streitross und eine herausragende Rüstung, nicht jedoch den Zaubergürtel. Der Protagonist begegnet dem Waldweib Ruel, das ihn fesseln konnte, da er nicht gegen eine Frau kämpfen will. Das Wiehern seines Pferdes, das Ruel in die Flucht treibt, und die Hilfe Gottes, der nach einem Gebet des Wigalois diesen von seinen Fesseln befreit, helfen aus der bedrohlichen Situation. In weiteren Kämpfen überwindet Wigalois den mit ungeheurer Kraft ausgestatteten Zwerg Karrioz, ein Rad, das mit Schwertern und Kolben besetzt ist und ihm den Weg versperrt, sowie das Mischwesen Marrîen, das über einen Feuerzauber verfügt. Das Feuer kann nur mit Marrîens Blut gelöscht werden. Schließlich gelangt Wigalois zur Burg des Teufelbündners Roaz. Hier muss er noch die beiden Torwächter bezwingen. Einen erschlägt Wigalois, den anderen, Adan, macht er sich zum Untertan. Es gelingt nach schwerem Kampf, auch Roaz zu besiegen, dessen Frau, Japhite, aus Liebesleid stirbt. Es findet eine prunkvolle Hochzeit statt, bei der auch Artusritter anwesend sind. Zu ihnen gehört Gawein. Gawein und Wigalois erkennen ihr verwandtschaftliches Verhältnis. Danach folgt eine weitere Herausforderung, von der es ausdrücklich heißt, dass es sich nicht um eine *âventiure* handelt. Auch aus dieser Auseinandersetzung geht Wigalois als Sieger hervor, wobei sich sein Vater Gawein als derjenige erweist, der die eigentliche militärische Leistung erbringt. Das Werk endet schließlich mit einem Ausblick auf das glückliche Leben des Paares, Lârîe und Wigalois. Wirnt erwähnt deren Sohn, Lifort Gâwânides, dessen Leben zu erzählen für ihn zu schwierig sei, weshalb ein anderer über ihn schreiben soll (V. 11627-11535).

3. Die Datierung: Grundlagen und Konsequenzen

Da Wirnt von Gravenberc urkundlich nicht bezeugt ist, was bereits Saran feststellte (Saran 1896, 254-255), kann die Forschung bei Aussagen über den Dichter ausschließlich auf literarische Zeugnisse zurückgreifen. Das heißt zunächst auf: 1.) Wirnts einziges bezeugtes Werk, den *Wigalois* selbst; 2.) die Erwähnung Wirnts bei anderen Dichtern, z.B. Heinrich von dem Türlîn, Rudolf von Ems; 3.) die Rezeption und Bearbeitung des Stoffes; sowie 4.) Konrads von Würzburg *Welt Lohn*.

Den Zeugniswert der zuletzt genannten Quelle hat Saran sicher bei weitem überschätzt, denn es handelt sich hierbei, wie Lienert zu Recht feststellt, um Fiktion: „Konrads Erzählung ist Fiktion - daß er das Motiv der Frau Welt auf Wirnt übertragen hat, läßt sich wohl aus dem religiösen Ethos und den Weltklagen in dessen Werk erklären." (Lienert 1991, 1). Unabhängig davon, ob man sich der Begründung für den Rekurs auf Wirnt anschließen will, liegt Lienert bei der grundsätzlichen

Einschätzung sicher völlig richtig. Streng genommen können die Aussagen Konrads über Wirnt für die Forschung nur dann einen Wert besitzen, wenn sie sich anderweitig stützen lassen. Während Saran noch glaubt, aus Konrads Werk Rückschlüsse auf Wirnts Leben ziehen zu können (Saran 1896, 255-256 und 275-278), dürfte heute kaum noch jemand diese Auffassung akzeptieren. Vor dem Hintergrund der Quellenlage ist es wenig erstaunlich, dass es verschiedene Datierungsvorschläge für Wirnts Wigalois gibt. Diese gilt es gemäß der einleitend formulierten Zielsetzung zunächst vorzustellen und gegeneinander abzuwägen. Die Argumente, die Saran anführt, um seine Datierung für den *Wigalois* als plausibel zu erweisen, sollen nicht im Einzelnen nachgezeichnet werden, als Fazit resümiert Saran, dass der *Wigalois* zwischen 1203 und 1209 entstand, er engt diesen Zeitraum sogar noch weiter ein, indem er weiter folgert: Der Durchschnittswert, welcher ziemlich genau sein dürfte, wären die Zahlen 1202-1205 (Saran 1896, 267-272, Fazit 272). Die Grundlage für diese zeitliche Festlegung bildet, was den Beginn der Arbeit Wirnts am *Wigalois* betrifft, die Auffassung, mit dem beweinten Fürsten (V. 8064) sei Berthold IV. von Andechs (Herzog Berthold I.) gemeint, der 1204 starb. Saran glaubt, auf Grund der Art der Schilderung der Trauer und ihrer Position im Werk schließen zu dürfen, dass Wirnt den *Wigalois* bereits bis zu der Stelle gedichtet hatte, an der er die Trauer beschreibt. Deshalb geht Saran davon aus, Wirnt habe spätestens 1203 den *Wigalois* begonnen. Als spätesten Zeitpunkt für die Beendigung des Werkes nimmt Saran das Jahr 1209 an, das Jahr der Kaiserkrönung des Welfen Otto. Die Grundlage dafür bildet eine Textstelle, in der es heißt:

> ez ist ein berc, der beste
> den ie dehein man gesach.
> ezn wære dehein wîp sô swach
> sine behieltez mit lîhter wer
> immer vor des küniges her. (V. 3634-3638).

Aus diesen Versen glaubt Saran schließen zu dürfen, dass Wirnt auf die kaiserlose Zeit des deutschen Reiches anspielt: „Da Wirnt hier auf die höchste ihm bekannte macht anspielen will, so erwartet man nach der sonstigen gewohnheit der mhd. Dichter *des keisers her.*" (Saran 1896, 270), ein Fazit, das nicht zwingend zu sein scheint. Auf diesen Aspekt wird später zurückzukommen sein. Allerdings sollte man eine voreilige rigorose Ablehnung in Anbetracht der Tatsache vermeiden, dass Wirnt auch sonst durchaus Bezüge zu seiner Lebenswirklichkeit herstellt. Diese sind bekanntermaßen keineswegs auf die Erzählerkommentare beschränkt. Wenngleich die Argumente Sarans im Einzelnen nicht zwingend sein mögen, sollte sein Vorgehen, die Zeitklagen mit in die Datierung einzubeziehen, viel stärker beachtet werden. Der Hinweis, solche würden ab dem zweiten Jahrzehnt des 13. Jahrhunderts häufiger auftreten, genügt, wie noch gezeigt werden wird, wohl kaum. Als Mäzene von Wirnt erschließt Saran die Grafen von Henneberg (Saran 1896, 172-175 und 278-281). Grundlage und Ausgangspunkt dafür bietet für Saran die Analyse des Textes selbst (z.B. erneut die Darstellung der Trauer um den verstorbenen Fürsten von Meranien), von der ausgehend Saran Schlüsse auf die historischen Verhältnisse, in denen sich Wirnt bewegt, zieht, wobei hier sicher zu sagen ist, dass Saran zu sehr darauf baut, in den Dichtungen die Lebensrealität zu finden. Dieser Aspekt wurde mit dem Hinweis auf die Bewertung von Konrads von Würzburg *Welt Lohn* bereits angesprochen.

Auch Neumann geht, jedenfalls wo es ihm für seinen Datierungsversuch zuträglich erscheint, davon aus, dass Konrads von Würzburg *Welt Lohn* reale Fakten aus Wirnts Leben spiegelt, denn er glaubt - wie Saran -, annehmen zu dürfen, Wirnt hätte sich am Kreuzzug 1217/18 beteiligt, denn dieser sei weitgehend ein Andechs-Meranier Kreuzzug gewesen (Neumann 1964, 53). Grundlage dieser Aussage ist die Auffassung, Wirnt sei im unmittelbaren Umfeld der Andechs-Meranier zu suchen. Durch seine Annahme bezüglich der Kreuzzugsteilnahme gewinnt Neumann einen *terminus ante quem*, als entsprechenden terminus post quem stellt dem Neumann den Tod des Grafen Berthold IV. gegenüber, denn auf diesen beziehen sich auch für ihn die Verse, die von der Trauer um einen Fürsten berichten. Weiter eingrenzen will Neumann diesen Zeitraum durch die lobende Erwähnung Wolframs durch Wirnt, aus der Neumann glaubt, schließen zu dürfen, dass der *Parzival* abgeschlossen und Wolfram mit diesem Werk zu „einem entscheidenden Hörer- und Leserkreis durchgedrungen ist." (Neumann 1964, 61). Daraus ergibt sich für Neumann eine Entstehungszeit von circa 1210-1215. Die Grundvoraussetzung für das Jahr 1210 erscheint streng genommen nicht zwingend.

Warum sollte ein Dichter einen 'Kollegen' nicht auch schon dann loben, wenn dieser noch nicht von einem für damalige Verhältnisse breiteren Publikum entdeckt worden war. In diesem Zusammenhang ist mit Nachdruck an die immer noch nicht völlig geklärte Entstehungsgeschichte gerade des *Parzival* zu erinnern und an die uneingeschränkt zu akzeptierende Feststellung Bumkes (2004, 248-249): „(...), daß die umfangreichen Werke in vielen Fällen nicht auf einmal entstanden sind und daß sie nicht erst nach Fertigstellung des ganzen bekannt gemacht worden sind, sondern daß es Frühfassungen, Teilveröffentlichungen, (...) und Parallelversionen gegeben hat." Als Ort der Entstehung nimmt Neumann den gesellschaftlichen Umkreis des Herzogs Otto I. von Meranien an (Neumann 1964, 61).

Kritisch setzt sich Neumann mit der bereits zitierten Textstelle (V. 3634-3638) auseinander. Er lehnt den Versuch Sarans ab, auch darin eine Stelle mit historischem Bezug zu sehen - hier bezogen auf die kaiserlose Zeit des Reiches. Für Neumann handelt es sich hierbei keineswegs um einen Hinweis Wirnts darauf, dass er in einer kaiserlosen Zeit lebt. Zu fragen ist allerdings, ob die Argumente Neumanns zwingender sind als diejenigen von Saran. Neumann weist auf den Namen der Burg hin und die Übersetzung Wirnts „ûf ir hûs ze Roimunt, - / daz tuon ich iu entiuschen kunt: / Küniges berc hieze ez hie - /" (V. 3755-3757). Inwiefern dies ein Gegenargument zu Sarans Auslegung der zuvor angeführten Verse darstellt, ist nicht ersichtlich, denn warum sollte eine Königsburg nicht von einem Kaiser angegriffen werden. Der Hinweis darauf, dass das von Roaz besetzte Korntin ein Königreich ist, würde als Argument gegen Saran nur dann anzuführen sein, wenn man gleichzeitig unterstellt, nur Roaz käme als König und Feind in Betracht, beides gibt jedoch der Text nicht her.

Ebenfalls ein eher schwacher Einwurf ist in dem Verweis auf die Titulierung des Kaisers als *rex Romanorum* zu sehen. Die gesamte Argumentation findet sich bei Neumann (1964, 52). Allein die Beobachtung, dass etwa der von Wirnt so geschätzte Wolfram von Eschenbach Otto als Kaiser bezeichnet „Do der keiser Otte / ze Rome truoc die krone" (393,30-394,1)[6], entkräftet diesen Einwand. Es bleibt als Fazit demnach eigentlich nur die Feststellung: Sarans Schlussfolgerung ist

---

[6] Zitiert nach: Wolfram von Eschenbach *Willehalm*. Text der Ausgabe von Werner Schröder. Völlig neu bearbeitete Übersetzung, Vorwort und Register von Dieter Kartschoke, Berlin, New York 1989.

zwar möglicherweise gewagt, die Argumente Neumanns widerlegen sie andererseits kaum. Der Hinweis auf die Benutzung der Bezeichnung 'keiser' durch Wolfram von Eschenbach darf und soll nicht so verstanden werden, dass Wirnt, wenn er es denn tat, auf den Kaiser als dem König übergeordnete Instanz nur in Abhängigkeit von Wolfram verweisen konnte. Sie ist nur als Indiz dafür zu sehen, dass sich die Verwendung der Titulierung „Kaiser" nachweisen lässt und mit dem Wort im Empfinden der Zeitgenossen sicher die höchste weltliche Macht angesprochen wurde.

Die Verwendungsweise der Bezeichnung 'Kaiser' im Werk selbst kann zumindest die These Sarans erhärten, dass Wirnt für die Benennung der höchsten Machtinstanz 'keiser' benutzt hätte. Bei der ersten Stelle handelt es sich um die Erwiderung Wigalois' auf die Bitte Lârîes, vor dem Aufbruch eine Nacht zu bleiben und auszuruhen:

> wæren mîn älliu rîche
> sô daz ich keiser wære
> der êren ich enbære
> ê ich verlieze iuwer gebot. (V. 4210-4213).

Diese Aussage kann zwar als eine Art Topos gewertet werden, dennoch belegt die Wortwahl die Annahme Sarans. Die zweite Stelle hat ebenfalls direkten Bezug zu Wigalois. Als Bêlêâre Wigalois eine neue Ausrüstung schenkt, beschreibt sie den Harnisch folgendermaßen:

> dar zuo gibe ich iu zehant
> daz aller beste îsengwant
> daz ie dehein keiser getruoc,
> darumbe Brîen Lâmêren sluoc
> an guoten triuwen dâ er lac. (V. 6066-6070).

Die Herkunft des Harnischs wird in dem Hinweis in V. 6069 nur angedeutet, derjenige, der Bêlêâres Mann den Harnisch anvertraute, war König Jorel. Durch die Differenzierung einerseits „königlicher Überbringer" und andererseits „kaiserwürdiger Harnisch" zeigt Wirnt auch hier die hierarchische Denkweise. Dass von Kaiserwürde die Rede ist, als es um einen Ausrüstungsgegenstand für Wigalois geht, wird wohl kaum als Zufall abgetan werden können.

Eine weitere Textstelle aus Wirnts Wigalois sollte bei der Bewertung der beiden Argumentationen ebenfalls berücksichtigt werden, denn auch sie spielt im Hinblick auf den Protagonisten eine Rolle. Es handelt sich um die Beschreibung von Flôrîe bei der Ankunft Gaweins an Jorams Hof. Mehrfach benutzt Wirnt Formen des Substantivs mhd. 'künegin': "ze kemenâten az diu künigîn" (V. 711); „diu küniginne in enpfie" (V. 722), als Wirnt jedoch Flôrîes Tugendhaftigkeit charakterisieren will, formuliert er: „si möhte wol keiserinne / von ir tugent sîn gewesen" (V. 734-735). Dies kann zwar nicht beweisen, dass Saran mit seiner Schlussfolgerung Recht hatte, aber es schwächt Neumanns ohnedies nicht sehr gewichtigen Gegenargumente im Zusammenhang mit den bereits erwähnten Textstellen weiter ab. Immerhin lässt sich dokumentieren: Für Wirnt bedeutet 'keiser' respektive 'keiserin' die hierarchisch höchste Position. Auch Wirnts Charakterisierung, die gerade die Tugendhaftigkeit Flôrîes als einer Kaiserin würdig ansieht, ist im Hinblick auf die Rolle, die der Sohn als idealer Herrscher dereinst spielen wird, sicher nicht zufällig, sondern absichtsvoll gewählt.

Im Verlauf des Werkes verwendet Wirnt noch einmal das Wort 'keiser', als Wigalois Gott um Beistand bittet:

> 'nu hilf, keiser, herre got,
> daz mich dirre tievels bot
> iht scheide von dem lîbe,
> daz ich dem süezen wîbe
> erledige ir gesellen
> du solt den tievel vellen,
> wand er der werlte schaden tuot.' (V. 5079-5085).

Hier geht es, wie das Zitat zeigt, um die höchste, allerdings himmlische Machtinstanz - Gott. Wirnt verwendet die Bezeichnung 'keiser' und Ableitungen davon nicht nur, wenn er die höchste irdische, sondern auch, wenn er die nach christlicher Vorstellung oberste himmlische Macht benennen will. Es scheint demnach naheliegend, im Sinne Sarans davon auszugehen, dass für Wirnt die höchste Macht und die Bezeichnung 'keiser' zusammengehören. Es ergibt sich daraus, unabhängig davon, ob man sich der Datierung Sarans anschließen will, dass er mit der Feststellung Recht hat, dass es auffällig ist, dass der mit einem herausragenden Lob ausgestatteten Burg als potentieller Angreifer nicht der Kaiser, sondern ein König gegenübergestellt wird. Folgendes lässt sich allerdings nicht von der Hand weisen: Sieht man von der Textstelle ab, in der Wigalois Gott als 'keiser' bezeichnet, dann kann bei allen Textstellen, an denen 'keiser' vorkommt, ein direkter Bezug zum Protagonisten nachgewiesen werden. Seine Mutter hat kaiserliche Tugenden, er benutzt das Substantiv selbst, wenn auch in Verbindung mit dem Irrealis in der Antwort an Lârîe für sich, und er erhält eine Rüstung, wie sie noch kein Kaiser trug. Darin liegt jedoch kein Widerspruch, denn Wigalois befindet sich erst auf dem Weg zu einem Herrscheramt.

Von einer Spätdatierung geht Honemann (1994, 347-362) in seiner Untersuchung zur Stellung und Bedeutung des Kampfes zwischen Wigalois und Hojir von Mansfeld, dem roten Ritter, aus. Er stellt in diesem Zusammenhang auch die Frage nach den möglichen Mäzenen, wobei er neben dem Umfang der Beschreibung und weiteren Besonderheiten des angesprochenen Kampfes, wie etwa der Tatsache, dass Wigalois gegen eine historisch belegbare Person antritt, das Interesse der Mansfelder am *Wigalois* heranzieht. Eine solche Zuweisung müsste allerdings, wie Honemann selbst ausführt, durch weitere eingehende Untersuchungen abgesichert werden, vorläufig sind die Schlüsse, die er aus der Hojir-Aventiure zieht, eher als Thesen zu betrachten.

Ausgehend von der Feststellung, dass es sich bei dem namengebenden Ort um Gräfenberg östlich von Erlangen gelegen handelt, der nie andechsisch war, sondern altes Eigengut der Zollern, versucht Mertens (1981, 14-31) zu erweisen, dass diese auch als Auftraggeber Wirnts anzusetzen sind. Er verwirft dabei eine frühe Datierung, wie sie Neumann vorgeschlagen hat, obwohl er als Datierung der Kölner Handschrift, auf die noch näher einzugehen sein wird, um 1220 angibt. Als Grund führt Mertens zunächst an: „Bei dieser Einordnung bleibt das Unbehagen, daß Wirnt sein superlativisches Lob Wolframs bereits nach einigen Büchern des *Parzivals* gesprochen haben soll"; und weiter: „ferner daß ein Werk mit der oben skizzierten literarischen Eigenart bereits zu so frühem Zeitpunkt geschaffen wurde und obendrein von den uns bekannten Literaturzentren relativ isoliert dasteht." (Mertens 1981, 24). Es wurde bereits darauf hingewiesen, dass es nicht recht einsehbar ist, warum ein Dichter die Qualität eines Kollegen nicht früher erkannt und gelobt haben soll, als dies ein breiteres Publikum tat. Außerdem ist hier erneut auf die Entstehungsgeschichte des *Parzival* hinzuweisen.

Den Aspekt, dass die Zollern und nicht die Andechs-Meranier als Gönner Wirnts anzusehen sind, vertieft Mertens weiter. Dabei zieht er auch die Möglichkeit heran, dass mit dem im *Wigalois* beweinten Fürsten von Meran (V. 8064) nicht Berthold IV. (gest. 1204), sondern Otto VII. (gest. 1234) gemeint sein könnte. In dem zitierten Hinweis auf das Haus Meran sieht Mertens kein Argument gegen seine Gönnerzuschreibung, denn seiner Meinung nach ist dieser: „auch als Huldigung eines anderen Auftraggebers für den befreundeten (oder verwandten) Meranier vorstellbar." (Mertens 1981, 25). Sicher ist diese Möglichkeit nicht auszuschließen, aber es scheint auch kein Argument zu sein, mit dessen Hilfe man ein anderes Geschlecht als das der Andechs-Meranier als Mäzene Wirnts plausibel machen kann.

Auf zwei weitere Argumente, die nach Mertens Meinung eine frühe Datierung des *Wigalois* unwahrscheinlich machen, soll abschließend noch kurz eingegangen werden. Ein Faktum, das gegen eine frühe Entstehung spricht, sieht er darin, dass Gottfried Wirnt in seiner „Literaturschau" nicht nennt, denn dies erklärt sich am einfachsten, so Mertens, daraus, dass von Wirnt um 1210/15 noch nichts bekannt war (Mertens 1981, 27). Ließe sich das Fehlen unter anderem nicht auch damit erklären, dass Gottfried einen 'Verehrer' Wolframs (V. 6343-6346) nicht unnötig erwähnen wollte, denn dies hätte doch seine eigene Position geschwächt und die Wolframs gestärkt, den er doch - mit an Sicherheit grenzender Wahrscheinlichkeit - in einem schlechten Licht erscheinen lassen wollte? Darüber hinaus handelt es sich nicht annähernd um eine exhaustive 'Liste' von Autoren, die vor Gottfried geschrieben haben. Weitere Beispiele nicht erwähnter Autoren und Werke könnten angeführt werden. Dieser Hinweis ist somit zu wenig zwingend, um eine Datierung darauf aufbauen zu können. Das letzte Argument, mit dem Mertens sich gegen eine Datierung ins erste Jahrzehnt des 13. Jahrhunderts stark macht, resultiert aus der Huldigung an einen Meranier. Eine solche war - nach Auffassung von Mertens - unmittelbar nach 1208, als das Haus Andechs-Meranien wegen seiner Beteiligung an der Ermordung Philipps von Schwaben in Bamberg der Acht verfiel, nicht unproblematisch (Mertens 1998, 178). Geht man davon aus, dass Wirnt nicht im Auftrag der Andechs-Meranier schrieb, wozu Mertens, wie bereits dargelegt, neigt, kann dieser Vorbehalt vielleicht ins Feld geführt werden, allerdings gilt es selbst dann zu berücksichtigen, dass das Verhalten der Meranier den bisherigen Kontrahenten im Streit um die Macht, Otto, der nunmehr seines Widersachers entledigt war, trotz der verhängten Acht, wohl kaum gestört haben dürfte. De facto schwerwiegende negative Konsequenzen von Seiten des jetzt alleinigen Anwärters waren kaum zu erwarten, möglicherweise sogar eher im Gegenteil positive. Wurde der *Wigalois* hingegen für das Haus der Andechs-Meranier verfasst, schlägt Mertens' Argumentation gar nicht zu Buche, denn dann gilt das bisher im Hinblick auf den zweiten Thronanwärter soeben Gesagte auch. Wenn dies aber als Argument abgelehnt werden sollte, kann darüber hinaus für die in Rede stehende Konstellation noch angeführt werden, dass die Huldigung durch den 'Hofdichter' als Versuch der Rehabilitierung des Geschlechts geradezu dessen Aufgabe war. Zumindest kann ihm aber unterstellt werden, dass er versuchte, einen Beitrag dazu zu leisten. Eine solche Huldigung in unmittelbarer zeitlicher Nähe zur Ermordung Philipps hat, das deutet der verwendete Begriff Rehabilitierung bereits an, auch Konsequenzen für die Beurteilung der Tat selbst, denn diese wurde dann unter Beteiligung von Mitgliedern eines als ehrenwert beurteilten Hauses durchgeführt. Die von Mertens vorgebrachten Argumente scheinen alles in allem eher vage und thesenhaft. Letztlich zeigt dies Mertens selbst, der zwar zunächst für eine späte Datierung um 1234 eintritt, danach einräumt, dass jedoch das, was er anführte, auch mit einer Datierung in die zwanziger Jahre vereinbar wäre (Mertens 1981, 28). Doch auch an dieser Datierung hält Mertens, wie noch gezeigt werden wird, im weiteren Verlauf seiner Forschungsarbeit nicht fest.

Die Datierung der frühesten Handschriftenfunde auf das erste Viertel bzw. die ersten drei Jahrzehnte des 13. Jahrhunderts lassen die zeitliche Festlegung von Honemann und Mertens aus paläographischen Erwägungen als wenig plausibel erscheinen. Es ist grundsätzlich zu bedenken, dass bei der Datierung von Handschriften, sieht man von dem Sonderfall, dass Handschriften Jahresangaben enthalten, die es erlauben, ihre Entstehungszeit genau festzulegen, ab, immer eine gewisse Ungenauigkeit bei der zeitlichen Fixierung zumindest als Möglichkeit bestehen bleibt, worauf Mertens zu Recht hinweist. Dies bedeutet aber keinesfalls, dass an der Datierung mittels der Schrift 'vorbeiinterpretiert' werden darf. Die Datierung der Fragmente durch Bertelsmeier-Kierst, auf die im Folgenden Bezug genommen wird, wurde erst 1992 publiziert. Da der Aufsatz von Mertens früher entstand, ging er bei seiner Datierung und dem Hinweis auf die möglichen 'Verschiebungen' bei Datierungen mittels der Schrift nur von der Kölner

Handschrift aus, allerdings kann auch deren Entstehung - wie noch dargelegt wird - kaum in die 30er Jahre des 13. Jahrhunderts datiert werden. Im vorliegenden Fall gilt dies in besonderem Maße, da es nicht nur eine Handschrift gibt, die eine Datierung auf nach 1234 unwahrscheinlich macht, sondern darüber hinaus drei Fragmente bekannt sind, die aus einer Handschrift stammen, deren Entstehung sehr wahrscheinlich ebenfalls vor 1234 liegt. Für die Fragmente stellt Bertelsmeier-Kierst (1992, 287) fest: „Aufgrund dieser Befunde dürfte die auf 1220-1230 zu datierende Handschrift E im österreichischen Raum, unweit Steiermark, abgefaßt sein."

Zur Kölner Handschrift, Stadtarchiv W*6, äußerst Schneider (1987, 46-47): „Die Entstehung der Kölner Handschrift bald nach der Abfassung des ‚Wigalois' und im Herrschaftsbereich der Andechser Grafen ist dennoch wahrscheinlich."[7] Um diese Aussage zu konkretisieren, ist anzumerken, dass Schneider die Datierung Neumanns zu Grunde legt, also 1210-1215. Schiewer (1988, 239) kommt für die Kölner *Wigalois*-Handschrift zu einer ähnlichen Datierung. Er gibt das erste Viertel des 13. Jahrhunderts als Entstehungszeitraum an.[8] Selbst wenn man geneigt sein sollte, entgegen diesen fundiert erarbeiteten Datierungen eine größere Ungenauigkeit anzunehmen und eine spätere Entstehung der angesprochenen Handschriften noch für möglich zu halten, sollte man nicht vergessen, dass es sich hier um Texte verschiedener Herkunft handelt, die nicht nur das Werk als Grundlage, sondern auch einen gewissen Bekanntheitsgrad voraussetzen. Dies macht die Spätdatierung von Wirnts Text auch dann unwahrscheinlich, wenn man von einer erhaltenen Überlieferung ausgeht, die bald nach der Entstehung des Werkes einsetzt. Spätestens die Datierung der Fragmente, die es erforderlich machen würde, für zwei unabhängig voneinander entstandene Handschriften sehr ähnliche Besonderheiten beim 'Produktionsvorgang' zu unterstellen, lassen den nachfolgend zitierten Hinweis von Mertens, mit dem er sich die Möglichkeit der Spätdatierung eröffnet, fast mit Sicherheit hinfällig, zumindest aber überaus zweifelhaft erscheinen: „Allerdings ist eine genaue Festlegung immer problematisch - regionale und persönliche Archaismen

---

[7] Zur Kölner Handschrift siehe außerdem: 883-885 sowie Abb. 35 und 36.
[8] Ein von Bertelsmeier-Kierst angekündigter Beitrag zur Datierung der Kölner Handschrift ist bisher nicht erschienen.

sind nicht auszuschließen, [...] kann leicht eine „Verschiebung" von zwanzig Jahren ausmachen.[20]" (Mertens 1981, 26). Mertens (1998, 178) ist später von der Spätdatierung abgerückt, was die Beurteilung der von ihm früher vorgebrachten Argumente bestätigt und der Datierung der Handschriften eher gerecht wird. Die von ihm gewählte Formulierung lässt jedoch weiterhin seine Ansichten über die Unsicherheit der Datierung erkennen: „Die Datierung kurz vor 1220 wird dem literarischen Charakter des *Wigalois* besser gerecht als eine Frühdatierung bald nach 1204 und den ersten *Parzival*-Büchern." (Mertens 1998, 178). Mit ähnlichen Argumenten plädierte Mertens zunächst für eine Spätdatierung. Obwohl sie offenkundig nicht besonders tragfähig sind, schließlich musste Mertens seinen ersten Datierungsansatz revidieren, hält er an dieser Art zu argumentieren fest. Lienert gibt als Lebensdaten für Wirnt von Gravenberg circa 1170/80-circa 1230 an, so dass auch dadurch eine Datierung des Werkes, wie sie unter anderem Mertens - zumindest ursprünglich - und Honemann vorgeschlagen haben, von vorne herein für sie kaum in Betracht kommt. Die durch „kaum" angedeutete eher vage Formulierung resultiert daraus, dass Wirnt urkundlich nicht belegt und von seinem Leben fast nichts gesichert ist. Für Lienert bezieht sich Wirnts Hinweis in V. 8064: „am wahrscheinlichsten auf den Tod Bertholds IV. am 12.8.1204." (Lienert 1991, 3).

Als Fazit aus den Datierungsvorschlägen und Gönnerzuweisungen lässt sich festhalten, dass es keinen wirklich triftigen Grund gegen eine Frühdatierung, wie sie Saran vorgeschlagen hat, gibt und schon gar nicht kann sie als widerlegt eingestuft werden. Vergleichbares lässt sich auch für die Gönnerfrage formulieren. Auch hier zeigt sich kein stichhaltiges Argument, das die Andechs-Meranier als Mäzene Wirnts unplausibel macht. Das Interesse anderer Adelsfamilien ist kein Beleg dafür, dass es sich um die Gönner handelt. Der Kampf des Wigalois gegen Hojir von Mansfeld mag zwar das Interesse der Grafen von Mansfeld an Wirnts Werk geweckt haben, aber es erscheint doch, besonders wenn gleichzeitig die Verbindung mit der Erwähnung der grenzenlosen Trauer über den Tod eines Mitgliedes des Hauses Andechs-Meranien gesehen wird, eher wahrscheinlich, dass hier eine Reminiszenz an den erfolgreichen, wenn auch lange zurückliegenden Kampf eines Verwandten dieses Geschlechts gegen Hojir, vorliegt (Honemann 1994). Neumann (1964, 56) spricht in diesem Zusammenhang von „einer kleinen Huldigung" an das Haus Andechs. Die heute überwiegend angenommene Bezugsnahme Wirnts auf den Tod Bertholds IV. legt es eigentlich nahe, den Zeitpunkt der Abfassung des Werkes nicht allzu weit vom Todesjahr Bertholds zu entfernen. Rechtfertigungsargumente dafür, dass dies doch möglich sei, wirken eher erzwungen als plausibel. Es stellt sich die Frage, ob es neben der bisher vorgestellten Vorgehensweise, andere Ansätze als die frühe Datierung mangels zwingender Argumente gegen diese anzuzweifeln, auch Hinweise gibt, die für eine frühe Datierung, wie Saran sie vorgeschlagen hat, sprechen. Wenn dies der Fall sein sollte, resultiert daraus eine solide Grundlage für die Beantwortung der Frage nach der Intention Wirnts.

Dabei ist, um Einwänden und Missverständnissen vorzubeugen, klar zu stellen, dass die Intentionen, die spätere Abschreiber mit ihrem Tun und dem Werk selbst verbanden, keineswegs identisch gewesen sein müssen mit denjenigen, die Wirnt bei seiner Arbeit verfolgte. Das Werk bietet, wie eigentlich alle literarischen Werke, nicht nur eine Deutungsmöglichkeit, sondern kann durchaus auf verschiedene Weise 'gelesen' und demzufolge interpretiert, gedeutet und letztlich einem Publikum in unterschiedlicher Wirkungsabsicht zur Rezeption unterbreitet werden. Dies gilt für Wirnts Roman möglicherweise mehr als für andere Werke. Es ist hier nicht nur an die alte Formel 'prodesse et delectare' zu denken, sondern auch an verschiedene Möglichkeiten innerhalb der beiden Oppositionsglieder. Dass der *Wigalois* so manchen Rezipienten in besonderer Weise dazu verlockt haben mag, nur den Aspekt des 'delectare' wahrzunehmen, sollte nicht dazu führen, das Werk als reinen Unterhaltungsroman zu apostrophieren, wie es etwa Haasch (1954, 54) tat, der den *Wigalois* als „reinen Aventiurenroman" bezeichnet. Das bereits zur Sprache gebrachte Argument Sarans, dass aus dem Text auf die kaiserlose Zeit vor der Krönung Ottos als Entstehungszeitraum zu schließen sei, soll dabei zumindest vorerst ausgeklammert bleiben, denn es beruht auf der Interpretation eines Textstückes der Erzählebene.

4 Die Erzählerkommentare

Einen anderen Status nehmen die Erzählerkommentare ein, denn sie haben - nach Wirnts Darstellung - einen direkten Bezug zur aktuellen

Realität und liegen deshalb auf einer anderen Ebene als der Erzähltext selbst. Es ist daher erwägenswert, den Inhalt der Aussagen des Erzählers zumindest zunächst als Realitätsbezug, als Lebenswirklichkeit des Autors und seiner Umgebung bzw. seiner Mitmenschen aufzufassen und infolgedessen auf eine andere Art zu beurteilen. In der älteren Forschung war es durchaus üblich, in den Erzählerkommentaren weit rigoroser als in der soeben geschilderten Art einen Rekurs auf die Realität zu sehen (z. B.: Latzke 1906, 961-985; Wild 1953). In den letzten Jahren ist man da eher vorsichtiger. In jüngeren Arbeiten zum *Wigalois* spielen die Erzählerkommentare kaum noch eine Rolle, sie finden eher am Rande Erwähnung. Schröder deutet sie sogar als ein Indiz für künstlerisches Unvermögen Wirnts, siehe: Werner Schröder (1986). Es stellt sich daher zunächst die Frage, ob die Erzählerkommentare tatsächlich Realität widerspiegeln oder ob mit Lienert (1997, 272), zu formulieren ist: „Zeitklagen sind (vielleicht mit Ausnahme weniger konkreter Anspielungen) umstandslos weder als autobiographische noch als historische Zeugnisse zu nehmen, sie belegen weder eine persönliche Misere des Autors noch zeitgeschichtliche Mißstände." Immerhin zeigt auch diese sehr rigide klingende Beurteilung durch die in Klammer gesetzte Formulierung eine Ansatzmöglichkeit zur Diskussion. Gerade Wirnts Werk bietet dazu allen Anlass, man denke nur an die nicht weg zu diskutierenden historischen Anspielungen innerhalb des eigentlichen Erzähltextes (s. etwa die Hojir-Aventiure). Außerdem gilt es bei Aussagen mit Bezug zur Lebenswirklichkeit der Rezipienten des Dichters zu berücksichtigen, dass diesen quasi notgedrungen auffällt, ob Wirnt bei dem, was er als aktuelle Wirklichkeit bezeichnet, tatsächlich die Realität schildert. Alles andere könnte ihm als Lüge ausgelegt werden, mit den entsprechenden Konsequenzen. Wie ist es vor diesem Hintergrund etwa um die Beurteilung des Dichters durch seine Rezipienten bestellt und vor allem, was bedeutet das für die Intention, die Wirnt mit seinem Werk verbindet. Muss man nicht davon ausgehen, dass die Möglichkeit, auf seine Rezipienten zu wirken, abnimmt, wenn diese bemerken, dass Wirnt in seinen Kommentaren nicht tatsächlich, wie er behauptet, auf die Realität hinweist.

Im Hinblick auf das Publikum, das Lienert (1997, 264) ebenfalls nur als fiktiv ansieht, gilt es, vergleichbare Überlegungen anzustellen. Man darf doch sicher annehmen, dass für den mittelhochdeutschen

Dichter das Publikum einen ganz anderen Stellenwert hatte, als es das für den heutigen Schriftsteller haben kann. Dies hängt schon allein damit zusammen, dass die Verbreitung von Literatur auf eine völlig andere Art vor sich ging. Die Bevölkerung war im Mittelalter zu über 90% weder lese- noch schreibkundig und selbst an den Höfen gab es viele Analphabeten. Demnach war auch der interessierte und intendierte Rezipient auf einen Vortragenden angewiesen, sei es der Sänger, sei es der Epiker selbst oder ein des Lesens Kundiger, der den Text zum Besten gab. Als Publikum ist zunächst die Hofgesellschaft zu denken und gerade diese dürfte für den Dichter, besonders den Epiker der damaligen Zeit weit mehr als Fiktion gewesen sein. Dies sollte zumindest für die Zeit der Entstehung eines epischen Werkes unterstellt werden. Dass der Vortragende verschiedene Rollen annehmen kann und auch seinem Publikum unterschiedliche Rollen zuschreibt, ist davon nicht tangiert.

Was die Erzählerkommentare betrifft, so sind diese nicht pauschal zu beurteilen, sondern zu differenzieren. Sentenzen etwa lassen keine unmittelbaren Rückschlüsse auf die Lebenswirklichkeit des Autors zu, auch wenn dieser sie als persönliche Stellungnahme äußert. Dies gilt auch für sich daran anschließende allgemein gehaltene Äußerungen, die der Rubrik laudatio temporis acti zuzuordnen sind. Gleichwohl gilt es auch bei jedem Erzählerkommentar der genannten Art zu bedenken, ob nicht eventuell durch die Auswahl im ersten bzw. die Stoßrichtung der Zeitklagen im zweiten Fall doch, wenn nicht unmittelbar, so doch mittelbar auf die Lebensumstände des Autors bzw. die zeitgenössischen Verhältnisse geschlossen werden kann.

Für die Datierung sind vor allem gesellschaftsbezogene Erzählerkommentare relevant. Die Aussagen Wirnts, die den Glauben, Gott, allgemein die Frömmigkeit zum Gegenstand haben, sind zwar besonders im Hinblick auf die Auslegungsmöglichkeit der verwendeten Symbole im Korntinteil, deren 'bezeichenunge', relevant, sie dürften aber bei einem Dichter, der sich glaubhaft als frommer Mensch zu erkennen gibt, auch etwas über das Verhältnis seiner Umwelt zum Glauben aussagen.

Auf die Kommentare im Einzelnen einzugehen, würde den Rahmen sprengen.[9] Nur auf den umfangreichen 'apokalyptischen' Kommentar

---

[9] Siehe dazu: Rochels 1901, Latzke 1906.

soll und muss später noch genauer eingegangen werden. Die zahlreichen Stellungnahmen zu Aspekten der Frömmigkeit erweisen in jedem Fall, dass Wirnt selbst fromm war, und sie dokumentieren, dass er Fehlverhalten in Sachen Glaube für die üblen Zustände verantwortlich macht, die zu seiner Zeit auf der Welt herrschen. Er klagt z.B. über den Aberglauben (V. 6182-6203) oder beschreibt die Güte und Allmacht Gottes (V. 6469-6484, 6874-6884). Insgesamt ist der Gesichtspunkt Glaube/Frömmigkeit so stark ausgeprägt, dass wohl kaum davon die Rede sein kann, dass dies nichts mit dem Autor, seinem Leben, seinem Denken zu tun hat. Auf der eigentlichen Textebene sind neben dem Korntinteil, der insgesamt auf die Frömmigkeit des Autors hin gedeutet werden kann, die zahlreichen Gebete ein Indiz für die Gläubigkeit des Autors, jedenfalls dann, wenn man davon ausgeht, dass Wirnt die Handlungsweise des Protagonisten und der anderen positiv dargestellten Figuren seiner eigenen Lebenshaltung entsprechend anlegte. Die Gesellschaftskritik bezieht sich auf verschiedene Bereiche. So beschäftigt sich Wirnt mit denjenigen seiner Zeitgenossen, die sich des Eidbruchs schuldig machen (V. 2146-2158). Meineidige wurden früher geächtet, weshalb man es tunlichst vermied, Eide zu brechen, und diese unbedingt einhielt. Dies wäre auch zu Lebzeiten Wirnts noch notwendig. Wirnt wählt hier eine drastische Sprache. Er bezeichnet denjenigen, der seinen Eid bricht, als „tôtsieche[n] man" (V. 2152). Außerdem wäre es früher so gewesen, dass derjenige als „an êren ligen tôt" (V. 2157) betrachtet wurde, der nicht zu seinem Wort stand. Daneben geißelt Wirnt die Habgier als um sich greifende Unsitte (V. 2317-2348). Als Ursache führt er den Mangel an Ehrgefühl und Standesbewusstsein bei den Mitgliedern der Ritterschaft an, der seinerseits daraus resultiert, dass Unwürdige in den Ritterstand erhoben werden. Beide Aspekte werden in dem noch zu besprechenden zeitkritischen, bereits unter der Bezeichnung 'apokalyptisch' erwähnten Kommentar, der dem Rachefeldzug gegen Lîon vorangeht, in gesteigerter Form erneut aufgegriffen. Auch das Verhalten gegenüber Jungfrauen und Damen ist beklagenswert, denn es hat sich ebenfalls ins Negative gewendet. Dargestellt wird dies V. 2358-2395. Früher war es ohne Weiteres möglich, dass Jungfrauen allein reisen konnten, heute müssen sie - so klagt Wirnt - befürchten, belästigt und mit übler Nachrede behelligt zu werden. Selbst Damen, die sich als ehr- und tugendhaft erwiesen hätten, wagten nicht mehr, das Haus zu verlassen, weil man ihnen schlechte Absichten unterstellt und sie mit üblen Gerüchten verfolgt. So siegt das treulose Verhalten gegen Anstand und Beständigkeit. In gewisser Weise wird auch dieser Aspekt im schon erwähnten „apokalyptischen" Kommentar zur Sprache gebracht, allerdings steht dabei das Sterben aus Minne im Vordergrund, für das jedoch nur das richtige Verhalten gegenüber den Frauen die Basis bilden kann.

Die Zeitkritik kulminiert schließlich in dem bisher ausgeklammerten, im Folgenden näher zu besprechenden Kommentar, der gelegentlich die Charakterisierung, „fast apokalyptische Ausmaße" anzunehmen, erfuhr. Diese Bezeichnung bezieht sich weniger auf die Art der Darstellung als vielmehr auf das Faktum, dass Wirnt sich hier nicht nur auf die Offenbarung des Johannes bezieht, sondern auch Formulierungen aus ihr - allerdings in geänderter Reihenfolge - übernimmt. Nach einer formelhaften Wendung, mit der Wirnt durch eine Frage auf das Folgende vorbereitet, schildert er, dass es kaum noch wahre Minne gibt, und derjenige, der wahrhaft liebt, Spott ausgesetzt wird. Danach beschreibt Wirnt das Verhältnis zu Gott und die aus diesem resultierenden Folgen:

> wîlen dô minten si got
> dô hêt ouch ers in sîner pflege.
> nu kêre wir alle von dem wege
> sîner gebot, diu er uns lie.
> dâ von solt wir bedenken wie
> diu werlt sich verkêret hât;
> ir vreude jæmerlîche stât;
> diu reht sint gevlœhet;
> ir gewalt der ist gehœhet;
> diu triuwe ist verschertet;
> untriuwe mit nîde hertet. (V.10254-10264)

Die betrüblichen Zustände folgen für Wirnt also daraus, dass die Menschen sich von Gott abgewendet haben, der Glaube ist mithin das Fundament einer funktionierenden Gesellschaft. Mit der Feststellung, dass sich die Zustände von Jahr zu Jahr verschlimmern, Habgier dazu führt, dass niemand ein friedliches Ende findet, leitet Wirnt über zur Offenbarung des Johannes, denn seine Auffassung ist:

> sî stêt nû, als wîlen sach
> Jôhannes, dâ von er sprach
> in dem hêren geiste.
> mit gotes volleiste
> sach er die himel offen stên;
> dar inne solhiu dinc begên
> daz im ze schrîben wart verboten. (V. 10273-10279)

Nachdem Wirnt auf den Text des Johannes eingegangen ist, wendet er sich noch einmal dem Fehlverhalten seiner Zeitgenossen zu, greift erneut das Motiv der Habgier auf und weist auf die Vergänglichkeit des irdischen Strebens hin:

> owê dir, rîcheit unde ruom!
> dîn zierlîch gebende
> wirt vil ellende
> nach des lîbes ende. (V. 10302-10305)

Es scheint doch mehr als fraglich, ob Wirnt seinem Publikum, mit dem er ja in unmittelbarer Verbindung stand, mit dem er eine Kommunikationsgemeinschaft bildete, eine Darstellung der Zeitverhältnisse in diesen Dimensionen zugemutet hätte, ohne einen realen Hintergrund. Es ist mithin spätestens hier zu fragen, ob man abseits literarhistorischen Unbehagens gegen eine 'Frühdatierung', wenn man dieses überhaupt teilt, nicht doch zugestehen sollte, dass dieses vernichtende Urteil über die Gegenwart am besten in das erste Jahrzehnt des 13. Jahrhunderts also in die Jahre der immer heftiger werdenden Thronstreitigkeiten im Reich passt. Bei der Bewertung ist auch die Stelle zu bedenken, an der Wirnt diesen Kommentar einflicht. Die Feierlichkeiten anlässlich der Hochzeit von Wigalois und Lârîe neigen sich dem Ende zu und mit ihnen, so könnte jedenfalls erwartet werden, auch das Werk, als ein Bote am Hof erscheint und das Hilfeersuchen Lîamêres, einer Verwandten Lârîes, vorträgt. Das Geschehen erfährt, wie es bereits durch den Aufbruch des Wigalois nach Korntin der Fall war, eine Ebenenverlagerung. Dies wird zwar schon bei der Beratung, was zu tun sei, und dem Entschluss zur Kampfansage deutlich, letztlich aber durch die Erwiderung Lîôns auch explizit ausgesagt: „hie enist niht âventiure" (V. 10182). Das bedeutet, der 'apokalyptische' Erzählerkommentar fällt in den Teil des Werkes, in dem es um den als realen Rachefeldzug zumindest suggerierten und weitgehend entsprechend dargestellten Kampf gegen Lîon geht. Das Publikum hört den Kommentar demzufolge nicht mit der gleichen Einstellung wie die Erzählerkommentare davor, sondern nimmt die Ausführungen Wirnts wahrscheinlich noch ernster.

Die Möglichkeit, auf Grund der Kommentare Wirnts auf die Person des Dichters, seine Denkweise und die zeitgenössischen historischen Verhältnisse schließen zu können, sollte vor dem Hintergrund des Gesagten nicht bezweifelt werden. Diese Aussage bezieht sich bewusst nur auf Wirnts Werk und beansprucht keine Allgemeingültigkeit. Erst eine nähere Betrachtung des jeweiligen Einzelfalls lässt den Stellenwert der Erzählerkommentare erkennen.

5 Gattungszugehörigkeit und Intention des Autors

In den Umkreis von Datierung und Bewertung der Intention Wirnts gehört auch die Frage nach der Klassifizierung bzw. Gattungszugehörigkeit des *Wigalois*, auf die deshalb nachfolgend eingegangen werden soll. Mertens bezeichnet das Werk als Legendenroman und den Protagonisten als Legendenheiligen. Diese Einschätzung ist schon deshalb unbefriedigend, weil sie kaum in Einklang zu bringen ist mit dem abschließenden Kriegszug gegen Lîon, dessen grundlegende Motivation rechtlich-politischer Natur ist, wobei nicht übersehen werden sollte, dass es auch um Rache geht. Beides Motive, die einem Legendenheiligen wohl kaum zu unterstellen sind (Mertens 1990, bes. 86-89). Tragfähiger scheint hingegen der schon geäußerte Ansatz, dass es in Wirnts *Wigalois* um die Darstellung idealer Herrschaft gehen könnte. Kaisers (1975, 410-443) Ansatz, Wirnt habe den *Wigalois* im Zusammenhang mit dem so genannten Territorialisierungsprozess für das Haus Andechs-Meranien verfasst, weist bereits in diese Richtung, es kann ihm aber aus chronologischen Gründen nicht zugestimmt werden. Reichert hat gezeigt, dass die von Kaiser angesprochenen Entwicklungen, wie Marktgründungen, der Aufbau von Gerichtsbezirken, die heftigen Auseinandersetzungen zwischen Landesfürst und Adel in Süddeutschland erst ab den 30er Jahren des 13. Jahrhunderts einsetzten. Davor ist Derartiges nicht erkennbar (Reichert, 1985, bes. 6-127). Dieser zeitliche Rahmen stimmt jedoch, wie gezeigt wurde, nicht zur handschriftlichen Überlieferung. Der gelegentlich anzutreffende Hinweis darauf, dass es sich bei dem Kampf von Wigalois gegen Roaz und Lîôn um einen Kreuzzug handelt, ja sogar um den Aufruf zu einem solchen (Brinker 1995, 87-100), vermag, was die erste Auffassung betrifft, bestenfalls dann einigermaßen gerechtfertigt erscheinen, wenn man unter Kreuzzug jeden Kampf gegen das Böse oder begangenes Unrecht verstehen will, was den zweiten Interpretationsansatz anbelangt, so regen sich doch erhebliche Zweifel an der Adäquatheit. Für die Bewertung als Kreuzzugsaufruf fehlen, um nur zwei Aspekte zu benennen, der göttliche Auftrag, dem Wigalois Folge leistet, oder der Gedanke zum Kampf aufzubrechen, um das Christentum auszubreiten oder doch zumindest zu verteidigen. Der Beistand Gottes und das Ersuchen darum deuten keinesfalls notwendigerweise auf Kreuzzugsgeschehen. Der Auffassung von Brinker erteilt auch Thomas (2005, 144-145) eine deutliche Absage. Die ganze Anlage des Romans, Aufbau und Ablauf, stehen ganz eindeutig im Dienste des Gedankens, den Werdegang des Wigalois zum idealen Herrscher darzulegen und diesen abschließend als einen eben solchen zu erweisen. Hierauf weist schon Heinzle (1973, 270) hin, wenngleich er diesem Aspekt keine weitere Aufmerksamkeit schenkt: „(…): bei der Übernahme der Herrschaft und während des Unternehmens gegen Lîôn ist Wigalois nicht mehr der Märchenheld des klassischen Artusromans, sondern erscheint in voller Kenntnis der Erfordernisse königlicher Machtpolitik zum Besten seines Landes umsichtig planend und geschickt agierend, als Herrschergestalt durchaus zeitgeschichtlichen Zuschnitts." Einschränkend zu Heinzle wäre anzumerken, dass Wigalois die Bahnen des Artusritters im 'klassischen' Artusroman nicht erst mit dem Aufbruch gegen Lîôn verlässt.

Verfolgt man den Aufbau des Romans und den Werdegang des Wigalois, fällt, sieht man vom so genannten epischen Achtergewicht ab, zunächst die klare Zweiteilung in Ritterfahrt oder Bewährung als Ritter und die deutlich davon abzuhebende, als Erlösungstat einzustufende Befreiung Korntins von Roaz auf. Diese beiden Teile erinnern an die Zwei-Schwerter-Lehre. Das weltliche Schwert, im Roman das arthurische, und das geistliche, das in den mit Gottes Hilfe bestandenen Herausforderungen wirksam wird, werden im Protagonisten geeint. Schon Mitgau (1959) weist in seiner Arbeit mehrfach auf die beiden Funktionen des Protagonisten als Aventiure- und Gottesritter hin. Dieses Gottesrittertum sollte jedoch, wie bereits erläutert wurde, nicht mit Kreuzrittertum verwechselt werden. Diese beiden Parameter, die Kombination aus weltlicher Macht und geistlicher Gewalt durch die sakrale Ausrichtung, belohnt durch göttlichen Beistand, machen Wigalois zum Repräsentanten des von Kirche und Staat gleichermaßen akzeptierbaren, idealen Herrschers. Dies zeigt der siegreiche Kampf in dem expressis verbis als 'Nicht-*Aventiure*' gekennzeichneten Kriegszug am Ende des Werkes, der nur als Bestätigung der idealen Herrscherqualitäten des Wigalois in der 'realen' Welt aufgefasst werden kann. Während Wigalois die arthurischen Bewährungsproben aus eigener Kraft meistern kann, ist er, wie bereits ausgeführt, bei der Erlösung Korntins auf die tätige Mithilfe Gottes angewiesen. Diese erbittet er sich stets demütig. Nur durch Gottes Eingreifen kann Wigalois alle Gefahren unbeschadet überstehen. Die einzige Ausnahme bildet die kurzzeitige 'Krise' nach dem Kampf gegen den Drachen Pfetan. Die Andersartigkeit der Auseinandersetzungen, mit denen Wigalois in Korntin konfrontiert wird, zeigt sich schon vor dem Abschied aus Roimunt:

> sîn muot in in die vreise
> und in solhen kumber stiez
> dar zuo im niemen trôst gehiez
> an gotes gnâde erz allez liez. (V. 4366-4369)

Auch die Messe, die am Morgen des Aufbruchs auf Wunsch des Protagonisten abgehalten wird, bietet Wigalois Gelegenheit, Gottes Beistand zu erbitten. Noch deutlicher wird der Unterschied durch das Verhalten des Priesters, der das Schwert des Wigalois segnet und gegen Zauber feit:

> der priester strihte im umb sîn swert
> einen breif, der gap im vesten muot:
> vür älliu zouber was er guot.
> des gnâter im und bevalch sich got. (V. 4427-4430)

Materiell gesehen hat Wigalois immer noch das arthurische Schwert in Händen, dennoch dürfte klar zu Tage treten, dass eine Veränderung stattgefunden hat. Die Haltung des Protagonisten ist eine andere als zuvor. Das Schwert, das er führt, ist eben durch die demütige Hinwendung zu Gott - besonders aber durch das Verhalten des Priesters - nicht mehr das arthurische, sondern das Schwert Gottes. Waffe und

Ritter sind Werkzeuge Gottes geworden. Offenkundig wird dies im Kampf gegen Roaz, denn es ist das gesegnete, mit dem Brief versehene Schwert, das das Eingreifen des Teufels zu Gunsten von Roaz verhindert:

> dô was gewarnet der junge man
> mit einem brieve, der im wart
> gestricket an sîner vart
> umb sîn swert mit gebet,
> und mit dem kriuze, daz er tet
> vür sich dô er zem tor în gie.
> dâ von getorste der tievel nie
> zuo im komen nâher baz. (V. 7334-7341)

Noch deutlicher als das Schwert verweist die „glävîe" auf die hier angesprochene Bedeutungsebene der christlichen Auslegung. Das wird bereits durch die Herkunft der Lanze hervorgehoben:

> und rît vür daz bürgetor;
> dâ stecket ein glävîe vor,
> die brâhte mir ein engel her
> niht ist daz dâvor gewer
> horn, stein noch îsengwant,
> man steche dâ durch unz an die hant. (V. 4747-4752)

Es handelt sich um die Waffe, mit deren Hilfe der Drache Pfetan getötet werden kann. Die im Text dargelegte, explizite Verbindung der Waffe mit Gott eröffnet eine weiter- und tiefergehende Deutung unter religiös-sakralem Aspekt.

Die Lanze lässt sich durch ihre Herkunft als Insignie des Himmelreichs werten. Sicher ist in diesem Zusammenhang auch an die Longinus-Legende zu denken, die Lanze als Zeichen der Erlösung zu sehen (Lohbeck 1998, 140-150). Da Wirnt jedoch die eigentliche, finale Erlösungstat, den Kampf gegen Roaz, nicht mit dieser Waffe verbindet, ist es nahe liegend, davon auszugehen, dass ein anderer Gesichtspunkt wichtiger ist. Es handelt sich dabei um die Bezugsetzung zum Reich bzw. zur Herrschaft über dieses. Die 'Heilige Lanze' gilt sowohl als Reliquie als auch als Herrschaftszeichen und gehört zum Reichshort (Knappe 1974, 131-132). Mit diesem Symbol stellt Wirnt seinen Protagonisten in Beziehung zu Karl dem Großen und dessen religiössakral begründetem Herrschertum. Dass diese Annahme keinesfalls als zu weit hergeholt abgetan werden darf, zeigt der Text im weiteren Verlauf an zwei Stellen. Im vorliegenden Zusammenhang mag die Erste als bedeutender angesehen werden, dennoch ist die Andere keinesfalls außer Acht zu lassen, denn auch sie unterstützt die Auffassung von der offenkundig lebendigen Erinnerung an die wohlgeordnete Herrschaft Karls des Großen. An der ersten, der soeben angesprochenen Textstellen regelt Wigalois die Angelegenheiten innerhalb seines Herrschaftsbereichs. Hier stellt Wirnt expressis verbis den Bezug zu Karl dem Großen her:

> dô er die vürsten hêt gewert
> ir lêhen, als si an gezôch
> ir deheines muot dâ von envlôch
> sine swüren im alle hulde dâ.
> Dô gebôt er den vürsten sâ
> daz si behielten Karles reht
> und diu gerihte machten sleht
> über allez sîn rîche.
> daz wart dô stæticlîche
> gevestent, als er in gebôt.
> sus hêt daz lant sîne nôt
> mit vreuden überwunden. (V. 9549-9560)

An der zweiten Stelle, die explizit Karl den Großen nennt, geht es um den Liebestod Lîamêres. Wirnt beschreibt ihre Treue V. 10037 mit der Formulierung, „ir triuwe wac vür Karles lôt", einer formelhaften Wendung, die auf Karls umfassende Rechtsordnung verweist.

Wirnt stellt demnach seinen Protagonisten nicht nur symbolhaft in die Tradition Karls des Großen, sondern auch, indem er diesen nennt. An der zweiten der angeführten Stellen ist der Bezug zu Wigalois nicht unmittelbar herzustellen, aber sie dokumentiert ebenfalls, dass Karl der Große in den Gedanken Wirnts als idealer Herrscher präsent war. Insgesamt muss in der Nennung Karls ein weiterer Hinweis darauf gesehen werden, dass Wirnt, wie bereits verdeutlicht wurde, seinem Werk bewusst konkrete historische Bezüge auch auf der Erzählebene verleihen will. Das Faktum, dass Wirnt hier nicht nur symbolisch, sondern auch unmittelbar und direkt auf ein im Bewusstsein seiner Zeitgenossen, seines Publikums als funktionierend angesehenes

Herrschaftsgefüge Bezug nimmt, sollte ein wichtiger Aspekt einerseits bei der Beantwortung der Frage nach Wirnts Intention sein, andererseits aber auch bei der Datierung des Werkes beachtet werden. Hier geht es nicht um Herrschaft auf Landesebene, der Fokus liegt auf der Herrschaft im Reich und auf der Frage, wie ein idealer Herrscher beschaffen sein muss (Sandrock 1931, Neuendorff 1979). Karl den Großen im Zusammenhang mit der Herrschaftsübernahme durch Wigalois anzuführen, betont den Weg, der Wirnt vorschwebt, zusätzlich, denn Karls Herrschaftsausübung war geprägt durch die Verbindung der beiden Komponenten, die nun auch Wigalois zum idealen Herrscher machen, weltliches und geistliches Schwert. Die Notwendigkeit der Hinwendung des Herrschers zu Gott wird gegen Ende des Werkes noch einmal in aller Deutlichkeit hervorgehoben, als Gawein seinem Sohn eine Fürstenlehre für sein künftiges Herrscheramt mit auf den Weg gibt, beginnt er:

> er sprach, got hât sîn wunder
> und sîn genâde an in getân.
> ir sult im wesen undertân
> und minnet in herzelîche.
> der sinne sît ir rîche,
> des guotes und der êren;
> daz sult ir allez kêren
> swâ ir muget nâch sînem gebot.
> swer herzelîche minnet got,
> der ist behalten hie und dort. (V. 11521-11530)

Der Inhalt macht das vor dem Zitat Gesagte zwar hinlänglich offenkundig, dennoch sollte, um den Stellenwert zu verdeutlichen, auf das Verhältnis von Gesamtumfang der Fürstenlehre zu dem Teil hingewiesen werden, der sich auf die Pflicht des Herrschers bezieht, sein Amt im Sinne Gottes auszuüben, weil dadurch die Dominanz des Gottesbezugs zusätzlich unterstrichen wird. Der Hinweis darauf, dass sich Wigalois am Willen Gottes und seinem Gebot zu orientieren habe, umfasst zehn Verse der 32-versigen Fürstenlehre. Die anderen Aspekte, die Gawein anführt, wirken dagegen eher als nachgeordnet. Bedeutsam ist in diesem Zusammenhang auch, dass Gaweins Fürstenlehre aufgeschoben wird, bis nach der Rückkehr vom Kriegszug gegen Lîon. Sie steht also nicht in Zusammenhang mit der Hochzeit und der

Krönung des Wigalois nach dem Sieg über Roaz, als Wigalois sein Amt antritt und beginnt, es auszuüben, sondern mit dem als real zumindest suggerierten und dem zeitgenössischen Publikum so vorgestellten Teil des Werkes. Dies ist sicher kein Zufall.

6. Abschließende Bewertung

Als grundlegende Prämissen für die abschließende Bewertung des Werkes dienen folgende Aspekte: Trotz intensiver Bemühungen entbehren die Versuche, Wirnts Werk entgegen dem Vorschlag Sarans, die Entstehung im ersten Jahrzehnt des 13. Jahrhundert anzusetzen, später zu datieren, wirklich überzeugender Argumente.

Vergleichbares gilt für Vorschläge, die im Hinblick auf den Auftraggeber Wirnts gemacht wurden. Es bleibt als einleuchtendste Möglichkeit, ein Mitglied des Hauses Andechs-Meranien als Mäzen anzunehmen. Dass unabhängig davon auch andere Adelsfamilien ein offenkundig lebhaftes Interesse an dem Werk zeigten, wie Honemann nachwies, widerspricht dieser Festlegung nicht, solange die deutlichsten Bezugsmöglichkeiten für das genannte Geschlecht als Gönner sprechen. Man sollte dem Autor konzedieren, dass er eine bestimmte Konzeption verfolgte, als er sein Werk verfasste, statt den Aufbau als ein mehr oder minder zufälliges, durch Beeinflussungen durch andere Werke und/oder Autoren entstandenes Konglomerat abzutun. Darüber hinaus sollte bedacht werden, dass es überaus problematisch ist, in der Zeit, in der Wirnts Werk - selbst eine relativ späte Datierung berücksichtigend - entstanden ist, von funktions- und intentionsloser Literatur, also von rein auf Unterhaltung abgestellten epischen Werken auszugehen.

Ein interpretatorischer Ansatz, der selbst den des Öfteren als konglomerathaft beanstandeten Aufbau von Wirnts Werk als sinnvoll erweisen kann, ist derjenige, der davon ausgeht, dass es im *Wigalois* um die Darstellung eines idealen Herrschers bzw. die Rechtfertigung von Herrschaft durch einen idealen Herrscher geht. Vor dem Hintergrund der mittelalterlichen Auffassung vom idealen Herrscher, für den nicht nur die weltliche Macht zählt, sondern auch der geistliche Aspekt, seine Hinwendung zu Gott und dessen Bereitschaft, dem Herrscher gnädig gesinnt zu sein, eine ganz entscheidende Rolle spielt, lässt sich der „Werdegang" des Wigalois als vom Dichter planvoll in Szene gesetzter Weg plausibel erklären. Wigalois gelangt in zwei Etappen zum Status des idealen Herrschers. Der Weg vom Artushof bis nach Roimunt macht deutlich, dass Wigalois weltlichen Bewährungsproben und Anforderungen gewachsen ist. Die Erlösung von Korntin zeigt, dass sich Wigalois der Hilfe Gottes sicher sein kann und deshalb sogar in der Lage ist, den Teufel zu besiegen, wobei im finalen Kampf gegen Roaz beide Aspekte zusammengeführt werden. Die Insignien des Glaubens, in denen sich die Verbundenheit mit Gott ausdrückt, vertreiben den Teufel und die weltlich-ritterliche Befähigung des Protagonisten macht den Sieg gegen Roaz möglich. Bei diesem Interpretationsansatz ergibt sich der dritte Teil des *Wigalois* nicht nur, sondern er ist geradezu notwendig, denn er liefert im „realen" Kontext die Bestätigung dessen, was in der Welt der 'âventiuren' schon deutlich gemacht wurde - Wigalois verkörpert den idealen Herrscher. Der Feststellung von Thomas (2005, 141): „Der einwandfreie Status des Protagonisten erweist sich als politisches/theologisches Programm des Dichters.", ist ohne Einschränkung zuzustimmen. Der Bezugsrahmen ist jedoch nicht, wie etwa Heinzle annimmt, die Landesherrschaft, denn dazu ist der *Wigalois*, wie bereits ausgeführt, selbst dann, wenn man entgegen dem handschriftlichen, recht eindeutigen Befund von einer relativ späten Datierung ausgeht, zu früh entstanden. Es bleibt, dies offenbar besonders der Korntinteil, nur der Bezug auf das Reich, das heißt, die Thronstreitigkeiten am Anfang des 13. Jahrhunderts sind, wie schon Saran vermutete, als Hintergrund für Wirnts Werk anzusehen.

Die Auseinandersetzungen um die rechtmäßige Nachfolge für den im Jahre 1197 überraschend verstorbenen Heinrich VI. begannen unmittelbar nach dessen Tod. Sie wurden zusehends radikaler, das Reich wurde in zwei Lager - ein staufisches und ein welfisches - gespalten. Der Staufer Philipp von Schwaben, Bruder Heinrichs VI., wurde ebenso zum König gewählt wie sein Kontrahent, der Welfe Otto IV., woraus sich ein erbitterter Kampf mit wechselndem Kriegsglück ergab. Während der Zeit der kriegerischen Konfrontation kam es immer wieder dazu, dass Anhänger einer Partei - auch mehrfach - die Seiten wechselten, wenn sie sich dadurch Vorteile versprachen. Ein Aspekt, der bei den Auseinandersetzungen eine immer stärker werdende Rolle spielte, war auch das Verhältnis der Kontrahenten zur Kirche. Während der Papst zunächst versuchte, sich aus den Streitigkeiten herauszuhalten, bezog er später immer mehr Position zu Gunsten Ottos IV., den er schließlich offen und nachhaltig unterstützte. Die Staufer wurden als Feinde der Kirche stigmatisiert, Philipp selbst als deren Verfolger, wohingegen Otto IV. von kirchlicher Seite als 'magis et idoneus', das Reich zu regieren, bezeichnet wird. An der Haltung der Kurie konnten auch Versprechungen Philipps gegenüber der Kirche nichts ändern. Selbst als Otto IV. herbe militärische Niederlagen hinnehmen musste, blieb Papst Innozenz III. zunächst bei seiner Haltung. Erst als Otto Gefahr lief, bedeutungslos zu werden, kam es zu einer Annäherung zwischen Innozenz III. und Philipp, allerdings wurden bei den Unterhandlungen, die dazu führten, strittige und schwierige Themen ausgeklammert. Durch die Ermordung Philipps am 21. Juni 1208 zeitigten die Verhandlungen keine Konsequenzen, und es ist nicht abzusehen, wohin sie geführt hätten. Beteiligt an der Meucheltat waren Mitglieder des Hauses Andechs, allerdings ist rätselhaft, welchen Nutzen sie davon hatten, bzw. was sie sich davon versprachen.

Nach Philipps Ermordung herrschte vorübergehend Chaos im Reich. Am 11. November 1208 hielt Otto IV. jedoch schon den ersten Hoftag ab. Mit der Ermordung Philipps schienen sich die Wünsche des Papstes zu erfüllen, es kam am 4. Oktober 1209 zur Kaiserkrönung Ottos, der jedoch kaum mehr als ein Jahr später schon die Entzweiung folgte. Papst Innozenz belegte Otto IV. am 18. November 1209 mit dem Bann. Am 5. Dezember 1212 wurde Friedrich II. zum König gewählt. Nach der Niederlage in der Schlacht bei Bouvines am 27. Juli 1214 verlor Otto IV. jeden Rückhalt und war fortan bedeutungslos. Zu den politischen Verhältnissen siehe z. B. Csendes (2003) und Engels (1994). In diesen Kontext fügen sich die in den Zeitklagen massiv verurteilten Erscheinungen, wie der Bruch des gegebenen Eides und die Habgier, denn sie war in der Regel der Grund dafür, das gegebene Wort zu brechen und die Seiten zu wechseln. Aber auch die Klage darüber, dass niemand mehr in Frieden seine Tage zu Ende bringt, wäre zu nennen. Die beiden zuletzt genannten Aspekte der Zeitklagen werden auch auffällig deutlich und drastisch im 'apokalyptischen' Erzählerkommentar hervorgehoben, auf dessen besonderen Stellenwert auch auf Grund seiner Position im Werk bereits hingewiesen wurde. Durch die Skizzierung der historischen Ereignisse wird noch deutlicher, wie wichtig gerade in dieser Zeit der Aspekt des Verhältnisses zu Gott war, als dessen Stellvertreter auf Erden der Papst gilt. Die

Verbindung von weltlicher Macht und Hinwendung zu Gott zur Verwirklichung der Herrschaft war ein dominierender Gedanke. Den Zeitgenossen Wirnts stand deutlich vor Augen, dass jeder der beiden Kontrahenten nur einen Bereich für sich verbuchen konnte, denn nach anfänglichen Erfolgen wurde Ottos militärische Position zusehends schwächer, allerdings hatte er die Kirche in Person des Papstes auf seiner Seite, während es bei Philipp genau umgekehrt war. Seine späten Versuche, sich der Kirche zu nähern, scheiterten zunächst. Später, als sie zum Erfolg zu führen schienen, wurde Philipp ermordet.

Wirnt zeigt mit seinem *Wigalois* die Unzulänglichkeit beider Kontrahenten auf, er offenbart, woran ihre Bemühungen letztlich scheiterten. Betrachtet man beide Komponenten der Herrschaft als gleichwertig und unterstellt damit quasi auch, dass Wirnt nicht Partei ergreifen, sondern nur aufzeigen will, wodurch sich der ideale Herrscher auszeichnet, wäre sein Werk vor der Ermordung Philipps anzusiedeln. Geht man hingegen davon aus, dass Wirnt demjenigen Anwärter auf die Kaiserkrönung den Vorrang einräumt, der sich der Zustimmung des Papstes sicher weiß, diese Möglichkeit besteht auf Grund der starken Betonung des Aspekts der Frömmigkeit durchaus, würde sich der Zeitrahmen bis zur Krönung Ottos IV. ausweiten möglicherweise sogar kurz darüber hinaus, aber bestenfalls wenige Monate, da sich schon bald danach die Entzweiung zwischen Papst und Kaiser anbahnte. Der Hinweis darauf, dass die Andechs-Meranier Parteigänger Philipps waren, ist kein Gegenargument. Es wurde bereits darauf hingewiesen, dass im Hause Andechs ein Sinneswandel stattfand, der Rätsel aufgibt. Ebenso ist unklar, wann sich das Haus Andechs entschloss, Philipp als Gegner zu betrachten. Die Frage, ob das Attentat auf einen plötzlichen Entschluss zurückgeht, oder ein lang geplantes Komplott dahinter steht, ist nach wie vor nicht beantwortet. Es kann deshalb auch nicht ausgeschlossen werden, dass Wirnt bereits vor der Bluttat im Interesse Ottos argumentierte.

Die Betonung des Glaubens, der Frömmigkeit wäre dann in Wirnts Werk auch unter dem Aspekt einer sich andeutenden antistaufischen Haltung zu sehen, denn Philipp war, wie bereits erwähnt, als Kirchenfeind verschrien. Geht das Attentat auf Philipp hingegen auf einen plötzlichen Entschluss zurück, gilt dies zwar ebenfalls, zusätzlich jedoch und in den Vordergrund rückend müsste der Aspekt der Rehabilitierung des an der meuchlerischen Tat beteiligten Hauses Andechs beachtet werden. Otto, der nach der Ermordung Philipps recht schnell allgemeine Anerkennung fand, war zumindest vorübergehend im dargelegten Sinn der ideale Herrscher. Als Spekulation ließen sich sogar Anspielungen auf das historische Dasein der beiden Prätendenten im *Wigalois* anführen, so könnte in der Vita des Wigalois die Herkunft aus einem fremden Reich als eine Parallele zu Ottos IV. Leben aufgefasst werden, denn Otto kommt aus dem Exil in England. Noch hypothetischer wäre eine Bezugsetzung zwischen Roaz und Philipp, dem mit dem päpstlichen Bann belegten und als Verfolger der Kirche verteufelten Staufer. Dies sind aber, wie gesagt lediglich Spekulationen, die sich zwar anstellen, aber nicht belegen lassen.

Unabhängig davon, wie man sich in dieser Frage letztlich entscheidet, die Datierung des Werkes in das erste Jahrzehnt des 13. Jahrhunderts erscheint durch das Gesagte überaus plausibel, ebenso wie die Absicht, den Protagonisten als Vorbild für den idealen Herrscher im Reich darzustellen. Ob Wirnt sein Werk erst nach dem Tode Bertholds im Jahr 1204 begann, kann auf der Basis der Position der Erwähnung im Roman nicht wirklich entschieden werden. Der unterbreitete Interpretationsanzsatz erlaubt es, den Aufbau des Werkes als sinnvolle und durchdachte Konzeption aufzufassen. Dass die einzelnen Aspekte aneinandergereiht, also additiv wirken, ist kein Mangel. Diese Vorgehensweise scheint im Hinblick auf das Publikum zur Verdeutlichung der Botschaft geradezu notwendig. Außerdem lässt sich in der Darstellungsweise die Wiedergabe eines stufenhaften Reifeprozesses sehen. Dass Wirnts Werk über diese Intention hinaus auf Grund seiner Anlage und Ausgestaltung ein breites Deutungsangebot bereithielt und entsprechend ohne größere Umgestaltungen verschiedenen Intentionen dienen konnte, wurde bereits gesagt. Dieses Faktum dürfte zur Beliebtheit des Werkes erheblich beigetragen haben.

Literaturverzeichnis

Textausgaben

Wirnt von Gravenberc, *Wigalois der Ritter mit dem Rade*, hrsg. v. J. M. N. Kapteyn. Erster Band: Text, Bonn 1926 (Rheinische Beiträge und Hülfsbücher zur germanischen Philologie und Volkskunde; Bd. 9).
Wirnt von Grafenberg *Wigalois. Text – Übersetzung – Stellenkommentar*. Text der Ausgabe von J. M. N. Kapteyn übersetzt, erläutert und mit einem Nachwort versehen von Sabine Seelbach und Ulrich Seelbach, Berlin, New York 2005.

Wolfram von Eschenbach *Willehalm*. Text der Ausgabe von Werner Schröder. Völlig neu bearbeitete Übersetzung, Vorwort und Register von Dieter Kartschoke, Berlin, New York 1989.

Sekundärliteratur

Bertelsmeier-Kierst 1992: Christa Bertelsmeier-Kierst, "Zur ältesten Überlieferung des "Wigalois" I. Die Handschrift E", in: *ZfdA* 121: 275-290.
Brinker 1995: Claudia Brinker, "»Hie ist diu aventiure geholt!« Die Jenseitsreise im Wigalois des Wirnt von Gravenberg: Kreuzzugspropaganda und unterhaltsame Glaubenslehre?", in: *Contemplata aliis tradere: Studien zum Verhältnis von Literatur und Spiritualität*, hrsg. von Claudia Brinker, u. a., Bern, u. a.., 87-110.
Bumke 2004: J. Bumke, *Wolfram von Eschenbach*, 8., völlig neu bearbeitete Auflage (Sammlung Metzler; Bd. 36), Stuttgart, Weimar.
Csendes 2003: P. Csendes, *Philipp von Schwaben. Ein Staufer im Kampf um die Macht*, Darmstadt.
Cormeau 1977: Ch. Cormeau, *>Wigalois< und >Diu Crône<. Zwei Kapitel zur Gattungsgeschichte des nachklassischen Artusromans* (Habil.-schrift, München 1973 / Münchener Texte und Untersuchungen zur deutschen Literatur des Mittelalters; Bd. 57), München 1977.
Daiber 1999: A. Daiber, *Bekannte Helden in neuen Gewändern? Intertextuelles Erzählen im 'Biterolf und Dietleib' sowie am Beispiel Keies und Gaweins im 'Lanzelet', 'Wigalois' und der 'Crone'* (Mikrokosmos. Beiträge zur Literaturwissenschaft und Bedeutungsforschung, Bd. 53), Frankfurt a. M., u. a.
Dietl 2003: Cora Dietl, "Wunder und zouber als Merkmale der âventiure in Wirnts Wigalois?", in: *Das Wunderbare in der arthurischen Literatur. Probleme und Perspektiven*, hrsg. von Friedrich Wolfzettel, Tübingen: 297-311.
Eming 1999: J. Eming, *Funktionswandel des Wunderbaren. Studien zum Bel Inconnu, zum Wigalois und zum Wigoleis von Rade* (Diss. Berlin 1996 / Literatur - Imagination - Realität; Bd. 19), Trier.
Engels 1994: O. Engels, *Die Staufer*, 6., überarbeitete und erweiterte Auflage, Stuttgart.
Fuchs 1997: St. Fuchs, *Hybride Helden: Gwigalois und Willehalm. Beiträge zum Heldenbild und zur Poetik des Romans im 13. Jahrhundert* (Diss. Frankfurt a. M. 1995 / Frankfurter Beiträge zur Germanistik; Bd. 31), Heidelberg.
Gottzmann 1979: Carola L. Gottzmann, "Wirnts von Gravenberg 'Wigalois'. Zur Klassifizierung sogenannter epigonaler Artusdichtung", in: *ABäG* 14: 87-136.
Grubmüller 1985: Klaus Grubmüller, "Artusroman und Heilsbringerethos. Zum >Wigalois< des Wirnt von Gravenberg", in: *PBB* 107: 218-239.
Hahn 1994: Ingrid Hahn, "Gott und Minne, Tod und triuwe. Zur Konzeption des Wigalois des Wirnt von Grafenberg", in: *Personenbeziehungen in der mittelalterlichen Literatur*, hrsg. von Helmut Brall, Barbara Haupt, Urban Küsters (Studia humaniora; Bd. 25), Düsseldorf, 37-60.
Haasch 1954: G. Haasch, *Das Wunderbare im höfischen Artusroman. Ein Beitrag zur*

Motivgeschichte mittelalterlicher Epik und zur Klärung des Verhältnisses von Artusroman und Märchen (Diss. masch.), Berlin.

Heinzle 1973: Joachim Heinzle, "Über den Aufbau des Wigalois", in: *Euphorion* 67: 261-271.

Henderson 1986: Ingeborg Henderson, "Dark Figures and Eschatological Imagery in Wirnt von Gravenberg's Wigalois", in: *The Dark Figure in Medival German and Germanic Literature*, hrsg. von Edward R. Haymes und Stephanie Cain van D'Elden (Göppinger Arbeiten zur Germanistik, Nr. 448), Göppingen, 99-113.

Honemann 1994: Volker Honemann, "Wigalois' Kampf mit dem roten Ritter. Zum Verständnis der Hojir-Aventiure in Wirnts Wigalois", in: *German Narrative Literature of the Twelfth and Thirteenth Centuries. Studies presented to Roy Wisbey on his Sixty-fifth Birthday.* Hrsg. von Volker Honemann, Martin H. Jones, Adrian Stevens, David Wells, Tübingen, 347-362.

Jäger 2000: A. Jaeger, *Ein jüdischer Artusritter. Studien zum jüdisch-deutschen »Widuwilt« (»Artushof«) und zum »Wigalois« des Wirnt von Gravenberc* (Conditio Judaica 32, Studien und Quellen zur deutsch-jüdischen Literatur- und Kulturgeschichte), Tübingen.

Kaiser 1975: Gert Kaiser, "Der Wigalois des Wirnt von Grâvenberc. Zur Bedeutung des Territorialisierungsprozesses für die „höfisch-ritterliche" Literatur des 13. Jahrhunderts", in: *Euphorion* 69: 410-443.

Knappe 1974: K.-B. Knappe, *Repräsentation und Herrschaftszeichen. Zur Herrscherdarstellung in der vorhöfischen Epik* (Diss. Kiel 1971/ Münchener Beiträge zur Mediävistik und Renaissance-Forschung, 17), München 1974.

Latzke 1906: Rudolf Latzke, "Über die subjektiven Einschaltungen in Wirnts 'Wigalois'", in: *Zeitschrift für die österreichischen Gymnasien* 75: 961-985.

Lienert 1991: Elisabeth Lienert, "Wirnt von Gravenberg (ca. 1170/80 - ca. 1230)", in: Fränkische Lebensbilder. Neue Folge der Lebensläufe aus Franken 14: 1-13.

— 1997: Elisabeth Lienert, "Zur Pragmatik höfischen Erzählens. Erzähler und Erzählerkommentare in Wirnts von Grafenberg Wigalois", in: *Archiv für das Studium der neueren Sprachen und Literaturen* 234: 263-275.

Lohbeck 1999: G. Lohbeck, *Wigalois. Struktur der bezeichenunge* (Diss., Heidelberg 1998 / Information und Interpretation, Bd. 6) , Frankfurt a. M., u. a.

Mertens 1981: Volker Mertens, "Iwein und Wigalois auf dem Weg zur Landesherrschaft" in: *GRM*, N.F. 31: 14-31.

— 1990: Volker Mertens, "'gewisse lêre". Zum Verhältnis von Fiktion und Didaxe im späten deutschen Artusroman", in: *Artusroman und Intertextualität. Beiträge der deutschen Sektion der Internationalen Artusgesellschaft vom 16. bis 19. November 1989*, hrsg. von Friedrich Wolfzettel (Beiträge zur deutschen Philologie; Bd. 67), Gießen, 85-106.

— 1998: Volker Mertens, *Der deutsche Artusroman*, Stuttgart (RUB; Nr. 17609; Literaturstudium).

Mitgau 1959: W. Mitgau, *Bauformen des Erzählens im „Wigalois" des Wirnt von Gravenberc* (Diss. masch.), Göttingen.

Neuendorff 1980: D. Neuendorff, *Studie zur Entwicklung der Herrscherdarstellung in der deutschsprachigen Literatur des 9.-12. Jahrhunderts* (Diss., Berlin 1979 /

Acta Universitatis Stockholmiensis, Stockholmer Germanistische Forschungen, 29), Stockholm.

Neumann 1964: Friedrich Neumann, "Wann verfaßte Wirnt den `Wigalois'?", in: *ZfdA* 93: 31-62.

Reichert 1985: F. Reichert, *Landesherrschaft, Adel und Vogtei. Zur Vorgeschichte des spätmittelalterlichen Ständestaates im Herzogtum Österreich*, Köln.

Ringeler 2000: F. Ringeler, *Zur Konzeption der Protagonistenidentität im deutschen Artusroman um 1200. Aspekte einer Gattungspoetik*, Franfurt a. M., u. a..

Rochels 1901: R. Rochels, *Über die religiösen und sittlichen Bemerkungen in dem Ritterroman 'Wigalois' des Wirnt von Gravenberg und anderen gleichzeitigen Dichtungen* (Wissenschaftliche Beilage zum Jahresbericht des Progymnasiums zu Eupen), Eupen.

Sandrock 1931: L. Sandrock, *Das Herrscherbild in der erzählenden Dichtung des deutschen Mittelalters* (Diss.), Emsdetten.

Saran 1896: Franz Saran, "Über Wirnt von Grafenberg und den Wigalois", in: *PBB* 21: 253-420.

Schiewer 1988: Hans-Jochen Schiewer, "Ein ris ich dar vmbe abe brach / Von sinem wunder bovme. Beobachtungen zur Überlieferung des nachklassischen Artusromans im 13. und 14. Jahrhundert", in: *Deutsche Handschriften 1100-1400. Oxforder Colloquium 1985*, hrsg. von Volker Honemann und Nigel F. Palmer, Tübingen, 222-278.

Schneider 1987: K. Schneider, *Gotische Schriften in deutscher Sprache. I. Vom späten 12. Jahrhundert bis um 1300, Text- und Tafelband*, Wiesbaden.

Schröder 1986: Werner Schröder, "Der synkretistische Roman des Wirnt von Gravenberg. Unerledigte Fragen an den Wigalois" in: *Euphorion* 80: 235-277.

Thomas 2005: N. Thomas, "Wirnts von Gravenberg Wigalois und die Auseinandersetzung mit der Parzival-Problematik", in: *ABäG* 60: 129-160.

Wennerhold 2005: M. Wennerhold, *Späte mittelhochdeutsche Artusromane. ,Lanzelet', ,Wigalois', ,Daniel von dem blühenden Tal', ,Diu Crône'. Bilanz der Forschung 1960-2000* (Diss. Würzburg, / Würzburger Beiträge zur deutschen Philologie; Bd. 27), Würzburg.

Wild 1999: G. Wild, "(Pseudo)-arthurisches recycling oder: Wie die Symbolstruktur des Artusromans im Spätmittelalter aufgehoben wird", in: *Erzählstrukturen der Artusliteratur. Forschungsgeschichte und neue Ansätze*, hrsg. von Friedrich Wolfzettel, unter Mitarbeit von Peter Ihring, Tübingen, 291-310.

Wild 1953: H. Wild, *Das Menschen- und Gottesbild des Wirnt von Grafenberg nach seinem Wigaloisroman* (Diss.), Freiburg.

THE HOLY ROOD IN THE NETHERLANDS AND NORTH GERMANY
A comparative study of nine Middle Dutch and two Middle Low German recensions of the legend about the Provenance of the Cross

by Annelies Roeleveld
in cooperation with Evert Wattel and Margit Rem [1]

Abstract

A comparison was made of all the known recensions and fragments in Middle Dutch (9) and Middle Low German (2) of the medieval legend of the Provenance of the Cross. Variants were written and weighted, and a computer-assisted stemma was produced. The stemma arranges the recensions into a few groups, but only a small number of conclusions can be drawn from it, e.g. that the two Low German texts, not surprisingly, are to be found at a larger distance from their nearest relatives than any of the Middle Dutch recensions. Both were very obviously translated from Middle Dutch, and it was already clear from the differing ways they solve translating problems that one was not copied from the other, nor did they have a close common ancestor; this is corroborated in the stemma. The dialects of the Middle Dutch texts were then determined by means of the computer-controlled method Rem and Wattel developed for the Corpus of 14th century charters and deeds; the results were entered into the stemma. It now turned out that one of the Low German recensions was relatively closely related to a Dutch text with Northern and Eastern traits. Both Low German texts, however, have as their second closest relatives early recensions which localise in Southern Brabant. All the early Middle Dutch recensions do in fact localise in Southern Brabant. The obvious conclusion is that an archetypical text must have been written in Southern Brabant.

1. Introduction

In 1997 Erika Langbroek and I published an edition of the story of Valentin and Namelos, which appears in several Middle Low German manuscripts (Roeleveld & Langbroek 1997). Our investigations brought a Middle Low German miscellany dating from about 1476 and known as the 'Hartebok' to our attention. It had been published only once, in 1731 (Staphorst 1731). In 2001 our diplomatic edition of the Hartebok was published as volume 8 in the series Middeleeuwse Verzamelhandschriften uit de Nederlanden (Langbroek & Roeleveld 2001a). It was published in the Dutch series because it had always been thought to have its origins in Bruges, but also and in particular because it is remarkable evidence of the relative unity of the Dutch

---

[1] And my thanks to Erika Langbroek for her cooperation.

and Low German linguistic and cultural areas in the late Middle Ages. It had been obvious for years that the second text in the miscellany, *Van deme holte des hilligen krutzes*, was a translation of a Middle Dutch text very similar to *DBoec vanden Houte* and *Van den drie gaerden*.[2] Further investigations established that the seventh and longest text in the Hartebok, *Van Namelos vnde Valentin*, must also be based on a Middle Dutch text.[3] Of the sixth text, the abecedarium *Vnser leuen vrowen rozenkrantz*, on the other hand, evidence showed that the existing Dutch parallel text, in a 1528 incunabulum, is very probably a translation from Middle Low German.[4] A number of these texts were investigated in the context of parallel and variant texts, and the investigation includes research into rhymes according to the method of Thomas Klein and the constructing of textual genealogies with the help of computer-assisted stemmatological techniques.[5]

2. The Holy Rood

In *Van deme holte des hilligen krutzes*, the second text in the Hartebok, the story is told of Adam's son Seth, who is sent by his dying father to Paradise to acquire the promised *olye der barmherticheit* (oil of mercy). There he is told that the crying baby in the tree of knowledge of good and evil is going to atone for the sins of mankind. He is given three *kerneken* (small kernels) to put under Adam's tongue when he is buried. From the *kernen* grow three *gherden* (shoots), which will grow into a cedar, a cypress and a palm tree. A portentous dream sends Moses to find the *roden* (twigs, rods) growing out of the *kernen*; he pulls them out and uses them in the desert to cast them into the bitter waters to make those sweet and eventually plants them in the field of Moab. King David is commissioned in a dream to fetch them and plant them in Jerusalem; on the way there, sick and lame folk are healed by their touch and three blackamoors get white skins. In the

---

[2] See e.g. Baert 1995: 39; 2001: 225.
[3] Langbroek & Roeleveld 1998b; Roeleveld, Langbroek & Wattel 2004.
[4] Roeleveld & Langbroek 2002.
[5] Methods in Klein 1997 (rhymes) and Wattel & van Mulken 1996a,b (stemmatology). Results in Langbroek 2003, 2004, Langbroek & Roeleveld 1997, 1998a, 1998b, 2001a, 2001b, 2005, Roeleveld & Langbroek 2002, Roeleveld, Langbroek & Wattel 2004.

court, the three *roden* grow into one tree with three crowns. When Solomon starts the building of the temple, a large beam is needed and the tree is cut down; however, the beam cannot be used, as it keeps changing size. It is left lying neglected in the temple court, until *Sibilla* foretells that the Son of God will hang on it. In fear it is then thrown into a small water, where it is used as a bridge, until the queen of Sheba refuses to set foot on the holy rood because she also knows what it is destined for. The rood is now trimmed with gold and jewels and is put over the entrance of the temple, until King Abya steals the gold and jewels and has the rood buried deep underground. It is found centuries later when a pond is dug and it is left to float in the pond until the Jews realize that it may be used for making a cross. When Jesus has died on the cross and the soldier pierces his side with the spear, there comes out the oil of mercy that had been promised to Adam.[6]

3. The origin of the story

For the origin of the story, see the very thorough research of Barbara Baert (2001). Erika Langbroek's article in this same volume (2010) continues the investigation into the themes and symbolism in the numerous different recensions of the story. The following paragraphs give a very condensed summary of their findings.

The elements of the story in the form under consideration are present in the C12 works in Latin of several authors; these elements, are amongst others, the prefiguration of the crucifixion, the symbolism of paradise and the principle of trinity - three trees grown into one. A Latin prose version from around 1220, the so-called *Legenda*, becomes the basis of a fast growing group of very comparable vernacular recensions: a C13 French prose version, translated from Latin and closely related to the *Legenda* text; a C14 French rhymed version; a C14 rhymed version in Middle English, the *Story of the Holy Rood*, comprising 860 verses and closely following the *Legenda*; a passage in the Middle English *Cursor Mundi* (an epic from about 1320, on history from the creation onward), which is a translation of the C14 French text. Moreover, there are the Middle Dutch recensions (1 prose

---

[6] For further details and for variants in other recensions, see Langbroek 2010.

one[7] and 9 rhymed ones) and the two rhymed Middle Low German ones (of which Baert mentions only the Hartebok recension).

There are a number of vernacular versions from before 1200, but in those the story takes different turns and contains different symbolisms. The story is also to be found in the *Legenda Aurea* of 1260, again with different turns. Some of the elements of the story, incidentally, are also to be found in the *Queste du Saint Graal* (C12).

4. Middle Dutch and Middle Low German

In an ideal investigation, the *Legenda* text, the French and English rhymed and prose recensions, the nine Middle Dutch rhymed recensions and the prose recension, and the two Middle Low German rhymed recensions should be put side by side. Comparing prose and rhyme in Latin and vernacular texts is certainly possible and can be very worthwhile, as was shown in the comparison of the very different *Valentin and Namelos* texts (Roeleveld, Langbroek & Wattel 2004); but in the case of the Holy Rood it seemed advisable, for the time being, to restrict the research to the Middle Dutch and Middle Low German recensions, which differ in many turns and details of the story of the French and English texts and the *Legenda* text. For the construction of a stemma is it quite possible to compare story elements, but the similarity of the Middle Dutch and Middle Low German recensions makes it possible to compare not elements but words. It was also decided to leave out the Middle Dutch prose recension for the time being.

5. The parallel texts

Before 1500 we have the texts in the following survey. ***C*** and ***H*** are the two Middle Low German texts. In addition to these, there are Dutch incunabula en also printed versions of later than 1500; these have not been included in the study.[8]

In the column verses *pf* = partly fragmentary, *pvf* = partly very fragmentary.

---

[7] Hermodsson 1959: 65, 66; Leidse Universiteits Bibliotheek, mark Letterk. 262.
[8] Jungman & Voorbij 1999.

The Holy Rood in the Netherlands and North Germany 179

ab-brev.	text	year	editions	verses
b	Haarlem, Stadsbibliotheek, 56 D 6:5 *Dit is dat boec vanden houte*.	1496	(consulted photocopy)	781
C mlg	Hamburg, Staats- und Universitäts-bibliothek, Conv. 4, f. 182r-199r.	C15	Schröder 1876	807
D	Düsseldorf, Hauptstaatsarchiv, no sign.	1400-1450	A. Birlinger in Germania 15 (1870), 360-64.	174 pf
G	Göttingen, Niedersächsische Staats- und Universitätsbibliothek, Luneb. 24a.	C14	(consulted photographs)	67 pf
H mlg	Hamburg, Staats- und Universitäts-bibliothek, 102c *in scrinio* ('Hartebok'), f. 11r-23v. *Van deme holte des hilligen krutzes*.	ca. 1476	Langbroek & Roeleveld 2001 (MVN 8), 79-100	771
Hu	Brussel, Koninklijke Bibliotheek, 15.589-623 ('Hs. Van Hulthem'), f.15va-19vb. *DBoec vanden houte*.	1405-1408	Brinkman & Schenkel 1999 (MVN 7), vol. 1, 177-196.	780
M	Brussel, Koninklijke Bibliotheek, II 5.580	1360	(consulted prints of micro-film)	171 pf
O	Oudenaarde, Stadsbibliotheek, 5576	1275-1325	Hermodsson 1959, 54-55	6
S	Groningen, Universiteitsbibliotheek, 405 ('Zutphense Hs.') f. 210va-214va. *Van den drie gaerden*	1339	Hermodsson 1959, 121-154.	840
T	's-Hertogenbosch, Archivum Capuccinorum Hollandiae, 4.	C15	P. Maximilianus in: Bijblad voor Taal en Letteren 2 (1914), 38-48.	192 pvf
U	Utrecht, Universiteitsbibliotheek, 1329, f. 34ra-37vb.	1438	(consulted microfilm)	567

6. Comparison of texts

The similarity of the eleven texts (for examples see section 8) makes the construction of a stemma very feasible. The writing of variants and the determining and valuing of categories is illustrated below. For a clear understanding of the matter it is particularly necessary to know that for determining the relationship between versions of a text, it is not spelling or notation that is taken stock of, but the use of certain words, terms and constructions. An important factor for the lineage is e.g. the difference between *grote schade* and *schade* or between *schade* and *vernoy*: which versions occur in which of the texts at that point. It is not important how *schade* and *vernoy* are spelt. Nor is it important for this purpose whether at a certain point the text says *zullen* or *zellen* or *zoelen*: important is whether a form of *zullen* is used or a form of *kunnen* or nothing at all. Whether *zullen*, *zellen* or *zoelen* is used, is of importance for the determination of the dialects, of course.

7. Linguistic differences and translation problems

For our purpose the Middle Low German and Middle Dutch texts may simply be put side by side; they are often almost literally identical. Important differences are often caused by the idiomatic and syntactic differences between the two languages. It is also evident that the Middle Low German versions were translated from Middle Dutch: there are obvious translation problems, as may be illustrated by the following examples from a small number of Middle Dutch manuscripts and the two Middle Low German ones.[9]

7.1	(*S*70	ic ben ghereet tedoen algader)
	*S*71	wat v is lief ende ghi gebiet
	*S*72	mer ic en weet des weghes niet
	*Hu*67	Dat v es lief en*de* ghi gebiet
	*Hu*68	Maer des weghes en wetic niet
	*D*2	Du lief is en*de* ghi ghebiet
	*D*3	Mer ic en kan des wegen niet

---

[9] The numeration of S is according to the manuscript and therefore differs from the numeration in Hermodssons critical edition.

	*C*71	wat gy willen unde wat gy beyt
	*C*72	mer ik enwiit des weghes nyt
	*H*69	Des juw is leff vnde ick bin plicht
	*H*70	Mehre ick wet des weges nicht.

The translators/editors are faced with two problems here: the Middle Low German equivalent of the verb *gebieden* is *(ge)beden* and their written language requires *nicht*, not the colloquial form *niet*. So *H* translates *ghi gebiet* as *ick bin plicht* and solves both problems. *C* uses the colloquial form *nyt* - the first and only time in the whole text - but Middle Dutch *ghi gebiet* remains a problem. The translator leaves things at a half-rhyme *gy beyt* and slightly adapts the first half of the sentence to it.

Rhymes more often cause translation problems.

7.2	(*S*56	Lieue kijnt gaet zonder beide)
	*S*57	op gherechte vaderlike minne
	*S*58	toten inghel Cherubinne
	*Hu*53	Op gherechte vaderlike minne
	*Hu*54	Toten inghel cherubinne
	*C*57	op rechte vaderlike mynne
	*C*58	to dem enghel Serubynne
	*H*55	Vp rechte vederlike truwe
	*H*56	To deme engel cherubynne

The word *minne* in Middle Low German has such sexual connotations that it is impossible to speak of *minne* for a father. *H* changes the word into *truwe* 'loyalty', but the angel is still *cherubinne*, so the rhyme is off. The editor of *C* does not see any problem or cannot think of a solution, as happens more often in the early part of the text. The off-rhyme solution of *H* has not been considered a variant, because it does not indicate anything about the relationship between the texts, but only illustrates a translation problem.

7.3	(*S*146	ende loept ouer een lant
	*S*147	dat heit Auelat)
	*S*148	dat maecsi met haren water nat
	*Hu*142	Met haren water net si dat

*U*150   Met hare*n* wate*r* net si dat
*b*150   Met haer water so net sy dat

*C*148   mit erer gude doet se dat
*H*143   Mit ereme water neret se dat.

The verb in three out of the four Middle Dutch recensions is *netten* 'to wet'; in Middle Low German, however, *netten* is a euphemism for passing water. In *H* the problem is solved by using *neren* 'to feed', the editor of *C* makes the river 'do' something out of her goodness, probably 'give'. Neither of the two solutions has been considered a variant.

7.4   *S*95   toten dale van Ebroene
      *Hu*89   Tote int dal van ebroene

      *C*95   hen in dem dale to Ebbrone
      *H*94   Went in den dal to ebron

Where Middle Dutch uses *van* in constructions with geographical names like these, Middle Low German uses *to*. Again, this is not to be regarded as a variant.

7.5   *S*140   Seth liet zine oghen omme gaen
      *Hu*143   Sij*n* oghe*n* lietti al o*m*me gaen

      *C*140   sine oghen dede he al umme gan
      (*H*   lacking)

The Middle Dutch recensions have *liet ... ommegaen*, *C* has *dede ... umme gan*. This is not a variant but a translation.

7.6   (*S*283   daer hi dede zijn einde)
      *S*284   waren duuel bi gheheinde
      *Hu*280   Was die duuel d*aer* ghehende

      *C*290   do was de dǔǔel dar behende
      *H*289   Do was de duuel dar behende

Middle Dutch *gehende* (stress on 2nd syllable) 'close, near' does not exist in Middle Low German. But Middle Low German does have *behende* (stress also on 2nd syllable); *behende* means 'skilful, nimble' and happens to fit nicely in the context: instead of '(at that time) the devil was around / devils were there' it now reads 'the devil was skillfully at work'. It is quite possible that both translators/editors did not even know the Middle Dutch word and mistook its meaning. Again, these 'translations' have not been regarded as variants.

7.7	*S*412	rijd enwech ouer die Iordane
	*Hu*394	Rijt wech ou*er* die jordane
	*C*406	vare henne over de Jordane
	*H*414	Vare hen auer de Iordane

In Middle Low German *rijden* is always on a horse, hence in *C* and *H* the command to go *varen* and cross the river Jordan. These are not variants. Moreover, *heen* + *varen* and *weg* + *rijden* are probably fixed combinations and therefore, again, not variants relevant for lineage and relationships.

8. The materials for the stemma

For the construction of a stemma the writing of variants is required.[10] Ten lines from the first part of the text may serve as an example. Since *S*, *Van den drie gaerden*, consists of the largest number of verses, that text and its numeration was chosen as a basis.

*S*11	Adaem was die ierste man
	die oyt menschen vorme ghewan
	ende hoe hi bi zijns wijfs rade
	creech swaer vernoy ende groten scade
*S*15	ende van eenre cleinre spise
	ghewijst waert vten paradise
	bi wat zaken dat dat ghesciede
	weten noch wael vele liede
	daer om laet ict achter bliuen
*S*20	dat ic daer niet af en wil scriuen

---

[10] See also Roeleveld & Langbroek 2002 for a description and explanation of the method of writing variants.

When these 10 lines were compared, only 6 other versions of the text were available. As an illustration, the first 4 of these lines in the other 5 recensions read:

*Hu*11   Adam was die ierste man
         Die t*er* werelt ye lijf ghewan
         En*de* hi bi sijns wijfs rade
         Groet v*er*noy nam en*de* scade

*C*11   Adam was de erste man
        de ye van mynschen forme gewan
        unde wo he by synen wyůes rade
        hat grot vordret unde schade

*U*11   ADam was dieerste ma*n*
        Die me*n*schelike vorme gewa*n*
        En*de* hoe hi bi sij*n*s wijfs rade
        V*er*noey gewan en*de* grote scade

*b*11   Adam was deerste man
        Die ye menschen form ghewan
        En*de* hoe hi by sijns wijfs rade
        Groot vernoy nam ende scade

*H*9   Adam was de erste man
       De gij mynschen formen wan
       Wo he na synes wyues rade
       Groten weddermo̊t wan vnde schade

The following variants were written:

line in S	variants	category	specification
12	HSCbHu/U	7	oyt, (ter werelt) ye / --
12	HSCb/Hu	8	oyt, ye / ter werelt ye
12	HCb/S	2b	ye / oyt
12	HSCUb/Hu	1	menschen, menscheliken vorme / lijf
12	HSCb/U	5	menschen vorme / menscheliken vorme

13	H/SHuCUb	8	-- / ende
13	HSCUb/Hu	8	hoe / --
14	HHuUb/SC	4	*OV / VO*
14	HSHuCb/U	8	groet, swaer vernoy / -- vernoey
14	HHuCb/S	2b	groet / swaer
14	HHuCb/SU	8	scade / groten scade
15	HSHuCb/U	8	ende / --
15	HCU/SHub	8	hoe hi / --
15	H/S/HuCUb	2b	vmme / van / bi
16	HU/SHuCb	4	*Vaux Vlex / Vlex Vaux*
16	HSHu/CUb	5	waert / was
16	HSHuCb/U	1	ghewijst / gheworpen
17	HHuCUb/S	3	*2 verses reversed or not*
17	H/S/HuCUb	2b	noch alle / noch wael vele / meest alle (S18)
18	H/SHuCUb	9a	* / *whole verse* (S17)
19	HSCU/Hub	6	*whole verse* / --
19	HSC/U	8	*id, t, es* / --
20	HSCU/Hub	6	*whole verse* / --

The categories are:

cate-gory	classification	weight factor
1	important semantic difference	2.3
2a	less important semantic difference	1.5
2b	marginal semantic difference	1.3
3	inversion/move over two or more verses	2.2
4	inversion/move within one verse	1.2
5	difference in grammatical structure	1.0
6	interpolation or omission (--) of one whole verse	2.4
7	important interpolation or omission	2.1
8	minor interpolation or omission	1.1
9a	*whole verse* completely different, no comparison possible (*)	2.0
9b	part of a verse completely different, no comparison possible (*)	1.4

The catagories are a reflection of the types of differences that were looked for. When comparing other types of texts, e.g. rhyme and prose or long and concise versions of the same story, categories and classification automatically become different. The weight allotted to a category of variants depends on the relevance the investigator attributes to it for the interconnection of the texts. Knowledge of the texts and experience in this type of investigation play a role. To avoid undue influence on the stemma it is mathematically necessary to use 1, 1.1 etc. for the lowest values and 2, 2.1 etc. for the highest. A weight factor must not be used more than once. The 1-values are used for what the investigator considers not very important differences, the 2-values for more important ones: in this case difference in grammatical structure is allotted the smallest weight factor, because it is seen as the result of dialectical difference or occasional sloppiness. In this way only very large differences in weight will lead to significantly different stemmas.[11]

9. The operating procedure

In line 11, the 6 available recensions show no relevant differences. In line 12 it was first established whether or not 'ever' (*oyt, ye* etc.) occurs: this was written as the first variant. The 5 recensions with 'ever' then divided into versions with only *oyt/ye* as against versions with *ter werelt ye*. Lastly, the difference between *oyt* and *ye* was also written, but it was regarded as marginal. In line 14 occur, amongst other things, differences in the order verb-object, in line 16 differences in the location of the auxiliary with respect to the main verb. Also inversion in the order of verses or the absence of one or more verses may be relevant for the relationship between the recensions.

There are variants which occur several or even many times in the text. Examples are Middle Dutch and Middle Low German *fonteine*, *borne* and *water*, which occur as variants in 6 places in the sections of which variants were written, and *piscine*, *dike*, *put* and *water*, which also occur as variants in 6 places; the passages in question deal with Paradise, the pond etc. The most striking instance is the word for 'twig, rod': *roede* with its diminutives *rodekin*, *rudelin*, and *gaerde* with its diminuative *gaerdeken*; these words appear in nearly 40

---

[11] For more details and explanation see Wattel & Van Mulken 1996b.

places. Variants of this often occurring type were included in the calculations, but were given a slighter weight factor.

Unfortunately, it was never possible to write variants from all the 11 recensions: the smaller fragments do not coincide anywhere. Variants were written from all the sections of which 6 or 7 versions exist; there is one small section where 8 versions were available, but there one recension was very fragmentary. In the end, variants were written for 377 verses; on a maximum total of 840 verses (in *S*) this is, in the computer-aided stemmatological practice, more than sufficient for constructing a reliable stemma. The definitive weights of the categories were decided on in consultation with Evert Wattel. Wattel then processed the variants in the computer, with the resulting stemma of fig. 1.

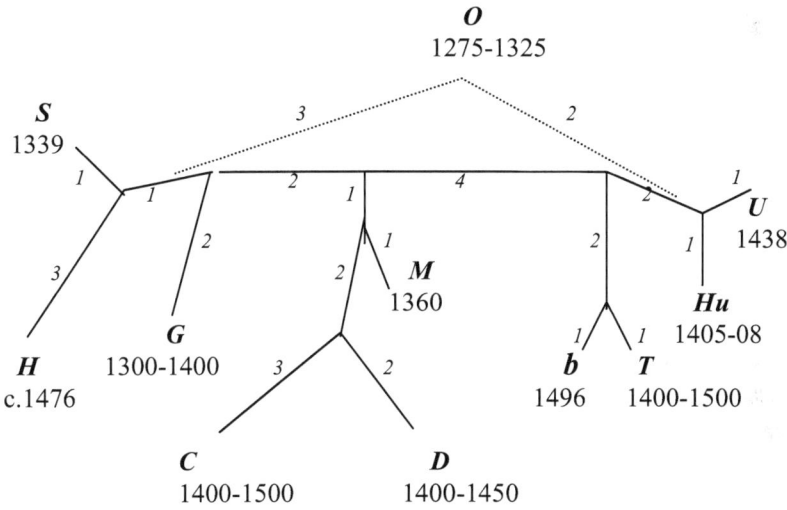

Fig. 1. Stemma of 11 recensions

From the computer calculations it is not clear whether recension *O*, which consists of no more than 6 verses and therefore yields extremely few variants, should be linked to cluster *S*+*H* or cluster *U*+*Hu*.

As no information is available about any original of which other recensions could have been copied, or about any copying among the recensions available to us, no point of suspension was chosen; a schematic representation is presented of the way in which the recensions turn out to be related.

The "junctions" indicate where recensions start differing; a lost mutual exemplar may be assumed here. The numbers by the connecting lines indicate the relative distances between the recensions. The orientation of the lines is random: a mirror image of the diagram is just as valid. *Hu* and *U* may change places, *C* and *D* may change places including the lines from which they are suspended, etc.

10. First conclusions

A number of observations can now be made.

10.1
The recensions divide into two large groups: on the one side *C*, *D*, *M*, *G*, *H* and *S*, perhaps *O*, on the other side *b*, *T*, *Hu* and *U*, perhaps *O*.

10.2
The dates of the recensions play a certain role in the relations. The entire right hand group *b-T-Hu-U* dates from C15, even if the oldest and youngest recensions differ by almost a century: *Hu* dates from 1405-8, *b*, the youngest recension of all, dates from 1496. The closely related cluster *Hu-U* is also close in dates. If *O*, by far the oldest recension, should be counted as one of the right hand group, it clashes badly with the rest, an indication that maybe *O* does not belong in this group, after all.

10.3
The left hand group is much more varied in dates: from 1339 for *S* to 1476 for *H*. If *O* should be counted as one of this group, it dates from 1275-1325 to 1476.

10.4
The distance of both manuscript *H* and manuscript *C* to the next "junction" is 3, the largest distance between a manuscript and a junction in the stemma. *H* has *S Van den drie gaerden* as its nearest relative, at a total distance of 4. *C* has the fragment *D* as its nearest relative, at a total distance of 5. These are the longest distances to a nearest relative in the whole stemma. From these two observations we may draw the conclusion that the two Middle Low German recensions are precisely the most divergent ones in the whole set. Both *H* and *C* are at a distance of 13 to *Hu DBoec vanden houte*, from which recension, in spite of the affinity they showed at first glance, they do differ considerably, after all.

10.5

The distance between ***H*** and ***C*** is 12; their mutual difference is hardly smaller than from ***Hu***. That they could not have been copied one from the other or from the same exemplar was already clear from the fact that again and again they have different solutions for the translation problems occurring in the adaptation from Middle Dutch (see section 7).

10.6

Similar observations can be made about all the mutual relationships of the manuscripts in the stemma. Another example is the distance between the two best-known Middle Dutch recensions, ***S*** *Van den drie gaerden* en ***Hu*** *DBoec vanden houte*, which is 11, not much smaller that the distance between *DBoec vanden houte* en its Middle Low German relatives.

10.7

More sweeping conclusions are not really possible, notably also because dialect data are lacking in the stemma.

11. Geographical origins of the Middle Dutch texts

Now an interesting question is whether the geographical origins of the different recensions are of greater relevance for the mutual relationships than the dates. For example: do the recensions that ***H*** and ***C*** are most closely related to originate from areas bordering on the Middle Low German region? Does the cluster (***O-***)***U-Hu*** locate in about the same dialect area? Could a hypothetical original text be located around Bruges, where the Hartebok was supposedly written or assembled?

Of all 9 Middle Dutch recensions dialect descriptions-inventories are available. Brinkman and Schenkel's provisional conclusion about the language of the copyist of the Van Hulthem manuscript ***Hu*** is 'that he hailed from the Southwest of Brabant or from the Southern border area between Flanders and Brabant,[12] which locates recension ***Hu*** *DBoec vanden houte* geographically, for the time being. Hermodsson, who produced a critical edition of ***S*** *Van den drie gaerden* in 1959, in which he also took stock of other versies, also defines ***Hu*** as Brabant,

---

[12] Brinkman & Schenkel 1999, vol. 1: 76.

with a few Flemisch features. Hermodsson defines *S*, *Van den drie gaerden*, als Guelders-Utrecht, but also notes that others characterised it als "Western Middle Dutch" or "South Holland-Utrecht tinged", and points out a number of very Northeastern, but also a number of Brabant features. He calls *D* Brabant with a small number of Eastern Middle Dutch features, *G* Western Holland, *M* Western Brabant, *O* Flemish, *T* Western Middle Dutch with marked Brabant features, *U* Eastern Brabant, and *b* Western Middle Dutch.[13] Here a number of points should be noticed:

1. In defining the dialects of a number of the recensions Hermodsson bases himself on conclusions from much older research, by other investigators.

2. Hermodsson bases his own conclusions, as was often customary half a century ago, on forms which struck him as Flemish, Brabant, Holland etc., and on rhyming couplets which struck the eye. An investigation into *all* the words and *all* the rhyming couplets in any of the recensions did not take place.

3. Defining certain forms as Brabant, Flemish, Holland, etc. was done until not very long ago on grounds which may not be unscientific or unacademic, but may now be out of date. For example: a certain manuscript could be proved to originate from a convent in Western Brabant, whereupon certain forms occurring in the manuscript were labelled "Western Brabant"; subsequently other manuscripts in which the same forms occurred were also labelled "Western Brabant". Such conclusions were completely logical and legitimate, but their soundness could never be properly verified.

For a more well-founded answer to the questions about the geographical origins and their relevance for the stemma of the legend about the Provenance of the Cross I applied to Margit Rem, who is engaged on the *Corpus veertiende-eeuws Middelnederlands* which was built up at the Amsterdam Vrije Universiteit. Her Corpus contained over 2700 dated original documents, charters and deeds from 345 different towns and villages, of which the geographical origin is known and which did not originate from too important persons, whose documents may not be in the local dialect. Literary texts are not included. The documents incorporated in the Corpus regulate and settle things

---

[13] Hermodsson 1959: 37-62.

on a fairly low and strictly local level, and therefore it may be assumed that the local dialect was used. From the Corpus documents, 101 linguistic oppositions were chosen as 'locators', linguistic variants on the basis of which a document can be located in a certain location. A few examples are: *achter* with spelling variants *aghter*, *hachter*, etc., as opposed to *after*, where *after* occurs especially in documents from Holland and Utrecht; *brief*, *brif*, etc. as opposed to *breef*, *breif*, where the latter forms occur in Northern documents. For the whys and wherefores of the complete method and the choice of the linguistic material I refer to Rem's Ph.D. thesis.[14] Unlocated documents may now be located on the basis of these locators: when Evert Wattel's computer programmes have checked a document for all the 101 locators, the computer produces a map in which the document is located in nuances of grey: the darker an area is, the more points of agreement there are with the language of the area.

In order to verify the reliability of the method, the data of certain charters and deeds were removed from the Corpus and the computer then tried to locate such a 'blind' charter or deed on the basis of the locators. All the charters and deeds did locate in the place where they hailed from or very close to it. In a few cases the complete material of a city was removed, after which the 'blind' charters and deeds nevertheless located in about the right area: the material from Bruges located unequivocally in Flanders, the material from Dordrecht in the Southwest of Holland. Evidently, with this method of locating, the occasional suggestion of mere guesswork need no longer disturb us.

Although the nine Middle Dutch texts in this investigation are literary, and only four of them (**G**, **M**, **O** and **S**) can be positioned in the fourteenth century, consultation with Rem and Wattel nevertheless made it clear that this method should be useful for aquiring an indication about the geographical origin of the texts. The difference between the dialects in C14 charters and deeds and the language in C14-C15 literary texts is probably not very substantial, with the result that the linguistic usage of the writers/copyists of these literary texts should be located reasonably correctly.

The locators on Rem's list were applied to the 9 Middle Dutch recensions, in their entirety. No selection took place of words or forms

---

[14] Rem 2003, chapters 2, 5 and 6.

which struck us for whatever reason: *all* the words of *all* the versions were passed in review. A few examples of locators and results are given below:

kocht 'bought'
b: cocht- 1, verkoft 1
D: verkoft 1
G: -
Hu: cochten 1, verkocht 1
M: vercocht 1
O: -
S: cochten 1, verkoft 1
T: vercocht 1
U: vercocht 1

lieden 'folk, people'
b: liede(n) 4, luden 3
D: lude 1
G: liden 1
Hu: liede(n) 8
M: liede 1, (tymmer)luden 2
O: --
S: liede(n) 8, luden 1
T: --
U: liede 6

zullen 'shall' (singular)
b: zal 25
D: sal 2
G: sal 1, sel 1
Hu: sael 1, sal 27
M: sal 3
O: --
S: zal 23
T: sal 8
U: sael 1, sal 25

zullen 'shall' (plural and infinitive)
b: sullen 4 (+ ghi sult 12, du sult 2, suldi 2)
D: -- (+ du sult 1)
G: -- (+ saltu 1, du salt 1)
Hu: selen 2 (+ seldi 4, ghi selt 5)
M: -- (+ du salt 1)
O: --
S: zoelen 2 (+ du zalt 1, zaltu 1, ghi zelt 2)
T: -- (+ seldi 1, ghi sult 2)
U: selen 1, sullen 1 (+ du salt 1, seldi 3, ghi selt 4, du sult)

The results in total were processed by Wattel. The results for eight out of the nine manuscripts were dialect geographical maps, see Figs. 3-10. For manuscript *O* (6 verses only) it turned out that a map could not be realised.

12. The locations

b (fig. 3). Version *b* (1496) locates as Western, with Dordrecht as its central point. This version is not in fact a manuscript but an early print; at the end of the text it says *Gheprent Thantwerpen by my*

Henrijc van Rotterdamme Littersnijder. Locating by means of Rem and Wattel's method appears to be very appropriate, even though it was here applied to a literary text from the end of C15. Flanders also colours slighty grey, but less grey than areas in North Holland. Hermodsson also located this version as Western.

D (fig. 4). Fragment *D* (1st half C15) locates in Kampen plus Holland/Utrecht. Hermodsson calls this version Brabant, with only a few Eastern Dutch traits.

G (fig. 5). Version *G* (C14) locates in Utrecht/Holland and to a much lesser degree in (Southern) Brabant. Hermodsson calls *G* Western Holland.

Hu (fig. 6). Version *Hu* (1405-1408) locates in (Southern) Brabant, fitting in with Brinkman & Schenkel's estimations and Hermodssons location (apart from his 'a few Flemish traits').

M (fig. 7). Version *M* (1360) locates in (Southern) Brabant. Hermodsson calls *M* Western Brabant.

O. Version *O* (1275-1325), the oldest text, did locate as very Eastern, but in the absence of sufficient data a map could not be realised. As mentioned before, *O* consists of 6 verses and the only locator is the word *ik*, which occurs twice: once as *ich*, once as *ic*. The author/copyist is uncertain when to use initial *h-*: he uses *ebbich* (line 3) where other recensions have *hebbich*, and *hende* where other recensions have *ende* (line 6). Because of the form *ich* and the uncertainty about when to use initial *h-*, Hermodsson locates *O* as Flemish.

S (fig. 8). Version *S* (1339) locates in Brabant. Hermodssons location is Gelders-Utrecht, with Northeastern as well as Brabant traits.

T (fig. 9). Version *T* (C15) locates in Brabant. Hermodsson calls *T* Western Middle Dutch with clear Brabant traits.

U (fig. 10). Version *U* (1438) locates in (Southern) Brabant. Hermodsson locates *U* as Eastern Brabant.

12.1. *Remarks on the locations*

The geographical location of version *D* differs significantly from the conclusion of earlier investigators. Also the location of *S* is rather different. Nevertheless, the reliability of the Rem-Wattel method appears to warrant abiding by their locations: Kampen plus Holland/Utrecht for *D*, and Brabant for *S*. The location of *O* is left out of consideration.

13. Locating the Middle Low German versions

For the Middle Low German texts an indication of their geographical origin can also be given. Both versions (again: all the words were passed in review) were checked on the features from the so-called Katalog, a list of dialect characteristics drawn up by Robert Peters for Middle Low German (Peters 1987, 1988 and 1990). The results are summarized here:

	Northern Low German	West-phalian	East-phalian	East of Elbe
H	47 + 10 –	25 + 31 –	27 + 28 –	26 + 13 –
C	42 + 14 –	29 + 27 –	22 + 34 –	24 + 16 –

For example, for *H*, the text in the Hartebok, it appears that 47 forms and phenomena were found which according to Peters are Northern Low German (*nordniederdeutsch*), as against 10 forms which as indicated by Peters do not belong in this dialect, 25 forms which are Westphalian (*westfälisch*) and 31 forms which are not Westphalian. The 25 Westphalian forms are almost without exception also Northern Low German, so that the fact that there are so many forms which are *not* Westphalian, is a weightier factor in the determination of the dialect.

So *H*, *Van deme holte des hilligen krutzes* in the Hartebok, is predominantly Northern Low German, with East of Elbe (*ostelbisch*) traits, a characteristic which, as a matter of fact, applies to all the other literary texts in the miscellany and which fits in with the geographical region of the home of the manuscript since time immemorial, the city of Hamburg. The version in manuscript *C* evidences virtually identical dialect characteristics; this manuscript has also dwelled in Hamburg for very long.

14. Complementary stemma

All these data were entered into the stemma of Figure 1, with the more complete stemma in Figure 2 as a result.

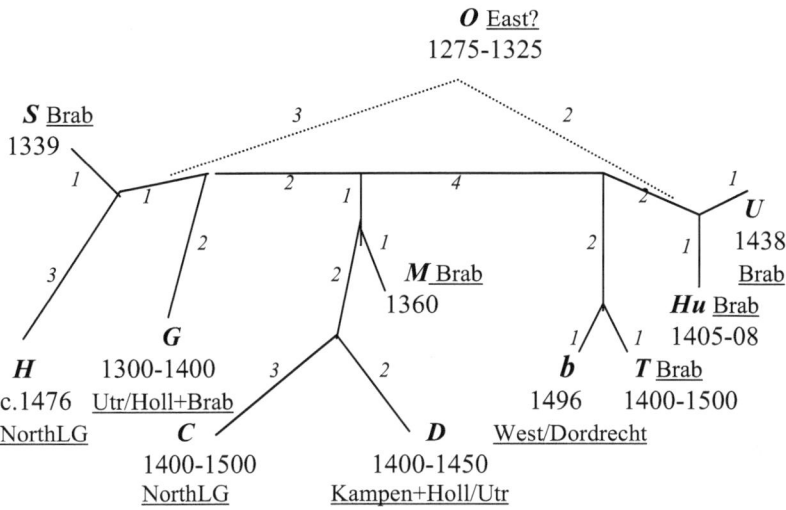

Fig. 2. Stemma with dialect data

15. More conclusions

A number of questions can now be examined anew.

D, the version most closely related to *C*, is indeed somewhat Eastern Middle Dutch tinged (Kampen+Holland/Utrecht). Both manuscripts date from C15, *D* from the first half. It is, therefore, quite possible that they go back on one and the same Eastern Middle Dutch exemplar, be it by way of one or more intermediate versions. The differences are too great for a more direct relationship. The version one branch away, the much older *M*, on the other hand, is Brabant. A tentative hypothesis could be that the postulated Eastern Middle Dutch exemplar and version *M* both go back on one and the same original; this original may have been Brabant, in view of the following observations.

The versions closest to *H* are Brabant (*S*) and Utrecht/Holland+Brabant (*G*). In addition to this it should be considered that *S* is much older than *H* (1339 and c 1476 respectively) and that *G* is also a C14 manuscript. About the precise relationship between *H*, *S* and *G* very little can be concluded on these grounds either. A very tentative conclusion might be that *H* may ultimately go back on a Brabant tinged version of the text.

The 4 versions in the "right-hand" group, *b*, *Hu*, *T* and *U*, form a fairly homogenous group. All these version date from C15, *Hu* just before 1410, *U* between 1425 and 1450, *b* 1496; *T* is only generally 'C15'. Only *b*, the 1496 print, is evidently not Brabant, the other three versions locate practically identically as Brabant. If *O* is counted as one of this group, the deviation is also serious: the dialect, as far as it can be determined for these 6 verses, is very Eastern. This is another indication that *O* should probably not be counted as one of this group.

If *O* is counted as one the "left-hand" group, the group becomes slightly more heterogeneous: *S* and *M* are unquestionably Brabant, *G* is partly Brabant, and for the rest the group is Utrecht/Holland, Kampen+Utrecht/Holland, "Eastern" and Low German. As established earlier, the dating of this group is also rather heterogeneous.

From the oldest version *O*'s position in the stemma and geographical location no conclusions can be drawn. In total, 5 out of the 8 usable versions locate as Brabant, 1 as possibly Brabant (*G*) and 2 as not Brabant (*b* and *D*). The youngest version, *b*, the 1496 print, also locates slightly as Flemish, but this is surely not an indication that the cradle of an original C13 or C14 text stood in Flanders. In none of the other versions is there any question of a dialect in which Bruges would fit, the town in which according to tradition the Hartebok texts were supposed to have been collected and copied (Langbroek & Roeleveld 2001a: 30-33).

If again we leave *O* out of consideration, the oldest texts (*S*, *G* and *M*) are from Brabant and the most homogenous subgroup (*b*, *Hu*, *T* and *U*) also locates in large measure in Brabant. It does, therefore, not appear inaccurate to conclude that the cradle of the rhymed Middle Dutch text probably stood in Brabant. Although the relationship is not very close, both Middle Low German texts are relatively similar to two of the oldest, Brabant texts, *M* and *S*. The conclusion appears to be obvious, that both recensions are translations, or go back on translations, of, again, Brabant exemplars.

16. Final conclusions

From the investigations reported in this article it is not yet possible to get a clear picture about the previous history of the Middle Dutch text about the Provenance of the Cross. The related Latin version *Legenda* (1220) is much older; also the *Legenda Aura* (1260) is somewhat older than the oldest Middle Dutch version *O* (1275-1325), although this does by no means rule out that a Middle Dutch translation could have been made of the version in that popular collection. Brabant is in all likelyhood the place where the rhymed Middle Dutch text, ultimately based on the *Legenda*, was created. Thus it is certainly possible that the first Middle Dutch text was translated from French; a version which was like the C13 and C14 rhymed French versions that have been preserved, may have been the exemplar. To the best of my knowledge, neither Barbara Baert, whose intimate knowledge all these texts is second to none, nor anyone else, has ever suggested this. Moreover, from the retold versions in Baert 2001, as mentioned in section 2, it appears that the Middle Dutch and Middle Low German versions do in quite a number of elements and turns of the story diverge from the French and English texts and the *Legenda* text.[15]

However, as remarked earlier, it is actually possible to do useful and succesful stemmatological research into the relationships between mutually quite divergent recensions of a story, in diferent languages, of different lengths, and rhymed and prose. It should, therefore, after the Middle Dutch and Middle Low German recensions from this investigation, be worth putting the Latin versions from the Legenda and the Legenda Aurea, the French and English recensions, and the Middle Dutch prose text, through a stemmatological analysis, as was carried out for the many different versions of *Valentin and Namelos* and in a slightly different way for the many versions of *Van dren konyngen* (the legend of three living and three dead kings) with striking results (Roeleveld, Langbroek & Wattel 2004; Langbroek 2003, respectively).

Literature

Baert 2001: Barbara Baert, *Een erfenis van heilig hout. De neerslag van het teruggevonden kruis in tekst en beeld tijdens de Middeleeuwen*, Leuven.

Brinkman & Schenkel 1999: H. Brinkman en J. Schenkel, *Het handschrift-Van Hulthem. Hs. Brussel, Koninklijke Bibliotheek van België, 15.589-623*, 2 dln. (MVN 7). Hilversum.

---

[15] See also Langbroek 2010.

Hermodsson 1959: Lars Hermodsson, *Dat boec van den houte. Eine mittelniederländische Dichtung von der Herkunft des Kreuzes Christi. Mit einer Einleitung neu herausgegeben* (Uppsala Universitets Årsskrift 1959, 1) Uppsala/Wiesbaden.

Jungman & Voorbij 1999: M.E.M. Jungman (i.s.m. J.B. Voorbij), *Repertorium van teksten in het handschrift-Van Hulthem (hs. Brussel, Koninklijke Biliotheek België, 15.589-623)*. Cd-rom met een Inleiding. Hilversum.

Klein 1997: Thomas Klein, "Die Rezeption mittelniederländischer Versdichtungen im Rheinland und Augustijns 'Herzog von Braunschweig'", in: *Amsterdamer Beiträge zur älteren Germanistik* 47: 79-107.

Langbroek 2003: Erika Langbroek, "Ein merkwürdiges Ende oder eine doppelte Erzählung? Probleme beim Aufbau der Versdichtung 'Van dren konyngen' im *Hartebok*", in: *Amsterdamer Beiträge zur älteren Germanistik* 58: 171-207.

— 2004: Erika Langbroek, " 'Dith is de kranshals' und [Frowenloff] im Hamburger Hartebok. Alte Fragen, neue Antworten", in: Niederdeutsches Jahrbuch 127, 65-84.

— 2010: Erika Langbroek, "Die Kreuzholzlegende im Hartebok und seine Verwandten", in: *Amsterdamer Beiträge zur älteren Germanistik* 66, 205-248.

Langbroek & Roeleveld 1997: *Valentin und Namelos. Mittelniederdeutsch und Neuhochdeutsch*. Herausgegeben, übersetzt und kommentiert van Erika Langbroek und Annelies Roeleveld unter Mitarbeit von Arend Quak (Amsterdamer Publikationen zur Sprache und Literatur 127), Amsterdam, Atlanta.

— 1998a: Erika Langbroek und Annelies Roeleveld, "Valentin bekommt einen Gefährten. Ein Vergleich der Reimpaare in den Handschriften S, H und K", in: *Amsterdamer Beiträge zur älteren Germanistik* 50: 149-165.

— 1998b: Erika Langbroek und Annelies Roeleveld, "Wie reimen sich die Nachbarn? Eine Untersuchung nach den ursprünglichen Reimen in 'Valentin und Namelos" in der Stockholmer Handschrift Cod. Holm. Vu 73, in: *Niederdeutsches Jahrbuch* 121: 85-131.

— 2001a: Erika Langbroek en Annelies Roeleveld (Hgg.), m.m.v. Ingrid Biesheuvel en met een codicologische beschrijving door Hans Kienhorst: *Het Hartebok. Hs. Hamburg, Staats- und Universitätsbibliothek, 102c in scrinio* (MNV VIII), Hilversum. (N.B.: A list of corrections of the printing errors which unfortunately occurred can be obtained from the publisher - Verloren, Hilversum).

— 2001b: Erika Langbroek und Annelies Roeleveld, "Eine Wolfenbütteler Himmelfahrt. *Van der hymmeluart marien* in Cod. Guelf. Helmst. 1084 und *Van der bort cristi* im Hartebok", in: *Amsterdamer Beiträge zur älteren Germanistik* 55: 193-221.

— 2005: Erika Langbroek und Annelies Roeleveld, "Ein stemmatologischer Versuch. "Dith is de kranshals" im *Hartebok*. Textvergleiche mit den überlieferte sonstigen Kranshalsgedichten", in: *Amsterdamer Beiträge zur älteren Germanistik* 60: 183-198.

Peters 1987: Robert Peters, "Katalog sprachlicher Merkmale zur variablenlinguistischen Erforschung des Mittelniederdeutschen. I", in: *Niederdeutsches Wort* 27: 61-93.

— 1988: Robert Peters, "Katalog sprachlicher Merkmale zur variablenlinguistischen Erforschung des Mittelniederdeutschen. II", in: *Niederdeutsches Wort* 28: 75-106.

— 1990: Robert Peters, "Katalog sprachlicher Merkmale zur variablenlinguistischen Erforschung des Mittelniederdeutschen. III", in: *Niederdeutsches Wort* 30: 5-17.

Rem 2003: Margit Rem, *De taal van de klerken uit de Hollandse grafelijke kanselarij (1300-1340)*. Naar een lokaliseringsprocedure voor het veertiende-eeuws Middelnederlands (Stichting Neerlandistiek VU 39. Doctoral Thesis, Vrije Universiteit), Amsterdam.

Roeleveld & Langbroek 2002: Annelies Roeleveld und Erika Langbroek, "Four Parallels to *Vnser leuen frowen rozenkrantz* in the Low German *Hartebok*: Pedigree, Rhymes and an Edition", in: *Amsterdamer Beiträge zur älteren Germanistik* 56: 179-197.

Roeleveld, Langbroek & Wattel 2004: Annelies Roeleveld, Erika Langbroek und Evert Wattel, "Valentin and Namelos discover their parentage: Narrative elements in the family tree of an international medieval tale", in: *Studies in Stemmatology II*, ed. Pieter van Reenen, August den Hollander and Margot van Mulken, Amsterdam-Philadelphia, 283-301. (Eerder verschenen als: Vrije Universiteit Amsterdam, Faculteit der Exacte Wetenschappen, Rapportnr. WS-531, 1999, Amsterdam).

Schröder 1876: C. Schröder, "Vom Holze des heiligen Kreuzes", in: Niederdeutsches Jahrbuch 2: 88-113.

Staphorst, N., (ed.),'"Dat Harte-Bock"; in: Hamburgische Kirchen-Geschichte, I, 4 (1731): 175-267 (copy Den Haag Kon. Bibl. 3062 A 11).

Wattel & van Mulken 1996a: E. Wattel and M. van Mulken, "Shock Waves in Text Tradition", in: *Studies in Stemmatology I*, ed. P. van Reenen and M. van Mulken, Amsterdam-Philadelphia, 105-121.

Wattel & van Mulken 1996b: E. Wattel and M. van Mulken, "Weighted Formal Support of a pedigree", in: *Studies in Stemmatology I*, ed. P. van Reenen and M. van Mulken, Amsterdam-Philadelphia, 135-167.

Fig. 3. Version *b*, 1496, 781 verses

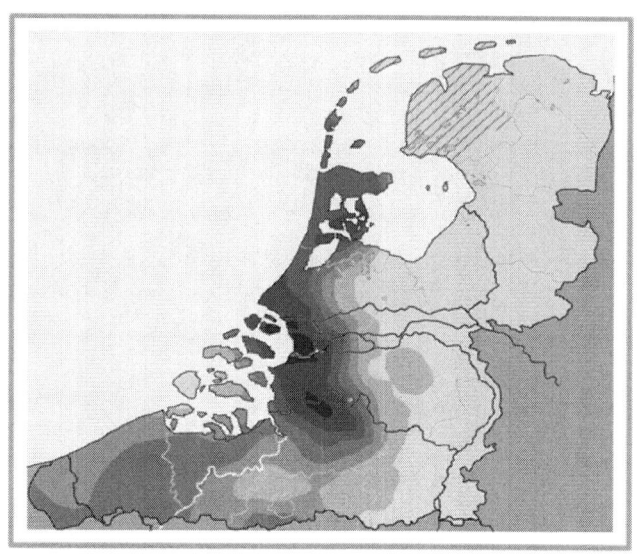

Fig. 4. Fragment *D*, 1400-1450, 174 verses

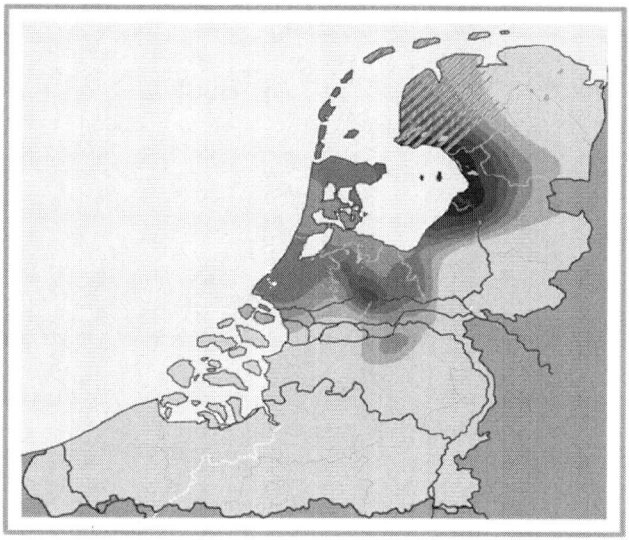

Fig. 5. Fragment *G*, C14, 67 verses

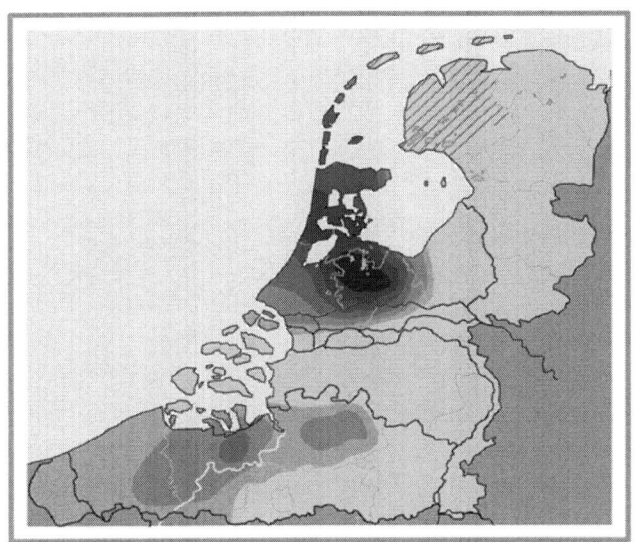

Fig. 6. Version *Hu*, 1405-1408, 781 verses

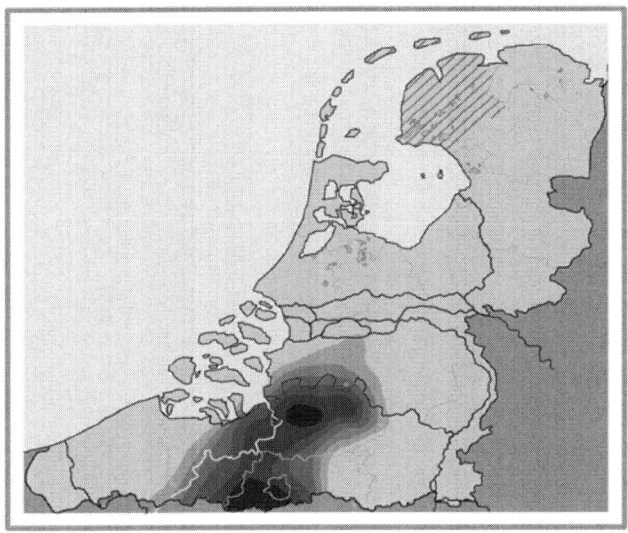

Fig. 7. Fragment *M*, 1360, 171 verses

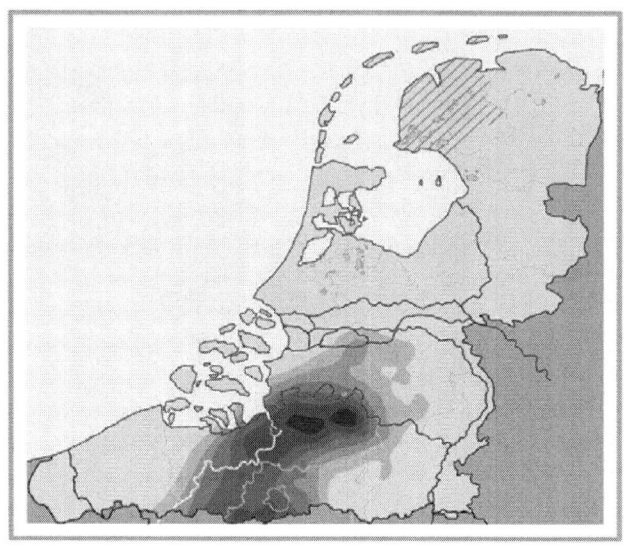

Fig. 8. Version *S*, 1339, 839 verses

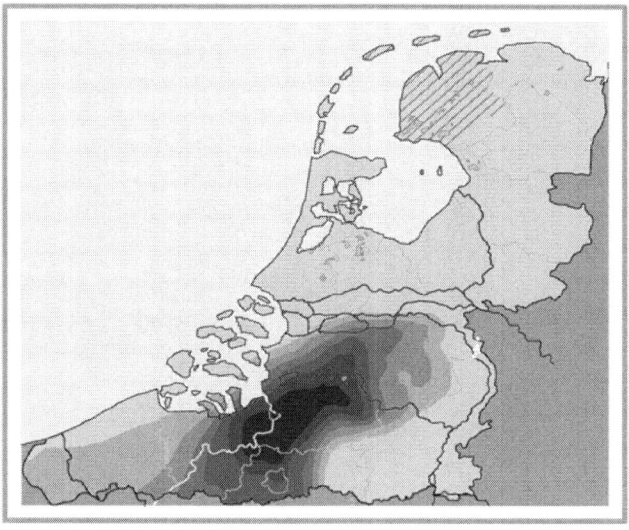

Fig. 9. Fragment *T*, C15, 177 verses

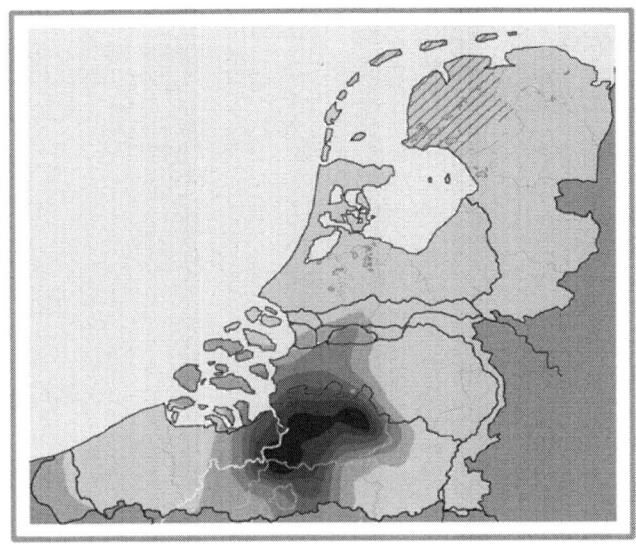

Fig. 10. Version *U*, 1438, 567 verses

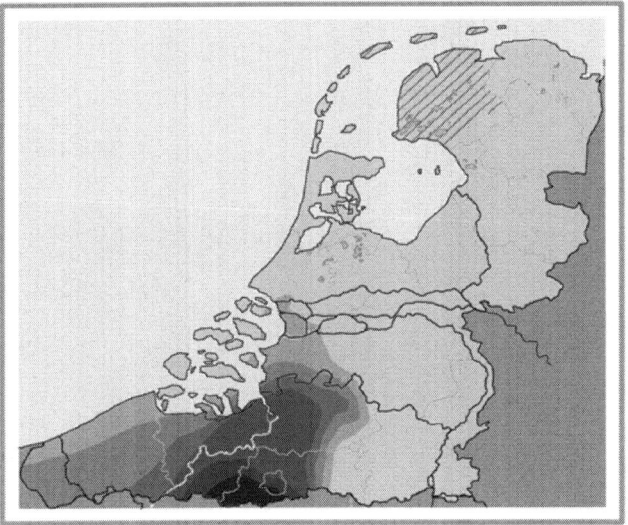

DIE KREUZHOLZLEGENDE IM 'HARTEBOK' UND IHRE VERWANDTEN

Erika Langbroek - Amsterdam

I. Die Kreuzholzlegende, Einleitung

In der Sammelhandschrift, die unter dem Namen 'Hartebok' (1476) bekannt geworden ist, heißt die zweite reimende Verserzählung *Van dem holte des hilligen krutzes*. Untersuchungen haben gezeigt, dass es hier um eine Übersetzung der älteren mittelniederländischen Versdichtung geht, die unter der Überschrift *Van den drie Gaerden* (Handschrift *S*) überliefert wurde und die Tideman (1844) *DBoec vanden Houte* nannte.[1] Die ausführliche Studie von Barbara Baert (2001), *Een erfenis van heilig hout*, in der sie die überlieferten Bildgeschichten, wie zum Beispiel die Fresken in Arezzo und Florenz, und die schriftlichen Hintergründe der Kreuzholzlegende genau untersucht, war für mich der direkte Anlass, die Erzählung im Hartebok und die mittelniederländischen verwandten Texte unter die Lupe zu nehmen; mit Hilfe der früheren Fassungen der Erzählung im Hinblick auf die variierenden Details wird eine Entwicklung von dem ältesten Text bis zur Überlieferung im 13. Jahrhundert skizziert. Die mittelniederländisch überlieferte Kreuzholzlegende und ihre mittelniederdeutschen Übersetzungen, die von Hermodsson *Vdh* (*Van den houte*) von mir aber *niederländische Kreuzholzlegende* (*NKh*) genannt wird, werden hier, was die wichtigen Teilelemente der Erzählung betrifft, untersucht.[2] *NKh* wird zur *Legenda-Gruppe* gerechnet (Baert 2001, 225), an deren Anfang eine lateinische Prosaversion steht, die *Legenda* (*Le*, 1220). Die ganze *Legenda-Gruppe* unterscheidet sich deutlich von anderen Fassungen; sie kennzeichnet sich unter anderem dadurch, dass die Legende bei Golgotha endet und dass nicht, wie zum Beispiel in der *Legenda Aurea* (*LA*, ± 1260), weiter über Kreuzfindung (Helena) und Kreuzhebung (Heraklius) erzählt wird. Obwohl Hermodsson die Da-

---

[1] Vgl. für die Übersetzungstechnik bei den mittelniederdeutschen Texten *H* und *C* in diesem Band, A. Roeleveld 'The Holy Rood in the Netherlands and North Germany'.
[2] Siehe für die Datierung von *Vdh* (1290?-1330) Hermodsson 1959, 30ff., 113.

tierung von *NKh* von *LA* abhängig zu machen scheint und also eine Entstehungszeit nach 1260 annimmt, wird sich zeigen, dass die *LA* kein direktes Vorbild für *NKh* sein kann. Die Untersuchung richtet sich vor allem darauf, wie *NKh* und *Le* von anderen Fassungen abweichen und wie sich *NKh* deutlich, trotz vieler Übereinstimmungen, von *Le* abhebt und mit biblischen 'Fakten' erweitert wird.[3]

II. Kurze Zusammenfassung des Inhalts von *NKh*

Kurzer Prolog: der Erzähler will über das Kreuzholz berichten [**1**].[4] Er fängt mit Adam an, der alt und krank ist [**2**] und darum seinen Sohn Seth ins Paradies sendet, das Öl der Barmherzigkeit zu holen. Im Paradies zeigt ein Engel Seth die vier Paradiesströme [**3a**], einen hohen, verdorrten Baum [**3b**], um den eine Schlange sich windet [**3c**]; Seth sieht bei den Wurzeln die Seele von Abel [**3d**]; oben im Baum ist ein neugeborenes Kind, das am Holz aus den drei Kernen (3K) des Apfels, von dem Adam gegessen hat, sterben wird [**3e**]. Seth empfängt dann 3K, die er Adam, wenn er gestorben ist, unter die Zunge legen soll [**3f**], die 3K werden zu drei Zweigen (3G, mnl. *gaerde* = Zweig) hochwachsen (Zeder, Zipresse und Kiefer/Palmenbaum) [**3g**]. Seth kehrt zu Adam zurück, erzählt von den 3K und 3G; Adam freut sich [**4**]. Als Adam stirbt, nimmt der Teufel seine Seele mit [**5a**]. Er wird in Hebron, wo er geschaffen wurde, von Seth begraben, der ihm die 3K unter die Zunge legt [**5b**]. Die 3K wachsen zu 3G, eine Elle lang, die sich während 3200 Jahre nicht verändern [**5c**].

Moses findet die 3G in Hebron [**6a**]. Er sieht sie gesondert um sein Bett, lässt sie aber stehen [**6b**]; dann sieht er die 3G um sein Bett in Elim und wiederum lässt er sie stehen [**6c**]. Als er sie zum dritten Mal um sein Bett sieht, in Rafidim, zieht er sie aus dem Boden; mit den 3G macht er bitteres Wasser süß [**6d**]. Moses kommt zum Berg Sinaï, geht später nach Moab und pflanzt die 3G dort; sie bleiben unverändert [**6e**].

In einem Traum erhält David von einem Engel ein Zeichen nach Moab zu gehen, die 3G zu finden und in seinen Hof zu pflanzen [**7a**]. David begibt sich nach Moab; er findet die 3G um sein Bett, zieht sie aus [**7b**]. Unterwegs nach Jerusalem heilt David Kranke: Lixsillus (Bixillus, Bixillas, Bexillas), Mohren und einen 'lazers' Mann, der bei Davids Ankunft schon geheilt war [**7c**]. David kommt in Jerusalem und stellt die 3G bei seinem Palast in ein Wasser [**8a**]. Über Nacht wachsen die 3G, tief wurzelnd, zusammen [**8b**].

---

[3] Zur *NKh* zählen die Texte (Handschriften) *b*, *D*, *G*, *Hu*, *M*, *O*, *S*, *T*, *U*, *H*, *C* (vgl. III).

[4] Im Folgenden wird immer auf diese Numerierung hingewiesen.

Der Baum wächst; David legt während dreißig Jahre jedes Jahr einen silbernen Ring um den Stamm [**8c**]. Er besucht den Baum oft und betet dort [**8d**]. Dann will David einen Tempel bauen, was er aber nicht darf [**8e**].

Als Salomo den Tempelbau anfängt, wird der Baum umgehauen [**9a**]. Die 30 Ringe werden in den Tempel gebracht und bleiben dort bis Judas' Zeit [**9b**]. Als Bauholz verändert das Holz dauernd seine Länge [**9c**] und wird nicht gebraucht; es bleibt dann im Tempel liegen [**9d**]. Eine Sibylle setzt sich auf das Holz und fängt Feuer [**10a**]; sie prophezeit, dass Gottes Sohn am Holz hängen wird [**10b**]; darauf wird sie in einen Kerker geworfen und stirbt [**10c**]. Das Holz wird, als Brücke, über ein Gewässer gelegt [**10d**].

Als die Königin von Saba zu Salomo kommt [**11a**], weigert sie sich, über die Brücke zu gehen, verehrt das Holz [**11b**]. Salomo wundert sich; die Königin von Saba prophezeit, dass 'der Welt Hoffnung' am Holz hängen wird [**11c**]; sie schenkt Silber und Gold, womit man das Holz beschlägt [**11d**]. Das Holz wird zum Tempel gebracht, quer über der Tür befestigt, damit sich jeder vor dem Holz verbeugen soll [**11e**]. Spätere Könige plündern das Gold und die Juwele; das Holz wird draußen tief vergraben [**12a**]. Da liegt es 200 Jahre [**12b**].

Man gräbt zum Waschen von Opferfleisch ein Wasserbecken (*piscina probatica*) [**13a**]. In Christus' Zeit, vor der Passion, schwimmt das Holz nach oben [**13b**]. Der Evangelist Johannes erzählt über Heilungen im Becken [**13c**]. Jesus wird von Judas verraten [**14a**], als Gefangener zum Hohenpriester gebracht [**14b**] und von vielen verschmäht [**14c**]; Jesus erscheint vor Pilatus [**14d**] und wird gegeißelt [**14e**]. Ein Jude weiß noch, dass in einem Wasser ein Stück Holz liegt [**14f**].

Die Zusammensetzung des Kreuzes wird beschrieben [**15a**]; Jesus trägt das Kreuz [**15b**], wobei Maria und Johannes zugegen sind [**15c**]. Jesus wird gekreuzigt [**15d**]. Marias Kummer sei zu groß, darüber etwas zu sagen [**15e**], ein Schwert durchschneidet ihr Herz [**15f**]. Jesus stirbt, es folgt eine Sonnenfinsternis, ein Erdbeben, die Felsen reißen [**16a**]. Ein Ritter durchsticht die Seite Jesus'; daraus strömt das Öl der Barmherzigkeit [**16b**]. Schlussgebet [**16c**].

III. Die Liste der Varianten (oder Teile) der Kreuzholzlegende

Die folgende Aufzählung enthält Werke, die von Baert für ihre Studie benutzt wurden oder die sich aus eigener Studie ergaben, in chronologischer Reihenfolge. Die jeweilige Seitenzahl nach dem Namen Baert (d.h. Baert 2001) und anderen (Baert; Gysseling u.ä.) vermerkt die Seiten, die uns die nötigen Fakten liefern. Die mittelniederländischen und mittelniederdeutschen Texte, die zu *NKh* gehören, werden mit * beziehungsweise ** vermerkt. Zwischen eckigen Klammern stehen die Texte, die zwar von mir untersucht wurden, in der Ausarbeitung der Fakten aber keine Rolle spielen. Die Abkürzungen der Texte werden unten immer beibehalten:

[*OS*   (2. Jh. v. Chr.-3./4. Jh. n. Chr.) *Oracula Sibyllina* (lat.) (Baert 267)]

VAE   (± 70) *Vita Adae et Evae* (lat.) (Baert 234)

arVae   (5. Jh.) *Übersetzung der Vita Adae et Evae* (armen.) (Baert 240)

PsENg   (5. Jh.) *Pseudo-Evangelium* von Nikodemus (gri.) (Baert 239f.)

[*DG*   (vor 470) *Descriptio Graeciae X,12,9* von Pausanias (lat.) (Baert 268)]

PJ   (8. Jh.) *Überlieferung* aus den Kreisen von Pope Jeremia (slav.; gri.) (Baert 241, 268)

[*BOH*   (9. Jh.) *Bericht* über St. Odilia von Hohenburg (lat.) (Baert 232)]

byzW   (842-887) *byzantinische Weltchronik* von Georgias Monachos (gri.) (Baert 267)

slK   (950) *Kreuzholzlegende der slavischen Bogomilen* (slav.) (Baert 242)

PsENl   (10. Jh.) *Pseudo-Evangelium* von Nikodemus (lat.) (Baert 239)

[*TS*   (vor 11. Jh.) *Übersetzung des Targum Scheni* (armen.) (Baert 255, 265)]

slVAE   (1000-1200) *Übersetzung der Vita Adae et Evae* (slav.) (Baert 240)

SpE   (± 1100) *Speculum ecclesiae* von Honorius Augustodunensis (lat.) (Baert 216)

El   (± 1100) *Elucidarium* von Honorius Augustodunensis (lat.) (Klunder 16ff.)

THL   (± 1100) *3. Traktat zum Hohen Lied* von Honorius Augustodunensis (lat.) (Baert 260)

[*Mi*   (4. Jh.-12. Jh.) *Midrasch* (hebr.) (Baert 228f.)]

LF   (1120) *Liber floridus* von Lambertus von Sint-Omaars (lat.) (Baert 219)

Hi   (vor 1150) *Historia* (lat.) (Baert 220f.)

IM   (vor 1155) *De imago mundi* von Honorius Augustodunensis (lat.) (Baert 217)

ESC   (1170) *De exaltatione sanctae crucis* von Johannes Belethus (lat.) (Baert 219)

HS   (vor 1178) *Historia scholastica* von Petrus Comestor (lat.) (Baert 217)

P   (± 1180) *Pantheon, XIV* von Gottfried von Viterbo (lat.) (Baert 218)

HD   (1180) *Hortus Deliciarum* von Herrad von Landsberg (lat.) (Baert

224, 227, 260)
[*IJ*   (1190) *Interrogatio Johannis* der Katharen (lat.) (Baert 242)]
[*Per*   (± 1190-1212) *'Perceval'* von Didot (afr.?) (Baert 251)]
CJ   (± 1210) *La citez de Jhérusalem* (lat.) (Baert 221)
OI   (1212) *Otia Imperialia* von Gervasius von Tilbury (lat.) (Baert 217)
Le   (1220) *Legenda* = *Prosaversion* (lat.) (Baert 225, 229f., 244)
CRC   (1250) *Chronica Regia Coloniensis* (lat.) (Baert 235)
QGra   (13. Jh.) *Queste du Saint Graal* (afr.) (Baert 222)
SHR   (13. Jh.) *Story of the Holy Rood* (me.) (Baert 225, Hermodsson 15)
LA   (± 1260) *Legenda Aurea* von Jakob de Voragine (lat.) (Graesse 303, Kap. 64)
NKh   (1290?-1330) *Niederländische Kreuzholzlegende* (s. die Texte mit * und **)
R   (1271) *Rijmbijbel* von Jacob van Maerlant (mnl.) (Gysseling)
*O**   (1275-1325) Hs. Oudenaarde, Stadtsbibliotheek, 5567 (mnl.) (Hermodsson 54f.)
RT   (14. Jh.) *Rood-Tree-Gruppe* (me.) (Hermodsson 16ff.)
Lu   (14. Jh.) *Lucidarius* (mnl.) (Klunder 29)
*G**   (14. Jh.) Hs. Göttingen, Niedersächsische SUB, 8° Cod. Luneb. 24a (mnl.)
Rb   (1332) *Rijmbijbel* von Jacob van Maerlant (mnl.) (Chavannes)
*S**   (1339) *Van den drie gaerden*, UB Groningen, Hs. 405, Bl. 210va-214va (mnl.)
[*PA*   (1355-1358) *Pélerinage de l'âme* von Guillaume de Deguileville (afr.) (Baert 253)]
*M**   (1360-1375) Hs. Brüssel, KB II 5.580 (mnl.)
*D**   (1400-1450) Hs. Düsseldorf, Hauptstaatsarchiv, ohne Signatur (mnl.)
*Hu**   (1405-1408) *DBoec vanden Houte*, Hs. Brüssel, KB 15.589-623, F. 15va-19vb (mnl.)
*U**   (1425-1450) *dit es vte tdiechs vanden houten*, Hs. Utrecht, UB, 1329, F. 34ra-37vb (mnl.)
OHK   (15. Jh.) *Om det heliga korset*; (Hg.) George Stephens, Stockholm, 1847 (altschw.)
LD   (15. Jh.) *De ligno domini*; (Hg.) George Stephens, Stockholm, 1847 (altschw.)
*T**   (15. Jh.) Hs. 's-Hertogenbosch, Archivum Capuccinorum Hollandiae, 4 (mnl.)
*C***   (15. Jh.) 'Vom Holze des heiligen Kreuzes', SUB Hamburg, Convent. 4, F. 182r-199r (mnd.)
*H***   (1476) *Van dem holte des hilligen krutzes*, SUB Hamburg, Hs.

	102c in scrinio, F. 11r-23v (mnd.) (Langbroek & Roeleveld)
bo	(1483) *Boec van den Houte*, (Druck) Culemborg (mnl.) (Baert 289f., 336, 353f.; vgl. auch Baert 1995)
b*	(1496) *Dit is dat boec vanden houte*, Haarlem Stadsbibliotheek, (Druck) Antwerpen (mnl.).[5]

IV. Bemerkungen anlässlich der Kreuzholzlegende in Wandmalereien [6]

Die Legende vom Paradiesbaum, der zum Kreuzholz wird, wurde in vielen Formen überliefert. Wahrscheinlich dienten den zahlreichen Abbildungen schriftliche Belege als Quelle, obschon man nicht mit Sicherheit sagen kann, welcher Text genau welcher Abbildung zum Vorbild war (Baert 2001, 378). In Italien sieht man erst am Ende des 14. Jhs. die erste Freskenreihe der Kreuzholzlegende, zum Beispiel die Malereien von Agnolo Gaddi (1388-1393) in der S. Croce in Florenz. Nördlich der Alpen sind die ältesten Abbildungen noch etwas später, z.B. in einer Kirche in Wiedenest (± 1455). Für meine Untersuchungen haben die Fresken, da sie erst nach 1300 gemalt wurden, wenig Bedeutung; doch möchte ich zu den Abbildungen einiges bemerken.

Bei den Freskenreihen in Italien sieht man nie Moses oder David dargestellt; die Bildgeschichte springt von Seth-pflanzt-einen-Zweig zur Königin von Saba (KvS), die bei Salomo zu Besuch kommt. Das fehlende Glied, warum das Holz nämlich als Brücke über den Bach Kidron gelegt wird, muss selbstverständlich bekannt gewesen sein.

Auffallend ist, dass in den Bilderreihen die Kreuzigung so selten dargestellt wird; eigentlich werden bei den Illustrationen im *Boec van den Houte* (1483) zum ersten Mal drei Szenen der Passion gewidmet: die Kreuztragung, die Kreuzigung und einige Personen, die neben dem Kreuz von Demonen geheilt werden: (zu Bild 17) *Daer stont dat heylighe cruys/ Hier gheschyede den duuel groot confuys/ Want alle die ghene die beseten sijn/ Die worden verlost van hoerre pijn*. Dem Text unter den Bildern im *Boec van den Houte* liegt *Van den drie Gaerden* (*S*, 1339) zu Grunde. Es ist eine Erzählung des *Legenda*-Typus, aus der Umgebung von Maerlant (Baert 1995, 40ff.; 2001, 347).

In den Fresken endet die Kreuzholzlegende nicht bei der Passion und dem Öl der Barmherzigkeit; es wird weiter 'berichtet' über die Kreuzauffindung (Helena), den Raub des Kreuzes (Chosroes) und die

---

[5] In der Literaturliste werden alle Texte in alfabetischer Reihenfolge aufgezählt.
[6] S. Baert 2001, 269ff.

Kreuzhebung (Heraklius); die gemalten Kreuzholzlegenden weichen also von *Le* und *NKh*, nicht aber von *LA* (± 1260) ab.

Als Heraklius mit dem Kreuz in Jerusalem hinein gehen will, wird er zu Demut gemahnt: er legt sein königliches Gewand ab, steigt vom Pferd und soll mit gebeugtem Haupt und barfuß mit dem Kreuz die Stadt betreten – dieses Element der Demut bei der Pforte sieht man in *NKh*, als das Holz von König Salomo über den Eingang des Tempels eingefügt wird, damit jeder das Holz mit gebeugtem Haupt verehren soll; vgl. z.B. *H*, Vss. 638-649:

      Vnde salomon de wyse here
      De leth nemen mit groter ere
640 Vnde in den tempel dregen do
      He leth mit stenen leggen to
      Alle doren grot vnde cleyne
      De dar weren sunder eyne
644 Vnde leth dat holt dar dwers in fogen
      So dat nemant scholde mogen
      Dar in gan vnde spreken sine bede
      He negede deme holte vnde der stede
648 De dat touorenn hadden betreden
      De mosten do alle anbeden.

Der Sieg über den Islam in Spanien (Alorcos, 1195 und Las Navas de Tolosa, 1212) wird als eine Art Kreuzzug betrachtet. Der Zusammenhang ist (durch die Kreuzzüge) natürlich der Sieg des Christentums (schon von Konstantin) über das Heidentum. Die Kreuzholzlegende gehört sicher zum größten Teil zum Gedankengut der Kreuzzüge, das im 14. Jh. noch immer aktuell war und durch den Fall von Konstantinopel (1453) noch aktueller wurde. In der bildenden Kunst wurden danach Darstellungen von Salomo und der KvS populär, weil das Verhältnis zwischen dem Osten und dem Westen prekär war. Der Fall von Konstantinopel ist leider für meine Untersuchungen zu spät, aber natürlich hatte er in der Entstehungszeit des Harteboks (*H*, 1476) noch große Aktualität.

Die Devotion der Kreuzreliquien, die in Europa zu sehen ist,[7] erin-

---

[7] Seit der Kreuzauffindung im 4. Jh. verbreitet sich die Reliquienverehrung des Kreuzes über Europa. Vgl. auch Kemper 2006, 214: Im Jahre 1108 schenkte Ansellus, cantor und Presbyter des heiligen Grabes in Jerusalem, dem Erzbistum Paris eine Reliquie des Heiligen Kreuzes; Kemper 2006, 231: Seit der Eroberung Jerusalems 1099 und Konstantinopels 1204 gelangten Kreuzreliquien in größerer Zahl nach Europa.

nert an die Kreuzzüge:

(± 70	Verwüstung von Jerusalem und Zerstörung des Tempels durch Titus)
1096-1099	erster Kreuzzug (mit Stürmung von Jerusalem)
1147-1149	zweiter Kreuzzug
(1187	Einnahme von Jerusalem durch Sultan Saladin)
1189-1192	dritter Kreuzzug
1202-1204	vierter Kreuzzug (der in Konstantinopel endete)
1212	Kinderkreuzzug (Kinder als Sklaven von Marseille nach Alexandrien verkauft)
1228-1229	fünfter Kreuzzug (Jerusalem, Bethlehem, Nazareth von den Christen erobert)
(1244	Eroberung von Jerusalem durch die Muslime)
1248-1254	sechster Kreuzzug
1270	siebter Kreuzzug
(1291	Akko, letzte Hochburg der Christen, von den Mamelucken erobert).

Zwischen 1096 und 1204, also in der Zeit bevor **Le** (1220) entstand, fanden vier Kreuzzüge statt. Daneben konnte jeder Pilger, der das Heilige Land und die heiligen Stätten besuchte, mit Reliquienverehrung im Heiligen Land konfrontiert werden. Als **NKh** (1290?-1330) entstand, waren alle Kreuzzüge gescheitert, das Heilige Land war in den Händen der Muslime.

V. Die Texte der Kreuzholzlegende: die wichtigsten Elemente

Gemeinschaftlich in den verschiedenen Fassungen der Legende ist der Gedanke, dass das Kreuzholz in direktem Zusammenhang mit dem Paradies steht. Die Sünde von Adam (und Eva), und somit die Erbsünde aller Menschen nach ihnen, kann nur durch Christus' Tod gesühnt werden. Adams Sünde besteht daraus, dass Adam sein Bündnis mit Gott brach, indem er vom Baum der Erkenntnis des Guten und Bösen aß.

V.1
[3a-e] Als Boten sendet Adam seinen Sohn Seth (und Eva) ins Paradies, um Vergebung zu bitten. Nicht in jeder Erzählung kann (können) Seth (und Eva) das Paradies betreten.

Dass Seth das Paradies nicht betritt, steht in der ältesten Erzählung

VAE (± 70). Das heißt, dass Seth und Eva keine Samen oder Zweige (einen Zweig) vom Engel bekommen, die (der) zu einem Baum des Kreuzholzes aufwachsen können (kann). Während der Reise zum Paradies werden Seth und Eva sogar von der Schlange herausgefordert und des Hochmuts beschuldigt, weil nur der Messias Adam retten kann. Sie bekommen das Versprechen, beim Erscheinen des Messias könne Adam vom Lebensbaum genießen und das ewige Leben bekommen. Hier entsteht also schon früh die Verbindung zwischen dem Baum der Erkenntnis vom Guten und Bösen und dem Lebensbaum.[8]

In späteren Übersetzungen der *VAE* gibt es insoweit eine Änderung oder Erweiterung, dass da schon von einem Zweig (*arVAE*, 5. Jh.) oder von Zweigen (*slVAE*, 1000-1200) die Rede ist, der (die) auf Adams Grab gepflanzt wird (werden). Übrigens soll dieses Grab sich nach *VAE* im Paradies befinden.

Ohne Ausbreitung der späteren Übersetzungen von *VAE* ist das Schema deutlich: Adam stirbt ohne Vergebung, wird im Paradies begraben und wartet auf das Kommen des Messias.

Die Zerstörung des Tempels in Jerusalem und die Vertreibung der Juden in die Diaspora (70 n.Chr.) könnten im Zusammenhang mit der Periode stehen, in der die *VAE* (± 70) entstand. Noch immer warten die Juden auf das Kommen des Messias. Das Ende des Judentums wird später in der Legende von der Sibylle und von KvS vorhergesagt [**10b-11c**].

V.2

Dass Seth wohl ins Paradies kommt und Samen oder einen Zweig erhält, ist die Voraussetzung für die Legende des Kreuzholzes. Beschreibungen von all dem, was Seth im Paradies sieht, und die Erklärung dazu [**3a-e**] findet man erst 1220 (*Le*).

Das Motiv, dass Seth Samen (vom Apfel) des Baumes der Erkenntnis des Guten und Bösen bekommt [vgl. **3f**], ist jünger als das Motiv, dass er einen Zweig oder Zweige bekommt; das Motiv des Zweiges (der Zweige) ist ab 1100 (*SpE*) bekannt und weit verbreitet (vgl. *LF*, 1120; *ESC*, 1170; *QGra*, 13. Jh.; *LA*, ± 1260; *OHK*, 15. Jh). In *Le* (1220), *NKh* (1290?-1330) und *R* (1271) ist der Baum der Erkenntnis

---

[8] Vgl. Kemper 2006, 236: Zur Gleichsetzung von Kreuz und Lebensbaum im 13. und 14. Jahrhundert trugen Bonaventuras Traktat 'Lignum vitae' und Ubertinos da Casale 'Arbor vitae crucifixae Iesu' bei.

des Guten und Bösen im Paradies verdorrt. Um dem verdorrten Baum ein längeres Leben zu sichern, sollen Zweige oder Samen gepflanzt werden, damit der Baum aufs Neue entsprießen kann.[9]

Als Motivvariante des Zweiges (der Zweige) bekommt Seth Samen [**3f-g**]. Dieses Element wie auch die Paradiesbeschreibung tritt erst nach 1200 (***CJ***, 1210) in die Geschichte ein. Es fällt auf, dass die Samen des Baumes der Erkenntnis des Guten und Bösen von drei verschiedenen Bäumen (Zeder, Zipresse, Olivenholz/Palmenbaum) stammen, um die heilige Dreieinigkeit zu bezeichnen. Seth erhält den Auftrag, die Samen unter Adams Zunge zu legen, das heißt, dass der Baum aus dem Körper von Adam wachsen und den Körper gleichsam in sich aufnehmen wird. Ob das beim Zweig, der auf Adams Grab gepflanzt wurde, auch der Fall ist, bleibt offen. In einer der ältesten Fassungen (*ar**VAE***, 5. Jh.) befindet sich das Grab im Paradies, und bleibt das Holz auch im Paradies.

V.3

Als Seth zurückkommt, ist Adam schon gestorben oder noch nicht gestorben [**4-5a**]; im zweiten Fall freut Adam sich und stirbt kurz darauf.

In **ar*VAE*** (5. Jh.), ***Le*** (1220), ***LA*** (± 1260) und ***OHK*** (15. Jh.) ist Adam schon gestorben. Dies nimmt dem Leser die Möglichkeit, sich mit und für Adam zu freuen. Übrigens ist Adam in der ältesten Vita (***VAE***, ± 70) noch nicht gestorben.

Dass Adam noch nicht gestorben ist, findet man außer in ***NKh*** und ***VAE*** (± 70) in ***LF*** (1120), ***ESC*** (1170), auch in ***slVAE*** (1000-1200) und ***LD*** (15. Jh.).

Dass Adam sich freut [**4**], wird auf verschiedene Weisen erzählt: in ***slVAE*** (1000-1200) flicht Adam sich von den 3G eine Krone und legt sie sich auf das Haupt; in ***ESC*** (1170) erkennt Adam gleich das Wunder des Zweiges. Aber das Lachen von Adam wird zum ersten Mal in ***NKh*** erwähnt; vgl. ***H***, Vss. 283-285:

> Do vorblindende [l. vorblidede] adam de olde
> 284 Vnde lachede mehre wen enewerff
> An sineme herten ehre he sterff.

---

[9] Kemper 2006, 223: "Die Kreuzholzlegende schafft (...) unmittelbare Verbindung zwischen dem Baum der Erkenntnis, an dem der Sündenfall stattgefunden hatte, und dem Kreuzesbaum, an dem durch Christus die Erlösung bewirkt wurde".

V.4

Neben den wenigen Fällen, worin Adams Grab im Paradies zu suchen ist, findet man sein Grab vor allem in Hebron [**5b-c**]. Als die Samen zu Zweigen aufgewachsen sind, ändert sich ihre Länge während vieler Jahre nicht. Dass Hebron in der Heilsgeschichte sehr wichtig ist, sieht man bei den Varianten, wo Adam auch in Hebron geschaffen wurde. In Hebron hätte David die 3G finden und nach Jerusalem mitnehmen können; aber so verläuft die Geschichte in keiner der Varianten. Die Frage ist also, wie die 3G (oder der Baum) befördert werden: durch die Sintflut, von Moses, von David, von jemand anderem, oder sie werden gar nicht befördert; fünf Möglichkeiten also.

Zuerst das Motiv, dass Adam an dem Ort begraben wird (Hebron), wo er geschaffen wurde; zum ersten Mal wird dies von Honorius Augustodunensis in *El* (± 1100) erwähnt. In *IM* (vor 1155) wird Adam zwar in Hebron geschaffen, aber auf dem Kalvarienberg begraben und erst später von einem Engel nach Hebron gebracht; in *CRC* (1250) wird Adam dort begraben, wo Gott ihn schuf, der Ort Hebron wird aber nicht genannt. In *R* von Jacob van Maerlant (1271) wird Adam bei Damas(kus) geschaffen und später wohl in Hebron begraben, wie in den Vss. 3346ff. erzählt wird (übrigens handelt es sich da um das Begräbnis von Jakob in Kanaan). Die Möglichkeit besteht, dass Gen. 3:19 zu diesem Motiv geführt hat, wo Gott nämlich zu Adam spricht: "(Im Schweiße deines Angesichts sollst du dein Brot essen,) bis dass du wieder zu Erde werdest, davon du genommen bist".

Die Sintflut als Beförderungsmittel kommt in *CJ* (± 1210) vor; hier wird der Baum zum Libanon gebracht, woher das Holz für Salomos Tempelbau kommt. Dass die Sintflut eben keinen Einfluss auf die Versetzung des Baumes hat, wird in einem Fall, in *QGra* (13. Jh.) explizit erzählt. Implizit ergibt sich daraus, dass der Baum bis Salomos Zeit auf Adams Grab stehen bleibt, wie auch in *LA* (± 1260) und *OHK* (15. Jh.).[10]

Dass die Zweige von einem Unbekannten oder einem Juden nach Jerusalem gebracht werden, wird nur zweimal erzählt: in *Hi* (vor 1150) und *OI* (1212). Es scheint eine Notlösung zu sein.

Der erste namentlich bekannte Überbringer ist Moses [**6a-d**]. Es ist

---

[10] Vgl. Addenda 1, 5.

ein kräftiger Eingriff in die alttestamentliche Geschichte, um Moses nach Hebron ziehen zu lassen, wo er nach der Bibel überhaupt nicht gewesen ist. Aber so erhält Moses seinen Platz in dieser Heilsgeschichte – obschon er die schon hatte, weil er das jüdische Volk aus Ägypten herausführte – und so wird er direkt mit dem Kreuzholz verbunden. Maerlant (*R*, 1271) nennt bei seinem Mosespassus das Kreuzholz indirekt und direkt, wenn man bedenkt, wie oft Moses mit seinem Stab 'Wunder' verrichtet: (Vss. 4212ff.) als Moses mit seinem Stab in das Rote Meer schlagen soll, (Vss. 4271ff.) wo Maerlant den Stab, mit dem das Wasser in Mara geschlagen wird, mit dem Kreuzholz in Zusammenhang bringt; auch da (Vss. 5879ff.), wo Moses mit seinem Stab auf einen Felsen schlägt, um daraus Wasser zum Vorschein zu bringen und (Vss. 5940ff.) als Moses echte Heilungen bewirkt, indem er eine metallene Schlange auf einen Stecken stellt. Dass Moses in Moab stirbt ist allgemein bekannt, aber dass er die 3G dort pflanzt, damit David sie in Moab findet, wird erst in *NKh* erzählt, denn in *Le* (1220) und *LD* (15. Jh.) pflanzt Moses die 3G auf den Berg Tabor.[11]

Wie schon bemerkt wurde, hätte David die 3G auch in Hebron finden können, denn da regiert er 7 Jahre. Auch die Verbindung von David mit Moab [7a-c] ist biblisch: Moab wird von David unterworfen und tributpflichtig gemacht. Weiter scheint der David-Passus eine Wiederholung oder Verdoppelung des Mosesabschnittes zu sein: David findet die 3G um sein Bett, zieht sie aus, weil er ein göttliches Zeichen bekommt; mit den 3G verrichtet er 'Wunder' oder Heilungen, er nimmt die 3G mit nach einem Ort, wo sie 'gefunden' werden können. Dass David Menschen heilt, wird schon in *HD* (1180) erzählt, aber die ganze Reihe von Motiven, vom Auffinden der 3G bis zur Überbringung nach Jerusalem [7b-8a], ist neu in *Le* (1220) und *NKh*; nur der Fundort in *Le* ist ein anderer als in *NKh*: David findet die 3G in *Le* auf dem Berg Tabor.

Davids visionärer Traum, der den Ort zeigt, wo die 3G gesucht und geholt werden müssen [7a], erinnert an den Traum von Konstantin dem Großen, der die Reise von Helena nach Jerusalem und die Heilungen, die das Kreuzholz bewirkt, nach sich zieht.[12] Sieht man nun

---

[11] Vgl. Addenda 2, 8c.
[12] Vgl. Baert 2001, 66, Abb. 6: Traum von Konstantin; seit Anfang des 9. Jhs. kommt dieser Traum in Abbildungen vor.

den Zeitpunkt, an dem der Traum von David in die Geschichte eintritt (*Le*, 1220 oder *NKh*, 1290?-1330), wäre vielleicht an eine spätere 'Konstantin'-Interpolation zu denken.

V.5
Dass die Zweige nach Jerusalem gebracht werden (müssen) [**8a-b**], scheint in den meisten Varianten der Kreuzholzlegende zu fehlen. Ohne Moses und David als Überbringer ist es einfach so, dass der ausgewachsene Baum zur Zeit von Salomos Tempelbau entdeckt wird. Wo er genau steht – auf Adams Grab in Hebron, auf dem Libanon oder sonstwo – ist offenbar nicht so wichtig. Wenn wir annehmen, dass in *Hi* (vor 1150), wo ein dreiästiges Stück Holz zum König gebracht wird, mit diesem König David (oder Salomo) gemeint ist, dann ist *Hi* die erste Quelle. Jerusalem wird zum ersten Mal in *OI* (1212) genannt.

Wo auch immer der Baum steht, das Holz ist für den Tempelbau (oder Palastbau) in Jerusalem [**9a**] bestimmt; zum ersten Mal in *LF* (1120), danach in *ESC* (1170) und *P* ($\pm$ 1180).

V.6
Das Holz erweist sich beim Tempelbau (oder Palastbau) als zu lang oder zu kurz [**9c**]. Dann gibt es ein paar Möglichkeiten: entweder wird das Holz weggeworfen oder es bleibt im Tempel liegen und wird danach weggeworfen [**9d-10d**]. Damit ist eine Prophezeiung oder sind zwei Prophezeiungen über das Ende des Judentums verbunden.

Dass das Holz weggeworfen wird, erzählt *LF* (1120) zum ersten Mal; da kommt die KvS in Jerusalem, erkennt die Bedeutung des Holzes und verehrt es, mit einer Prophezeiung. In dem Fall, dass das Holz im Tempel (oder im Palast) liegen bleibt, gibt es offenbar zwei Varianten: im Palast erkennt die KvS die Bedeutung des Holzes und prophezeit danach, in *HS* (vor 1178). Oder: im Tempel prophezeit die Sibylle Christus' Tod (1. Prophezeiung), das Holz wird weggeworfen, wonach die KvS auch prophezeit (2. Prophezeiung). Um es weiter zu komplizieren, wird das Holz an der Tempelpforte verehrt und erst später weggeworfen und begraben [**11e-12a**], wie vielleicht schon *P* ($\pm$ 1180), aber auf jeden Fall *Le* (1220) und *NKh* erzählen. Um es kurz übersichtlich darzustellen:

aa	Holz weggeworfen + Prophezeiung KvS + Holz bleibt draußen liegen	*LF* (1120)
ab	Holz weggeworfen + Prophezeiung KvS + Holz in *piscina probatica*	*ESC* (1170)
ba	Holz bleibt im Palast + Prophezeiung KvS + Holz begraben (= *pisc. prob.*)	*LA* (1260), *R* (1271)
bb	Holz bleibt im Palast + Prophezeiung KvS + in den Tempel gebracht + weggeworfen	*HS* (vor 1178)
ca	Holz bleibt im Tempel + Prophezeiung KvS + Holz bleibt im Tempel	*CJ* (± 1210)
cb	Holz bleibt im Tempel + Prophezeiung KvS (erst später) + Holz weggeworfen	*Hi* (vor 1150)
cc	Holz bleibt im Tempel + Prophezeiung Sibylle + ???	*PJ* (8. Jh.)
da	Holz bleibt im Tempel + Prophezeiung Sibylle + Holz an Tempelpforte aufgestellt + Prophezeiung KvS im Palast (undeutlich) + Holz beseitigt	*P* (± 1180)
db	Holz bleibt im Tempel + Prophezeiung Sibylle + Holz beseitigt als Brücke + Prophezeiung KvS + Holz begraben, bei *piscina probatica*	*Le* (1220)
dc	Holz bleibt im Tempel + Prophezeiung Sibylle + Holz beseitigt als Brücke + Prophezeiung KvS + Holz in Tempelpforte eingefügt + Holz weggeworfen	*NKh* (1290?-1330)

Die Variante in *NKh* (1290?-1330) ist also eine Verdoppelung der Prophezeiung (wie in *Le*, 1220), eine Verdoppelung des Holzes im Tempel und eine Verdoppelung der Beseitigung des Holzes.

V.7

Wenn Jesus am Kreuz hängen wird und die Verheißung an Adam Wahrheit wird [**15d**], bedeutet dies das Ende des Judentums. Obschon Moses (Maerlant vergleicht den Stab von Moses schon mit dem Kreuzholz: *R*, 1271; Vss. 4271-4287), David und Salomo das Holz verehren und als heilig anerkennen, ist die messianische Prophezeiung der heidnischen Sibylle [**10b**][13] oder der (heidnischen) KvS [**11c**] vorbehalten, die in *Le* (1220) *Sibilla* und in *R* (1271) Königin *Cibille* genannt wird.

Von einer Prophezeiung ist die Rede in *PJ* (8. Jh.), in *LF* (1120), in

---

[13] Vgl. für die Sibylle als erste Zeugin des christlichen Glaubens Dronke 1990, 7f.

Hi (vor 1150), in *ESC* (1170), in *HS* (vor 1178), in *LA* (± 1260); zwei Prophezeiungen sieht man erst (abweichend) in *P* (± 1180) und *Le* (1220). Die KvS hat den Ruf, sehr weise Fragen stellen und Rätsel aufgeben zu können (*byzW*, 842-887). Als *regina austri* ist sie die Präfiguration von Maria, weil sie als Geliebte von Christus gesehen wird (*THL*, ± 1100), oder sie vertritt die *ecclesia gentium*, die sich bekehrt (*P*, ± 1180).

Aber eigentlich war das Kommen Christi schon vom Engel [3a] in *VAE* (± 70) verheißen.

V.8
Die Menschheit kann durch das Kreuzholz geheilt werden, weil Christus daran hängt [16b]. Dieses Motiv kann selbstverständlich in der ältesten Version, *VAE* (± 70), nicht vorkommen, denn da ist von einem Baum oder von einem Zweig (von Zweigen) oder Samen noch keine Rede.

Sobald die 3G von Menschen ausgezogen werden [6d, 7b-c], zeigen sie ihre heilende Wirkung, bei Moses (schon in *slK*, 950) und bei David (zuerst in *HD*, 1180). Auch in der *piscina probatica* [13c] bringt das Holz Heilungen zu Stande (*SpE*, ± 1100).[14] Den Übergang vom heilenden Holz zur Genesung durch Christus am Kreuzesholz sieht man eigentlich erst in *LA* (± 1260).

VI Einzelheiten, in denen die *Legenda* (1220) von früheren Varianten abweicht

Erweiterungen und Änderungen in der Kreuzholzlegende finden dauernd statt. Aber die Änderungen, die in der *Le* zum ersten Mal vorkommen, sind:

VI.1 [3b-f] *Seth sieht im Paradies (vier Paradiesströme), einen hohen, verdorrten Baum, eine Schlange, die Seele von Abel in der Hölle, ein neugeborenes Kind; Seth empfängt 3K, die er Adam unter die Zunge legen soll.*
Es betrifft dasjenige, was Seth in einer Vision im Paradies sieht und

---

[14] Es könnte sein, dass die *piscina probatica* eines der Becken ist, die Salomo zum Waschen des Opferfleisches bei seinem Tempel graben ließ (2 Chron. 4:6); vielleicht ist aber das Wasserbecken (Bethesda genannt) bei der Schafspforte gemeint, wo Kranke geheilt wurden; vgl. Joh. 5:2-4: *piscina probatica*, von gri. προβατικός, 'Schafsteich' (zum Waschen der Opferschafe).

die Erklärung dazu, und die Anweisungen an Seth, was er mit den 3K tun soll. All diese Elemente sind unbiblischen Ursprungs. In *Le* sieht Seth zum ersten Mal den verdorrten Baum, der hier aus drei Teilen besteht – dem Lebensbaum, dem Baum von Jesse und der Frucht, die Christus ist – und er sieht die Seele von Abel. In *OI* (1212) wird aus den Samen eines Apfels, den Adam heimlich mitgenommen hat, ein Zweig wachsen. In *slVAE* (1000-1200) bekommt Seth drei Zweige, in *LF* (1120) nur einen Zweig.

VI.2 [**5b**] *Seth begräbt Adam in Hebron; er legt die 3K unter Adams Zunge.*
Eigentlich ist es eine Wiederholung von [3f]. Es betont nur, dass Seth die Anweisungen des Engels im Paradies befolgt; es ist unbiblischen Ursprungs. Abweichend sind *VAE* (± 70), wo das Grab sich im Paradies befindet, *IM* (vor 1155), wo ein Engel Adam einen Samen in den Mund legt, und *arVAE* (5. Jh.), *LF* (1120), *ESC* (1170), wo Seth einen Zweig bekommt.

VI.3 [**6a**] *Moses findet 3G in Hebron.*
Moses findet in *Le* keine 3G sondern Bäume in Hebron. Dass Moses in Hebron kommt, ist (wie in *NKh*) unbiblischen Ursprungs. In *slK* (950) findet er die 3G in Mara.

VI.4 [**6d**] *Moses findet die 3G, zieht sie aus, macht Wasser süß.*
Mit *NKh* teilt *Le*, dass Moses Wasser süß macht; in *Le* schlägt er jedoch süßes Wasser aus einem Felsen. Das ist eine Vermischung von zwei oder drei Bibelstellen: Ex. 15:25 (Moses ist in Mara, wo er bitteres Wasser süß macht) und Ex. 17,5-6 (Moses schlägt auf einen Felsen, damit Wasser herausströmt) oder Num. 20:11 (wo Moses gegen das ausdrückliche Verbot Gottes nicht zum Felsen spricht, sondern auf ihn schlägt). Die heilende Wirkung des Paradiesholzes wird biblisch begründet, aber nicht ganz korrekt.

VI.5 [**7c**] *David heilt Ethiopier, einen Aussätzigen und einen Eremiten.*
Das Holz hat auch in Davids Händen eine heilende Wirkung; dies ist unbiblischen Ursprungs. Schon in *HD* (1180) bringt David Ethiopier mit dem Holz in Kontakt (er tauft sie); weiter heilt er einen Aussätzigen. In *Le* heilt er Ethiopier, einen Aussätzigen und einen Eremiten.

VI.6 [**8a-c**] *David bringt die 3G nach Jerusalem und stellt sie in einen Brunnen.*
Mit David kommen die 3G (oder die Bäume) [siehe VI.3, **6a**] nach Jerusalem, wo er sie (vorläufig) in einen Brunnen stellt; die 3G wachsen in einer Nacht zusammen und sind im Boden fest verwurzelt. David legt danach jedes Jahr einen silbernen Ring um den Baum. All diese Motive sind unbiblischen Ursprungs. In *Hi* (vor 1150) bringt ein Jude ein dreiästiges Stück Holz zum König und in *OI* (1212) wird nur ein Zweig nach Jerusalem gebracht.

VI.7 [**9a**] *Salomo will einen Tempel bauen; der Baum in Jerusalem wird umgehauen.*
Beim Tempelbau von Salomo fehlt ein Baum. Dieses Motiv ist unbiblischen Ursprungs. Schon in *LF* (1120) und *ESC* (1170) benutzt man das heilige Holz für den Tempelbau, der Baum steht aber (noch) auf Adams Grab. Obwohl der Baum in *P* (± 1180) in Jerusalem steht, weicht die Geschichte zu sehr von der in *Le* beschriebenen Legende ab (Jonitus, Sohn von Noach, pflanzt drei Früchte, aus denen ein Baum wächst; außerdem wird das Holz für den Palastbau benutzt). In *CJ* (± 1210) wird der Baum sogar von der Sintflut auf den Libanon gebracht, woher das Holz für den Tempel kommen sollte.

VI.8 [**10(a-)b**] *Die Sibylle setzt sich auf das Holz und fängt Feuer; sie prophezeit, Gottes Sohn werde am Holz hängen.*
Die Textstelle, wo die Sibylle Feuer fängt, ist auch unbiblischen Ursprungs; es ist ein Element, das seit dem 8. Jh. (*PJ*) bekannt ist. Die Prophezeiung der Sibylle, dass Gottes Sohn am Holz hängen wird [**10b**], ist schon eine Hinzufügung in *Le*, aber auch unbiblisch. Dass die Sibylle die erste von zwei Prophetinnen ist, wird zum ersten Mal in *P* (± 1180) und *Le* erzählt.

VI.9 [**11c**] *Salomo wundert sich; die KvS prophezeit, 'der Welt Hoffnung' werde am Holz hängen.*
KvS prophezeit Christus' Tod und damit das Ende des Judentums. Ihr werden prophetische Worte in den Mund gelegt, die aber unbiblischen Ursprungs sind. Abweichend sind *Hi* (vor 1150) und *HS* (vor 1178), wo die KvS zwar das Holz wiedererkennt, es aber Salomo nicht oder erst später mitteilt. Übrigens sieht die KvS in *HS* (vor 1178) das Holz im Palast, im *domus saltus*.

VI.10 [16b] *Das Ende der Legende nach Christus' Tod.*
Erst in *Le* endet die Kreuzholzlegende mit der Passion. Da hat das Holz seine Aufgabe erfüllt, nämlich Adam zu erlösen. Selbstverständlich ist nach dem NT Christus' Kreuzestod die Erlösung der Menschheit.

VII. Kurze chronologische Übersicht der Legende vor *NKh* (1290?-1330)

Fettdruck zeigt, wann ein Motiv zum ersten Male vorkommt; kursiv sind die Motive, die zwar vorkommen, aber in ihrem Zusammenhang erheblich abweichen, und zwischen Klammern stehen schließlich die Motive, die nur indirekt von Bedeutung sind:

± 70 (*VAE*)
    Seth + Eva
    Grab im Paradies
    Verheißung -> **Messias** rettet

5e e. (*arVAE*)
    Zweig auf Grab (im Paradies)

8e e. (*PJ*)
    Sibylle
    (Messias)

950 (*slK*)
    Moses

1100 (*SpE*)
    Seth
    Zweig
    Moses
    KvS
    piscina probatica

1120 (*LF*)
    Seth
    Zweig
    Tempel von Salomo
    [pisc. prob.] -> irgendwo

vor 1150 (*Hi*)
    Moses
    (*David?*)
    (*Jerusalem?*)
    KvS
    piscina probatica

vor 1155 (*IM*)
    Hebron
    (Messias)

1170 (*ESC*)
    Seth
    Zweig
    Tempel von Salomo
    Brücke
    KvS
    piscina probatica

vor 1178 (*HS*)
    (Palast von Salomo)
    KvS
    piscina probatica

± 1180 (**P**)
David
(*Jerusalem*?)
Tempel von Salomo
(Palast von Salomo)
(*Sibylle*).
KvS

± 1210 (**CJ**)
Seth
Samen
(Baum)
Tempel von Salomo
(Messias)

1212 (**OI**)
Jerusalem

1220 (**Le**)
Seth
Samen
Moses
David
Jerusalem
Tempel (oder Palast) von
       Salomo
Sibylle
KvS   ↑

Brücke
piscina probatica
Passion
Messias

13. Jh. (**SHR**)
Hebron
(Baum)

± 1260 (**LA**)
Seth
Zweig (Baum)
(Palast von Salomo)
KvS
Brücke
piscina probatica
Passion
(Messias)

1271 (**R**)
Seth
Hebron
Moses
David
Tempel von Salomo
KvS
piscina probatica
Passion

VIII. Einzelheiten, in denen *NKh* von *Le* (1220) und anderen Fassungen abweicht

VIII.1 [1: *Prolog*]

In *NKh* sagt der Erzähler, er habe über das Kreuzholz gelesen; vgl. *H* (1476), Vs. 3: "Dat hebbe ick lesen wo dat was". Er ist nicht so explizit wie Jacobus de Voragine in *LA* (± 1260), der sich auf das Evangelium vom Nikodemus (*(Ps)EN*, 5. und 10. Jh.) bezieht; auch in *OHK* (15. Jh.) steht: "Scriuas j laest nichomedi [l. nichodemi] ...".[15] Während der Aufzeichnung von *NKh* können zahlreiche Varianten der Er-

---

[15] Im zweiten Teil des *PsEN*, wo Christus die Hölle aufschließt, erzählt Adam, dass er am Ende seines Lebens Seth ins Paradies sandte, um das Öl der Barmherzigkeit zu holen, damit Seth ihn salbte; danach bestätigt Seth Adams Aussage.

zählung bekannt gewesen sein. Auf jeden Fall appelliert der Erzähler an eine Autorität (er habe hierüber 'gelesen'), weil er die Wahrheit so gut wie möglich berichten will.

VIII.2 [3a] *Seth sieht im Paradies die vier Paradiesströme, worüber ausführlich berichtet wird.*
In *Le* bekommt Seth drei Visionen; in der ersten Vision sieht Seth einen Brunnen mit den vier Weltströmen. Vergleichbar mit *Le* ist *LD* (15. Jh.). *NKh* berichtet ebenfalls vom Brunnen und den Strömen, aber viel ausführlicher. Somit ist der Bericht mit Gen. 2:10-14 vergleichbar: "Und es ging aus von Eden ein Strom, zu wässern den Garten, und teilte sich von da in vier Hauptwasser. Das erste heißt Pison, das fließt um das ganze Land Hevila; und daselbst findet man Gold. Und das Gold des Landes ist köstlich; und da findet man Bedellion und den Edelstein Onyx. Das andere Wasser heißt Gihon, das fließt um das ganze Mohrenland. Das dritte Wasser heißt Hiddekel (Tigris), das fließt vor Assyrien. Das vierte Wasser ist der Eupfrat". Auch in *R* (1271; Vss. 413-416) erzählt Maerlant über den großen Brunnen, der die ganze Welt mit Wasser versieht, und verbindet damit einen Vergleich: Jesus ist der Brunnen, Maria ist das Paradies. In *R* (Vss. 491ff.) wird der Brunnen nochmals genannt, zusammen mit den Strömen, die daraus entspringen (*fisons = ganges*; man findet Gold in ihrem Sand; *Gion = nilus*, der fließt durch Ethiopien; *tygris* und *eufrates*, die in der Erde verschwinden und an anderer Stelle wieder auftauchen können). Obwohl mit dem Baum, von dem Seth 3K empfängt, der Baum der Erkenntnis vom Guten und Bösen gemeint ist, erinnert die Schilderung hier an den Lebensbaum, der oft bildlich mit den vier Paradiesströmen dargestellt wird.[16]

VIII.3 [4] *Seth kehrt zu Adam zurück, erzählt über 3K und 3G; Adam freut sich und lacht mehrmals.*
Über Adams Freude steht in *Le* nichts. Vor allem das letzte Motiv in *NKh*, dass Adam lacht, gibt dem Leser die Möglichkeit, sich mit Adam zu freuen. Es weist schon auf das Ende der Erzählung hin, wo Christus Adam retten wird; im NT wird Adam einmal direkt mit Jesus in Verbindung gebracht, im Lukasevangelium (Lk. 3:38), wo am Ende von Jesus' (Josephs) Geschlechtsregister steht: ".. (Seth), der war ein

---

[16] Wie z.B. im Apsismosaik der S. Clemente in Rom; vgl. Lassen 2009, 236f.

Sohn Adams, der war Gottes..". Das Lachen könnte man als Äußerung der Lebenslust betrachten, als Hoffnung, dass die Macht des Todes gebrochen wird.[17] Außer in **NKh** findet man nur in **LD** (15. Jh.) das mehrfache Lachen Adams: "Tha war adam mykith gladhir. oc lo aat. ey vtan en tiidh".

VIII.4 [5a] *Adam stirbt; der Teufel nimmt seine Seele mit.*
Dieses Element verstärkt Punkt [4]: die Freude von Adam. Ebenso wie Abel kann Adam noch nicht an dem Moment seines Todes gerettet werden. Dies setzt auch voraus, dass Adam aus der Hölle befreit wird, als Christus nach seinem Tod zur Hölle hinabfährt und die Höllenpforte aufschließt. In der mnl. 'Übersetzung' **Lu** (14. Jh.; Hs. B1) von **El** (± 1100) steht (Kursivierung von mir):

1937	Ende opten derden dach daer naer
	Ter tijt vander minnacht rechte
	Verloste hi vter *hellen* zijn knechte
1940	Abrahame ende zijn andre vrient
	Die niet der hellen hadden verdient
	Ende *adame* den ersten man
	Ende menige die ic niet genoemen can
1944	Vut den torment vander *hellen*
	Ende vter leeder duuele quellen
	Ende leedese int soete paradijs
	Des maect ons die scrifture wijs

Auch im lateinischen **El** (± 1100) findet man ähnliches, denn eine der Fragen lautet (1.160): "Quo ivit anima ejus [= Chr.] post mortem", die mit **Lu** (14. Jh.; Vss. 1932-33) übereinstimmt: "Waer omme doe [l. voer] ons sceppers geest / Als hi sciet vter werelt tempeest". Als Maerlant die Frauen am Ostermorgen beim leeren Grab von Christus erwähnt, lässt er den Engel sagen (**Rb**, F. 149v; Kursiviering von mir):

> Doe sagen si den steen af gedaen
> Die sere groot was sonder waen
> Enten ingel diere oec vp sat
> Onse here was verresen vor dat

---
[17] Handwörterbuch des deutschen Aberglaubens 5, Sp. 868ff.

> Enter *hellen* oec geuaren
> Sine vriende verloste hi te waren
> *Adam* entie ghesellen sine
> Mar die quade bleuen in die pine

Die Reihenfolge der Geschehnisse nach Christus' Tod – zur Hölle hinabsteigen und Auferstehung – weicht, wie in ***Rb*** und ***R***, auch in manchen frühmhd. Texten ab; obwohl die Reihenfolge meistens Hinabsteigen–Auferstehung ist, kommt also auch die umgekehrte Reihenfolge Auferstehung–Hinabsteigen vor. Weil nämlich das Hinabsteigen als Sieg über den Tod und den Teufel betrachtet wird, bekommt das Hinabsteigen zur Hölle die größere Betonung, an welcher Stelle nur darüber erzählt wird.[18]

Sehr abweichend ist ***CRC*** (1250), wo Engel Adam nach seinem Tode direkt in den Himmel bringen; die Konsequenz wäre dann, dass das Kreuzholz für Adams Rettung überflüssig ist.

VIII.5 [5c] *Die 3K wachsen zu 3G aus, die sich während 3200 Jahre* (in ***C*** aber *172 Jahre*) *nicht ändern.*
Wie lange die Periode ist, bis Moses kommen wird, ist nicht bekannt, obwohl viele Berechnungen der Zeit bis zur Ankunft des Messias gemacht worden sind. ***R*** (1271; Vss. 21290ff.) berichtet, dass die Geburt Christi nach 5199 Jahren stattfand. ***PsEN*** und ***LA*** (± 1260) nennen in diesem Zusammenhang 5500 (oder auch 5952) Jahre. Die Bemerkung in ***NKh*** ist eigentlich überflüssig, denn wenn es geheißen hätte, 'sie standen da sehr lange', wäre die Mitteilung dieselbe gewesen. Es scheint eine historisierende Verstärkung zu sein, dass Moses auserwählt ist, die 3G zu finden. Im Zusammenhang mit Jesus erinnern die Zweige vielleicht an (Jes. 11:1): "Und es wird eine Rute aufgehen von dem Stamm Isais, und ein Zweig aus seiner Wurzel Frucht bringen". In ***LA*** (± 1260) kommt Moses, wie schon bemerkt wurde, als Entdecker der 3G nicht vor. Jacob de Voragine hat nur die Bemerkung, dass der Baum auf Adams Grab bis Salomos Zeiten stehen bleibt.

---

[18] Vgl. Jacobs 1987, 17ff.; s. auch Graesse 1890, 235ff., ***LA*** (Cap. CIV, *De resurrectione domini*), wo zuerst über Auferstehung und die Erscheinungen Christi und danach erst über das Hinabsteigen zur Hölle erzählt wird.

VIII.6 [**6b-d**] *Moses sieht die 3G gesondert um sein Bett stehen und lässt sie stehen, in Hebron* [**6b**] *und in Elim* [**6c**]. *Moses sieht in Rafidim die 3G zum dritten Mal um sein Bett stehen; er zieht sie aus, macht Wasser süß* [**6d**].

Die Tatsache, dass die 3G in der Wüste hinter Moses her ziehen, ist eine Verdreifachung des Zeichens, das Moses bekommt. Und damit die 3G von Moses wirklich wiedererkannt werden, stehen sie immer um sein Bett. Wiederum wird betont, dass Moses auserwählt ist. Dieses Auserwähltsein beinhaltet, dass Moses die 3G als die Dreieinigkeit anerkennt und sie an eine Stelle bringt, wo David sie finden kann. So bekommt Moses seinen Platz in dieser Heilsgeschichte. Das ist natürlich in *Le* auch der Fall, wird dort aber nicht betont. Das Herausführen des jüdischen Volkes aus Ägypten verbindet Moses mit Pesach. Und um den Kreuzestod während Pesach zu ermöglichen, soll Moses das jüdische Volk aus Ägypten führen und soll er das Kreuzholz finden. Die Orte, an denen Moses sich befindet, sind biblisch: Ex. 17:1 (Moses in Rafidim), Ex. 15:25 (Moses in Mara, wo er aus bitterem Wasser süßes Wasser macht). Vgl. für die letzte Bibelstelle auch *slK* (950), wo Moses die 3G in Mara findet und damit bitteres Wasser süß macht.

VIII.7 [**6e**] *Moses kommt zum Berg Sinai; Moses zieht nach Moab, pflanzt die 3G dort.*

Der Berg Sinai kommt in den anderen Erzählungen der Legende nicht vor; selbstverständlich kennt der Bearbeiter der Erzählung die Bibel gut und erwähnt also, dass Moses da die zehn Gebote empfing (vgl. Ex. 20:1-7). Auch dass Moses das gelobte Land nicht betreten darf, weiß er (vgl. für Moses in Moab Num. 20:7-8; 21:10ff.), und dass Moses in Moab stirbt (vgl. Deut. 34:5). In *R* (1271), die den Geschehnissen der Bibel genau folgt, kommt Moses in Vs. 5979 in Moab, in den Vss. 6424-25 stirbt Moses. Bemerkt werden muss, dass in *NKh* gerade nicht über Moses' Tod erzählt wird, weil nicht sein Tod, wohl aber seine Rolle als Überbringer der 3G wichtig ist. In *Le* und *LD* (15. Jh.) stirbt Moses auf dem Berg Tabor.

VIII.8 [**7a**] *Im Traum erscheint David ein Engel, der ihn nach Moab sendet, die 3G zu holen und in seinen Hof zu pflanzen;* [**7b**] *David zieht nach Moab; er bekommt ein Zeichen, dies seien die 3G; sie stehen gesondert um sein Bett, er zieht sie aus.*

In *Le* gibt es keinen Traum; da steht nur, dass David die 3G auf dem Berg Tabor findet. Obwohl David die 3G in *Le* auch nach Jerusalem bringen wird, sieht man in ***NKh*** deutlich die göttliche Absicht: der Engel ist ein Bote Gottes. Durch diesen Boten wird David in diese Heilsgeschichte eingefügt. Dass David nach Moab zieht und das moabitische Volk besiegt, wird an mehreren Stellen im AT erzählt: 1. Sam. 22: 3-4 (David bringt seine Eltern vor Saul in Sicherheit), 2. Sam. 8:12 [= 1. Chron. 18:11] (David hat Moab besiegt), 2. Sam. 23:20 [= 1. Chron. 11:22] (ein Held von David hat zwei Helden von Moab geschlagen), 1. Chron. 18:2 ("Auch schlug er [= D.] die Moabiter, dass die Moabiter David untertänig wurden und Geschenke brachten"); vgl. auch Ps. 60:10 [= Ps. 108:10] und Ps. 83:7. Der Erzähler kennt also die Bibel. Durch die Art und Weise, wie David die 3G findet, wird er mit Moses verbunden. Dass er danach auch mit den 3G 'Wunder' verrichten wird, ist nur die logische Folge. Auch in ***LD*** (15. Jh.) träumt David von einem Engel, der aber ihn zum Berg Tabor sendet.

VIII.9 [**8c**] *Die 3G wachsen zu einem Baum zusammen; um den Baum legt David jedes Jahr einen Ring, insgesamt dreißigmal; manche glauben, die 30 Ringe seien die 30 Silberlinge.*
In ***Le*** und ***LD*** (15. Jh.) wird zwar erzählt, dass jedes Jahr ein silberner Ring um den Baum geschlagen wird, aber dass es 30 Ringe werden, steht nur in ***NKh***. Die 30 Jahre beziehen sich wahrscheinlich auf die Regierungsperiode von David in Jerusalem (eigentlich 33 Jahre); vgl. 2. Sam. 5:5 ("In Hebron regierte er [= D.] sieben Jahre und sechs Monate über Juda; aber zu Jerusalem regierte er drei und dreißig Jahre über ganz Israel und Juda"); so auch in 1. Kön. 2:11; 3:4; 29:27; hier könnte man ebenfalls sagen, dass die Erzählung biblisch erweitert wird. Außerdem wird eine Verbindung mit dem späteren Verrat von Judas gemacht: dadurch, dass nach manchen Leuten die 30 silbernen Ringe die 30 Silberlinge seien, tritt Judas ebenfalls in diese Heilsgeschichte ein. Ohne Verrat sind der Kreuzestod und die Erlösung nicht möglich.

VIII.10 [**8d**] *David besucht den Baum oft und betet dort.*
In einigen Varianten, ***P*** (± 1180), ***Le*** (1220) und ***LD*** (15. Jh.) komponiert (und liest) David unter dem Baum seine Psalmen. Nur in ***NKh*** wendet David sich dort mit Gebeten an Gott. Obwohl dieser Unterschied klein zu sein scheint, ist das Dichten der Psalmen unter dem Baum unbiblischen Ursprungs, weil die Psalmen von David während seines ganzen Lebens komponiert wurden. Auch in ***R*** (1271) sagt

Maerlant, übrigens nicht am Ende von Davids Leben (Vss. 10641ff.):

> Doe dauid an elke side.
> Jn rusten was van allen stride.
> Maecti den souter sonder waen.
> Daer .c. ende .l. salm in staan.

Vielleicht erinnert der 'Wunderbaum' an den Baum in Ps. 1:3: "Der ist wie ein Baum, gepflanzt an den Wasserbächen, der seine Frucht bringt zu seiner Zeit, und seine Blätter verwelken nicht".

VIII.11 [8e] *David will einen Tempel bauen; er darf das wegen seiner vielen Kriege nicht.*
Diesen Abschnitt kann man auf zwei Weisen betrachten. Die erste ist, dass David zu viele Menschen getötet hätte, wie in **R** (1271, Vss. 10133ff.): David will einen Tempel bauen, aber darf es nicht (Vss. 10144-6): "Want hijs besturd met menscen bloede./ Sijn sone die na hem sal sijn here./ Sal maken een huvs in mijn here". So liest man auch in **LD** (15. Jh.), wo David ein 'Menschentöter' genannt wird ("at han war mandrapare"), der unter dem Baum das Psalterium las und seine Sünden beweinte: "oc gik vnder that sama traedh oc graet sina syndir. oc togh at laesa psaltarin". Die zweite, biblische, Erklärung ist, dass es Davids Aufgabe war, die ihn umlagernden Feinde zu schlagen (vgl. 1. Kön. 5:2-4: "Und Salomo sandte zu Hisram und ließ ihm sagen: Du weißt, dass mein Vater David nicht konnte bauen ein Haus dem Namen des Herrn, seines Gottes, um des Krieges willen, der um ihn her war, bis sie der Herr unter seiner Füße Sohlen gab. Nun aber hat mir der Herr, mein Gott, Ruhe gegeben umher, dass kein Widersacher noch böses Hindernis mehr ist"). In 2. Sam. 7:12-13 soll Nathan David sagen, Gott habe immer in einem Zelt gewohnt, und wenn er eine zederhölzerne Wohnung haben wollte, hätte Gott ihm schon den Auftrag dazu gegeben und: "Wenn nun deine Zeit hin ist, dass du mit deinen Vätern schlafen liegst, will ich deinen Samen nach dir erwecken, der von deinem Leibe kommen soll; dem will ich sein Reich bestätigen. Der soll meinem Namen ein Haus bauen, und ich will den Stuhl seines Königreichs bestätigen ewiglich"; darum sagt Salomo (1. Kön. 5:5): "Siehe, so habe ich gedacht, ein Haus zu bauen dem Namen des Herrn, meines Gottes, wie der Herr geredet hat zu meinem Vater David und gesagt: Dein Sohn, den ich an deine Statt setzen wer-

de auf deinen Stuhl, der soll meinem Namen das Haus bauen". In *Le* dagegen steht, dass David mit dem Bau beginnt. Biblisch an der Fassung in *Le* ist, dass David dem noch jungen Salomo für den Tempelbau viel Material (Holz, Gold und Kostbarkeiten) sammelt (1. Chron. 27:2-5; 29:1-9).

VIII.12 [9b] *Die 30 Ringe werden in den Tempel gebracht; sie bleiben dort bis Judas' Zeit.*
In *Le* werden die 30 Ringe überhaupt nicht erwähnt. Nachdem der Baum umgehauen ist, werden die 30 Ringe in den Tempel gebracht; sie können da liegen bleiben, bis Judas für seinen Verrat die 30 Silberlinge empfängt. Zum zweiten Mal kommt also Judas nebenbei in die Geschichte hinein, als Vorbereitung für seine Rolle in der Heilsgeschichte während der Passion; eine Rolle, die schon von Moses und David (und Salomo) vorbereitet wird. Die Verbindung zwischen Judas und David/Salomo sind die silbernen Ringe, die David um den Baum legt und die Salomo später in den Tempel bringen lässt. In *NKh* wird insgesamt dreimal an Judas referiert. Die 30 Silberlinge sind biblischen Ursprungs, die 30 silbernen Ringe natürlich nicht.

VIII.13 [10c] *Die Sibylle wird in den Kerker geworfen, wo sie stirbt.*
Es mag deutlich sein, dass die Sibylle als eine solche Wahrsagerin oder Zauberin betrachtet wird, die in Ex. 22:18 gemeint ist: "Die Zauberinnen sollst du nicht leben lassen" (vgl. auch Deut. 18:10). Nur in *RT* (14. Jh.) und in *NKh* stirbt die Sibylle im Gefängnis. In *Le* wird sie außerhalb der Stadt gesteinigt, wie auch in *LD* (15. Jh.): "tha togho the hona oc stendo hona i hael"; vgl. dazu Lev. 20:27: "Wenn ein Mann oder Weib ein Wahrsager oder Zeichendeuter sein wird, die sollen des Todes sterben. Man soll sie steinigen; ihr Blut sei auf ihnen". In *LD* wird noch hinzugefügt, dass die Sibylle, die Maximilla heißt, die erste Märtyrerin war: "oc hon war then første martir Fore thy at hon tholde først martirium oc pino fore ihesu christi nampn".

VIII.14 [11b] *Die KvS weigert sich beim Bach, über die Brücke zu gehen; sie verehrt das Holz.*
In *Le*, *OHK* (15. Jh.) und *LD* (15. Jh.) wird die KvS Königin Sibilla genannt; *LA* (± 1260) und *NKh* halten sich aber an die Bibel (1. Kön. 10:1-13), wo sie keinen Namen trägt, wie schon in *LF* (1120) und *ESC* (1170).

VIII.15 [11d] *Die KvS schenkt Silber und Gold, womit das Holz beschlagen wird.*
Dieses Element fehlt in **Le**. In **NKh** wird wiederum auf die Bibel Bezug genommen, 1. Kön. 10:1-13 und 2. Chron. 9:1-12, wo die KvS mit Kamelen, Spezereien, Gold und Juwelen kommt. Durch die Verehrung des Holzes kann die KvS die Präfiguration von Maria werden in **THL** (± 1100) oder zur Geliebten Christus', u.a. in **HD** (1180), die die *ecclesia gentium* vertritt.

VIII.16 [12a] *Spätere Könige plündern das Gold und die Juwele; sie lassen das Holz hinaus bringen; das Holz wird in einer sehr tiefen Grube vergraben.*
Die späteren Könige *Roboam* und *Abia* (wahrscheinlich sind Rehabeam und sein Sohn Abia gemeint) erwähnt nur **NKh**; über sie wird im AT (1. Kön. und 2. Chron.) erzählt. Auch in **R** (1271) wird über die späteren Könige ausführlich berichtet; in Vss. 12260ff. plündert Roboam die Tempelschätze, Abia wird u.a. in Vs. 12285 genannt.

VIII.17 [12b] *Das Holz liegt da 200 Jahre.*
In anderen Fassungen kommt das Holz in die *piscina probatica*, die offenbar schon gegraben wurde, wie in **R** (1271), Vss. 11963ff.: das Holz wird in der Erde begraben, aber kommt in der *piscina probatica* zum Vorschein. Oder es wird absichtlich in der *piscina probatica* zurückgelassen, in **ESC** (1170). Über die Periode, die vorbeigeht, bis das Holz wieder sichtbar ist, wird in **Le** nichts gesagt. Worauf sich diese 200 Jahre beziehen ist undeutlich, oder es sollte sein, dass diese Periode mit den 200 Jahren verwirrt wird, dass das Kreuz *nach der Passion* unbemerkt liegen bleibt, wie **LA** (± 1260) erwähnt. In den meisten Fällen liegt das Holz unbemerkt bis Jesus kommt, und das ist bestimmt nicht nach 200 Jahren.

VIII.18 [14a] *Jesus wird von Judas, der ihn küsst, verraten.*
Dies fehlt in **Le**. Es ist das zweite Mal, dass Judas in der Geschichte genannt wird, und das dritte Mal, dass an ihn referiert wird. Selbstverständlich ist dieser Passus in den vier Evangelien zu finden (Mt. 26:47-50; Mk. 14:43-46; Lk. 22:47-48; Joh. 18:2-9). Der Erzähler zeigt nicht nur seine biblischen Kenntnisse, sondern betont die heilsgeschichtliche Bedeutung von Judas.

VIII.19 [14b] *Jesus wird gefangen genommen und zum Haus des Hohenpriesters gebracht.*
Fehlt in *Le*, ist aber aus dem NT bekannt (Mt. 26:57-66; Mk. 14:53, 55-64; Lk. 22:63-71; Joh. 18:12-24) und *R* (1271; Vss. 26094ff.).

VIII.20 [14c] *Jesus wird verspottet; man zieht ihn an dem Bart.*
Fehlt in *Le*. Die Verspottung Jesus' ist bekannt aus Mt. 26:67-68 ("Da spieen sie aus in sein Angesicht und schlugen ihn mit Fäusten. Etliche aber schlugen ihn ins Angesicht und sprachen: Weissage uns, Christe, wer ist's, der dich schlug?"), Mk. 14:65 ("Da fingen an etliche, ihn zu verspeien und zu verdecken sein Angesicht und ihn mit Fäusten zu schlagen und zu ihm zu sagen: Weissage uns! Und die Knechte schlugen ihn ins Angesicht"), Lk. 22:63-64 ("Die Männer aber, die Jesum hielten, verspotteten ihn und schlugen ihn ins Angesicht und fragten ihn und sprachen: Weissage, wer ist's, der dich schlug? Und viele andere Lästerungen sagten sie wider ihn") und Joh. 18:22 ("Als er aber solches redete, gab der Diener einer, die dabeistanden, Jesu einen Backenstreich und sprach: Sollst du dem Hohenpriester also antworten?"). Vgl. hierzu *R* (1271), Vss. 26125-7: "Een knecht gaf hem eenen plat./ Ende seide andwordstu dat./ Den bisscop die vor di staet." Das Detail, dass Jesus am Bart gezogen wird, ist unbiblischen Ursprungs, aber von sehr vielen Abbildungen war bekannt, dass Jesus einen Bart trug, z.B. ist Christus schon auf den geschnitzten Holztüren der S. Sabina in Rom (5. Jh.) bei der Kreuzigung mit Bart dargestellt. Auch das Apsismosaik der S. Pudenziana in Rom (5. Jh.) zeigt Christus mit Bart als Würdezeichen.[19]

VIII.21 [14d] *Jesus vor Pilatus, der dem Willen des Volkes folgt: Jesus soll gekreuzigt werden.*
Fehlt in *Le*, ist nur aus dem NT bekannt (vgl. Mt. 27:1-2, 11-26; Mk. 15:1-15; Lk. 23:1-7, 13-25; Joh. 18:28-40; 19:4-16); siehe auch *R* (1271), Vss. 26191-26268.

VIII.22 [14e] *Jesus wird gegeißelt.*
Fehlt in *Le*, ist aber aus dem NT bekannt (vgl. Mt. 27:30 und Mk. 15:19); siehe auch *R* (1271), Vss. 26364-68 en 26391-96. In Psalterien des 9. Jhs. kommt die Geißelung vor, z.B. in einem Stuttgarter Psalter

---

[19] LCI, 1, 363; Timmers, 32f.

(Stuttgart LBibl. Cod. 23) aus 820-830.[20] Dass Christus an seiner Geißelsäule steht, wird in *NKh*, z.B. in *H* (Vs. 711-2) erzählt: "Men bant ene vmme eyne sule vaste / Vnde gheyselde ene mit haste". Erst vom 15. Jh. an entsteht in der Malerei, Plastik, Graphik der von Pilatus zur Schau gestellte *Ecce homo* als einzelnes Andachtsbild nach Joh. 19:4-5.[21]

VIII.23 [**15a**] *Vom Holz wird ein Drittel (Zeder) abgehauen, das ist der senkrechte Teil des Kreuzes; quer darauf wird ein Balken (Zipresse) befestigt; die Nägel sind aus Olivenholz.*
Das Kreuz besteht also aus zwei Teilen; die Nägel, die beide Teile verbinden, sind auch aus Holz. Die verschiedenen Baumsorten kommen schon früher vor [**3g**], wo in *Le* und *NKh* erzählt wird, dass die 3K zu 3G einer Zeder, Zipresse und Kiefer (oder eines Palmenbaums) hochwachsen werden, und [**8b**], wo die 3G einer Zeder, Zipresse und Kiefer zu einem Baum aneinanderwachsen. Eventuell muss man die Stellen hinzunehmen, wo im Holz die Dreieinigkeit erkannt wird. Insoweit ist der Erzähler konsequent. In *LA* (± 1260) werden aber vier Teile des Kreuzes (der senkrechte Teil, der Querbalken, der *titulus* und der Stamm, worauf das Kreuz steht [oder, in einer Variante: das Fußbrett]) und ihre Holzsorten (Palme, Zipresse, Zeder, Olivenholz) genannt. In *R* (1271) besteht das Kreuz aus denselben vier Holzsorten (Vss. 26445ff.) und hat es ebenfalls vier Teile: der Fuß steht im Felsen, darauf senkrecht zwei drittel des Holzes, ein Drittel ist der Querbalken und der *titulus*. Auch in *OHK* (15. Jh.) besteht das Kreuz aus vier Teilen (Sockel, Stamm, Querbalken, *titulus*), wozu *vier* Holzsorten gehören (Palmen-, Zeder-, Zipressen- und Olivenholz). Diese vier Teile, die aus anderer Tradition stammen, sind vor allem merkwürdig, weil doch nur drei Zweige aneinanderwachsen.[22] In *Le* fehlt die Zusammensetzung des Kreuzes. Weil die 3G die Dreieinigkeit vertreten [**3g**], ist in der Legende eine Spaltung in drei Teile, die zusammen das Kreuz bilden, theologisch korrekter als vier Teile.

---

[20] LCI, 2, 127ff.
[21] Reclam, 134; LCI, 1, 558.
[22] Vgl. Kemper 2006, 212ff.: Die vier Teile und die vier Holzsorten des Kreuzes stammen aus einer anderen Tradition als der der Kreuzholzlegende. In der Passionsliteratur des Spätmittelalters schreiben vor allem Autoren, die in Paris tätig waren (Petrus Comestor, Bonaventura, Franciscus de Mayronis, Michael de Massa).

VIII.24 [15b] *Jesus trägt sein Kreuz.*
Fehlt in *Le*. Die Kreuztragung Christi ist nur aus dem Johannesevangelium (Joh. 19:17) bekannt; in den übrigen Evangelien trägt Simon von Kyrene das Kreuz (Mt. 27:32; Mk. 15:21; Lk. 23:26). *R* (1271; Vss. 26399ff.) will allen Evangelien Recht tun: zuerst trägt Jesus das Kreuz, dann Simon von Kyrene. Schon in frühchristlicher und frühmittelalterlicher Zeit wird die Kreuztragung Christi bildlich dargestellt, z.B. auf einem Elfenbeintäfelchen, um 420-430, Rom (British Museum) und auf einer Miniatur des Egbertcodex, um 980. Die Buchmalerei jedoch lässt Simon von Kyrene mit dem Kreuz voranschreiten.[23]

VIII.25 [15c] *Dabei sind Maria und Johannes.*
Fehlt in *Le*. Maria und Johannes stehen auf Abbildungen meistens neben oder unter dem Kreuz, wobei Jesus Johannes zu Marias Sohn und Maria zu Johannes' Mutter macht, vgl. Joh. 19:26-27. Auf einem alten Fresko in der S. Maria Antiqua (750) auf dem Forum in Rom steht Maria links und Johannes rechts vom Kreuz. Bei frühen Kruzifixen (bis 1200) steht Maria im Allgemeinen ebenfalls links vom Kreuz und Johannes rechts. In den Evangelien werden weiter genannt: (Mt. 27:55-56) Frauen (nicht Maria), (Mk. 15:40-41) Frauen (nicht Maria), (Lk. 23:49) Bekannte, auch Frauen (nicht Maria); nur im Johannesevangelium (Joh. 19:25) stehen in der Tat neben Maria Klopas, Maria Magdalena auch Maria und Johannes. *R* (1271; Vss. 26498ff.) folgt ungefähr dem Johannesevangelium (Joh. 19:25).

VIII.26 [15d] *Jesus wird gekreuzigt: zwei Nägel gehen durch seine Hände, einer durch seine Füße.*
Fehlt in den Evangelien, in *Le* und *R*. In dieser Szene hat Christus die Füße aufeinander. In Abbildungen findet man Jesus mit den Füßen nebeneinander oder aufeinander. Aus der Beschreibung der Zusammensetzung des Kreuzes (vgl. **VIII.23 [15a]**) in *LA* könnte man schließen, dass drei oder vier Nägel verwendet wurden. In den ältesten Abbildungen, wie z.B. auf den geschnitzten Holztüren der S. Sabina in Rom (5. Jh.) ist Christus mit seinen Händen ans Kreuz genagelt, aber seine Füße stehen frei auf dem *suppedaneum* (Fußstütze), sein Körper

---

[23] LCI, 2, 649ff.; Reclam, 134.

ist recht; nicht zu sehen ist, ob seine Füße durchbohrt sind. Auf einem Fresko in der S. Maria Antiqua auf dem Forum in Rom (750) ist Christus mit vier Nägeln ans Kreuz geschlagen, so wie es bis etwa 1200 in Abbildungen üblich bleibt.[24] Aus Konstantinopel wurde zwar vom 4. Kreuzzug (1202-1204) ein neuer, mehr realistischer Kruzifixtypus mitgebracht, aber Jesus hat die Füße noch nebeneinander hat. Seit ± 1250 findet man in Italien bei Kruzifixen eine naturalistische Abbildung: der Körper Christi hängt schwer an den Armen, die Füße sind überkreuzt und mit einem Nagel am Kreuz festgehalten. Beide Typen, Füße nebeneinander oder überkreuzt, bleiben noch eine Zeit lang bestehen. Die Erwähnung von nur drei Nägeln findet man in schriftlichen Quellen schon im 12. Jahrhundert, z.B. in Vs. 10390 der 'Kaiserchronik' (± 1150) und in *P* (± 1180).[25]

VIII.27 [15e] *Marias Kummer ist zu groß, darüber zu erzählen; weil die Passion darüber nicht spricht, will der Erzähler nicht so anmaßend sein, dies wohl zu tun.*
Fehlt in *Le*; auch in den vier Evangelien wird über Marias Kummer tatsächlich nicht erzählt. Offenbar kannte der Bearbeiter die Evangelien gut.

VIII.28 [15f] *Ein Schwert durchschneidet Marias Herz.*
Fehlt in *Le*. Auch hier stellt sich heraus, dass der Bearbeiter sich im NT gut auskennt; er weist auf die Szene hin, wo Maria und Joseph mit Jesus in den Tempel kommen (Lk. 2:34-35): "Und Simeon segnete sie und sprach zu Maria, seiner Mutter: Siehe, dieser [Jesus] ist gesetzt zu einem Fall und Auferstehen vieler in Israël und zu einem Zeichen, dem widersprochen wird und es wird ein Schwert durch deine *Seele* dringen, auf dass vieler Herzen Gedanken offenbar werden", wo Marias Kummer von Simeon vorhergesagt wird. Der Unterschied ist nur: Seele (lat. *anima*) statt Herz. In *R* (1271) sagt Maerlant, dass Simeon prophezeit (Vss. 21475-7): "Ende vorseide die passie ons heren./ Die pine ende dien groten rouwe./ Dier omme soude doghen onse vrouwe." Diese kleine Variation, Herz statt Seele, könnte mit

---

[24] Kemper 2006, 211 und 265.
[25] H. van Os, mündliche Mitteilung; vgl. auch LCI, 1, 415. Nach Kemper (2006, 265ff.) vollzieht der Wandel vom Viernagel- zum Dreinagelkreuz sich schon in der Mitte des 12. Jhs.

bildlichen Darstellungen der Schmerzen Marias, vor allem in den Niederlanden (Flandern), zusammenhängen, wo (sieben) Schwerter Marias Herz durchstechen (die Zahl der Schwerter liegt nicht fest).[26]

VIII.29 [16a] *Jesus stirbt; die Sonne verbirgt ihren Schein, die Erde bebt, Felsen reißen, sagt Johannes, der die Wahrheit kennt.*
Fehlt in *Le*. Dass dem Bearbeiter der Legende hier ein kleiner Fehler unterläuft, wird deutlich aus den vier Evangelien; die Kombination von Sonnenfinsternis und Erdbeben und reißenden Felsen steht nur bei Matthäus: Mt. 27:45 und 27:51-52. Markus und Lukas sprechen nur von Finsternis. Und gerade im Johannesevangelium steht nichts darüber. Aber da Johannes hier unter dem Kreuz steht, muss er, nach dem Erzähler, die Finsternis und Bebung miterlebt haben. Darum muss man davon ausgehen, dass der Erzähler den Apostel Johannes und den Evangelisten Johannes als dieselbe Person betrachtet.[27]

VIII.30 [16b] *Ein Ritter durchsticht Jesus' Seite; daraus strömt das Adam verheißene Öl der Barmherzigkeit.*
Fehlt in *Le*. Dieser Passus ist nur aus dem Johannesevangelium bekannt: (Joh. 19:34) "... sondern der Kriegsknechte einer öffnete seine Seite mit einem Speer und alsbald ging Blut und Wasser heraus". Daran anknüpfend erzählt Maerlant in *R* (1271) die Legende "van den ridders een", der blind war und durch das Blut von Christus sehend wird (Vss. 26625 und 26638ff.). So auch in *HS* (vor 1178): 'Sed unus militum lancea ejus dextrum perforavit, et continuo exivit sanguinis, et aqua, et qui lanceavit eum, ut tradunt quidam, cum fere caligassent oculi ejus, et casu tetigisset oculos sanguine ejus, clare vidit'. In beiden Texten *HS* und *R* ist der Ritter ohne Namen. In *NKh* wird weder sein (legendärer) Name Longinus noch seine Blindheit erwähnt. Auch Joseph von Arimathia (nach anderen Simon von Kyrene), der mit dem Abendmahlskelch unter dem Kreuz steht, das Blut Christi aufzufangen, findet man in *NKh* nicht; es gibt also keine Verbindung zur Longinuslegende oder zur Gralslegende. Das Element des Trostes und der Rettung von Adam wird schon in anderen Fassungen genannt, aber das Öl der Barmherzigkeit wird außer in *NKh* nur in *LD*

---

[26] Vgl. Timmers, 142; LCI, 4, 85ff.
[27] In letzter Zeit wird angenommen, dass der Apostel Johannes und der Evangelist Johannes nicht dieselbe Person sind; vgl. McGinn 1992, 3-19.

(15. Jh.) erwähnt: 'das Holz trug die Frucht, die sowohl Adam als der ganzen Menschheit das Öl der Barmherzigkeit ("miskunnena olio") gab'.[28] Das aus der Seite strömende Blut bedeutet das Öl der Barmherzigkeit. Daher ist der Moment der Rettung in *NKh* ziemlich exakt: als Jesus durchstochen wird. In den anderen Fassungen ist dies weniger genau: beim Kommen Christi in *VAE* (± 70), nach 5500 Jahren in *PsEN* (5. und 10. Jh.), wenn der Zweig Frucht trägt, das heißt, wenn Christus am Kreuz hängt in *LA* (± 1260). In allen Fassungen, wo von der Rettung Adams durch Christus' Kreuzestod die Rede ist, wird das Holz, das aus Samen oder Zweigen des Baumes der Erkenntnis vom Guten und Bösen entstanden ist, zum Lebensbaum, der Adam das ewige Leben gibt.

IX Schlussfolgerungen

IX.1
Es ist tatsächlich so, wie frühere Untersucher festgestellt haben, dass *NKh* mit *Le* die meisten Übereinstimmungen teilt. Und weiter, dass *NKh* seine Form nur dank *Le* erhalten haben kann.

IX.2
Dass *Le* viele Varianten der Legende vereint und zu einem anderen Ganzen als z.B. *LA* macht, mag aus den Vergleichen (in **VI**, **VII** und **VIII**) deutlich sein.

IX.3
Die Arbeitsweise des Bearbeiters der *Le* zeigt sich aus Kapitel **VI**: der Textteil, in dem Seth auftritt, erwähnt nun einiges von dem, was im Paradies zu sehen ist [**3b-f**]; auch der schon bekannte Moses-Passus wird erweitert [**6a** und **6d**]. Der Abschnitt mit David wird nachdrücklicher als zuvor durch die wunderbare Wirkung der 3G bestimmt [**7c**, **8a-c**]. Als Überbringer der 3G nach Jerusalem ist David die Figur, die am meisten auf der Hand liegt; in Jerusalem soll man selbstverständ-

---

[28] In *LA* wird zwar über das *oleum misericordiae* berichtet, aber nicht in Cap. LXVIII, *De inventione sanctae crucis*, sondern in Cap. LIV, *De resurrectione domini*; vgl. Graesse, 243. Auch im zweiten Teil des *PsEN* erzählen Adam und Seth den Patriarchen und Propheten in der Hölle, dass Seth das Öl der Barmherzigkeit holen sollte.

lich statt der 3G einen Baum vorfinden [**9a**]. Auch erweitert der Bearbeiter von *Le* eine Prophezeiung über Christus' Tod zu einer doppelten Prophezeiung der Sibylle und der KvS [**10a-b**, **11c**]. Und schließlich kennzeichnet *Le* sich durch ihr Ende; nicht die Kreuzauffindung durch Helena oder die Kreuzhebung durch Heraklius sondern das Einlösen von Gottes Verheißung an Adam beim Tode Christi [**16b**] bildet das Ende.

IX.4

Die Erweiterungen, Verdoppelungen oder das Betonen anderer Akzente erfolgen in *Le* aber nicht auf Grund alt- und neutestamentlicher Kenntnis. Eine kleine Ausnahme betrifft vielleicht **6d**, wo Moses mit den 3G süßes Wasser aus einem Felsen schlägt.

IX.5

Die Legende in *NKh* wird, anders als in *Le*, biblisch unterbaut; das ist vielleicht schon im Prolog [**1**] zu sehen, wo der Bearbeiter sich wahrscheinlich auf die Bibel beruft. Ganz deutlich ist es der Fall bei **3a**, **6c-e**, **7b**, etwas weniger bei **8c**, aber bestimmt bei **8e**, **11b** und **11d**, **12a**, **14a-e**, **15b-f** und **16a-b**. Das ist in so vielen Punkten, dass anzunehmen ist, der Bearbeiter lege großen Wert darauf, dass man erkennt, die Legende sei (fast) biblisch. Das Verfahren erinnert an die Arbeitsweise von Petrus Comestor (***HS***, vor 1178) und Maerlant (***R***, 1271), die die Bibelgeschichte in die damals bekannte Weltgeschichte einfügen. In dieser Hinsicht ist die Arbeitsweise des Bearbeiters von *NKh* zwar keine einzigartige, aber doch eine besondere. Dadurch, dass der Text Longinus und seine wunderbare Genesung nicht erwähnt (Petrus Comestor und Maerlant nennen wohl noch die Genesung), zeigt sich, dass die Erzählung gerade von Legendärem befreit werden soll. Der Bearbeiter von *NKh* bezieht sich dauernd auf 'das Buch' (siehe *S*, Vs. 322: "dat zegghet boec alzonder waen", Vs. 635: "als ic heb horen lesen", Vs.797: "als ict beschreuen vant"), oder auf 'die Wahrheit' (siehe *S*, Vs. 134: "dat dar ic zegghen ouerwaer", Vs.216: "dat was waer", Vss. 241 und 335: "des zijt ghewes", Vs. 547: "dats ware dinc"); dass er damit die Bibel meint, zeigt sich aus den regelmäßigen Hinweisen auf das Alte Testament und die Evangelien, vor allem das Johannesevangelium. Man muss daraus folgern, dass der Bearbeiter von *NKh* sich mit biblischen Geschichten gut auskennt.

IX.6

Im Übrigen fällt auf, dass in *NKh* bestimmte Akzente dadurch stark betont werden, dass Verdoppelungen in die Legende eingeführt werden. Zu nennen sind die Wiederholungen bei der Auffindung der 3G durch Moses und die Wiederholung dieses Motivs, als David auftritt; über die Verehrung des Holzes bei und an dem Tempel von Salomo wird zweimal erzählt; es gibt zwei Prophetinnen; zweimal wird das Holz weggeworfen; Judas wird zweimal genannt, und auf seinen Verrat wird dreimal Bezug genommen; Marias Kummer wird zweimal erwähnt.

IX.7

Bei einigen Passionsmotiven in *NKh*, bei **14c** (Christus wird am Bart gezogen), **14e** (Christus wird an der Geißelsäule gegeißelt), **15b** (die Kreuztragung Christi), **15c** (Maria steht links, Johannes rechts vom Kreuz), **15d** (drei Nägel gehen durch Christus' Hände und Füße) und **15f** (ein Schwert durchschneidet Marias Herz), muss festgestellt werden, dass die Schilderungen mehr durch Kruzifixe und gemalte oder geschnitzte Passionsvorstellungen beeinflusst sein könnten, als bei *Le* zu sehen ist.

IX.8

Der Text von *NKh* stammt ungefähr aus den Jahren 1290?-1330.[29] Unsicherheit bei der Datierung (1290?) entsteht durch das Textfragment *O*, das 1275-1325 datiert wird. Gerade in der daran vorangehenden Periode schreibt Maerlant seine *R* (1271). In jener Zeit entstanden auch viele Passionsbearbeitungen und Evangelienharmonien.[30] Auch die *R* könnte man als eine Art Evangelienharmonie betrachten. Es geht vielleicht zu weit, zu behaupten, dass der Bearbeiter der mittelniederländischen *NKh*-Legende die *R* kannte. Aber auf jeden Fall ist für den Bearbeiter von *NKh* von einem Geistlichen auszugehen, der in der Bibel gut unterrichtet war. Hermodsson (1959, 113ff.) geht der Frage nach, ob Jacob van Maerlant der Dichter von *NKh* sein könnte. Seiner Meinung nach spricht aber gegen Maerlant, der ein großer Verehrer der Gottesmutter war, das wichtige Argument, dass über Marias

---

[29] Hermodsson 1959, 30ff., 113.
[30] Vgl. Langbroek 2008, 42 und die einschlägige Literatur.

Kummer beim Kreuz nicht berichtet wird [**15e**]. Maerlant hätte bestimmt an dieser Stelle eine 'Marienklage' eingefügt. Aus eigener Beobachtung wurde außerdem festgestellt, dass im Gegensatz zu *R*, worin man bei passender und unpassender Gelegenheit Mariavergleiche findet, in *NKh* die Rolle von Maria, ebensowie in der Bibel, klein ist.[31]

Literatur

Bächtold-Stäubli 2000: Hanns Bächtold-Stäubli (Hg.), *Handwörterbuch des deutschen Aberglaubens*, Bd. 5, Berlin-New York.
Baert 1995: Barbara Baert, *Het "Boec van den Houte"*. Verhandelingen van de Koninklijke Academie voor Wetenschappen, Letteren en Schone Kunsten van België, Klasse der Schone Kunsten, Jaargang 57, Nr. 62, Brüssel.
Baert 2001: Barbara Baert, *Een erfenis van heilig hout. De neerslag van het teruggevonden kruis in tekst en beeld tijdens de Middeleeuwen*, Leuven.
Chavannes 2008, s. *Rb*.
Dronke 1990: Peter Dronke, *Hermes and the Sibyls*. Continuations and creations. Inaugural Lecture, Cambridge-New York-Port Chester-Melbourne-Sydney.
Graesse 1890, s. *LA*.
Handwörterbuch des deutschen Aberglaubens, s. Bächtold-Stäubli.
Hermodsson 1959, s. *S*.
Jacobs 1987: Jef Jacobs, "Der *Descensus ad Inferos* als Bericht und Exempel in frühmittelhochdeutscher religiöser Dichtung", in: *ABäG* 26, 17-34.
Die Kaiserchronik eines Regenburger Geistlichen, Hg. von Edward Schröder, MGH 1,1, München, 1984.
Keller 1968: Hiltgart Keller, *Reclam Lexikon der Heiligen und der biblischen Gestalten*. Legende und Darstellung in der bildenden Kunst, 5. durchgesehene und ergänzte Auflage 1984, Stuttgart.
Kemper 2006: Tobias A. Kemper, *Die Kreuzigung Christi*. Motivgeschichtliche Studien zu lateinischen und deutschen Passionstraktaten des Spätmittelalters, Tübingen.
Klunder 2005, s. *Lu*.
Langbroek & Roeleveld 2001, s. *H*.
Langbroek 2008: Erika Langbroek, "Welche Vorlage suchen wir? Untersuchung der 'Niederlandismen' in: Zürich, Zentralbibliothek, C 170 App. 56", in: *Nothern Voices. Essays on Old Germanic and Related Topics*, Offered to Professor Tette Hofstra, Leuven - Paris- Dudley, MA, 41-69.
Lassen 2009: Annette Lassen, "The God on the Tree", in: *Greppaminni*, Reykjavík, 231-246.
LCI: *Lexikon der christlichen Ikonographie*, 1-4, allgemeine Ikonographie, Rom-Freiburg-Basel-Wien, 1994.
McGinn 1992: Bernard McGinn, "Introduction: John's Apocalypse and Apocalypse Mentality", in: Richard K. Emmerson & Bernard McGinn (Hgg.), *The Apocalypse in the Middle Ages*, Ithaca - London.

---

[31] Mit ihrem Namen wird Maria genannt in: Mt. 1:16, 18-25; 2:11-23; Lk. 1:26-56, 2:1-52; Joh. 2:1-12, 19:25; Apostelgesch. 1:14.

Reclam, s. Keller, 1968.
Roeleveld 2010: Annelies Roeleveld, "The Holy Rood in the Netherlands and North Germany. A comparative study of 9 Middle Dutch and 2 Middle Low German recensions of the legend about the Provenance of the Cross", in: *ABäG* 66, 175-203.
Tideman 1844: J. Tideman (Hg), *Jacob van Maerlant, DBoec vanden Houte*. Werken uitg. door de Vereeniging ter bevordering der oude Nederlandsche letterkundige Werken, 1:2, Leiden.
Timmers 1978: J.J.M. Timmers, *Christelijke symboliek en ikonografie*, Haarlem.

Quellen der Texte, die unter III genannt wurden

Mit * sind die Texte vermerkt, die zur Gruppe der niederländischen Kreuzholzlegende gehören, die mit ** bezeichnen die mittelniederdeutschen Übersetzungen der *NKh*:

b* (1496): *Dit is dat boec vanden houte*, (Druck) Haarlem Stadsbibliotheek, Antwerpen. (Fotokopien; 781 Vss.).
bo (1483): *Boec van den Houte*, (Druck) Culemborg, s. Baert 1995.
BOH (9. Jh.): *Bericht über Odilia von Hohenburg*, Th. Graesse 1890 (Hg.), *Jacobi a Voragine, Legenda Aurea* (reprogaphischer Nachdruck von 1890, Osnabrück, 1969, Cap. CXC, 876f.
byzW (842-887): *byzantinische Weltchronik* von Georgias Monachos, Muralt, Petrepoli (Hg.), 1859, Kap. XLIII; MPG 110.
C** (15. Jh.): 'Vom Holze des heiligen Kreuzes', SUB Hamburg, Hs. Convent. 4, F. 182r-199r; C. Schröder (Hg.), *NdJb* 2 (1876), 88-113 (807 Vss.).
CJ (Anfang 13. Jh.): *La citez de Jhérusalem (Chronique d'Ernoul)*, T. Tobler (Hg.), *Descriptiones terrae sanctae es saeculo VIII. IX. XII et XV, 7, La citez de Jhérusalem*, Leipzig, 1874, 216; H. Michelant und G. Raynaud, *Itinéraires à Jhérusalem et descriptions de la terre sainte rédigés géographique*, Bd. 3, *Itinéraires français*, Genf, 1882, 45-47.
CRC (1250): *Chronica Regia Coloniensis*, Hs. Brüssel, Koninklijke Bibliotheek Albert I, ms. 467, F. 1v.
D* (1400-1450): Hs. Düsseldorf, Hauptstaatsarchiv, ohne Signatur; A. Birlinger (Hg.), in: *Germania* 15 (1870), 360-364 (174 Vss., teils fragmentarisch).
DG (vor 470): *Descriptio Graeciae X,1,2,9*; W. Schubart (Hg.) 1889-1891, Leipzig; M.H. Rolma-Pereira, *Graecia Descriptio*, Leipzig, 1981.
El (± 1100): *Elucidarium* von Honorius Augustodunensis, (Hg.) Y. Lefèvre, *L'Elucidarium et les lucidaires. Contribution, par l'histoire d'un texte, à l'histoire des croyances religieuses en France au moyen âge.* Bibliothèque des écoles françaises d'Athènes et de Rome 180, Paris, 1954.
ESC (1170): *De exaltatione sanctae crucis*, in: *Rationale divinorum officiorum, von Johannes Belethus*, MPL 202, Sp. 152-153.
G* (14. Jh.): Hs. Göttingen, Niedersächsische Staats- und Universitätsbibliothek, 8° Cod. Luneb. 24a (Fotos; 67 Vss., teils fragmentarisch).
H** (1476): *Van dem holte des hilligen krutzes*, SUB Hamburg, Hs. 102c in scrinio, F. 11r-23v; Erika Langbroek und Annelies Roeleveld (Hgg.), *Het Hartebok. Hs. Hamburg, Staats- und Universitätsbibliothek, 102c in scrinio*, Hilversum, 2001, MVN 8, 79-100 (771 Vss.).
HD (1180): *Hortus Deliciarum* von Herrad von Landsberg; Hs. im Jahre 1870 verbrannt, Rekonstruktion und Facsimile, R. Green, *Herrad of Hohenbourg. Studies*

of the Warburg Institute, 36, 1979, 2, 264-265, Nr. 520.
Hi (vor 1150): *Historia*, Hs. MSB, München, Clm 14442, F. 1r; (engl. Übers.) J. Wilkinson, *Jerusalem Pilgrimage, 1199-1185*, London, 1988, 75.
HS (vor 1178): *Historia scholastica* von Petrus Comestor, MPL 198.
Hu* (1405-1408): *DBoec vanden Houte*, Hs. Brüssel, KB 15.589-623, F. 15va-19vb; H. Brinkman & J. Schenkel (Hgg.), *Het handschrift-Van Hulthem. Hs. Brussel, Koninklijke Bibliotheek van België, 15.589-623*, Hilversum, 1999, MVN 7, 177-196 (780 Vss.).
IJ (1190): *Interrogatio Johannis der Katharen*; R. Nelli, *Ecritures cathares*, Paris, 1968; J. Ivanov, *Livres et légendes bogomiles. Aux sources du catharisme*, Paris, 1976.
IM (vor 1155): *De imago mundi* von Honorius Augustodunensis, Hss. München, SB, Clm 22225 und 23387a.
LA (± 1260): *Legenda Aurea*; Th. Graesse (Hg.), *Jacobi a Voragine, Legenda Aurea* (reprographischer Nachdruck von 1890), Cap. LXVIII, *De inventione sanctae crucis* und Cap. LIV, *De resurrectione domini*, Osnabrück, 1969.
LD (15. Jh.): *De ligno domini*; George Stephens (Hg.), in: *Svenska Medeltidens Kloster-Helgona-Bok. En samling af de Äldste Legender och Äfventyr II, Ett fornsvenskt Legendarium, Första Bandet*, Stockholm, 1847, 89ff.
Le (1220): *Legenda = Prosaversion*; Hs. Cambridge, University Library, Ms. I 14; W. Meyer (Hg.), *Die Geschichte des Kreuzholzes vor Christus*. Abhandlungen der philosophisch-philologischen Classe der königlich bayrischen Akademie der Wissenschaften, 16, 2, München 1882, 131-149.
LF (1120): *Liber floridus* von Lambertus von Sint-Omaars; A. Derolez (Hg.), *Lamberti S. Audomari Canonici Liber Floridus. Codex autographus Bibliothecae Universitatis Gandavensis*, Gent, 1968, 5, F. 2r.
Lu (14. Jh.): *Lucidarius*, Hs. B1, Brüssel, KB 15642-51, F. 1r-61v; Nolanda Klunder (Hg.), *Lucidarius. De Middelnederlandse Lucidarius-teksten en hun relatie tot de Europese traditie*, Amsterdam, 2005, 385-459.
M* (1360-1375): Hs. Brüssel, KB II 5.580 (Mikrofilm; 171 Vss.).
Mi (4. - 12. Jh.): *Midrasch*; G. Salzberger, *Salomons Tempelbau und Thron in der semitischen Sagenliteratur*, Berlin, 1912, 22-30.
O* (1275-1325): Hs. Oudenaarde, Stadtsbibliotheek, 5567; Lars Hermodsson (Hg.), *Dat Boec van den Houte. Eine mittelniederländische Dichtung von der Herkunft des Kreuzes Christi*. Uppsala Universitets Årsskrift 1959:1, Acta Universitatis Upslaliensis, Uppsala-Wiesbaden, 1959, 54f. (6 Vss.).
OHK (15. Jh.): *Om det heliga korset*; George Stephens (Hg.), in: *Svenska Medeltidens Kloster-Helgona-Bok. En samling af de Äldste Legender och Äfventyr II, Ett fornsvenskt Legendarium, Första Bandet*, Stockholm, 1847, 88f.
OI (1212): *Otia Imperialia* von Gervasius von Tilbury; Th. N. Hall, 'The Cross as Green Tree in the Vindicta Salvatoris and the Green Rod of Moses in Exodus', in: *English Studies*, 72, 4, 1991, 305.
OS (2.Jh. v.Chr. - 3./4. Jh. n.Chr.): *Oracula Sibyllina*; W. Grebe, *Sibyllen Weissagung*, Köln 1989; A. Krufess, *Sibyllinische Weissagungen*, Berlin, 1951, 5-23.
P (± 1180): *Pantheon, XIV* von Gottfried von Viterbo, MPL 198, Sp. 872ff.; W. Meyer, *Die Geschichte des Kreuzholzes vor Christus*. Abhandlungen der philosophisch-philologischen Classe der königlich bayrischen Akademie der Wissenschaften, 16,2, München, 1882, 112-114.
PA (1355-1358): *Pélerinage de l'âme* von Guillaume de Deguileville, Hs. Paris, Bibliothèque Nationale, ms. fr. 602; u.a. J. Flynn, *Pilgrimage of the Soul. A Fifteenth*

Century English Porse Translation of the Pèlerinage de l'âme, New York, Garland, 1990.
Per (± 1190-1212): *'Perceval'* von Didot, in: W. Roach, *The Continuations of the Old French "Perceval" of Chrétien de Troyes*, Philadelphia, 1949.
PJ (8. Jh.): *Überlieferung aus den Kreisen von Pope Jeremia*: u.a. Anastasius Sinaitica (650), *Anagoricorum contemplationum in hexaemeron*, MPG 89, Sp. 944-945.
PsENg (5. Jh.) und **PsENl** (10. Jh.): älteste lateinische Fassung, 10. Jh., *Pseudo-Evangelium von Nikodemus*, Codex Einsidlensis 326, Einsiedeln, Stiftsbibliothek; vgl. auch *The Gospel of Nicodemus, or Acts of Pilate*. From "The Apocryphal New Testament", M.R. James-Translation and Notes, Oxford, 1924.
QGra (13. Jh.): *Queste du Saint Graal*; A. Pauphilet, *Etude sur la queste del Saint Graal*, Paris, 1921, 36-46 u. 84ff.
R (1271): *Rijmbijbel* von Jacob van Maerlant; Hs. Brüssel, KB 15.001 (1275-1300), Maurits Gysseling (Hg.), in: *Corpus van Middelnederlandse Teksten (tot en met het jaar 1300)*. Reeks II: Literaire handschriften, Deel 3, Rijmbijbel/tekst, Leiden, 1983.
Rb (1332): *Rijmbijbel* von Jacob van Maerlant, in: Claudine A. Chavannes-Mazel, *Maerlants Rijmbijbel in Museum Meermanno. De kracht van woorden, de pracht van beelden*, Hs. 10 B 21, Den Haag, 2008.
RT (14. Jh.): *Rood-Tree-Gruppe*, (Hg.) A. Napier, *History of the Holy Rood-tree*, (EETS. O.S. 103), 1894, 41ff.
S* (1339): *Van den drie gaerden*, UB Groningen, Hs. 405, Bl. 210va-214va; Lars Hermodsson (Hg.), *Dat Boec van den Houte. Eine mittelniederländische Dichtung von der Herkunft des Kreuzes Christi*. Uppsala Universitets Årsskrift 1959:1, Acta Universitatis Upslaliensis, Uppsala-Wiesbaden, 1959, 121-154.
SHR (13. Jh.): *Story of the Holy Rood*, Hs. London, British Library, Harley Ms. Nr. 4196.
slK (950): *Kreuzholzlegende der slavischen Bogomilen*; A.R. Miller, *German and Dutch Versions of the Legend of the Wood of the Cross. A Descriptive and Analytical Catalogue*, (unhgg.) Oxford, 1992, 47.
SpE (± 1100): *Speculum Ecclesiae* von Honorius Augustodunensis. *De inventione sanctae Crucis*, MPL 172, Sp. 945.
T* (15. Jh.): Hs. 's-Hertogenbosch, Archivum Capuccinorum Hollandiae, 4; P. Maximilianus (Hg.), in: *Bijblad voor Taal en Letteren* 2 (1914), 38-48 (192 Vss., teils fragmentarisch).
THL (± 1100): *3. Traktat zum Hohen Lied* von Honorius Augustodunensis, MPL 172, Sp. 453.
TS (vor 11. Jh.): *Übersetzung des Targum Scheni*; M. Grünbaum, *Neue Beiträge zur Semitischen Sagenkunde*, Leiden, 1893, 211ff.
U* (1425-1450): *dit es vte tdiechs vanden houten*, Hs. Utrecht, UB, Ms. 5.F.12,1329, F. 34ra-37vb (Mikrofilm; 567 Vss.).
VAE (± 70): *Vita Adae et Evae*; W. Meyer (Hg.), *Vita Adae et Evae. Abhandlungen der philosophisch-philologischen Classe der königlich bayerischen Akademie der Wissenschaften*, 14, München, 1879.
arVAE (5. Jh.): *armenische Übersetzung der Vita Adae et Evae*; E. Preuschen, 'Die apokryphen gnostischen Adamschriften aus dem armenischen übersetzt und untersucht', in: *Festgruss B. Stade*, 1900, 163-252.
slVAE (1000-1200): *slavische Übersetzung der Vita Adae et Evae*; A.R. Miller, *German and Dutch Versions of the Legend of the Wood of the Cross. A Descriptive and Analytical Catalogue*, (nicht hg.) Oxford, 1992, 45.

Addenda

Ein Vergleich von *LA* (± 1260) mit *OHK* (15. Jh.) und von *Le* (1220) mit *LD* (15. Jh.)

Die relativ spät überlieferten altschwedischen Texte *Om det heliga korset* (***OHK***) und *De ligno domini* (***LD***), die in den Untersuchungen von Baert (2001) unbeachtet bleiben, zeigen große Übereinstimmungen mit der *Legenda Aurea* (***LA***) beziehungsweise der *Legenda* (***Le***), wie folgende Vergleiche zeigen.

1 Der Vergleich von *LA* mit *OHK*.

In beiden Texten sind die Abweichungen unterstrichen; kursiv ist der Inhalt, der an anderer Stelle erscheint; fehlende Motive sind mit waagerechten Strichen (---) markiert; so zeigt sich, dass das Ende von *LA* (10a und 10b) in *OHK* fehlt:

	Legenda aurea		**Om det heliga korset**
1	Der Erzähler bezieht sich im Prolog auf das Evangelium von Nikodemus	1	=
2	Adam ist alt und krank; er sendet Seth zum Paradies für das Öl der Barmherzigkeit.	2	=
3a	Der Engel Michael[32] sagt Seth, es geschehe erst in 5500 Jahren.	3a	Der Engel Michael sagt Seth, es geschehe in 5000 Jahren.
3b	Seth empfängt einen Zweig des Baumes, an dem Adam sündigte.	3b	=
3c	Seth soll den Zweig auf den Berg Libanon pflanzen	3c	=
3d	Wenn der Baum Frucht trägt, wird Adam gesund.	3d	=
4	Adam ist bei Seths Rückkehr schon gestorben.	4	=
5	Seth pflanzt den Zweig auf Adams Grab, der zu einem großen Baum wächst.	5	=

---

[32] In Gen. 3:24 wird der Erzengel Michael beim Garten Eden nicht genannt, sondern ein Cherub. Michael findet man (im AT) in Dan. 10:13; 10:21; 12:1 und (im NT) in Jud. 9 und Offenb. 12,7. In *PsEN* trägt der Engel, der bei der Paradiespforte das Öl verhieß, ebenfalls den Namen Michael.

6a	Salomo sieht den schönen Baum, er haut ihn für seinen Palastbau (= *domus saltus*) um.	6a	Salomo fängt mit dem Tempelbau an [hier stimmt **OHK** mit **NKh** und anderen überein].
6b	Das Holz passt nicht, die Bauleute erklären es für untauglich.	6b	=
6c	Das Holz wird außerhalb der Stadt über einen Teich gelegt.	6c	Das Holz wird draußen hingelegt.
7a	KvS kommt über den Teich.	7a	KvS kommt.
7b	KvS hat eine Vision vom Tode Christi [s. **Hi**: dies ist das Ende des Judentums].	7b	KvS prophezeit den Tod Christi und das Ende des Judentums.
7c	Salomo lässt das Holz begraben.	7c	=
8a	Ein Teich zum Waschen der Opfertiere wird gegraben (= *piscina probatica*).	8a	=
8b	Ein Engel berührt das Wasser: *es finden Heilungen durch den Engel und das Holz statt.*	8b	-------
8c	Beim Herannahen der Passion schwimmt das Holz nach oben.	8c	=, bei Johannes gelesen: der Erste, *der bei einer Berührung ins Wasser kommt, genest.*
9a	Die Juden zersägen das Holz, machen daraus das Kreuz.	9a	=
9b	Das Kreuz besteht aus 4 Holzsorten.	9b	=
9c	Die 4 Teile des Kreuzes sind: 1. *senkrechter Teil*, 2. *waagerechter Teil*, 3. *titulus*, 4. *Stamm* (oder, nach Gregorius von Tours: 4. *das Fußbrett*).	9c	Die 4 Teile des Kreuzes sind: 1. *Stamm*, 2. *senkrechter Teil*, 3. *waagerechter Teil*, 4. *titulus*.
10a	Erklärung von dem, was der Apostel (Paulus) in seinem Brief an die Epheser meint (3:18): 'Gewurzelt und gegründet in die Liebe, werdet ihr dann, zusammen mit allen Heiligen, verstehen können, wie groß die Breite und Länge und Höhe und Tiefe ist'.	10a	-------
10b	Augustinus erklärt Eph. 3:18: 'die Breite: daran waren die Arme ausgebreitet, die Länge: daran hing der Körper, die Höhe: über dem Querholz, da hing sein Haupt, die Tiefe: unter der Erde, wo das Kreuz in den Boden ging'.	10b	-------

2 Der Vergleich von *Le* mit *LD*

Beide Texte, *Le* und *LD*, stimmen, vom Anfang abgesehen, in manchem überein, obwohl auch andere Erzählungen, wie *NKh*, bei der Bearbeitung von *LD* eine Rolle gespielt haben könnten. In beiden Texten sind die Abweichungen unterstrichen; fehlende Motive sind mit waagerechten Strichen (---) markiert:

	Legenda		**De ligno domini**
1a	-------	1a	Adam wird aus dem Paradies verbannt; Gott hatte ihn wohl das Öl der Barmherzigkeit versprochen [s. *NKh*].
1b	-------.	1b	Adam lässt sich in Hebron nieder: Adam und Eva bekommen 30 Söhne und 70 Töchter, neben Kain und Abel [s. *R* (1036ff): 30 Söhne und 30 Töchter].
2	-------	2	Die Geschichte von Kain und Abel [s. *NKh* und *R* (791f. und 845-872)].
3	-------	3	Nach 100 Jahren erkennt Adam Eva aufs Neue: Seth wird geboren [s. *NKh* und *R* (835ff.)].
4a	Als Adam 930 Jahre <u>alt ist</u>, ruft er <u>Eva und seine Söhne, um sie auf seinen Tod vorzubereiten</u>.	4a	Als Adam 932 Jahre in <u>Hebron gelebt hat</u>, ruft er <u>Seth</u> .... [s. *NKh* und andere Fassungen].
4b	Adam will das Öl der Barmherzigkeit und erklärt Seth den Weg ins Paradies: wiederzuerkennen an den verdorrten Fußspuren.	4b	=
5a	Seth hört vom Engel im Paradies, dass das Öl erst nach 5228 Jahren gegeben wird; Chr. wird Adam aus der Hölle erlösen und ihn taufen.	5a	------- [s. aber *LD* 16]
5b	Der Engel sagt zu Seth, an der Pforte des Paradieses hinein zu schauen.	5b	=
5c	Seth sieht einen Brunnen mit 4 Strömen, einen kahlen Baum, die Schlange, oben im Baum ein kind (= Gottes Sohn), an den Wurzeln die Seele von <u>Abel</u>.	5c	= , an den Wurzeln befindet sich aber die Seele von <u>Kaïn</u>.

5d	Der Engel gibt 3K: Seth soll sie bei Adams Tod in dessen Mund legen; daraus werden wachsen: 1. Zeder (= Vater), 2. Zipresse (= Sohn), 3. Kiefer (= heiliger Geist).	5d	=
6	Adam wird begraben im Hebrontal.	6	Adam freut sich und lacht [s. *NHk*]; Seth begräbt Adam in Hebron.
7	Die 3K werden 3G; sie bleiben unverändert, bis Moses kommt.	7	Die 3K wachsen 1 Elle hoch, [s. *NKh*] bis Noach kommt, bis zu den Tagen von Abraham und bis Moses kommt.
8a	Moses findet die 3G, begrüßt sie im Namen der Dreieinigkeit, zieht sie aus.	8a	Moses kommt [nach dem Durchzug durch das Rote Meer] in Hebron, findet die 3G, erkennt sie an und zieht sie aus.
8b	Die Kraft der 3G lässt süßes Wasser aus einem Felsen strömen.	8b	Moses wickelt die 3G in pure Seide, legt sie in ein Kästchen; und alles, was in die Nähe kommt, wird gesund.
8c	Moses pflanzt die 3G auf den Berg Tabor und stirbt.	8c	=
8d	-------	8d	Die 3G stehen dort 1000 Jahre.
9a	-------	9a	David erhält im Traum von einem Engel den Auftrag, nach Tabor zu gehen [s. *NKh*].
9b	David findet die 3G auf dem Berg Tabor, bringt sie nach Jerusalem; unterwegs gibt es Heilungen.	9b	=
9c	Die 3G wachsen aneinander.	9c	=
9d	Jedes Jahr schlägt David einen silbernen Ring um den Baum.	9d	=
9e	Unter dem Baum komponiert David Psalmen und beweint seine Sünden.	9e	David liest unter dem Baum seinen Psalter und beweint seine Sünden.
9f	David beginnt mit dem Tempelbau.	9f	David will einen Tempel bauen, darf das aber nicht [s. *NKh*].
10a	Salomo baut den Tempel, der Baum wird umgehauen, das Holz ändert dauernd seine Länge.	10a	=
10b	Das Holz wird zur Verehrung in den Tempel gestellt; oder: über dem Türpfosten befestigt, zur Verehrung.	10b	= (ohne die zweite Variante)
11a	Eine Frau, Maximilla, setzt sich auf das Holz, fängt Feuer; sie prophezeit.	11a	=
11b	Maximilla wird außerhalb der Stadt gesteinigt.	11b	= , sie war die erste Märtyrerin.

12a	Das Holz wird in einen Sumpf begraben (= *piscina probatica*).	12a	=
12b	Ein Engel berührt das Wasser und gibt ihm heilende Kraft.	12b	= , aber der Engel kommt <u>jeden Tag</u>.
13	Die Juden holen das Holz aus dem Wasser: es dient als Brücke.	13	=
14	Sibilla (KvS) kommt, verehrt das Holz und <u>prophezeit</u>.	14	Sibilla, Königin vom Osterland, kommt und verehrt das Holz.
15	Das Holz bleibt da unehrenvoll liegen bis zum Moment, dass die Juden daraus ein Kreuz machen.	15	=
16	-------	16	Der Baum trägt Frucht; das Holz gab Adam und der ganzen Menschheit das Öl der Barmherzigkeit [s. *NKh*].

LEHRER UND PROPHETEN IM LUZERNER OSTERSPIEL

von Elly Vijfvinkel — Rotterdam

1. Einleitung

Die drei Hauptgattungen der mittelalterlichen Literatur, Epik, Lyrik und Drama, kennen einen vergleichbaren Überlieferungsstand. Von allen Vertretern dieser Gattungen sind in den meisten Fällen mehrere handschriftliche Fassungen aus unterschiedlichen Zeiten überliefert. Vorliegende Betrachtungen beziehen sich auf das Luzerner Osterspiel, dessen Entwicklungsstufen sich seit dem 15. Jahrhundert verfolgen lassen.

Aus acht Handschriften von einem mittelalterlichen *osterspil* lässt sich ein Passionsspiel rekonstruieren, welches in regelmäßigen Abständen im schweizerischen Luzern aufgeführt wurde, und das als 'Luzerner Osterspiel' (LO) bekannt ist. Die Handschriften, die in der Luzerner Zentralbibliothek zusammen mit anderen auf Spielaufführungen bezogenen Manuskripten aufbewahrt werden, überliefern uns, kurz gefasst, Folgendes: den Spieltext vom 2. Tag für 1545 (45); eine Teilhandschrift vom 1. Spieltag anno 1571 (71); unvollständige Abschriften 1583 (83 und 83a); eine für 1597 bestimmte Textrevision (97); drei Manuskripte, die mit der letzten Aufführung des Spiels 1616 (16) zusammenhängen. Nach unterschiedlichen älteren Teilveröffentlichungen hat Wyss 1967 zum ersten Mal eine vollständige Ausgabe dieses Spiels herausgebracht. Diese erfolgte nach den jeweils ältesten Handschriften für die beiden Spieltage und dabei liegt der Szenengliederung die Aufführungsbeschreibung von 83 zugrunde. Die Ausgabe wurde für diese Arbeit benutzt.

Um 1480 entstand die, erstmals, von Hartl beschriebene und publizierte Handschrift des 'Donaueschinger Passionsspiels' (DP).[1] Auf die großen Ähnlichkeiten der beiden, zwei Spieltage füllenden geistlichen

---

[1] a. Hartl 1942; b. Touber 1985. Diese Ausgabe wurde für diese Studie benutzt.

Dramen hat Dinges schon 1910 (105ff.) hingewiesen. Viele gleich lautende oder fast gleich lautende Textstellen sind vorhanden. Ein auffallender Unterschied zwischen dem Donaueschinger Passionsspiel und den späteren Luzerner Fassungen ist der Umfang. Umfangreicher wurden die Texte namentlich durch Aufnahme neuerer biblischer Ereignisse. Die Beschränkung auf die detaillierte Passion Christi im Donaueschinger Spiel wurde noch durch die franziskanische Umgebung, für die das Spiel gemeint war, geprägt. Das Luzerner Spiel dagegen war ein Produkt der reichen, politisch mächtigen Stadt Luzern, wo die Überprüfung des Textes in den Händen des etablierten Stadtklerus lag.

Das Surplus an Textumfang verdankt das 'Luzerner Osterspiel' zum Teil den alttestamentlichen Szenen, Propheten- und Lehrersprüchen. Alttestamentliche Szenen und Lehrersprüche finden sich nicht, Prophetensprüche weniger im 'Donaueschinger Passionsspiel'. Beide Spiele, nicht unwichtig für die Forschung, gehen wohl auf ein unbekanntes Luzerner Spiel zurück und haben sich selbständig weiter entwickelt (1986: 86, 107). Das Stemma könnte folgendermaßen aussehen:

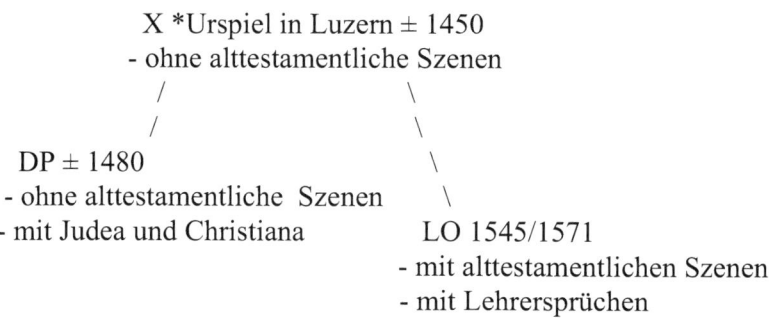

Die Luzerner Entwicklung lässt sich anhand der verschiedenen Textüberlieferungen weiter verfolgen.

Unsere Studie hat den Textzuwachs durch Sprechtexte, oder Sprüche, der Lehrer, auch Kirchenväter genannt, und die der Propheten zum Gegenstand. Die Forschung kann in diesem Fall aus reicher, wenn auch nicht immer erschlossener Überlieferung schöpfen. Dank dem fleißigen Regisseur, Dokumentensammler Cysat, der von 1575 bis 1614 Luzerner Stadtschreiber war, blieb Material erhalten, das uns viele Belege für die Spielentwicklung bietet (Evans 1961: 39). Erwähnenswert in unserem Zusammenhang ist MS. 167 I.fol.5r-15v von Hans Salat, Spielleiter für 1538. Weiter sind die Textrevisionen von Zacharias Bletz, der 1545 und 1561 Spielleiter war, und von Renward Cysat, Regisseur 1583, 1597, teils 1571 von Bedeutung. Evans (1961: 68) meint, dass das Alttestamentliche und die Pro- und Epiloge der Lehrer möglicherweise schon um 1500 zum Luzerner Spiel gehörten; ein Rodel der Luzerner Bekrönungsbruderschaft, welche für Spielaufführungen mitverantwortlich war, erwähnt nämlich Beträge für Requisiten, die mit dem Paradies zusammenhängen. Auch die Listen (Evans 1961: 174ff.) von Hans Salat führen Spielernamen und Requisiten auf, die alttestamentliche Szenen und die *leerer* betreffen.

2. Lehrer

Die auftretenden „leerer", Ambrosius, Augustinus, Gregorius, Jeronimus und Chrisostomus, unterrichten am Anfang oder Ende einer Spielszene u.a. über noch nicht oder schon Gespieltes. Ein Beispiel zeigt, wie Augustinus in seinem Spruch, Anfang Actus 7, rückwärts auf den Auszug aus Ägypten schaut, V.2144-2148: *Ir hand gesehen mitt figuren,/Wie Moyses zeigtt sim schwäher an/Die gnad, so inen gott hatt than,/Vnd sy durch sin göttliche hand/Erlößt, gfürtt vß Egipttenland* und auch vorwärts auf die David- und Goliathgeschichte, V. 2182-2184: *Ir werdend ouch harnach vernän,/Wie Dauid ein grossen Risen mitt fuog/Durch Gottes krafftt zuo tod erschluog.* In der ältesten uns bekannten Luzerner Textüberlieferung, 45, steht ein Kirchenväterspruch jeweils am Ende einer Szene, später, in 71 und 83, besonders im ersten Teil des ganzen Spieltextes, ist der Platz am Anfang einer Szene auch üblich (Wyss 1967: I, 27). Wo die Einschübe anfangs platziert wurden, lässt sich ohne dazwischen liegende Überlieferungen und ohne Berücksichtigung der möglichen andern Vorlagen schwer bestimmen. Die Stadt Luzern kennt eine lange Tradition in der Manuskriptbearbeitung.

Es ist nicht bekannt welche Vorlagen genau der damalige Bearbeiter Bletz bei der Vorbereitung für die Aufführungen von 1545 und 1560 benutzte (Wyss 1967: I, 16). Man kann nicht ausschließen, dass er außer Osterspielhandschriften auch andere Manuskripte zurate ziehen konnte.

Der neben den vier lateinischen Kirchenvätern einzig griechische Lehrer, Chrysostomus, tritt ab 83 auf und wird 97 wieder aus dem Spiel entfernt (Evans 1961: 128 und Wyss 1967: III, 195, Anm. 531). Offensichtlich haben sich die Bearbeiter der Handschrift 45, möglich für die Aufführung vom Jahre 1545, am meisten mit den Lehrersprüchen und deren Sprechern befasst. Diese älteste Textüberlieferung weist in zwei von sechs Lehrersprüchen Korrekturen, zugleich auch Umbenennungen auf. Der zweite Spruch vom 2. Spieltag, V. 6349-6384, wird Augustinus in den Mund gelegt. Vielleicht von Bletz selbst (Wyss 1967: I, 13-25) wurde die Namensänderung vor V. 6349 vorgenommen: „Augustinus" ersetzt gestrichenes „Ambrosius". In derselben Spruchüberschrift wurde auch schon „Gregorius" gestrichen. Letzteres geschah auch im Laufe dieses Spruches neben V. 6356: „Augustinus" unter gestrichenem „Gregorius". Der, soweit uns bekannt, ursprüngliche Lehrer Gregorius wird durch Augustinus ersetzt. Weil von Ambrosius in diesem Actus sonst nicht die Rede ist, deutet das gestrichene Ambrosius eher auf einen Schreibfehler als auf Umbenennung hin. Ein solcher Abschreibfehler könnte mit dem vorhergehenden Actus, Lehrerspruch V. 6293-6308, der Ambrosius zugewiesen wurde, zusammenhängen.

Der dritte Lehrerspruch, V. 6639-6700, wurde dem Chrisostomos zuerteilt. Vor V. 6639 wurde Jeronimus gestrichen. Dieses Wegstreichen blieb im Verlauf des Spruches zweimal unterlassen, so dass am linken Rande neben V. 6646 und neben V. 6676, nicht zu Recht, Jeronimus stehen geblieben ist. Die vielen Änderungen und die Abweichungen in der Schreibweise in Hs 45 lassen auf mehrere Kopisten zu Bletzens Zeit schließen. Umbenennungen dieser Art finden sich nicht in den Lehrersprüchen von 71 - eine Reinschrift - und 83, als Cysat Stadtschreiber und Spielleiter war. In der Teilhandschrift 83, die die gleichen Lehrersprüche wie 71 aufweist, verschrieb sich der Kopist einmal und hat man in der Spruchüberschrift vor V. 629 Ambrosius, das A ausgenommen, mit Augustinus überklebt.

Auf der Bühne haben diese Lehrer, abweichend von den andern Spielern, einen festen Platz am Katheder. Die Bühnenanweisungen 71 vor V. 105: *GREGORIUS Enmitten im platz, stat in einem sonderbaren, harzuo gerüsten Cantzel oder stand, wol oben har under dem Paradys gestellt, den tragt man fürher, so offt ein Leerer reden sol, dann die Leerer gand nit am platz vmbher.* Blakemore Evans (1961: 192 und

Wyss 1967: III, 195, Anm. 531) berichtet von Quellen, die uns über Bekleidung dieser Lehrer informieren. Sie gehen wie hohe Geistliche gekleidet, haben ein Buch in der Hand und werden von einem Knaben begleitet.

Der Donaueschinger Proclamatorspruch, DP V. 24-59 kommt fast wörtlich in Luzern V. 21-57 vor. Große Übereinstimmung weisen die Verse DP 60-81, über Judenschuld, Christi Wunderzeichen, das Leiden und das Sterben für uns, mit LO V. 77-96 auf. Die dazwischen liegenden Verse 57-76 in LO kündigen die Paradiesszene und Gottes Menschwerdung an, welche beide in DP nicht vorkommen. Ein Beispiel mag den Mehrtext der Luzerner Fassung illustrieren. DP V. 57-59: *vnd betrachten sin biter sterben vnd liden/das er für vns geliten hat/durch der valschen iuden rat* und LO V. 54-65: *Betrachtten das bitter stärben vnd lyden,/Das alles Jesus gelitten hatt/Für vns, die sünder, durch fallschen Raat/der Juden, wie der Christlich gloub ertreit./Die heilig gschrifft dasselb gar grundtlich seit,/Wie anfangs Gott Adam vnd Eua schuoff,/Alls ir nun hörend nach minem ruoff/Vnd sähen werden, wie mitt sondrem flyß/Gott vatter sy satztt inns Paradys/Vnd wie sy brachend das gebott,/So inen gab der ewig Gott./Darumb sy vß dem Paradyß vertriben.* LO gibt einen Hinweis auf die Bibel, deren Inhalt hier dramatisiert wird. Zugleich stellt die Erwähnung vom Paradies eine Verbindung zu dem Wesen der Leidensgeschichte her. Im Paradies entstand ja die Sünde der Welt, die Christus auf sich nahm und die zu dessen Erlösungstod, zur Klimax des Spiels führt. Alttestamentliches wird in LO als essenzielle Ursache, fehlend in DP, der neutestamentlichen Folge hinzugefügt.

Die letzten Spruchverse, LO 97-104, beinhalten einen Aufruf zum Gebet und eine Bitte ans Publikum, am Platz zu bleiben und sich das, was zu Ehren Gottes gespielt wird, anzusehen. Nach dem Proclamatorspruch in DP fängt das Spiel mit der Szene „Weltleben der Maria Magdalena" an; der 1. Spieltag. In LO folgt der Lehrerspruch von Gregorius.

LO 71/83 eröffnet den 1. Spieltag mit, der Reihe nach, dem Schildknappen, dem Fähnrich, dem Proclamator und Gregorius' Lehrerspruch. Die Verse des Proclamatorspruchs 57-66, die, wie schon bemerkt, DP nicht aufweist, beziehen sich auf die Schöpfung und die Vertreibung aus dem Paradies, Alttestamentliches also. Ähnliches wird im Gregoriusspruch wiederum erwähnt.[2] Die Verse 67-76 vom Proclamator nehmen Bezug auf den darzustellenden Englischen Gruß, auf Jesu Menschwerdung und Jesu Kreuzestod für uns. Gregorius kündigt dies nicht im erwähnten Lehrerspruch an. Auf den Englischen Gruß und die Geburt Jesu jedoch, Neutestamentliches also, greift er zurück in seinem Prolog von Actus 14, schon ziemlich weit im Spiel. Den Kreuzestod erwähnt er an dieser Stelle nicht. Während der Darstellung der alttestamentlichen Szenen weisen die Lehrersprüche, ausgenommen Gregorius Actus 6, auf den Tod Christi hin. Die neutestamentlichen Darstellungen werden noch nicht angekündigt. Gregorius als einziger spricht in der Einleitung zum ganzen Spiel vom Englischen Gruß und von der Geburt Christi, die zweifellos einen Höhepunkt bilden, ohne den der Erlösungstod, die Klimax, nicht möglich gewesen wäre. Die übrigen Lehrersprüche, die es vor der neutestamentlichen Stoffdarstellung gibt, deuten auf den Tod Christi voraus und bilden damit einen gewissen Leitfaden.

Der Proclamatorspruch ist in sowohl DP als auch LO vorhanden. Geht man von der Annahme, dass LO eine Weiterentwicklung von einer DP-ähnlichen Vorlage war, aus, so führt die Aufnahme alttestamentlichen Stoffes erwartungsgemäß zu einer Anpassung des Proclamatorspruches. Ebenfalls führte Erweiterung mit Lehrersprüchen zu weiteren Änderungen hinsichtlich einer Vorlage, wie z.B. in der Szenenfolge (Vijfvinkel 1990: 111-116). Der Gregoriusspruch nach der Grablegung Christi in LO V. 9572-9681 hängt zusammen mit dem Fehlen der Streitgespräche zwischen Judea und Christiana vom DP-Text (Vijfvinkel 2005: 199-208). Die Disputationen I und II mit ihrem kämpferischen Charakter gibt es nicht im Luzerner Spiel, stattdessen jedoch fasst Gregorius den Weg zum Kreuzestod zusammen und bereitet er die Erlösung der Menschheit durch die Auferstehung vor.

Die Lehrersprüche greifen nicht alle auf eine vorangehende Szene zurück. Augustinus, 2. Tag, Actus 4, zum Beispiel, erwähnt Lazarus' Auferweckung, Actus 1, aber nicht die Judenberatung, Actus 3. Chrisostomos, 2. Tag, Actus 9, jedoch, hat wohl Mitteilungen über die

---

[2] Der Platz der Schöpfung ist in der Reihenfolge beim Spruch des Gregorius, beim Spruch des Pater Aeternus und in der Bibel, die gleiche. Die Ungenauigkeit, die Wyss (1967: III, 192, Anm. 105-210) erwähnt, bezieht sich auf die Zahlen am linken Rande 83. Sie ist m.E. Verzählung oder Nachlässigkeit, die bei Verwendung und Verarbeitung verschiedener Handschriften entstehen konnte.

Judenberatung von Actus 8 gemacht. In 71 und 83, 1. Spieltag, eröffnen die Lehrersprüche die Szenen 1–8 und 14; sie kündigen jeweils deren Inhalt an. In den übrigen Lehrerepilogen an beiden Spieltagen ist es kein festes Prinzip, die nächste Szene anzukündigen. Und nur für Actus 10 [27], Emmauspilger, gilt, dass sich dafür weder eine vorausdeutende noch eine rückblickende Bemerkung in irgendwelchem Lehrerspruch finden lässt.

Verhältnismäßig wenig wird in einem Lehrerspruch das Publikum zur Danksagung aufgefordert. Man soll dankbar für Christi Opfer- oder Kreuzestod und die Erlösung sein. Eine zusätzliche Dimension, Belehrung in der Danksagung, stellen wir in Actus 4, 2. Tag fest, wo Lazarus' Gastmahl dargestellt wird. In dieser Szene stellt Augustinus in seinem Epilog den Zuschauern Lazarus als konkretes Beispiel, dem sie folgen sollen, hin. Mit dem Mahl will Lazarus den Dank für seine Auferweckung, hier wird auf Actus 1, 2. Tag zurückgegriffen, zum Ausdruck bringen. Man kann in diesen Worten des Augustinus eine Antizipierung auf Christi Auferstehung heraushören. In diesem Lehrerspruch sind Belehrung, Danksagung, Rückwendung und Vorausdeutung eng miteinander verwoben.

Man wird in diesen Sprüchen auch über den Opfertod belehrt. Es zeigt sich, dass allgemein christliche Werte von den auftretenden Kirchenvätern aufgeführt werden. *„Bereut die Sünden"*, *„betrachtet das Leiden"*, *Christi Opfertod* und *ewiges Leben* sind bei diesen *Leerern* die wichtigsten Parolen. Daneben wird z.B. über den Wert der Demut oder über Judenbestrafung unterrichtet. Im Ambrosiusspruch V. 7208-7250 fällt eine Warnung vor Gotteslästerung und Schwören auf. Diese belehrende Bemerkung stammt wohl vom Kopisten, Bletz, her (Wyss 1967: III, 216, Anm. 7208-7250) und bezieht sich auf die Gesellschaft und Gewohnheiten zur Zeit der Aufführung des Spieles in Luzern.

Die Lehrersprüche von Actus 2 bis einschließlich Actus 8 vom 1. Spieltag verarbeiten Präfigurationen. Der Chrisostomusspruch, der den alttestamentlichen Teil abschließt, erwähnt eine Reihe davon und sogar mehr als im Spiel selbst dargestellt wurden. Nur einmal am 2. Spieltag gibt ein *Leerer* eine vorwegnehmende Darstellung. Augustinus erwähnt V. 6369 ff. den alttestamentlichen Zachariastext über den Einzug in Jerusalem und kündigt damit zugleich auch die nächste Szene „Christi Einzug in Jerusalem",Actus 5, an.

Das Luzerner Osterspiel und das Donaueschinger Passionsspiel gleichen sich in so hohem Maße, dass eine gemeinsame Vorlage unverkennbar ist. Durch ihre jeweilige Weiterentwicklung sind zwischen den Spielen Unterschiede entstanden. Die Aufnahme der Pro- und Epiloge der „Leerer" in das Luzerner Osterspiel hat die Aufgabe des Passionsspiels, Gott zu loben und ehren, unterstützt.

3. Propheten

Chrysostomus, der Lehrer, LO vor V. 2403, *„Beschlüßt das Allt Testament vnd facht damitt das nüw an."* In Chrysostomus' Rede zum Publikum beim Übergang von den alttestamentlichen zu den neutestamentlichen Szenen werden, LO V. 2493-2496, fünf Weissager angekündigt: *"Kurtz zeigend die Fünff propheten an,/Was wytter sol mercken wyb vnd man,/ Dem nüwen Testamentt zum yngang,/ Mitt wenig wortten, nitt zuo lang."* Für das Auftreten der fünf Propheten, *Malachias, Isayas, Jeremias, Ezechiel* und *Micheas* V. 2511-2568, und für Jesajas Auftritt nach Christi Geburt fehlen Entsprechungen in DP. Vermutet wird (Evans 1961: 68), dass die Lehrersprüche und die alttestamentlichen Szenen schon 1500 im Spiel vorhanden waren: Gilt dies aber auch für diese fünf Propheten? Sie sind im Spielplan für 1583 belegt (Evans 1961: 41). Die Liste von Hans Salat, 1538, für Bekleidung liefert uns Hinweise für „prophetische" Kleidung von nur *Esaya* und *Jeremias*. Salats Spielerliste für den Einzug (Evans 1961: 161) am 1. Spieltag führt *ii propheten* - wie auch für den 2. Spieltag, die Vorhölle – auf. Am 2. Spieltag treten sowohl in DP, einer Vorstufe für die Luzerner Textüberlieferungen, als auch in dem Luzerner Spiel, Jesaja und Jeremia in der Vorhölleszene auf. Nicht unwichtig ist hier der Verweis auf die Bibel in der Regiebemerkung zwischen LO V. 9871-9872: „*Hie söllend die personen in der vorhell nach der ordnung der bibel reden...".* In LO erscheint dieses Duo obendrein zusammen mit den drei andern als Weissager am 1. Spieltag. Immerhin bilden Jesaja und Jeremia seit 1538 den belegten Kern der Prophetengruppe. Ob die übrigen Weissager zugleich mit dem Kernduo in LO aufgenommen wurden, lässt sich nicht nachweisen.

In den Regiebemerkungen zwischen LO V. 2504 und V. 2505 werden, so wie in Chrysostomos' Rede, der *„ANFANG DEß NÜWEN TESTAMENTS"* und die Propheten, *„...Kommend die Propheten, ye einer nach dem andern fürher vnd redendt zum volck, gand Am platz* *vmbher.*" angekündigt. Diesen Bühnenanweisungen entnehmen wir auch, dass die Propheten, im Gegensatz zu den *„Leerern"*, die an einem Pult stehen, auf der Bühne umhergehen. Nach diesem Auftritt verlassen die Propheten die Bühne und machen sie diese für *Pater Aeternus* und Engel *Gabriel*, für die Annunziations- und Geburtsszene frei.

Etwas weiter im Spieltext (Wyss 1967: I,200), vor LO V. 2777, tritt der Prophet Jesaja auf: *„Isayas mitten Am platz zum volck".* Dieser bestätigt, V. 2777-2784, die Geburt des Kindes von der erwählten reinen Jungfrau und kündigt dann auch die Erlösung an, LO 71 und 83. Die Bibel jedoch überlässt im Neuen Testament einem Engel die Aufgabe, von der Geburt zu berichten. Genau betrachtet also ist Jesaja hier fehl am Platz. Die späteren LO-Handschriften, 97 und 16 (Wyss 1967: III, 202, Anm. 2777-84), haben das Spiel in biblischem Sinne berichtigt und Jesaja durch einen Engel ersetzt. Hier fällt wiederum noch genauere Anlehnung an die Bibel auf.

Zwei von den fünf Propheten, Jesaja und Jeremia, werden - hier stimmt der LO-Text mit dem DP-Textüberein - am 2. Spieltag in der Vorhölleszene von dem erstandenen Christus gerettet.

In LO prophezeien am Anfang der neutestamentlichen Szenen die fünf Weissager, dass die Jungfrau Maria den Erlöser in Bethlehem gebären wird. Für diese Sprüche sind Belege in den entsprechenden Bibelbüchern vorhanden.

Dem ersten Propheten,[3] *Malachias*, „mein Bote", wurde vom Geist Gottes offenbart, wann Christi Geburt sein wird und dass jeder sich auf Gottes Wegbereiter einstellen soll, LO V. 2511-2518. Das Bibelbuch Maleachi, das viele Drohungen an Israel und die Lehre, die Menschen sollen sich bereit machen für den Tag des Herrn, enthält, wird dem Publikum vermittelt.

Isayas, der als zweiter auftritt, teilt aus dem Inhalt des Bibelbuches Jesaja, die Verheißung Gottes, dem Volk ein Zeichen zu geben, mit, V. 2521. Das Zeichen, das gemeint wird, ist die jungfräuliche Geburt Christi, zum Trost der Menschheit.

Der Personifikation des Bibelbuches Jeremias, *Jeremias*, V. 2529-2544, hat Gott eine Prophezeiung bekannt gemacht, die die Geburt des

---

[3] Die Reihenfolge der Propheten im Spiel weicht ab von der der Bibelbücher Jesaja, Jeremia, Hesekiel, Micha und Maleachi. Vgl. Young 1933: I,125 ff.

gerechten Königs aus dem Geschlecht Davids, zur Seligkeit des Volkes, betont.

Eine Präfiguration der jungfräulichen Geburt lesen wir im Spruch des *Ezechiel*. Das Bild – porta clausa - des verschlossenen Tores, LO V. 2545-2556, durch das nur Gott ein- und ausgehen darf, stimmt mit der Bibel, Hesekiel 44, überein.

Der fünfte Weissager, *Micheas*, LO V. 2556-2568, verkündigt, wie Gottes Freund Micha, in dem so benannten Bibelbuch, Kapitel 5, den Heiland und teilt mit, dass Gott Bethlehem als Geburtsort auserwählt hat.

Den Sprüchen dieser Propheten im Spiel liegen also alttestamentliche Prophezeiungen, die auf die, ebenfalls in LO dargestellte Geburt Christi hinweisen, zu Grunde. Die fünf bereiten die Annunziation und Geburt Christi vor, die nach ihrem Bühnenabgang in demselben Auftritt gespielt wird. Mit Hesekiels präfigurierendem Bild und mit ihren Voraussagen, lassen die Weissager die alttestamentlichen Darstellungen in die des neutestamentlichen Teiles übergehen. Der in der Bibel verankerte Spieltext belehrt das zuschauende Publikum zu gleicher Zeit über den Wert dieser Geburt. Über Christus also, der der Menschheit zum Trost und zur Seligkeit geboren wird, derselbe, der später, ebenfalls im Spiel dargestellt, den Erlösungstod stirbt und damit endgültig die Weissagung erfüllt.

4. Zusammenfassung

Die bibelgetreuen Prophetensprüche bilden in LO einen passenden Übergang von den alt- zu den neutestamentlichen Szenen. Sie kündigen die direkt bevorstehende Geburt Christi an und lenken zu gleicher Zeit die Aufmerksamkeit auf dieses Ereignis, das von großer Bedeutung ist für den Hauptzweck des Passionsspiels, das Publikum über den Erlösungstod zu belehren.

Die Prophetengruppe verstärkt mit den Prophezeiungen die vorangehenden, präfigurierenden alttestamentlichen Szenen, den neutestamentlichen gegenüber. Zur Belehrung des Publikums ist die Darstellung von biblischer Prophezeiung und deren Erfüllung ein visuelles Mittel bei der Vermittlung von Bibelstoff.

Aufnahme von neuem Spielstoff hat Änderungen hinsichtlich einer potenziellen Textvorlage zur Folge. Neue Namen treten auf und andere Zusammenhänge entstehen. Die hier behandelten Luzerner Erweiterungen, die Lehrer- und Prophetensprüche, verstärken durch ihren didaktischen Wert und dramatischen Charakter die Aufgabe und Wirkung einer Passionsspielaufführung im Mittelalter. Das Publikum soll durch die dargestellte Heilsgeschichte im Glauben an Gott und die Erlösung durch dessen Sohn Christus gestärkt und dabei auch zum Lob Gottes angeregt werden.

Wie im Sinne des übrigen Spieltextes sind alle Lehrersprüche in der Tat zur Belehrung des Publikums gemeint. Der didaktische Weg führt über die verschiedenen biblischen Werte zu der Bedeutung von dem Kreuzestod Christi. Die Sprüche der Kirchenväter weisen Präfigurationen auf, wie sie auch für das Spiel, in das diese „Leerer" eingeschoben wurden, kennzeichnend sind, sie deuten Kommendes voraus und greifen auf das, was gespielt wurde zurück, verarbeiten jedoch nicht alle den Spielstoff in gleicher Weise und nach demselben Aufbau. Die meisten dieser Sprüche geben einen Hinweis auf die Passionsklimax, den Erlösungstod.

Die Propheten, umhergehend auf der Bühne, betonen in ihren Texten die Geburt des Erlösers, als unumgängliches Ereignis auf dem Weg zum Hauptziel. Sie übernehmen u.a. die Präfiguration von Hesekiels Bild des verschlossenen Tores und weisen eine, dem Luzerner Osterspiel kennzeichnende Bibeltreue auf. Durch diese Propheten wird Alttestamentliches kunstvoll mit Neutestamentlichem verknüpft und verläuft der Übergang von Szenen der Voraussagung zu Szenen der Erfüllung fließend.

Durch die Lehrer, die an einem Pult unterrichtend, retrospektiv und antizipierend auftreten, werden mittels ihrer Sprüche verschiedene Szenen des 1. und 2. Spieltags verbunden.

Das Luzerner Osterspiel bildet mit den verarbeiteten Erweiterungen eine Einheit im Aufbau und liefert einen Beitrag zum frommen Unterricht und zur Erbauung des Publikums im Sinne des traditionellen Glaubens. Denn hier lässt sich ebenfalls, wie schon früher festgestellt wurde (Touber 2004: 267-268 und 271-272; Vijfvinkel 1986 und 2005; Vijfvinkel 1994: 384; Vijfvinkel 2001: 332 und 340-41), eine Tendenz herauslesen, die Luzerner, alte Religionsauffassung der neuen gegenüber, standhaft zur Schau zu tragen. Die Reformation, nach der die Bibel die einzige Glaubensquelle war, bedeutete sicherlich eine Drohung für das großartige Spiel der Stadt Luzern: Calvins Verbot des religiösen Dramas, Luthers Billigung der biblischen Dramen nur aus moralischen Motiven und, besonders nahe in Zürich, der Reformator Zwingli, der sich gegen die religiöse Kunst äußerte. Zwar waren die alttestamentlichen Texterweiterungen zusammen mit den Lehrersprüchen vermutlich schon 1500 im Spiel vorhanden (Evans 1961: 68), aber sie konnten in späteren Bearbeitungen gut verwendet werden. Die *Leerer* unterrichteten am Pult aus der ganzen Heiligen Schrift. Im Proclamatorspruch *Die heilig gschrifftt dasselb gar grundtlich seit*, LO V. 58, wird schon auf die biblische Basis des Spiels hingewiesen. Diese Betonung der Bibel als Quelle nähert sich dem Prinzip der Reformation, dass nur die Bibel als Autorität gilt, an. Man kann in Cysats Heranziehung der katholischen Gegenbibel von Dietenberger[4] - insbesondere für die Spielbearbeitung 97 und 16 - ein Mittel im Streben, dem katholischen Glauben treu zu bleiben, sehen.

Literatur

Dinges 1910: G. Dinges, *Untersuchungen zum Donaueschinger Passionsspiel* (Germanistische Abhandlungen 35), Breslau.
Evans 1961: M. B. Evans, "Das Osterspiel von Luzern". Eine historisch-kritische Einleitung. Übers. des engl. Orig.-Textes [von 1943] von Paul Hagmann, in: *Schweizer Theater-Jahrbuch 27*.
Hartl 1942: E. Hartl (Hrsg.), *Das Donaueschinger Passionsspiel*, Leipzig (Reprogr. Nachdr. Darmstadt 1966).
Touber 1985: Anthonius H. Touber, *Das Donaueschinger Passionsspiel*, Neuausgabe mit Einleitung und Kommentar, Stuttgart.
— 2004: Anthonius H.Touber. "Passionsspiel und Ikonographie", in: *Ritual und Inszenierung*, Tübingen, 261-272.
Vijfvinkel 1986: Elly Vijfvinkel, *Das Donaueschinger Passionsspiel im Luzerner Osterspiel* (Diss.), Amsterdam.
— 1990: Elly Vijfvinkel, "Die Szenenfolge im Donaueschinger Passionsspiel und im Luzerner Osterspiel", in: *ABäG* 30: 111-116.
— 1994: Elly Vijfvinkel, "Das letzte Abendmahl in dem Donaueschinger Passionsspiel, dem Luzerner Osterspiel und in der Bibel", in: *ABäG* 38-39: 377-

---

[4] Als Luthers Übersetzung des Alten und Neuen Testaments, nach den neuzeitlichen Ansichten aus den ursprünglichen Sprachen, 1534 veröffentlicht wurde, erschien auch die erste Dietenberger Bibelübersetzung. Diese war noch auf die lateinische Vulgata gegründet und es dauerte fast hundert Jahre bis auch eine katholische Bibelrevision, zurückgreifend auf den Urtext, erschien. Vgl. auch Wyss 1967: I, 69; III, 195 Anm. 668; III, 239; III, 250ff.

385.
— 2001: Elly Vijfvinkel, "Die Christusgestalt in der Luzerner Osterspieltradition", in: *Wodan* 79, 331-342.
— 2005: Elly Vijfvinkel, "Die Integration des alten Osterspiels in den mittelalterlichen geistlichen Spielen von Donaueschingen und Luzern", in: *ABäG* 60: 199-208.
Wyss 1967: H. Wyss (Hrsg.), *Das Luzerner Osterspiel*, III Bde, Bern.
Young 1933: Karl Young, *The drama of the Medieval Church*, II Bde, Oxford.

BESPRECHUNGEN

Christian Schneider, *Hovezuht. Literarische Hofkultur und höfisches Lebensideal um Herzog Albrecht III. von Österreich und Erzbischof Pilgrim II. von Salzburg (1365-1396)* (Beiträge zur älteren Literaturgeschichte). Universitätsverlag Winter, Heidelberg 2008. 260 S. (ISBN 978-3-8253-5454-1).

In seiner für den Druck leicht überarbeiteten Heidelberger Dissertation bemüht sich Christian Schneider sehr eindrucksvoll darum, einen kulturhistorischen Ansatz zu verfolgen, um das höfische Lebensideal an den zwei Literaturzentren, Salzburg und Wien, anhand einer sorgfältigen Interpretation eines recht umfangreichen Textcorpus kritisch zu beleuchten. Dabei richtet er sich stark nach den Ergebnissen, die sein Doktorvater Fritz Peter Knapp mit seiner umfangreichen Literaturgeschichte vorgelegt hatte, und kombiniert diese zunächst sehr gelungen mit der jüngeren Diskussion um Norbert Elias' Theorie des Zivilisationsprozesses.

Sowohl unter Herzog Albrecht III. von Österreich (1365-1395) als auch unter Erzbischof Pilgrim II. von Salzburg entfaltete sich in den jeweiligen Städten bzw. an den Höfen eine neue literarisch und auch sonst kulturell hoch gebildete Intellektuellen-Schicht, die offensichtlich, wenn man alle Aspekte zusammennimmt, wie sie sich in der Dichtung jener Zeit finden lassen, wozu auch örtliche Bürgerhäuser und Fresken zu rechnen sind, sich einem neuen Lebensstil verschrieb, der teils religiös, teils weltlich-courtoise ausgerichtet war. Schneider erinnert uns vor allem an die Wiener Schule, die eine volkssprachliche Frömmigkeitstheologie förderte, geht dann auf die Reimspruchdichtung Peter Suchenwirts und Heinrichs des Teichners ein, zieht auch die Wiener Neidhart-Tradition zur Unterstützung heran, um mit einem Ausblick auf die Weltchronik Heinrichs von München zu enden. In Salzburg dominierte hingegen der berühmte Mönch von Salzburg, wozu noch die *Erweiterte Christherre-Chronik* zu rechnen ist.

Schneider entwickelt auf der Grundlage dieses Überblicks, der zugleich gut historisch untermauert ist, Überlegungen zur Entwicklung einer Hofkultur, die städtisch verankert war. Zunächst identifiziert er das Konzept der Selbstvergewisserung und Identität, mithin der Selbsterkenntnis, dann dasjenige der Selbstdisziplinierung und sozialen Kontrolle, was alles auf die zentrale Idee der *zuht* und *sitichait* hinzielt, also eine Form der verinnerten Selbstdisziplin, die nach außen strahlt und das Zusammenleben in der Gemeinschaft bestimmt. Das entscheidende Instrumentarium, um diese Form der Zivilisation zu realisieren, besteht in der Erfahrung von *scham*, was sich freilich als Idee schon durch die ganze mhd. Literatur zieht und gar nicht ein wirklich innovatives Element aus dem späten 14. Jahrhundert sein dürfte. Dass diese Form der intensivierten Hofkultur sowohl in Wien als auch in Salzburg zu entdecken ist, wäre nicht zu bezweifeln, aber man fragt sich doch, worin der Unterschied zwischen der Welt des 12./13. und des 14. Jahrhunderts bestehen soll. Schneider weist u.a. darauf hin, dass der Körper nun als mögliches Opfer der geistigen Unreinheit (Sünde) erschien, dass die Dichter bzw. Autoren auf die Zusammenführung von Sein und Schein insistierten (außen und innen), danach drängten, die "moralische und gesellschaftliche Integrität einer Person" (131) zu erreichen und sorgfältig zwischen notwendiger diplomatischer Verhaltensweise einerseits und Heuchelei und falscher Schmeichelei andererseits zu unterscheiden. Weiterhin betonten die Autoren, wie sehr ein öffentlich tragbares Verhalten der zwei Geschlechter vonnöten sei, um die Verfallserscheinungen der Zeit zu überwinden, die sich u.a. besonders an der falschen Kritik der Klaffer oder *rumœr* an Frauen zu erkennen gebe. Letztlich betont z.B. der Mönch in aller Deutlichkeit, wie sehr die erotische Liebe der inneren Aufrichtigkeit bedürfe, was auch die Betonung auf Treue und offene Zuneigungsbekundung einschließe.

Wenn aber Schneider hervorhebt, "Liebe beim Mönch erscheint stets auf Ausschließlichkeit, Beständigkeit, Aufrichtigkeit, Selbstlosigkeit, Dienstbereitschaft angelegt, immer schon gegenseitig und erfüllt zu sein" (167), hätte man gerne gewußt, ob dies tatsächlich eine differenzierte Position reflektiert. Worin besteht denn der Unterschied zur Liebeslehre etwa von Walther von der Vogelweide? Dass überall Klaffer auftreten, überrascht eigentlich auch nicht, aber noch wichtiger als ein möglicher Vergleich mit der klassischen mhd. Dichtung wäre wohl gewesen, das Auftreten dieses Themas in den Liederbüchern des 15. und 16. Jahrhunderts zu verfolgen. Schneiders Ansatz bietet auf jeden Fall viele Anregungen zu weiteren Forschungen (wobei er aber auch eine Reihe wichtiger Arbeiten gerade zum Mönch unterschlagen hat, z.B. Doris Sittig, *Vyl wonders machet minne*, 1987; vielfach Ulrich Müller).

Der wichtigste Aspekt in dieser neuen Hofkultur dürfte in dem Bemühen bestanden haben, zeitgleich sowohl Gott als auch der Welt zu gefallen, d.h. den Körper mit der Seele in Harmonie zu bringen, was jedenfalls am Wiener Hof zur Forderung nach der Kombination von weltlicher Bildung mit innerer Frömmigkeit führte. Die häufig formulierte Zeitkritik (etwa bei den Spruchdichtern) zeigte ebenso auf, wie weit entfernt man von diesem Ideal war, insoweit als viele Höflinge als Versager, als Weichlinge, als Schmeichler oder geldhungrige Menschen erscheinen. Hier wiederholt sich aber zunächst der alte Topos vom Hof als Ort des moralischen und ethischen Verfalls, wie es schon 1985 C. Stephen Jaeger deutlich herausgearbeitet hatte (*Origins of Courtliness*), und andere vor und nach ihm ebenfalls, was jedoch hier nicht berücksichtigt wird. Schneider greift dann auch auf das Konzept des literarischen Spiels zurück, um den wesentlichen Charakter der neuen Hofgesellschaft zu erfassen ("agonales Spiel", 217), was durchaus triftig sein könnte, nur irritiert hier die völlige Nichtbeachtung einschlägiger Forschung (siehe z.B. meine eigenen Studien "Das Spiel mit der Liebe - Leben als Spiel: Versuch einer Neuinterpretation des *Morîz von Craûn*," in: *GRM* 40, 4 [1990]: 369-398; "Erotik als Spiel, Spiel als Leben, Leben als Erotik: Komparatistische Überlegungen zur Literatur des europäischen Mittelalters," *Mediaevistik* 2 [1989]: 7-42; "Minnesang als Spiel. Sinnkonstitution auf dem Schachbrett der Liebe," *Studi Medievali* Serie Terza, XXXVI, 1 [1995]: 211-239). Seine am Ende formulierte These, dass mittels der an den Höfen entstandenen Dichtung Leitwerte geschaffen worden seien, um den eigenen Stand abzusichern, wäre unter Hinweis auf viele höchst kritische Spruchdichtungen des Teichners zu hinterfragen, obwohl Schneiders Überlegung, dass sich sowohl in Wien als auch in

Salzburg (dann aber auch wohl an vielen anderen spätmittelalterlichen, stadtorientierten Höfen) eine neue zivilisatorisch innovative Kulturform entwickelte, durchaus zu unterstützen wäre. Nur scheint hinterfragbar, ob es dabei wirklich um die Ausgrenzung der bürgerlichen Stände ging, vor allem wenn man an die Integration der neuen Intelligentsia in den Verwaltungsapparat denkt.

Damit müssen wir uns auch Schneiders theoretischen Grundlagen zuwenden, denn zu Beginn setzt er sich erfreulich nachvollziehbar und gut verständlich mit den wesentlichen Thesen Norbert Elias', denjenigen C. Stephen Jaegers und den Überlegungen Niklas Luhmanns auseinander. Er wägt ihre Aussagen einsichtig gegeneinander ab, befürwortet aber vor allem Luhmanns Gedanken, dass Literatur "in ihrer Semantik auch als Kommunikationsregulative zu sehen sei" (32), was indirekt am Ende auch auf die Hofkultur in Wien und Salzburg zuzutreffen scheint. Es möge mir aber gestattet sein auf die Tatsache aufmerksam zu machen, dass ich 2002 mit meiner umfangreichen Monographie *Verzweiflung und Hoffnung* wesentlich umfangreicher diesen Gedanken schon verfolgt und anhand vieler wichtiger Texte in der mhd. Literatur expliziert habe, ohne dass hier davon überhaupt ein Wort zu vernehmen wäre. Ich stützte mich vor allem auf Jürgen Habermas, der hier ebenfalls völlig unterschlagen wird. Schneider entwickelt zwar durchweg sehr klug und auf hohem Wissensstand seine Überlegungen, aber wissenschaftsgeschichtlich fliegt er über weite Felder dahin und beansprucht, überall neu zu ackern, wo schon längst sehr viel Saat aufgegangen ist. Ein krasses Beispiel: zwar behandelt er die bedeutende Gruppe der höfischen Unterhalter, kennt aber noch nicht einmal die entscheidende Studie von Maria Dobozy (*Re-Membering the Present: The Medieval German Poet-Minstrel in Cultural Context*, 2005). Vielleicht gibt es aber in Heidelberg keine neueren wissenschaftlichen Arbeiten aus dem nichtdeutschen Bereich? Ein Blick in Schneiders Bibliographie bestätigt nämlich, dass er sich praktisch nur an deutschsprachige Publikationen gehalten hat, und auch dies recht lückenhaft.

Zuletzt muß aber auch die Frage aufgeworfen werden, welche Relevanz seine ganze Diskussion zu Norbert Elias, C. Stephen Jaeger oder Niklas Luhmann für seine Analysen der Texte besitzen mag. Gewiß entdeckt man auch Rüdiger Schnells Sammelband *Zivilisationsprozesse* (2004) in der Literaturliste, aber mit dessen sehr triftigen Kritik an Elias hat sich der Autor praktisch gar nicht auseinandergesetzt. Kann man wirklich von einem Zivilisationsprozeß sprechen? Worin bestehen die Unterschiede zwischen der Welt um 1200 und der um 1400? Wo steht denn nun Schneider hinsichtlich der großen Debatte um Elias und seine Thesen? So klug und verständnisvoll er auch durchweg argumentiert, und dies auf der Basis recht guter Textkenntnisse, bleibt doch der kulturhistorische Ansatz deswegen stecken, weil die zu vergleichenden Parameter nicht mit in die Betrachtung einbezogen werden.

Albrecht Classen

Martin Schuhmann, *Reden und Erzählen. Figurenrede in Wolframs* Parzival *und* Titurel. (Frankfurter Beiträge zur Germanistik, 49). Universitätsverlag Winter, Heidelberg, 2008. 259 S. (ISBN 978=3=8253-5441-1).

Auch wenn die Wolfram-Forschung schon lange und in vielerlei Hinsicht ihre Aufmerksamkeit auf die individuellen Figuren und die Art und Weise ihrer Kommunikation gerichtet hat, bemüht sich Martin Schuhmann in seiner jetzt in den Druck gegebenen Frankfurter Dissertation von 2006, dieses Thema anhand von sorgfältig durchgeführten Analysen umfassender in den Griff zu bekommen. Anhand von Figurenreden lassen sich, wie er sehr nachvollziehbar argumentiert, wichtige Erkenntnisse über inhaltliche Aspekte gewinnen, denn anhand der funktionierenden oder scheiternden Kommunikation vermag man zentrale Aussagen des Textes wahrzunehmen (siehe dazu A. Classen, *Verzweiflung und Hoffnung*, 2002, hier nicht konsultiert). Reden kommen auf vielen verschiedenen Ebenen zum Einsatz, so auf der Handlungsebene, derjenigen des Erzählers und derjenigen der Figuren. Schuhmann strukturiert seine Arbeit dementsprechend in die folgenden Themenfelder: 1. die Beziehung zwischen Rede und Figur, um die Charakterisierung der Figur herauszufinden; 2. die Bedeutung der Figurenrede für die Entwicklung der Handlung, besonders bezogen auf Sigune; 3. die Relevanz von Reden für thematische Aspekte; 4. die Unterschiede in Redegestaltung bei Chrétien und Wolfram, was auch auf wichtige Unterschiede in der inhaltlichen Gestaltung aufmerksam macht; und 5. der Beitrag der Figurenrede für die Entwicklung der Narration.

So sehr man auch dem Autor insgesamt zustimmen muss, hat man auf weite Strecken kaum den Eindruck, dass hier wirklich neue Erkenntnisse angeboten werden. Natürlich wirft die Interpretation der Rede einer Figur wichtiges Licht auf ihren Charakter, aber darf man wirklich behaupten, hier öffnete sich ein noch ganz unbeackertes Feld? Schuhmann argumentiert weiterhin, dass die metrische Gestalt der Redeverse sorgfältig behandelt werden muss, um zu genauen Ergebnissen zu gelangen, dem man auch ohne weiteres zustimmen kann. So widmet er sich der Reimstruktur, dem Enjambement und der Anakoluthie, um darauf endlich konkret in die Arbeit einzusteigen und die unterschiedlichen Redepositionen der zentralen Figuren im Vergleich miteinander herauszukristallisieren oder individuelle Haltungen zu erkennen. Dabei konzentriert er sich auf die Reden Parzivals vs. Gawans, auf diejenigen des jungen Parzivals, dann auf innere Stimmungen und Ängste der Protagonisten, wie sie sich in den Reden spiegeln, und auf Selbstironie. Das längere Kapitel über die Reden der Sigune liest sich zwar durchaus einsichtig, aber der Erkenntniswert ist relativ gering angesichts der bisherigen Forschung. Schuhmann bezieht dann auch Wolframs *Titurel* ein und kann so zusätzliche Perspektiven offenlegen, hat sich aber nur relativ wenig mit der kritischen Literatur zu diesem Text auseinandergesetzt (es fehlen z.B.: A. Classen, *Utopie und Logos*, 1990; A. Sager, *Minne von mæren*, 2006). Er beobachtet insbesondere, was als wertvoll anzusehen wäre, dass die Figurenreden von einer gewissen Krise zeugen und Probleme aufweisen, was natürlich auch durch die inhaltliche Gestaltung mitgeprägt ist. Selbstverständlich redet hier Sigune ganz anders als im *Parzival*, was freilich mit ihrer Jugend und Unerfahrenheit zusammen-

hängt, während sie im *Parzival* vom Tod ihres Geliebten gezeichnet ist.
Schließlich widmet sich Schuhmann der Rede Trevrizents im *Parzival*, die viele innere Widersprüche aufweist und von Spannungen bestimmt wird. Auch die Fürstenrede im *Willehalm* wird noch beachtet, wo der Autor die wichtige Dialektik von antiheidnischer Propaganda und Schonungsgebot betont. Zum Abschluss bietet er einen sehr zu begrüßenden Vergleich zwischen der Figurenrede in Chrétiens *Perceval* und Wolframs *Parzival*, wobei er zum ersten Mal wirklich innovative Perspektiven entwickelt, denn seine Analyse deckt auf, dass der erstere z.B. im Gespräch zwischen Mutter und Sohn den jungen Perceval als einen Menschen zeichnet, der gar nicht richtig zuhört, und der dann bei Jeschute (wie sie Wolfram nennt) geradezu bewusst gegen den Rat seiner Mutter handelt. Wolfram gestaltete das Kommunikationsproblem anders, aber gegen Schuhmann würde ich behaupten, dass Parzival weiterhin erhebliche Probleme aufweist, nur sind diese, wenn auch immer noch kommunikativ bestimmt, anders gelagert. Sogar die Wechselrede zwischen dem Fräulein und ihrem Geliebten ist bei Chrétien anders als bei Wolfram (sie ist z.B. viel ängstlicher), besonders wenn man an die viel erotischere Zeichnung Jeschutes denkt. Man wünschte sich, dass Schuhmann viel stärker in diese Kerbe gehauen hätte, denn erst hier gelangt er zu neuen Einsichten und vermag überzeugend vor Augen zu führen, wie wichtig die genaue Interpretation der Figurenrede für den Vergleich der beiden Texte sein kann. Seine Studie ist jedoch insgesamt zufriedenstellend organisiert, die Argumentation entfaltet sich überzeugend, und gelegentlich vermag der Autor wirklich spannende und neuartige Entdeckungen vorzustellen.

Albrecht Classen

Heinric van Veldeken, *Sente Servas. Mittelniederländisch, Neuhochdeutsch.* Herausgegeben von Jan Goossens, Rita Schlusemann und Norbert Voorwinden mit Stellenkommentar, kritischem Apparat, Namenverzeichnis und Bibliographie (Bibliothek mittelniederländischer Literatur 3). - Agenda Verlag, Münster 2008. 417 S. (ISBN 978-3-89688-332-2). EUR 39,80.

Mit der *Servas*-Ausgabe ist die Reihe der Bibliothek mittelniederländischer Literatur jetzt auf drei Bände angewachsen. Die ersten zwei Bände (*Karel ende Elegast /Karl und Ellegast* und *Reynarts historie*) können als gelungene Ansätze zu einer neuen Auseinandersetzung von deutschsprachigen Lesern mit der mnl. Literatur betrachtet werden. Der vorliegende Band passt ausgezeichnet in diesen Rahmen, denn Heinrich von Veldeke verkörpert wie kein anderer Dichter die Überschneidung der deutschen und niederländischen Literatur. Der *Sente Servas* ist aber nicht nur deshalb eine vorzügliche Wahl. Die Ausgabe – die erste zusammen mit einer nhd. Übersetzung – macht das Stiefkind der Veldeke-Forschung wie nie zuvor einem deutschen Publikum zugänglich.

Obwohl Veldekes *Eneasroman,* vor allem wegen der Überlieferungslage und der sprachlichen Form, als Lieblingsstreitpferd der germanistischen Mittelalterphilologie des 20. Jhs. mehr Aufmerksamkeit auf sich gezogen hat, darf der *Sente Servas* sich in den letzten Jahren eines erhöhten Interesses erfreuen. Neben der vorliegenden mittelniederländisch/neuhochdeutschen Ausgabe wurde bereits 2006 eine zweisprachige Ausgabe mit einer Übersetzung ins Englische vorgelegt, für die Jan Goossens mit einem kurzen Vorwort auch einen bescheidenen Beitrag geliefert hat (Veldeke 2006). Dass diese erneute Beachtung verdient ist, wird nicht nur aus der dramatischen Heiligenlegende selber, sondern auch aus dem Nachwort, das der neuen Ausgabe beigegeben ist, ein für allemal klar. Dort wird der Leser in Hauptzügen auf den letzten Stand der Dinge gebracht und über den Dichter, die literarischen und politischen Hintergründe zum Text, die Stoff- und Editionsgeschichte, sowie die kodikologische Beschaffenheit zum *Servatius* unterrichtet. Die Bibliographie, in der Forschungsliteratur zu allen für den *Sente Servas* relevanten Aspekten der Veldeke-Forschung aufgelistet ist, ist ausgezeichnet.

Beachtenswert im Nachwort ist vor allem die Beschreibung der Stoffgeschichte. Es wird dort u.a. im Abschnitt 3.2 in gekürzter Form der Kern von Goossens' Artikel über Heinrichs Quellen für den *Sente Servas* präsentiert (Goossens 2008). Eine heikle Frage, denn die Herausgeber des vorliegenden Bandes bemerken ganz richtig: „Vielmehr ist die lateinische Überlieferung der Legende ein Dickicht, in dem die bisherige Forschung noch keine befriedigende Ordnung hat schaffen können" (S. 355). Dass der Dichter Heinrich „ziemlich frei" mit seinen Quellen umgegangen sei, verwundert niemanden. Trotzdem geben die Herausgeber genügend stichhaltige Argumente über die Übereinstimmungen und Abweichungen zwischen dem *Sente Servas* und der lateinischen Servatius-Tradition, um die Forschung einem besseren Verständnis vom Quellengebrauch des Autors näher zu bringen. Die Besprechung führt auch zu einer höheren Anerkennung für dessen meisterhafte Fähigkeit, ziemlich klischeeartiges hagiographisches Material in eine kleine literarische Perle umzuwandeln. Hilfreich in diesem Kontext ist auch die Namenkonkordanz, in der der Leser den Vergleich zwischen den verschiedenen Versionen des Servatius-Stoffes (Heinrich von Veldeke *Sente Servas*, Jocundus *Actus, Gesta, Vita*) machen kann.

Die Prosa-Übersetzung gibt das Orginal ausgezeichnet wieder und lässt sich auch durch die impressionistische Verseinteilung leicht lesen. Es sind mir nur sehr wenig Irrtümer aufgefallen. Darunter ist aber die etwas befremdende Übersetzung „Duutsch" (6175, 6184 – Wie spricht man das aus?) für *in dutschen* als verständliche Kompromissform zwischen „Niederländisch", „Deutsch" und „Limburgisch." Man wollte wahrscheinlich nicht in das nationalistische Minenfeld um den Autor geraten. Die Übersetzung als Ganzes ist manchmal ziemlich frei oder etwas zu blass, sodass der Sinn des Orginals an einigen Stellen schwer zu erkennen ist. Fragwürdig sind Stellen wie „(dann) ereignete sich die Katastrophe" (3301). Dieser Ausdruck, der im mnl. Text gänzlich fehlt, ersetzt eine Apposition zum Subjekt (*die ovele nae ghebueren*). Eine Übersetzung des ganzen Satzes ohne eine solche starke Abweichung wäre allerdings möglich gewesen: „Als sie sich zurückziehen wollten, / diese bösen Belagerer, / brachen die Mauer der Stadt zusammen / und ebenfalls die Tore und Türme." Ebenfalls ist „wurde er von brennender Liebe zu Gott erfüllt" (305) als Übersetzung von *doen waert hij vuyrich ende vroe* zwar sinngemäß, jedoch sehr frei. Natürlich ist es nicht möglich den Ton des mnl. Orginals in allen Fällen genau zu treffen. So ist „(dann) wurden alle Häuser eingeäschert wesentlich blasser als *daer en bleyff nyet onverbrannt* (3312) mit seiner typisch mittelalterlichen Untertreibung. Aber eine wortwörtliche Übertragung als „da blieb nichts unverbrannt" wäre m.E. keine gute Alternative, denn sie wirkt unnatürlich. Mit solchen Abweichungen muss man eben vorlieb nehmen. Schließlich kann die Wiedergabe eines Prosatextes in Verszeilen den Text manchmal etwas zerstückelt erscheinen lassen. So ist

Sie ließen die Stadt,
der Gott gnädig gewesen war,
als der Heidenkönig erschien, in Ruhe. (3403-05)

bestimmt keine schlechte Übersetzung. Trotzdem wird das Auge hier irregeführt; die Bindung von „in Ruhe" an das Verbum „ließen" ist ziemlich verloren gegangen. Kritische Bemerkungen dieser Art ließen sich bestimmt noch mehren, aber es ist nicht meine Absicht, diese Rezension mit solchen Kleinigkeiten unnötig zu belasten. Die Herausgeber bieten auf jeden Fall eine gut lesbare Übersetzung.

Der kritische Text beruht auf der einzigen vollständigen Handschrift, dem Leidener Codex BPL 1215 aus dem späten 15. Jh. Die Herausgeber haben verhältnismäßig wenig normalisiert und der Text weicht im Wortlaut in nennenswerten Einzelheiten nicht von der Ausgabe von G. A. van Es ab (Veldeke 1976). Fehler habe ich keine gefunden. Folgendes ist m.E. ein bedauerliches und überflüssiges Zugeständnis an einen veralteten textkritischen Brauch: die Vereinheitlichung und Modernisierung der Groß- und Kleinschreibung (auch bei den verschiedenen Bezeichnungen für Gott), die Modernisierungen der Schriftzeichen *u* und *v*, sowie *ij* und *y* gegenüber der Handschrift, die stillschweigende Auflösung aller Abkürzungen und die Hinzufügung der handschriftlich gänzlich fehlenden Interpunktion. Die Unterlassung dieser Emendationen hätte das Textverständnis oder den Gebrauch auch für einen mit dem Mnl. wenig vertrauten Leser keineswegs im Wege gestanden. Das Textbild der Handschrift wäre so auch für andere Zwecke, d.h. nicht nur für das literarische Verständnis besser bewahrt geblieben. Für manches muss der Philologe jetzt weiter auf van Es ausweichen, der allerdings auch eine moderne Zeichensetzung in seinem Text durchgeführt hat. Dass der eigentlich recht spärliche kritische Apparat am Ende des Buches anstatt im Stellenkommentar integriert erscheint, macht die Verwendung des Buches etwas umständlich.

Mit dieser Ausgabe und dem anregenden Nachwort tritt die *Servatiuslegende* nach langer Zeit auch in der deutschsprachigen Forschung sehr verdient wieder voll ins Rampenlicht. Die nhd. Übersetzung wird von vielen Nicht-Experten im mittelniederländischen Forschungsbereich enthusiastisch begrüßt werden. Auch der mittelniederländische Text ist, abgesehen von den erwähnten philologischen Schwächen, durchaus verlässlich. Da diese Ausgabe recht preisgünstig ist, kann sie auch ohne weiteres als Unterrichtstext in Mittelalterseminaren verwendet werden.

Michel van der Hoek

Literatur

Goossens 2008: Jan Goossens. „Zu den Quellen von Veldekes Servatius", in: *Zeitschrift für deutsche Philologie* 127: 1-14.
Veldeke 1976: Hendrik van Veldeke. *Sint Servaeslegende. In dutschen dichtede dit Heynrijk die van Veldeken was geboren.* Naar het Leidse handschrift uitgegeven door Dr. G.A. van Es met een beschrijving van het handschrift door Dr. G.I. Lieftinck. 2. Auflage.,Culemborg.
Veldeke 2006: Heinrich von Veldeke. *The Life of Saint Servatius. A Dual-Language Edition of the Middle Dutch Legend of Saint Servatius by Heinrich von Veldeke and the Anonymous Upper German Life of Saint Servatius*. Translated, with Commentary and Introduction by Kim Vivian, Ludo Jongen and Richard H. Lawson. Lewiston/Queenston /Lampeter.

R.B. Bremmer, *An Introduction to Old Frisian. History, Grammar, Reader, Glossary* - John Benjamins Publishing Company, Amsterdam-Philadelphia 2009. XII, 327. (ISBN 978-90-272-3255-7 (geb.); ISBN 978-90-272-3256-4 (Ln.)).

Es steht außer Zweifel, dass dieses Buch neben einigen klassischen Grammatiken (z.b. Steller 1928, *Abriss der Altfriesischen Grammatik* Halle, Heuser 1903, *Altfriesisches Lesebuch* Heidelberg, van Helten 1890 *Altostfriesische Grammatik* Schaan/ Liechtenstein, Sjölin 1969, *Einführung in das Friesische*, Stuttgart) in diesem Bereich eine wichtige Rolle spielen wird. Teil 1 des Buches bietet einen sehr ausführlichen Überblick über die Geschichte von Literatur und Gesellschaft der Friesen im Mittelalter. Es folgen Kapitel über die Phonologie, Morphologie, Wortbildung und Syntax des Altfriesischen. Insbesondere in zwei Kapiteln (Chapter VI: Dialectology, the faces of Old Frisian, Chapter VII: Two Long-standing problems, the periodization of Frisian and the Anglo-Frisian complex) werden die engen Beziehungen zwischen dem Altfriesischen und Altenglischen vertieft. Teil 2 enthält 21 verschiedene Texte mit ausführlichen Kommentaren und einem ausführlichen Glossar.

Die altfriesische Sprache ist der gemeinsame Vorfahre der modernen friesischen Dialekten. Sie ist überliefert in Rechtsbüchern und Urkunden aus dem 13. bis 16. Jahrhundert aus dem Gebiet zwischen Weser und IJsselmeer („the earliest manuscripts with Frisian texts to have been preserved date back to c. 1300.", Bremmer 2009: 15:). Altfriesisch hat eine recht altertümliche Form und kann daher auf dieselbe Entwicklungsstufe wie das Altenglische, Altniederdeutsche oder Althochdeutsche gestellt werden, auch wenn es eher zur Zeit des Mittelenglischen, Mittelniederdeutschen und Mittelhochdeutschen benutzt wurde. Laut Bremmer (2009: 125-128) hat das Altfriesische mehrere Lautentwicklungen gemeinsam mit dem Altenglischen durchlaufen, während das Altniederdeutsche eine Zwischenstellung zwischen dem Althochdeutschen, Altfriesischen und Altenglischen einnimmt.

Das Friesische wurde im Mittelalter in einem wesentlich größeren Gebiet gesprochen als heute. Darauf weist Bremmer gleich zu Beginn seines Buches hin, „As a spoken language, it enjoys a relatively healthy existence, owing to a fair-sized number of speakers (comparable e.g., to the number of speakers of Icelandic)" (2009: 1). Die

Siedlungsarchäologie hat für die Zeit um Christi Geburt fünf germanische Kulturgruppen (Nordgermanen, Nordseegermanen, Weser-Rhein-Germanen, Elbgermanen und Oder-Weichsel-Germanen) festgestellt, aus welchen, vor allem während der Völkerwanderung, die einzelnen Stämme (Friesen, Sachsen, Angeln, Chauken usw. an der Nordseeküste) hervorgegangen sind. Durch nordseegermanische Neuerungen ergibt sich bereits eine Differenzierung zwischen ‚Vorhochdeutsch' und ‚Vorniederdeutsch'. Unter jenen Westgermanen lassen sich nach der Völkerwanderung, was die Sprache angeht, zwei Gruppen unterscheiden, die man nach ihren Kerngebieten als die donaualpenländische und die Niederrhein-Nordsee-Gruppe bezeichnet hat. Dadurch, dass das spätere Oberdeutsch diese Neuerungen mitgemacht hat, ergeben sich in bestimmten Zügen Parallelen zwischen dem Gotischen und dem Oberdeutschen: – Nasalschwund vor stimmlosen Spiranten (Ersatzdehnung des vorausgehenden Vokals) af. *ôther*,ae. *ôder* vs. got. *anþar*, ahd. *andar*. – Einheitsplural im Paradigma der Verbflexion: z.B. Präsens: af. 1.2.3.Pers. *farat*, ae. 1.2.3.Pers. *far-að*.

Obwohl Bremmer selber sagt: „For historical linguists, the existence of dialects in older stages of a given language is undisputed" ((2009:118) scheint es im Allgemeinen nicht so einfach zu sein, zu bestimmen, welche Kriterien für die Dialektgliederung älterer Sprachen funktionieren könnten. Über die verschiedenen Kriterien z.B. von Lass (2000; dual, inflected definitive article or adjective inflection usw.) oder de Haan (2001; absence of full vowels in unstressed syllables, presence of a relative rich system of prepositions usw.) hinaus, nimmt Brenner auf phonologischer, morphologischer, morphologischer und lexikalischer Ebene im Rahmen der ganzen germanischen Sprachen Kriterien der Diversifikation und Einheitlichkeit für „Old Weser Frisian", „Old Ems Frisian" und „Old West Frisian" an (2009:109-118). Wie Bremmer meint, ist die Erforschung des Altfriesischen mit geschichtlich und kulturell wichtigen Texten im Bereich der vergleichenden Philologie der germanischen Sprachen immer ‚vielversprechend': „Old Frisian, though studied for such a long time, still remains a promising field of study" (2009: 19).

Yasushi Kawasaki

Literatur

Haan 2001: Germen de Haan, "Why Old Frisian is really Middle Frisian", in: *Folia Linguistica Historica* 22: 179-206.
Lass, 2000: Roger Lass, "Language Periodization and the Concept of "Middle"," in: *Placing Middle English in Context*, eds. I. Taavitsainen, T. Nevalainen, P. Pahta and M. Rissanen. Berlin and New York, 7-41.

Jakob Ruf. Leben, Werk und Studien. Konzipiert und herausgegeben von Hildegard Elisabeth Keller in Verbindung mit Linus Hunkeler, Andrea Kauer, Clemens Müller, Seline Schnellenberg Wessendorf, Stefan Schöbi und Hubert Steinke, unter Mitarbeit von Anja Buckenberger. 5 Bände im Schuber mit 2 CD-ROM. - Verlag NZZ Libro, Zürich 2008. 3550 S. (ISBN 978-3-03823-415-9).

Der erste Band dieser fünfbändigen Ausgabe hat die Biografie von Jakob Ruf zum Inhalt, Band 2 bis 4 enthalten die erste kritische Gesamtausgabe aller Werke von Jakob Ruf, in Band 2 die Werke bis 1544, in Band 3 die von 1545-1549 und in Band 4 die von 1550-1558. Zwei Werke, die ihm lange Zeit zu Unrecht zugeschrieben wurden, wurden ebenfalls aufgenommen. Band 5 ist ein Studien- und Bildband.

Jakob Ruf war ein Zeitgenosse von Paracelsus und des Zürcher Arztes und Gelehrten Konrad Gessner, aber im Gegensatz zu diesen berühmten Zeitgenossen war über ihn bis jetzt nur sehr wenig bekannt. Die jetzt vorliegende fünfbändige Ausgabe, die Hildegard Elisabeth Keller zusammen mit den Mitarbeiterinnen und Mitarbeitern ihres Projektteams herausgebracht hat, ändert diese Situation.

Fest steht, dass Ruf in Konstanz geboren wurde, wahrscheinlich im Jahre 1505 oder 1506 und dass er am 20. Februar 1558 in Zürich gestorben ist. Weniger sicher ist der Name Ruf; damals bestand für Namen keine verbindliche Schreibweise, so kommt der Familienname Ruf in verschiedenen Formen vor, wie z.B. Rûf oder Rûff, Ruef oder Rueff. Dies erschwerte die Forschung nach seiner Person, weil unter den in verschiedener Weise geschriebenen Namen Werke auf mehreren Gebieten überliefert sind. Die Germanistik kannte Jakob Ruf als den Verfasser des ersten protestantischen Passionsspiels, aber bei mehreren der kaum oder gar nicht bekannten Werke (Flugblätter, Lieder, Einblattdrucke, gewisse medizinische Werke) war der Nachweis, dass sie tatsächlich von Ruf verfasst wurden, erst noch zu erbringen.

Der erste Band trägt den Titel »Mit der Arbeit seiner Hände«, nach einer indirekt überlieferten Aussage Jakob Rufs. In neun Kapiteln entfaltet sich die Biografie, die sich auf archivalische Funde stützt. Die Umstände, unter denen Ruf in Konstanz aufwuchs, waren ungünstig. Strenge Winter und eine Pestepidemie suchten die Stadt heim, wo die Familie in ärmlichen Umständen lebte. Nach dem Tod des Vaters 1520 bekamen die jüngeren Kinder einen Vormund. Jakob, der älteste Sohn, lebte dann schon in einem Kloster. Um 1525 trat er aus; ein Dokument bestätigt, dass er das Geld, das er beim Eintritt ins Kloster eingebracht hatte, zurückforderte, weil er es für eine Lehre brauchte. Er entschied sich für eine Lehre bei einem Scherer. Die Arbeit eines Scherers bestand neben Haarschneiden, Rasieren und Aderlass, auch in der Behandlung von Wunden und Hautproblemen, zudem, im Falle von spezialisierten Scherern, auch aus chirurgischen Eingriffen.

In seiner Gesellenzeit bereiste Jakob Ruf das Bodenseegebiet und gelangte nach Lindau, wo er die Meisterprüfung ablegte. Im Jahre 1532 ist er im protestantischen Zürich, er bekommt das Bürgerrecht und wird Chirurg im Dienst der Stadt. Chirurgen waren Handwerker, dies im Gegensatz zu den akademisch gebildeten Ärzten.

Neben der täglichen Arbeit als Stadtchirurg und später auch als Arzt, schrieb Jakob Ruf ab etwa 1530 seine Werke. Er verfasste medizinische Schriften und Theaterstücke, betätigte sich auch als Spielleiter, schrieb Flugblätter und Kalenderblätter, Lieder und Spruchgedichte. Teilweise sind sie in Druck überliefert, einige aber sind nur als Handschrift erhalten geblieben. Das gilt z.B. für den *Weingarten*, der in nur einer Handschrift mit 76 Federzeichnungen überliefert ist.

In diesem ersten Band findet sich neben den neun Kapiteln mit der Biografie eine Übersicht aller Texte, die zum Gesamtwerk Jakob Rufs gehören (mit Kurzbeschreibungen des Inhalts), weiter die Quellen zur Biografie sowie ein Panorama zu Jakob Rufs Zürich. Von A (*Adam und Eva*) bis Z (*Zwingli*) wird in vierzig Artikeln die Stadt Zürich im 16. Jahrhundert und die zu der Zeit darin lebenden Menschen vorgestellt. Diese Beiträge enthalten Abbildungen von Holzschnitten, Federzeichnungen, Stichen und Realien. Eine Bibliografie schließt den Band ab. Zu dem Band gehört weiter eine Audio-CD mit Texten zu Jakob Rufs Werk.

Der zweite Band »Jakob Ruff. Werke bis 1544« fängt an mit einer Einleitung, in der die Recherchen zu Rufs Gesamtwerk, die editorischen Prinzipien und die Verantwortlichkeiten innerhalb des Projektteams dargelegt werden. Nachzugehen war am Anfang des Projekts an erster Stelle, welche Texte Jakob Ruf wirklich zugeschrieben werden konnten, was ihm im Laufe früherer Untersuchungen zu Unrecht zugeschrieben wurde und welche zusätzlichen Texte ihm, nach den neuesten Recherchen, zuzuschreiben sind. Aus dem Jahr 1929 stammte die einzige (unvollständige) Bibliografie von Rufs Werken.[1] Zwischen 1929 und 2004 (Anfang des Projekts) wurde nur ein Text neu entdeckt und vorgestellt und zwar die *Augenheilkunde*.[2] Die wichtigste zeitgenössische Bibliografie stammt von Konrad Gessner, der Ruf persönlich kannte, ihn seinen Freund nannte und auch mit ihm zusammenarbeitete. In seiner umfangreichen Bibliografie *Bibliotheca universalis* (1545) und in *Pandectae* (1548/49), dazu in den regelmäßig erscheinenden Ergänzungen, nennt er mehrere Werke von Ruf; darunter sind einige, die mit Rufs Namen und manchmal auch seinem Exlibris, einem Greifenkopf mit Schriftzug („Steinschneider zu Zürich") publiziert wurden. Wieder andere erschienen anonym oder nur mit den Initialen I.R. Zwei der von Gessner genannten Texte müssen endgültig als verloren gelten, das Spiel *Paulina* und das Flugblatt von der *Wiler Mondersscheinung*. Die spätere Forschung schrieb Ruf zwei Spieltexte zu, die Gessner in seiner Bibliografie nicht nennt. Nach Prüfung der Texte kam die Forschergruppe zu dem Schluss, dass sie in der Tat nicht von Ruf stammen. Dennoch wurden sie in die Gesamtedition aufgenommen, unter den Namen *Zürcher Hiob* und *Zürcher Joseph*. Im Anhang zu dieser Einleitung werden die zeitgenössischen Quellen in Wortlaut gegeben, mit Übersetzung ins Deutsche.

Die Spieltexte boten Jakob Ruf die Möglichkeit Religion und Politik in einer Weise zu verbinden, die kennzeichnend war für die innerschweizerische Situation. Auch konnte er in den Texten Gegenwartskritik äußern, zumal da er der Meinung war, dass die dramatische Form sehr geeignet war Wissen an ein großes Publikum zu vermitteln.

---

[1] Wildhaber 1929.
[2] Funder 1981.

Sechs Spiele hat er geschrieben, fünf davon sind überliefert. Das erste Spiel, *Etter Heini*, ist nur handschriftlich bewahrt geblieben, in zwei Abschriften, eine aus dem Jahre 1538, die andere aus dem Jahre 1542. Das Spiel ist nicht in Druck erschienen und im 16. Jahrhundert nicht aufgeführt. Das könnte mit den antikatholischen Akzenten des Spieles zu tun haben. Erst im Jahre 1978 erlebte es die Uraufführung in Zürich.

Vom *Weingarten* ist die Aufführung am Pfingstmontag, dem 26. Mai 1539, archivalisch belegt. Auch dieser Text ist nur in einer handschriftlichen Abschrift überliefert. Dass es nicht gedruckt wurde, hat vielleicht mit der seit 1523 bestehenden Buchzensur zu tun, denn das Spiel enthält antikatholische Polemik. Die Information auf dem Titelblatt weist das Manuskript als eine reformierte Spielhandschrift aus. Es ist als ein neues Spiel angekündigt ('Ein huipsch nuiw spil'), die zugrunde liegenden Bibelstellen werden genau genannt, wie auch das Aufführungsdatum, der Aufführungsort und von wem es gespielt wurde. Gezeigt wurde in diesem Spiel die neutestamentliche Parabel von den untreuen Winzern (Mt 21,33-46) aus reformatorischer Sicht.

Wilhelm Tell ist in einem gedruckten Exemplar überliefert. Das Spiel wurde Neujahr 1545 in Zürich uraufgeführt, in demselben Jahr ist es auch gedruckt worden. Der Stoff bot Ruf die Möglichkeit die Eidgenossenschaft zur Einheit aufzufordern, trotz religiöser Unterschiede. Als Textvorlage benutzte er ein *Urner Tellenspiel*, das er beträchtlich erweiterte. Es ist Rufs einziges Spiel, das schon einige Male ediert wurde (1843, 1893, 1946, hier zusammen mit dem Urner Tellenspiel).

Das *Passionsspiel* von Jakob Ruf ist das einzig erhaltene protestantische Passionsspiel der Eidgenossenschaft, es erschien 1545 in Druck. Obwohl das Spiel geschrieben war 'also das man es spylen möcht', ist es nicht sicher, dass es tatsächlich gespielt wurde, denn Belege für eine Aufführung hat man auch jetzt, nach der intensiven Beschäftigung mit Jakob Ruf und seinen Werken, nicht gefunden. Dazu kommt, dass in Zürich keine katholische Spieltradition bestand, wie in Luzern, wo bis 1616 Aufführungen belegt sind.

Vor allem die Bibelauslegungen (Herold, Jesus, Johannes, Engel) gebrauchte Ruf um die protestantische Lehre an die Zuschauer bekannt zu machen. Dass es sich um ein reformatorisches Spiel handelt, zeigt sich u.a. in den sehr kurzen Marienklagen; diese waren in den mittelalterlichen, katholischen Passionsspielen ja sehr dazu geeignet das Mitleiden der Zuschauer hervorzurufen. Auch in der Ecce homo-Szene merkt man den Unterschied zu katholischen Spielen, Pilatus betont nicht das Bild des Mitleidens mit Christus, sondern er ruft ein Bild des Schreckens auf. Mit dieser Interpretation trägt Ruf Luthers Ablehnung der *compassio* und *identificatio* mit dem leidenden Christus Rechnung. Das Spiel ist damit nicht nur ein Bibeldrama, sondern auch Schul- und Bürgerspiel.

Rufs letztes Spiel ist *Adam und Eva*, der Inhalt bildet die Schöpfungsgeschichte bis zur Sintflut. Es steht damit in der Tradition der mittelalterlichen religiösen Spiele, wie Passions-, Oster- und Fronleichnamsspiele. Überliefert ist es in einem Druck aus dem Jahre 1550. In demselben Jahr wurde es unter Rufs Leitung an zwei Tagen in Zürich aufgeführt. Am Ende der Aufführung wurde er von den Schauspielern mit einer Ehrenmedaille geehrt. Hierin kann man ein Zeichen der Anerkennung sehen für seine Tätigkeit als Verfasser von Spieltexten und als Spielleiter, neben seiner Arbeit als Chirurg und Arzt in Zürich.

Einige Manuskripte wurden – manchmal reich – illustriert. Von den zwei Exemplaren von *Etter Heini* hat eines ein illustriertes Titelblatt. Der *Weingarten* hat 76 Federzeichnungen, sie sind mitsamt Kommentar im Bildteil des fünften Bandes gedruckt und in digitaler Form auch auf der CD-ROM verfügbar. Dasselbe gilt auch für die zwanzig Holzschnitte, mit denen das Manuskript von *Wilhelm Tell* ausgestattet ist. Der Druck der *Passion* war mit vierzehn Holzschnitten ausgeschmückt. Auch diese Abbildungen findet man im Bildteil des fünften Bandes und auf der CD-ROM stehen die kolorierten Holzschnitte mit Kommentar, dazu einige Textseiten.

Wichtig ist, dass Rufs Spieltexte jetzt der Germanistik vollständig zugänglich sind in Editionen, die man als beispielhaft bezeichnen kann. Mit äußerster Sorgfalt wurden die Texte notiert, nach editorischen Prinzipien, wie sie im zweiten Band für alle Texte formuliert wurden. Die spezifisch editorischen Eingriffe für die einzelnen Spiele werden vermerkt, die Manuskripte sorgfältig beschrieben und die Szenenübersichten gegeben. Darüber hinaus geben die literar- kulturhistorischen Einordnungen einen Einblick in die innerschweizerische Situation, unter der die Spiele zustande gekommen sind, nach welchen Prinzipien Ruf arbeitete und was er mit seinen Spielen bezweckte. In diesem Teil wird wiederholt auf den anschließenden Kommentar verwiesen; diese Kommentare sind sehr ausführlich, es wird darin für das ganze Spiel der Gang der Handlung in allen Facetten beleuchtet. Es werden Verbindungen zwischen verschiedenen Szenen gelegt, wo nötig wird erklärt, warum und in welcher Weise Ruf von einer Vorlage abwich und in die Handlung eingriff.

Von Jakob Rufs medizinischen Schriften ist das im Jahre 1554 erschiene *Trostbüchlein* wohl seine erfolgreichste Publikation. Das Buch wurde in deutscher Sprache und in einer lateinischen Version herausgebracht. Von beiden Fassungen erschienen Nachdrucke, Neuauflagen, Bearbeitungen und Übersetzungen, wie ins Englische, Tschechische und Niederländische. Diese Nachwirkung dauerte bis ins 17. Jahrhundert. Jakob Ruf schrieb das *Trostbüchlein* in seiner Funktion als städtischer Instrukteur und Prüfer von Hebammen. Die deutsche Version war für Hebammen, schwangere Frauen und interessierte Laien bestimmt, und war mit 69 Holzschnitten versehen. Auch diese Abbildungen stehen teilweise im Bildteil des fünften Bandes gedruckt, auf der CD-ROM findet man zudem die kolorierten Abbildungen aus der deutschen Fassung des *Trostbüchleins* von 1554 und 1580 sowie der Neuauflage von 1580, mit Kommentar. Sie visualisieren den Text, indem sie beispielsweise den Zyklus, der die Entwicklung eines Embryos darstellt, veranschaulichen. Auch ganz praktische Abbildungen kommen vor, wie die eines Gebärstuhls und der Einrichtung eines Kindbettzimmers und eines geburtshilflichen Instruments, des sogenannten Entenschnabels. Weiter zeigen die Abbildungen mögliche Missgeburten, so etwa siamesische Zwillinge. Die Edition stellt eine seitengleiche Parallelausgabe des deutschen und lateinischen Textes dar; letzterer war für gelehrte Ärzte bestimmt.

Ebenfalls ediert sind erstens die Zürcher Archivalien zur Geburtshilfe des 16. und 17. Jahrhunderts (damit lässt sich nachweisen, dass Rufs Buch tatsächlich als Lehrbuch für die Hebammenausbildung verwendet wurde) und zweitens die Titelblätter und Vorworte der Neuauflagen, Übersetzungen und Adaptionen. Die erfolgreichste Rezeption erfuhr die Übersetzung ins Niederländische; sie erschien unter dem Titel *T'Boeck vande Vroet-Wijfs* und erlebte zwölf Auflagen in 90 Jahren.

Der fünfte Band, mit dem Titel »Die Anfänge der Menschwerdung«, hat einen Studien- und Bildteil. Der Band widmet Ruf als Schriftsteller, sowohl von medizinischen Texten, wie von Spieltexten, viel Aufmerksamkeit. Der Beitrag über die Literaturgeschichte der Ärzte (Hildegard Elisabeth Keller) beschäftigt sich mit akademisch gebildeten und handwerklichen Ärzten, wie Chirurgen, Scherer und Bader. Ihre Verdienste lagen auf literarischem und kulturellem Gebiet; es war bestimmt kein Zufall, dass Vertreter dieser schreibenden Berufsgruppen oft mit Druckern und Verlegern zusammenarbeiteten. Da ihre Publikationen im Druck erschienen, wurde ihr Wissen auch außerhalb der eigenen Region bekannt und konnte sich manchmal sogar über Europa verbreiten. Rufs Ausbildung in der Klosterschule, die ihm seine Lateinkenntnisse vermittelte, ermöglichte es ihm die bedeutende mittelalterliche Fachliteratur zu lesen und auch selber auf Lateinisch zu publizieren. In seinen Publikationen vereinigten sich das praktische Wissen des Schnittarztes und das theoretische des gelehrten Stadtarztes. Diese Kombination und die Art und Weise, wie er sein Wissen und seine Erfahrungen auch schriftlich auszudrücken vermochte, bewirkte, dass seine Schriften weit über die Grenzen der Eidgenossenschaft gelesen, übersetzt, bearbeitet und wieder gedruckt wurden. Die Übersicht der Werk- und Lebensporträts von 'schreibenden Ärzten, Chirurgen, Scherern und Badern' vom Anfang des 15. bis Ende des 16. Jahrhunderts zeigt, dass Rufs Werdegang durchaus Gemeinsamkeiten mit demjenigen anderer hatte, z.B. auf der Seite der Scherer mit Hans Folz (1435/40-1513) und auf der Seite der akademischen Ärzte mit dem Zürcher Stadtarzt Christoph Klausner (um 1490-1552), der mehr als zwanzig Jahre Rufs Vorgesetzter war, sowie mit dem bereits erwähnten Konrad Gessner (1516-1565). Die Kombination von Praxis und Theoriewissen in Rufs Schaffen war jedoch einzigartig.

Wie Theorie und Praktik kombiniert wurden, zeigt sich im Beitrag 'Geburtshilfe zwischen Mittelalter und Moderne' (Hildegard Elisabeth Keller). In Zürich ist gut dokumentiert, wie die Ausbildung von Hebammen geregelt war. Überliefert sind verschiedene Dokumente, die dies bezeugen. Das Dokument *Frag und Antworten* ist nur in einer Abschrift aus dem Jahre 1703 überliefert. Es ist ein Lehrbuch für Hebammen und zeigt, dass die städtschen Hebammen sich in Zürich einer Prüfung unterziehen mussten. Wann diese eingeführt wurde, ist allerdings nicht bekannt. Der Text dieses Frag- und Antworten-Katalogs geht direkt zurück auf Rufs *Trostbüchlein*.

Rufs Werke fanden auf dem niederländischen Buchmarkt einen reißenden Absatz, das galt nicht nur für das *Trostbüchlein*, sondern auch für das *Tumorbüchlein*. Dies erschien im Jahre 1662 unter dem Titel *Tractaet van de Phlegmatijke Geswellen*. Der Übersetzer war Hendrick van Roonhuyse, dessen beruflicher Werdegang mit dem von Jakob Ruf vergleichbar ist. Er absolvierte eine Lehre als Scherer und spezialisierte sich als Wundarzt. Im Jahre 1646 wurde er in die Amsterdamer Chirurgengilde aufgenommen, er war Vorsteher der städtischen Geburtshilfe und für die Ausbildung der Hebammen zuständig. In seiner Widmungsvorrede auf das *Trostbüchlein* (datiert auf September 1660) lobt er Ruf als einen sehr kundigen Arzt aus Zürich (*den seer experte Iacobus Ruff, Heel-meester tot Zurich*). Die Verbindung von Theorie und Praxis, die Ruf vorstand, fand somit Anklang im Kreis der hervorragenden Amsterdamer Spezialisten.

Das Kapitel über Theater in diesem Band trägt den Titel 'Theater zwischen Aufführung und Schrift'. Im ersten Beitrag handelt es sich um die Überlieferung der Spiele in Handschriften und Drucken (Seline Schellenberg Wessendorf). Ruf schrieb seine Spiele zwischen 1538 und 1550, einer Zeit, in der in Zürich viele Spiele im Druck erschienen. Damit änderte sich die Funktion von Spieltexten als 'nur' Aufführungstexte. Das Titelblatt gewann zunehmend an Bedeutung, es sollte informativ sein und zum Kaufen anregen. Die Illustrationen hatten eine ähnliche Funktion, denn mit Bildern kann man sehr viel ausdrücken, sie sollten die Neugierde reizen und zum Lesen anregen. Aus dem Vergleich aus den Städten mit einer katholischen Spieltradition – vor allem Luzern – zeigt sich, dass da die mündliche Überlieferung viel länger anhielt und dass da weniger Texte gedruckt wurden und dann noch oft in anderen Städten.

Der zweite Beitrag (Stefan Schöbi) geht der Frage nach, welche Funktion das Theater im 16. Jahrhundert erfüllte. Sie dienten nicht nur zur Belehrung, sondern auch zur Kurzweil, wie es wiederholt auf dem Titelblatt vermerkt wird. Die Titel der Werke lassen nicht vermuten, dass sie sehr gegenwartsbezogen waren und sich in den politisch-religiösen Zustand mischte. In Zürich gibt es wenig Dokumente, die explizit auf die Spielaufführungen zurückgehen. Ein wichtiges Zeugnis ist die Spielerliste von Jakob Rufs *Weingarten*. Da es ebenfalls biografische Dokumente gab, war es möglich zu rekonstruieren, aus welchen sozialen Kreisen die Spieler stammten. Im Anhang dieses Beitrags findet man die biografischen Angaben der 66 Spieler.

Trotz des Umfangs der bibliophil gestalteten Halbleinenbände ist es leicht sich darin zurechtzufinden. Das fängt schon beim Aufschlagen des ersten Bandes an. Das Inhaltsverzeichnis und die Einleitung bieten dem Leser eine schnelle Orientierung, sowohl über den ersten Band als auch über die gesamte Reihe. Die unterschiedlichen Farben auf den Umschlägen, die sich im ersten und im fünften Band auch in der Schmuckfarbe sowie in den Schutzblättern zwischen den verschiedenen Teilen wiederholt, springen ins Auge. Jeder Band schließt mit einer Bibliografie, der fünfte Band außerdem mit einem Gesamtregister (Sachregister und Register der historischen Namen und Forschernamen). Eine Fülle von Material wurde zusammengetragen, geordnet und in gut lesbaren Texten verarbeitet. Die fünf Bände bieten weit mehr als der Titel verspricht. Nicht nur das ungewöhnliche und interessante Leben von Jakob Ruf wird aus verschiedenen Perspektiven vorgeführt, sondern auch seine Werke vortrefflich ediert, dazu wird ein Zeitbild entworfen, das interessante Einblicke in die damalige Gesellschaft ermöglicht.

Cobie Kuné

Literatur

Wildhaber 1929: Robert Wildhaber, Jakob Ruf. Ein Zürcher Dramatiker des 16. Jahrhunderts, St. Gallen.

Funder 1981: Wolfgang Funder, "Über eine bisher unbekannte ophtalmonologische Monographie von Jakob Rüff (um 1500-1558)", in: *Klinische Monatsblätter der Augenheilkunde* 179: 297-298.

Sylvia Weigelt (Hg.), *Johannes Rothe. Thüringische Landeschronik und Eisenacher Chronik.* (Deutsche Texte des Mittelalters herausgegeben von der Berlin-Brandenburgische Akademie der Wissenschaften, Bd. LXXXVII). Akademie Verlag, Berlin 2007 (ISBN 978-3-05-004406-4).

Sylvia Weigelt erfreut sich im *Vorwort* der Tatsache, dass die schon lange vorgesehenen Editionen von Rothes Thüringischer Landeschronik (LChr) und Eisenacher Chronik (EChr) nun vorliegen. Weil seit 1990 der Zugang zu den Bibliotheken in ganz Deutschland möglich wurde und neue Handschriften gefunden wurden, muss jetzt die Überlieferungsgeschichte der Texte völlig neu geschrieben werden.

In der *Einleitung* werden nach allgemeinen Bemerkungen zur Person Johannes Rothe und seinem historiographischen Standort der Forschungsstand, die Quellen, die Überlieferung, die Sprache von LChr und EChr ausführlich besprochen; Weigelt schließt die Einleitung mit den Editionsgrundsätzen, die von Hübner 1934 für die Reihe 'Deutsche Texte des Mittelalters' aufgestellt wurden, ab; in etwas modifizierter Weise hält Weigelt sich für beide Editionen an diese Grundsätze.

Johannes Rothe (ca. 1360-1434) war als Kleriker und Stadtschreiber in Eisenach tätig; er hinterließ Rechtssammlungen, Ratsgedichte, ein Ritterspiel, geistlich-allegorische Werke, Legenden und insgesamt drei Chroniken (*EChr*, um 1414; *LChr*, um 1418/19; *WChr* [die Thüringische Weltchronik], 1421). Mit seinen volkssprachlichen Chroniken richtete Rothe sich auf verschiedene soziale Gruppen: städtisches und landgräfliches Publikum und auch Gönner und Freunde. Den Anlass zu seinen Chroniken sieht Weigelt in der großen Unsicherheit, die 1410 wegen eingreifender Besitzverhältnisse der Landgrafen entstand: entweder sollte Thüringen aufgeteilt oder mit osterländischer Herrschaft regiert werden. Aus dieser Unsicherheit wuchs wohl der Bedarf, die Vergangenheit für die Gegenwart und die Zukunft festzuhalten.

Leider ist die Überlieferung der *WChr* noch unzureichend erschlossen. Wohl ist deutlich geworden, dass es mehr Hss. gibt, als bis jetzt bekannt war. Eine kritische Neuedition bleibt aber fürs erste ein Desiderat der Forschung. Kurz zum Inhalt der WChr sei vorläufig gesagt: die WChr ist der Landgräfin Anna von Schwarzburg dediziert. Es ist eine Weltchronik mit regionaler Tendenz; Kap. 1-151 widmen sich der Universalgeschichte, erst seit Kap. 329 konzentriert sich die Darstellung auf die Geschichte Thüringens; es ist also eigentlich eine Landeschronik mit universalen Einschüben.

Die *LChr* widmet Rothe durch ein Akrostichon im Versprolog dem Amtmann der

Wartburg Bruno von Teutleben (*DEME GESTRENGE BRVNEN VON TEITELEIBIN AMCHTMANE VF WARTBERG*), der aus einem alten thüringischen Ministerialengeschlecht stammt. Urkundlich ist Bruno 1385 und 1391 belegt. Nicht auszuschließen ist, dass Rothe durch Bruno in Kontakt zum landgräflichen Hof kam und dass die LChr von ihm initiiert wurde. Hintergrund der Festlegung der Landesgeschichte ist natürlich die anstehende Herrschaftsteilung und die damit verbundene Besitzveränderung. Erzählt wird die Geschichte der Landgrafschaft Thüringen von ihren ersten Anfängen bis zum politisch bedeutenden Landesfürstentum. Die Fürsten, Grafen, Edelleute und Städte werden, wie üblich, in die Heilsgeschichte eingebunden; daher fängt die LChr mit der Schöpfung an. Obwohl sie eigentlich regionale Geschichtsschreibung sein sollte, wählt Rothe die Perspektive der Landgrafen, in deren Umfeld andere politisch wichtige Ereignisse vorkommen (z.B. der Kreuzzug des Kaisers Friedrichs I., weil Landgraf Ludwig III. daran teilnimmt). Besondere Aufmerksamkeit gilt der Rechtsprechung und den Besitzveränderungen, die durch unbelegbare Herkunftssagen verantwortet werden.

Der bisherigen Forschung war nur eine Handschrift bekannt. Die Chronik, die Neumann die 'Thüringische Landeschronik' nannte, wurde mit Ausnahme des Prologs noch nicht ediert. In der Forschung herrschte bis jetzt große Unsicherheit über die Trennung zwischen LChr und WChr. Nun aber 39 (oder vielleicht noch mehr) Textzeugen der LChr aus dem 15. bis 18. Jh. vorliegen und man daraus schließen könnte, dass das Landesbewusstsein der Rezipienten und ihr Interesse an der Geschichte des Landes und seiner Regenten sehr groß war, ist die Dringlichkeit einer Edition groß. Die Datierung der LChr, 1418/19 geschieht auf Grund der Dedikation und der von Rothe benutzten Quellen. Diesen Quellen entnimmt Rothe fast kritiklos alle Darstellungen, aber wenn ihm etwas nicht gefällt, werden Tatsachen ignoriert. Er fügt Kommentare, moralisch-didaktische Unterweisung und manchmal mündliches Erzählgut zu. Die sieben von ihm benutzten Quellen sind: die *Historia Scholastica* (für den Abschnitt von der Schöpfung bis zu Noah), die *Historia Pistoriana* (für den Abschnitt von den Söhnen Noahs bis 1402/3), die *Historia Eccardiana* (thüringische Geschichte, Papst- und Kaisergeschichte von 1025 bis etwa 1414), die *Erfurter Quellen* ('Cronica Sancti Petri Erfordensis moderna', 'Cronica minor Minoritae Erphordensis', 'Liber cronicorum sive annalis Erfordensis'; 1340-1350), die *Legenda Bonifacii* (geschrieben nach 1365), *die Iringsage - Widukind von Corvey 'Res gestae Saxoniae'* (über den Untergang des Thüringer Königreiches durch die Landnahme der Sachsen) und *Das Leben des heiligen Ludwig'* (geschrieben 1314/18-1323 von *Friedrich Köditz*, über Ludwig IV.). Für die Edition der LChr wird Hs. G (Erfurt/Gotha, UFB - FB Gotha, Cod. Chart. B 180, Papierhs., 1487, f. 185r-288r) als Leithandschrift gewählt. Weiter werden noch zwei Hss. für die Edition herangezogen: Hs. L (Leipzig, UB, Rep. II.4.137, Papierhs., 1485/1581, f. 16r-116v) und Hs. W (Weimar, Thüringisches Hauptstaatsarchiv, F 1866, Papierhs., 1555/60). Diese drei Hss. werden in der Einleitung ausführlich, die sonstigen Hss., die aus der Neuzeit stammen, nur kurz beschrieben. Bei den 39 Textzeugen findet man weder einen Autographen noch einen fest umrissenen Archetypus. Klassifizierung der Handschrift-verhältnisse und Fassungen erfolgte nach ausgewählten Abschnitten. Über die Sprache der Leiths. G sagt Weigelt, man könne in der Abschrift G Rothes Schreibsprache noch sehen; im Allgemeinen ist die westthüringische Vorlage und die Bearbeitung des ostthüringischen Schreibers Urban Schlorff gut erkennbar. Für die Details der Schreibweise verweise ich auf S. LXVII-LXXV der Edition.

Die *EChr* schildert die Entwicklung der Stadt Eisenach von ihren Anfängen bis in die Gegenwart des Chronisten, der wohl mehr als zehn Jahre Stadtschreiber der Stadt Eisenach war (ca. 1395-1407/12). Sie ist erstens auf Sicherung in der Vergangenheit erworbener Positionen der Stadt gegenüber dem Landgrafen gerichtet und erzählt zweitens die Geschichte der Landgrafen von Thüringen. Höhepunkt in der Beschreibung ist die Zeit um 1200, als Eisenach durch das Wirken von den Bürgern und dem Landgrafen eine Stadt wurde. Da das Hauptziel die Harmonisierung der Vergangenheit mit Blick auf die Gegenwart und Zukunft sein sollte, werden keine Skandale erwähnt. Die Geschichte wird in der Erzählung Rothes etwas 'sagenhafter', indem er bestimmte Ereignisse, die bekanntlich nicht in seiner Stadt stattfanden, nach Eisenach verlegt: eine Schlacht gegen die Ungarn, die Hochzeit von Ludwigs IV. Schwester Agnes; außerdem soll Bonifatius die Kirche auf dem Eisenacher Petersberg geweiht haben.

Dass das Interesse an der EChr wahrscheinlich kaum über die Lebenszeit von Rothe hinausging, zeigt sich daraus, dass sie nur in zwei Hss. überliefert ist. Obwohl es aus 1753 einen Druck der EChr, deren Verfasser damals unbekannt war (*auctore ignoto*) gibt, bestand in der Forschung bis heute ein weitgehendes Desinteresse an der EChr, weil vom alten Druck nur noch wenige Exemplare existieren. Der Druck entspricht nicht den heutigen Anforderungen an eine Textausgabe. Die Datierung von EChr (nach 1412/14 und vor 1418) ist u.a. auf Grund einer der Quellen, die 1414 fertiggestellt wurde. Es gibt keinen Adressaten, vielleicht weil der Prolog fehlt. Es könnte aber Ratsmeister Reinhard Pinkernagel gewesen sein. Als Quellen gelten wohl: die *Historia Eccardiana* (für die Zeit von 1015-1408), die *Historia Piccardiana*, mündliches Erzählgut und vielleicht Kirchenbücher. Die EChr ist in zwei Hss. überliefert: Hs. B (Berlin, SBB - PK, Ms. germ. quart. 252, Papierhs., 2. Viertel/Mittel 15. Jh.) und Hs. D (Dresden, SLUB, K 362, Papierhs., 1567); die Hs. D ist von Hs. B abhängig: Korrekturen und Ergänzungen von B wurden in D übernommen, manches ist vom Schreiber von D missverstanden. Die Sprache der Hs. B ist ostmitteldeutsch-westthüringisch.

Aus dem Text der *LChr* (Hs. G, f. 158v-188r; Edition S. 1-90), der sehr viele schöne und interessante Tatsachen enthält, greife ich nur einiges heraus, das die Chronik interessant zu lesen macht: der Prolog (f. 158v) fängt an mit:

*D*urch lust in myner jogunt schreib ich unde tychte.
*N*ach mynes synnes mogunt ich mancherleye ußrichte.

Rothe schließt seinen Prolog hoffnungsvoll mit (f. 160v):

*G*uter bilde nemmet war hyrinne von den fromen.
*S*o mag uch ditz buchelin gar zu nutcze wol kommen.

Das *D* von *Durch* ist der erste, das *G* von *Guter* der letzte Buchstabe des Akrostichons. Insgesamt widmet Rothe fast 20 Seiten der alttestamentlichen Geschichte: von Adam und Eva bis zum *thorm zu Babilonia*. Als die Welt 900 Jahre existierte, nahm Gott Enoch auf ins Paradies; danach fügt Rothe kommentierend hinzu:

> *Drye hat got genommen uff in das paradiß: einen vor deme gesetcze, das was disser Enoch, den andern in dem gesetcze, das was Helias, unde den drittem nach dem gesetcze, das was Johannes der ewangelista*

(obwohl die dritte Person bekanntlich einer der Übeltäter neben Christus am Kreuz sein sollte). Schön ist der erste Übergang zur thüringischen Geschichte: Trier wurde von *Trebeta* gebaut, der von Semiramis aus Babylonien vertrieben wurde und sich an der Mosel niederließ; nachdem Trebeta lange über die deutschen Lande und über Thüringen regiert hatte, wurde Troja zerstört. Teils flohen die Trojaner nach Italien, aber *Senno*, Anthenors Sohn, kam nach Thüringen, wurde in Trier König; dessen Sohn *Markomet* regierte über Thüringen und Böhmen *biß an die sehe* 'bis an die See'. Diese Periode, die bis Kaiser Julius dauerte, bildet den Übergang zur römischen Geschichte. In diesem Zusammenhang werden einige etymologische Erklärungen von Burgnamen im 'thüringischen Land' aufgezählt:

> *Alzo buwete her* [= Julius] *uff die Missener unde Osterlendere eine borgk, die nante her nach sime namen Juliborg, die wir nue nennen Yleborg ... in Doringen* [= Thüringen] *eyne borg bie deme Harcze, die nante her Confusio, das sich dutit 'eine vorstorunge', wan da mitte vorstorte her das konnigriche der Doringe. Die nennen wir nue Kuffehußen.*

Manche große Persönlichkeiten werden nur kurz und nebenbei genannt, z.B. Alexander der Große und König *Etczil*, der bei Köln 11.000 Jungfrauen erschlug. Fließende Übergänge von 'deutscher' zu thüringischer Geschichte seien z.B. an Karl dem Großen, Bonifatius und Kaiser Friedrich I. gezeigt: Karl der Große errichtete 734 zu Aachen ein Münster und baute in Thüringen Städte. Im Jahre 724 kam Bonifatius nach Thüringen, baute dort eine Kirche; im nächsten Jahr

> *quam her kein* [= gegen] *Geißman in Westfalen unde warf da nidder eyn großen bawm, den die heiden erten in der ere ores aptgotis Jovis, unde buwete an die stat eine kirche in sente Peters ere.*

In diesen Jahren wurde auch der erste *Doring*, *Hug der alde*, bekehrt und auf dem *Aldenberge* getauft. Kaiser Friedrich I. zog nach Polen und besuchte auf dem Rückweg die Stadt Naumburg (f. 214r); im Jahre 1180,

> *da wart herczoge Heinrich von Brunswig des keißers fient* (f. 218v)

zu 1190 (f. 221r)

> *Keißer Friddrich der wolde obir mer mit vil fursten czihen unde das heilige grab gewynnen. Da nam Loddewig der milde* [= Landgraf Ludwig III.] *das crucze an sich und czoch mit om*

(N.B. der Tod Friedrichs I. wird erst zum Jahr 1192 erwähnt) und brachte *ein banir*, das Wunder bewirkte und auf die Wartburg gebracht wurde. Es wundert nicht, dass im letzten Teil der Chronik spezifisch thüringische Vorfälle in der Mehrheit sind, z.B. *der krigk von Wartperg*, wo Rothe Walther von der Vogelweide neben anderen Sängern nennt und *meister Clingsor* vieles offenbaren lässt. Die Berichte über Thüringen aus der für Rothe jüngsten Vergangenheit werden selbstverständlich immer länger. Rothe beschließt seine Chronik mit:

Also man schreib nach Cristi gebort tußent CCCCVI jar [1406], *da starb landtgrave Balthazar zcu Wartpergk uf deme sloße in guteme volligen aldere und wart gefurt kein Reynhartsborn ... In deme andern jar darnach* [1407] *starb syn bruder Wilhelm, dem got gnade.*

Als extra Lesehilfe werden in der Edition (ab f. 172r, S. 18) am Rande neben dem Text die Jahreszahlen mit arabischen Ziffern angegeben (28, 330, 458, 515 usw.).

Auf den ff. 182r-190v der Hs. wurde offenbar die *Legenda Bonifacii* eingefügt, die in der Edition gesondert nach der Chronik herausgegeben wird (S. 90-98); sie fängt mit der Kreuzerhebung von Eraclius (620) an. Schon nach einigen Zeilen wird die Zeit von Karl dem Großen und Bonifatius geschildert: Wie Bonifatius Bischof wurde, wie er Thüringen bekehrte, wie die Ungarn Thüringen bedrohten und von Bonifatius geschlagen wurden. Und weiter wie Karl der Große durch einen Boten die Wartburg bauen ließ, wie Karl einen Landgrafen ernannte und die Rechtsprechung einführte. Das Land wurde in vier Teile geteilt; in diesem Passus werden viele thüringische Ortsnamen genannt. Gleich danach schließt die Legende (fast) mit:

Nue ist das landt zu Doringen ußgericht unde vornamet alzo: Wartperg heißet das houbt des landis, Elgirßborg der rechte arm, Ebirßborg der lingke arm, Wissensehe das hercze, Eckerßberge die fuße unde treten uf die Sale.

Das Bild der zusammengehörenden Körperteile (Haupt, Arme, Herz, Füße) soll wohl verdeutlichen, dass nach Rothe Thüringen nicht aufgeteilt werden sollte.

Der Text von *EChr* (Hs. B, f. 1r-59r; Edition S. 99-135) konzentriert sich vor allem auf die Geschichte der Stadt Eisenach; teilweise werden Fakten, die in der LChr erwähnt wurden, auch hier erzählt. Wieder erscheinen am Rande der Edition die jeweiligen Jahreszahlen in arabischen Ziffern (152, 740, 889 usw.). Die Chronik fängt mit der Vertreibung der Thüringer durch die Sachsen und die Landnahme der Thüringer in wendischem Gebiet an; nach

In den geczíten also dy Sachsin dy Doringe vortrebin von der sehe, do sũ vor woniten, obir den Harcz in dit land das nũ Doringin genant ist, vor Cristus gebort, und dy Doringe vort uß trebin dy Wendin, dy dit land ynne hatten und besaßin ...,

erzählt Rothe, dass noch viele Dörfer und Städte ihre wendischen Namen tragen. Wo die Thüringer am Vischbach Eisen fanden, ließen sie sich nieder und gründeten den Marktflecken *zcu Ysinmache* oder *zcu Isennach* (152 n. Chr.). Die EChr berichtet über die Könige in *Doringen*, wie Karl III. die Könige absetzte und zu Herzögen machte; auch erzählt er ausführlich über Bonifatius, die Ungarn, Klingsor, die heilige Elisabeth (gest. 1235). Aber doch vor allem darüber, wer wann regierte, wer welche Kirche baute, in welchem Jahr Eisenach durch Hungers- und Wassersnöte und strengen Frost heimgesucht wurde. In der Tat wird diese Chronik vor allem den Einwohnern von Eisenach von Interesse gewesen sein. Die Chronik schließt mit einem Geschehnis aus dem Jahr 1409, als die Stadt den neuen Erben der Landgrafschaft in ihre Stadt hinein ließ:

Abir dy gemeine der stad dy tadin dy thor uff und lißin on yn, wan her eyn erbe des landis was. Da was eyn krankir man uff dem kerchoffe sente Niclauwes, der wart also fro mit den luten, dy sich des frouwetin, das her vor froydin da starb.

Es freut mich dieses Buch gelesen zu haben, denn es gibt einen schönen Einblick und Durchblick in die Weise, wie Historiographie in Rothes Zeit verstanden werden muss. So weit ich nach den drei hinzugefügten Bildern am Ende der Edition (LChr f. 158v u. 197v, EChr f. 1v) kontrollieren kann, ist die Transkribierung sorgfältig; natürlich könnte man darüber streiten, ob die Abkürzungen (Nasalstriche für *m, n*; *r*-Haken für *er, ra, r, e, a* etc.) eigentlich durch besondere Druckweise hervorgehoben werden sollten; aber die Arbeitsweise der Herausgeberin entspricht offenbar den Prinzipien der ganzen DTM-Reihe. Nun liegt der Forschung ein schönes Werk da, das zu vielen Studien über Rothe und Geschichtsschreibung führen kann und soll. Weigelt nimmt nach der Edition noch zwei Verzeichnisse (Personennamen, S. 137-150; Ortsnamen, S. 151-165), ein Glossar (S. 167-176) und ein ausführliches Quellen- und Literaturverzeichnis auf. Das Glossar bietet eine Auswahl seltener, schwer verständlicher, in besonderer Bedeutung gebrauchter und thüringisch geprägter Wörter. Mit den Verzeichnissen und dem Glossar werden für den interessierten Leser alle Leseschwierigkeiten aufgehoben.

Erika Langbroek

Karl G. Johansson and Maria Arvidsson (eds.). *Barlaam i nord: Legender om Barlaam och Josaphat i den nordiska medeltidslitteraturen.* (Bibliotheca Nordica 1). - Novus forlag, Oslo 2009. 207 pp. (ISBN 9788270995196).

Robert Volk. *Historia animae utilis de Barlaam et Ioasaph (spuria): Einführung.* (Die Schriften des Johannes von Damaskos VI/1. Patristische Texte und Studien 61) - Walter de Gruyter, Berlin/New York, 2009. 597 pp. (ISBN 9783110194623).

The last decade or so has seen a revival of interest in the story of Barlaam and Josaphat (Joasaph), one of the most popular tales of the Middle Ages. Originally based on the life of Buddha, this Christian conversion narrative underwent conversions of its own by way of Georgia and Greece and was spread throughout much of Europe, the Middle East, and North-Eastern Africa. Readers unfamiliar with the broad dissemination of this tradition are encouraged to consult its grand if imperfect stemmatological representation at the end of Hiram Peri's *Der Religionsdisput der Barlaam-Legende* (1959), which must be unfolded several times. Among valuable reprints, dissertations, and smaller contributions, three recent works concerned with *Barlaam* deserve special mention, namely the edition of what might be the oldest surviving Latin translation by José Martínez Gázquez (1997), the critical edition of the widespread Latin "vulgate" version by Óscar de la Cruz Palma (2001), and the critical edition of the Greek version by Robert Volk (2006). Volk's monumental introduction to his edition appeared as a separate volume in 2009 and will be discussed briefly below, but not at once.

A conference entitled "Barlaam und Josaphat in der Literatur des Mittelalters" will take place in 2010, at the Universität Wien, in the wake of another symposium, "Barlaam und Josaphat in der europäischen Tradition," which was held at the Albert-Ludwigs-Universität Freiburg in 2007. Before both of these, in 2004, a meeting was held in Oslo devoted strictly to the Scandinavian versions of the story; the book *Barlaam i nord: Legenden om Barlaam och Josaphat i den nordiska medeltidslitteraturen*, edited by Karl G. Johansson and Maria Arvidsson, contains expanded versions of the papers delivered at that conference. The slim but informative volume consists of seven articles, a fifteen-page bibliography, and accurate indices. The first chapter, "De nordiske versjonen av Barlaam-legenden" by Johansson and Odd Einar Haugen (pp. 11-30), offers background information regarding the history of the Barlaam story in Georgia and Greece; surveys the Latin versions that lie behind the Scandinavian translations, namely the "vulgate" version represented in Palma's edition, the *Speculum Historiale* by Vincent of Beauvais, and the *Legenda Aurea* by Jacobus de Voragine; and then introduces the Scandinavian versions at greater length. There are four of these: 1) the Old Norwegian *Barlaams ok Josaphats saga*, written ca. 1250, which survives in three complete medieval manuscripts and a number of fragments; 2) an Old Swedish *Sagan om de helige Barlaam och Josaphat*, from the beginning of the fourteenth century, which is preserved in the *Old Swedish Legendary*; 3) a younger Swedish version – *Barlam och Josaphat* – written ca. 1440, which is based on both the *Speculum Historiale* and the Old Norwegian version; and 4) a sixteenth-century Icelandic translation from Low German, *Barlaham og Josaphat*, which is based ultimately on the *Legenda Aurea* and which survives in *Reykjahólabók*, a collection of hagiographic texts.

Magnus Rindal's "*Barlaams ok Josaphats saga* i det norske literære miljøet" (pp. 31-45), the second contribution, begins by repeating a good deal about the Old Norwegian version that was discussed in the first chapter, but goes into greater detail about its manuscript tradition. The remainder of this article presents a survey of the history of literary production in medieval Norway: The earliest translations into Norwegian were of religious and didactic Latin texts, followed later by translations of the French romances. The settings of literary culture were the monastery and the royal court, and the didactic story of Barlaam and Josaphat was created in the latter. There is nothing of surprise in this chapter, which is a pity; Rindal, who is the scholar best qualified to discuss the Norwegian *Barlaam*, says little about it, but this was not his charge.

Characteristic of the Greek narrative and that of its derivatives is the inclusion of several digressions from the main story. In the third chapter, "Forteljingane i forteljinga: Interpolasjonane i *Barlaams ok Josaphats saga*" (pp. 47-73), Haugen analyses the traditional "interpolations" and those unique to the Norwegian version in terms of their failure or success as rhetorical *exempla*, i.e., brief stories that illustrate a moral lesson and support the argument of the main narrative. He distinguishes three types of interpolation – apologues, parables, and "legendarisk og bibelsk materiale" (unique to *Barlaams saga*) – and argues that the translator was aware of these distinctions, since a different word is (normally) used for each: *dømisaga* for the apologues, *saga* for the parables, and *dømi* for the legendary or biblical digressions. Perhaps Haugen is right, but it seems that the body of evidence is too small and inconsistent to lead to firm conclusions. He argues further that the apologues and parables do function as *exempla*, but that the unique Norwegian interpolations fail to do so by not firmly supporting the argument of the story. Perhaps this is also true but, as Haugen admits, the medieval understanding of the term *exemplum* was inexact, as it still is.

Barlaams ok Josaphats saga is often considered to be a loose translation from Latin, which is likely true (its precise exemplar is unknown). As expected, the translator's style reveals or reflects aspects of courtly culture in medieval Norway, and this is the focus of Vera Johanterwage's "Kung Avennir i *Barlaams ok Josaphats saga* – en hövisk härskare?" By identifying deviations from the Latin *Vorlage* and, in turn, comparing these deviations with analogous scenes in Old Norse romances, she demonstrates how the translator manipulated the saga to suit its new courtly environment. This manipulation is clearest, according to Johanterwage, in the translator's representation of courtly splendor, hierarchy, and the figure of the chancellor, and also in the preponderance of such terms as *sæmð/soma* 'honor', *kurteisi*, *hæverska* 'courtliness', *riddaraskapr* 'chivalry', *ásti* 'love, affection', *blíða* 'friendliness', *litilæti* 'humility', among others. Her comparative method may be simple, but it bears fruit; more of her findings can be found in her 2007 dissertation – *Die Barlaams ok Josaphats saga: Eine höfische Legende am norwegischen Königshof* – which, as I am writing, awaits publication.

The next article in the collection, Jens Eike Schnall's "Grundkedelig og lidet norsk? Om forholdet mellem *Barlaams ok Josaphats saga* og *Kongespejlet*" (pp. 99-130), questions the longstanding modern opinion that *Barlaams ok Josaphats saga* is a dull and un-Scandinavian piece of literature. Its medieval readers must have held it in far higher esteem, Schnall argues, since it served as an important source for the Old Norwegian *Konungs skuggsjá*. The two works are often associated with one another, since both are dialogic, didactic, courtly, mid-thirteenth-century, and Norwegian, but their similarities seem to be more than incidental. Schnall presents a striking number of structural, thematic, and lexical parallels – especially from the section of Barlaam that preserves the *Apology* of Aristides – that left me convinced that the authors of the *Konungs skuggsjá* had indeed been influenced by the Norwegian *Barlaam*. This realization must have come as a surprise to Schnall, too, whose excellent dissertation on the didactic strategies of the *Konungs skuggsjá* (2000) contains not a single reference to *Barlaams ok Josaphats saga*. In *Barlaam i nord* he has done well to take care of unfinished business.

Scholars of medieval literature are not always fully aware of the work of art historians, and vice versa, and so the contribution by the art historian Kristin Bliksrud Aavitsland, who has written elsewhere on the "rhetoric" of images, is therefore especially welcome. In "Fra tekst til bilde: Ikonografisk transformasjon av enhjøringfabelen fra Barlaam-legenden i nordeuropeisk middelalder" (pp. 131-52), she demonstrates how medieval illustrators would manipulate their textual source material for artistic ends without vitiating its intended message. With the help of ten illustrations, half of which are in color, it is shown how the famous parable of the man and the unicorn could be represented with a number of iconographic substitutions – the abyss could be fashioned as a tree of life, the dripping honey as fruit, for instance – and yet the fundamental moral would be left intact: The transient pleasures of worldly existence can distract us from striving for the eternal salvation of our souls. The final article in this volume is also furnished with excellent illustrations; Maria Arvidsson's "Den fornsvenska översättningen av legenden om Barlaam och Josaphat i Holm A 49" (pp. 153-76) offers paleographic and orthographic analyses of the younger Old Swedish version, that which is based both on the *Speculum Historiale* and the Old Norwegian saga. Her investigation is useful, since Gustaf Klemming, in the late nineteenth century, provided no such discussion in his edition of this text; and it is insightful, since she demonstrates beyond doubt that three hands were involved in its production.

A quarter of this book is of an introductory nature and some of the rest is derived from earlier studies by the contributors, but all in all it is recommendable as a convenient anthology concerned with the northernmost branch of the *Barlaam* tradition. It should be noted, too, that *Barlaam i nord* is the inaugural volume of a new series, Bibliotheca Nordica, which is under the editorial supervision of Haugen, Johansson, and Jon Gunnar Jørensen. These scholars must be congratulated for founding this new publication venue and for securing its production with the Novus forlag. May many more volumes follow the one in hand.

As mentioned at the beginning of this review, a critical edition of the Greek *Barlaam and Joasaph*, by Robert Volk, was published in 2006. This book represents the greatest single advancement in *Barlaam* scholarship to date, and it is unlikely to be surpassed. Before its appearance, the preferred edition of the Greek version was that of the Loeb Classical Library (Woodward & Mattingly 1967), which was borrowed primarily from Boissonade's text from 1832, based on few manuscripts. Volk's edition takes the entire known manuscript tradition into account and is painstakingly thorough. His introductory volume to this edition has just been published (2009). Though *Amsterdamer Beiträge* might not seem to be the most appropriate place to discuss a contribution to Byzantine Studies, this book should be made known to everyone interested in the Germanic versions of the *Barlaam* story.

After a long bibliography (XIII-XL), the *Einführung* begins with a comprehensive chapter on the author of the Greek version (pp. 1-95). According to the Latin tradition, the romance was written by John of Damascus, who died in the middle of the eighth-century, and it is because of this tradition that Volk's books are part of the series "Die Schriften des Johannes von Damaskos." It has been argued for some time, however – and Volk's chapter strengthens this case – that the "author" was rather Euthymius of Athos (ob. 1028), who translated into Greek and amplified a Georgian *Vorlage* known today as the *Balavariani*. This thesis was reached only after much debate, often heated and politically biased, and Volk surveys its developments. The second chapter is concerned with source material (pp. 96-140); beyond his reliance on the *Balavariani*, Euthymius drew upon a number of other works, namely the *Life of Mary of Egypt*, the *Narratio* of (Pseudo) Nilus Ancyranus, the *Homilies* of John Chrysostom, the *Apology* of Aristides (which has a complicated history of its own), the *Fürstenspiegel* of Agapetus Diaconus, and the Bible. The pre-history of the main narrative – when and where the legend of the Buddha was Christianized – remains obscure, and Volk is too cautious to offer novel speculations. It is thought, for instance, that the Georgian *Balavariani* is based on the Arabic *Kitāb Bilawhar wa Būḏāsf*, which in turn derives from a lost Middle Persian work, itself a translation from Sanskrit. Could things be so? What faith can be had in the critical value of the Arabic text, which survives only in very late copies? Does Syriac have no place in this conjectural genealogy? The discovery of new manuscripts, it is hoped, will shed light on such questions.

The next chapter sketches the literary influence of the Greek *Barlaam* in the Middle Ages and beyond ("Das Fortwirken," pp. 141-57), and it is the only cursory section of the book. Since his *Einführung* concerns, strictly, only the Greek version and since *Barlaam and Joasaph* exists in so many languages across the globe, Volk's restraint here is understandable. To deal in full with the broader *Barlaam* tradition, as he and earlier scholars have remarked, is to confront a *mare magnum*, and so he focuses his survey on the influence of the text on later Byzantine literature. This section is followed by an 81-page summary of the story (pp. 158-239). Impatient readers will find this helpful, perhaps, but a full translation would have been only three times as long (Burchard's 1924 translation is 299 pages, and that of the Loeb edition is similar). The remainder and bulk of this book (pp. 240-594) consists of an exhaustive catalogue of 219 Greek manuscripts, each described in detail; a description of all the translations of the Greek text and their manuscript sources; a list of previous editions and their manuscript sources; a description of planned editions that were never completed; an account of various illustration cycles and their captions, which will be of benefit to art historians; and a manuscript stemma that, in the spirit of Hiram Peri, unfolds from the back to a width that is six times that of the closed book. Together, Volk's edition and introduction would be a praiseworthy accomplishment for a team of scholars; that they are the work of one man is a small wonder.

Valentine A. Pakis

Bibliography

Boissonade 1832: Jean François Boissonade, ed., "Vita Barlaam et Joasaph," in *Anecdota Graeca*, 5 vols., Paris, 4:1-365.

Cruz Palma 2001: Óscar de la Cruz Palma, ed., *Barlaam et Iosaphat, versión vulgata latina con la traducción casellana de Juan de Arce Solorceno (1608)*, Nueva Roma 12, Madrid.

Johanterwage 2007: Vera Johanterwage, *Die Barlaams ok Josaphats saga: Eine höfische Legende am norwegischen Königshof* (Doctoral diss.), Münster.

Martínez Gázquez 1997: José Martínez Gázquez, ed., *Hystoria Barlae et Iosaphat (Bibl. Nacional de Nápoles VIII.B.10)* (Nueva Roma 5), Madrid.

Peri 1959: Hiram Peri (Pflaum), *Der Religionsdisput der Barlaam-Legende, ein Motiv abendländischer Dichtung (Untersuchung, ungedruckte Texte, Bibliographie der Legende)* (Acta Salamanticensia: Filosofía y Letras 14/3), Salamanca.

Schnall 2000: Jens Eicke Schnall, *Didaktische Absichten und Vermittlungsstrategien im altnorwegischen »Königsspiegel« (Konungs skuggsjá)* (Palaestra 307), Göttingen.

Volk 2006: Robert Volk, ed., *Historia animae utilis de Barlaam et Ioasaph (spuria): Text und zehn Appendices* (Patristische Texte und Studien 60), Berlin.

Woodward & Mattingly 1967: George R. Woodward and Harold Mattingly, trans., *St. John Damascene: Barlaam and Joasaph*, 2nd ed. (Loeb Classical Library), London.

Klaus Düwel, *Runenkunde*. 4., überarbeitete und aktualisierte Auflage (Sammlung Metzler 72). - Verlag J. B. Metzler, Stuttgart-Weimar 2008. XII + 278 S. (ISBN 978-3-476-14072-2).

Die vierte und aktualisierte Auflage von Düwels verdientem Handbuch ist 2008 erschienen. Es handelt sich um eine korrigierte und ergänzte Neuauflage, die, was den Darstellungsteil betrifft, seitengleich ist mit der dritten Auflage. Das stattliche Literaturverzeichnis (S. 236-71) ist neben der sachlichen und klaren Darstellung der große Pluspunkt dieses Werkes. Aber auch das Fundortregister ist wertvoll für einen schnellen Einblick. So auch die Konkordanz für Runeninschriften im älteren Futhark auf S. 231-35.

Arend Quak

Yasushi Kawasaki, *Eine graphematische Untersuchung zu den HELIAND-Handschriften*. - Iuducium Verlag, München 2004. 111 S. (ISBN 3-89129-415-8).

In seiner Einleitung gibt der Autor zunächst eine kurze Übersicht über die Handschriften des 'Heliand' und das Verhältnis zwischen den erhaltenen Handschriften und Fragmenten, wobei selbstverständlich im Hinblick auf das Erscheinungsjahr der Studie das später gefundene Leipziger Fragment außer Betracht bleibt. Darauf werden die verschiedenen Ansätze einer historischen Graphematik im 20. Jahrhundert behandelt (S. 21-25). Für diese Untersuchung wurden die Schreiber der einzelnen Handschriften genau auseinander gehalten und die Texte dann vollständig ausgewertet. Dabei wurden alle Handschriften buchstabengetreu transkribiert und in Form alphabetischer Arbeitsindices mit Häufigkeitsangaben und Zeilennachweisen vollständig erschlossen. Die Untersuchung konzentriert sich auf die Wiedergabe der Dentale < þ d ð t> in allen Positionen im Wort. Für die Handschrift M kann festgestellt werden, dass sich die beiden Schreiber nicht strukturell unterscheiden. Im Anlaut wird /þ/ fast immer durch <th> repräsentiert (3815x). Nur beim Lexem *thurb-* finden sich neben 19mal <th> auch 7mal <d> und einmal <dh> im Anlaut. Im Auslaut findet sich hier auch 5mal <t>. Handschrift C hat im Anlaut 7324x <th> und nur zweimal <dh> und zwar auch beim Lexem **thurb-*. Dabei steht auch einmal <t> in *tegan*, aber man wäre mit dem Autor geneigt, im Hinblick auf die sonstigen Formen, einen Schreibfehler für <th> anzunehmen, denn alle Handschriften und auch die Fragmente haben im Anlaut sonst ausschliesslich <th> und nie ein anderes Graphem. Auf diese Art und Weise werden alle Positionen, wo /þ/ vorkommen kann, untersucht. Bei der Handschrift C fällt im Vergleich mit M weiter auf, dass C bei Nasalschwund und nach /r/ eine Vorliebe für <th> aufweist, während M dieses Graphem in dieser Position überhaupt nicht benutzt. Die Fragmente P, V und S haben im In- und Auslaut dagegen nie <th> sondern nur <d> oder <dh>.

Das Verdienst dieser Studie liegt darin, dass sie die Basis legt für weitere Forschung nach den Graphemen im Altsächsischen. Die nächste Frage wäre nämlich die nach den Hintergründen der einzelnen Schreibungen. Man fragt sich etwa, aus welchem Grund nur die Wurzel *thurb- aus der Reihe tanzt. Es handelt sich somit um eine nützliche und interessante Studie.

Arend Quak

Der Codex Vindobonensis 2681 aus dem bayerischen Kloster Wessobrun um 1100.
Diplomatische Textausgabe der Wiener Notker Psalmen, Cantica, Wessobrunner Predigten und katechetischen Denkmäler. Mit Konkordanzen und Wortlisten auf einer CD, herausgegeben von Evelyn Scherabon Firchow unter Mitarbeit von Richard Louis Hotchkiss. - Olms-Weidmann, Hildesheim-Zürich-New York 2009. Geb. xlviii + 468 S. und 4 Abb. (ISBN 978-3-487-13968-5).

In der verdienten Reihe der Ausgabe der Werke Notkers des Deutschen hat Evelyn Scherabon Firchow einen neuen Band herausgebracht. Diesmal handelt es sich um die Edition des Codex Vindobonensis 2681, der die bairische Übersetzung und Bearbeitung der Psalmen Notkers, die katechetischen Denkmäler und Fragmente der sogenannten Wessobrunner Predigten enthält. Die Handschrift wurde um 1100 im Kloster Wessobrunn geschrieben und wird hier zum ersten Mal vollständig herausgegeben, was zu begrüßen ist im Hinblick darauf, dass solche Ausgaben ganzer Sammelhandschriften von großer Bedeutung für die Forschung sind. Erst dann bekommt man einen Einblick in den Kontext und in die Entstehungsgeschichte der einzelnen Texte. Mit Recht betont auch die Herausgeberin, dass man zunächst eine zuverlässige Ausgabe der handschriftlichen Überlieferung haben soll ohne die "Verbesserungen" der einzelnen Editoren (S. xii). Dann folgt die Beschreibung der Handschrift (S. xiii-xviii), wobei die seltsame Reihenfolge auffällt. Vier Schreiberhände haben die Texte geschrieben, die im erhaltenen Kodex in folgender Reihenfolge stehen: Predigtbruchstücke, Notkers Psalmen, Wessobrunner Glaube und Beichte, Notkers Psalmen, Predigtbruchstücke, Notkers Psalmen, Vaterunser, Symbolum apostolorum, Canticum Zachariae, Canticum Sanctae Mariae, Athanasisches Glaubensbekenntnis, Predigtbruchstücke. Der Psalter diente, wie die Hg. wohl mit Recht annimmt (S. xix), für Lesungen. Der Text von Notker wurde weitgehend verdeutscht, wobei diese Übersetzung oft mit den Glossen der St. Galler Handschrift (R) übereinstimmt (xxi). Der lateinische Psalmentext und die Übersetzung stammen aus verschiedenen Quellen. Die anderen Pergamentbruchstücke der Predigtsammlungen A, B und C gehörten ursprünglich auch zur Handschrift 2681 und wurden wahrscheinlich im späten Mittelalter oder in der frühen Neuzeit aus der Handschrift geschnitten (xxiii). Die Handschrift begann ursprünglich mit den Psalmen. Als Provenienz scheint Wessobrunn wahrscheinlich, aber die Geschichte der Handschrift lässt sich nur bis ins 16. Jahrhundert zurückverfolgen, als sich der Kodex in der Bibliothek von Wilhelm, dem Grafen von Zimmern (1549-1594), befand. Sie wurde 1576 dem Erzherzog Ferdinand II. von Tirol geschenkt. Die fehlenden Psalmen 51-100 standen wohl im jetzt verschollenen dritten Teil der ursprünglich aus drei Teilen bestehenden Psalmenhandschrift. Die Sprache der Handschrift ist bairisches Althochdeutsch. Der Text der Handschrift ist vermutlich eine Abschrift, wie etwa aus falschem *zaheren* auf 2vb3 hervorgeht, das getilgt wurde (s. Zeile 7). Interessant sind auch die jüngeren Glossen, die vermutlich auf einen Benutzer zurückgehen, der den Text verdeutlichen wollte, etwa *dero chenun rates*, das durch *e weibs* erklärt, oder *Pediu*, das mit *Darumb* verdeutlicht wird. Dabei hatte der Benutzer offensichtlich auch Probleme mit den Graphemen, denn einige Male wird <z> über das betreffende Graphem der Handschrift hinzugeschrieben.

Natürlich hat sich die Hg. auch Gedanken gemacht über die Absicht dieser Übersetzung der Psalmen. Möglicherweise war sie für Frauen betsimmt und könnte man daraus schließen, dass es schon um 1100 herum in Wessobrunn eine Frauengemeinschaft gab, obwohl der älteste Hinweis darauf erst aus dem Jahre 1138-39 stammt. In der 'Wessobrunner Beichte' erscheinen einige weibliche Formen, die einen weiteren Hinweis darauf bilden, dass dieser Text für Frauen betsimmt war und auch in den Psalmen gibt es zwei solcher Wendungen.

Der Text ist in dieser Ausgabe genau nach der Handschrift abgedruckt worden und folgt ihr so eng wie technisch möglich ist. Die editorischen Eingriffe beschränken sich auf die Auflösungen der handschriftlichen Abkürzungen, die allerdings kursiviert werden. Am Schluss der Einleitung finden sich eine Bibliographie (xxxiii-xl), Abkürzungsverzeichnisse (xli-xlviii) und vier Abbildungen aus der Handschrift. Zu begrüßen ist auch, dass ein CD-Rom - für PC und Macintosh - mitgeliefert wird, der viele Suchmöglichkeiten bietet. Alles in allem eine ausgezeichnete Ausgabe!

Arend Quak

Quellen zur Alltagsgeschichte im Früh- und Hochmittelalter. Zweiter Teil. Ausgewählt und übersetzt von Ulrich Nonn (Ausgewählte Quellen zur deutschen Geschichte des Mittelalters. Freiherr-vom-Stein-Gedächtnisausgabe. Bd. XLb). - Wissenschaftliche Buchgesellschaft, Darmstadt 2007. Geb. 284 S. (ISBN 978-3-534-03159-7).

Mit diesem zweiten Teil liegen jetzt beide Bände der Quellen zur Alltagsgeschichte im Früh- und Hochmittelalter vor, vgl. Besprechung in dieser Zeitschrift, Band 61 (2006), 333-34. Die Prinzipien der Auswahl sind dieselben wie für Band I. Dieser Band enthält vier Abteilungen. Die erste enthält Quellen zur Geschichte des Bauerntums aus der Zeit von 789 bis ins 13. Jahrhundert (S. 13-57). Man staunt über die Tatsache, dass es dem Herausgeber gelungen ist, über diesen in den Quellen doch vernachlässigten Stand eine schöne Auswahl zu machen. Doch wird zugleich deutlich, dass chronologische und geographische Unterschiede existiert haben müssen. Während die 'Kaiserchronik' (um 1150) ausdrücklich sagt, dass ein Bauer, der ein Schwert trägt, verprügelt werden soll, erlaubt eine Waffen- und Kleiderordnung vom Jahre 1244 wenigstens den Hauswirten ein Schwert zu tragen. Und dies obwohl beide Quellen bairisch sind. Es wird auch deutlich, dass die Heerfahrt eine schwere Belastung für die Bauern gewesen sein muss (Nr. 5 und 6). Bei manchen Texten kann man nachdenklich werden. So wenn die Bauern von einem Geistlichen im 12. Jahrhundert nachdrücklich dazu angehalten werden, ihre Zehnten zu zahlen (Nr. 7). Es ist überhaupt deutlich, dass die Quellen besonders die Pflichten der Bauern ins Auge fassen. Die Landflucht der Bauern (Nr. 26) lässt sich denn auch verstehen. Die ausgewählten Quellen behandeln mehrere Aspekte des bäuerlichen Lebens, wobei der Weinbau einen ziemlich großen Platz einnimmt.

Die zweite Abteilung umfasst Handwerk, Gewerbe und Handel (S. 58-111). Interessant ist, dass besonders die älteren Quellen dazu noch die meisten Angaben enthalten und zwar in der Form der Wergelder, aus denen die Bedeutung hervorgeht, die man bestimmten Berufen beimaß (vgl. S. 59). Auch in dieser Abteilung findet man eine reiche Variation an Quellen aus den verschiedensten Zeiten und Gebieten.

Die dritte Abteilung betrifft das klösterliche Leben (S. 119-209), wofür die Quellen erwartungsgemäß reichlicher fließen. Das Mönchtum genoss hohes Ansehen und war in großer Anzahl vorhanden, so dass es fast eine Art dritten Stand zwischen Klerikern und Laien bildete. Hier findet man natürlich die Benediktinerregel als wichtige Quelle, aus der auch hier fleißig zitiert wird, vgl. u.a. Nr. 56, 59, 60, 63, 65 usw. Man fragt sich dabei immer wieder, wie das Verhältnis zwischen dem Ideal der Quellen, wie etwa der Benediktinerregel, und der alltäglichen Wirklichkeit war. Weiter wird auch der Gegensatz zwischen dem Leben im Kloster und dem Leben der Bauernbevölkerung ganz deutlich.

Der letzte Abschnitt umfasst Texte zum Rittertum und zum höfischen Leben (S. 210-81). Hier wird die Frage gestellt nach der Wirklichkeit hinter dem Ideal, das in der höfischen Literatur beschrieben wird (S. 210). Selbstverständlich finden sich hier häufiger volkssprachige Texte wie etwa Gottfrids 'Tristan' (Nr. 83), aber auch der französische Text von Chrestiens' 'Erec et Enide' wird herangezogen. Besonders der *miles christianus* wird in den lateinischen Quellen sichtbar. Wichtige Quellen dabei sind Beschreibungen des großen Hoftags von 1184 in Mainz (Nr. 89, 90); dabei natürlich die Beschreibung des Unwetters durch Otto von St. Blasien, das wohl einem göttlichen Eingreifen zuzuschreiben sei. Im Zusammenhang damit stehen wohl auch die kritischen Bemerkungen von geistlicher Seite zu den ritterlichen Turnieren (Nr. 92-95), was auffällt, da die Geistlichkeit auf der anderen Seite das Rittertum als wichtige Stütze im Kampf gegen die Heiden sah, vgl. Nr. 96 über die *nova militia*.

Das Buch bietet eine repräsentative Auswahl aus den Quellen und dürfte auch deswegen nützlich sein, weil die Übersetzungen mitgeliefert werden, was heutzutage wohl eine Notwendigkeit ist. Ein Sachregister am Schluss des Bandes ergänzt diese schöne Ausgabe.

Arend Quak

Die Weltchronik Heinrichs von München Neue Ee. Herausgegeben von Frank Shaw, Johannes Fournier und Kurt Gärtner (Deutsche Texte des Mittelalters. Hg. v.d. Berlin-Brandenburgischen Akademie der Wissenschaften. Band LXXXVIII). - Akademie Verlag, Berlin 2008. LXXII + 589 S. 3 Tafeln (ISBN 978-3-05-004460-6).

In der Reihe 'Deutsche Texte des Mittelalters' ist ein neuer Band erschienen, der zum ersten Mal die 'Neue Ee' die Geschichte von der Zeitenwende bis ins Mittelalter, zugänglich macht. Erst in den 1980er Jahren des 20. Jahrhunderts wurde die Erforschung der spätmittelalterlichen deutschen Reimchroniken richtig möglich. Bis dahin waren von den vier großen Weltchroniken eigentlich nur das Werk von Rudolf von Ems (1915) und die Weltchronik des Jans Enikels (1900) leicht erreichbar. Als dann um 1980 die Arbeit an der 'Christherre-Chronik' begann, die in den nächsten Jahren erscheinen soll (S. IX), wurde auch das Werk von Heinrich von München aktuell. Im Gegensatz zu den anderen Chroniken waren hier mehrere Autoren für mehrere Auftraggeber tätig: Redaktion α und β. Heinrich von München wird nur in Redaktion β genannt im Prolog und vermutlich war er nicht der Autor des gesamten Werkes. Als Auftraggeber kommen österreichische Adlige in Betracht und die Entstehungszeit liegt um 1380 (S. XII).

Der Typus der Weltchronik kennt die Einteilung nach Weltaltern, wobei allerdings die Redaktion β nur sechs Zeitalter nennt. Die vorchristlichen Zeitalter werden in der 'Alten Ee' behandelt und das letzte Zeitalter somit in der 'Neuen Ee'. In der Einleitung wird die Stelle behandelt, die Heinrichs Werk im Komplex der mittelalterlichen Reimchroniken einnimmt, wobei es besonders um die Vorstufen und Quellen geht, s. das Verzeichnis auf S. XVII. Die Grundlage für die Sprache Heinrichs von München bilden die von ihm selbst aus dem Lateinischen übersetzten Stellen oder solche, die aus deutscher Prosa versifiziert wurden. Auf Grund dessen kann man feststellen, dass die Sprache bairisch war. Die Überlieferung kennt die Handschriften H1-H19, wobei H1 die Erstfassung bildet, H2-H7 die Redaktion α und H8-H19 die Redaktion β. Die einzelnen Handschriften und Fragmente werden beschrieben auf S. XXIV-XXVII. Die Überlieferung konzentriert sich in den letzten Jahrzehnten des 14. Jahrhunderts im Bairischen. Ursprünglich war wohl die Geschichte bis Ludwig den Frommen geplant - *piz auf kayser Ludwegs zeit* (Prolog I,54) -, aber die Redaktion β führt sie weiter bis Friedrich II: *Piz auf chaiser fridreichs czeit* (S. 3, Plusverse Z.18 in H15 und H8). Beide Teile werden in dieser Ausgabe abgedruckt. Die Herausgeber begründen ihre Entscheidung, den ganzen Text herauszugeben, damit, dass es ein Totalkonzept gegeben habe und dass es einen Eindruck von den literarischen Werken vermittelt, die am Ende des 14. Jahrhunderts rezipiert wurden. Für Teil I gilt H1 (Cod. Guelf. 1.5.2. Aug.fol.) als Vorlage, s. die Erklärung S. XXXIII-XXXV. Die Einrichtung der Ausgabe geschieht nach den Prinzipien der Reihe DTM. Im Lesartenapparat werden die wesentlichen Abweichungen aufgenommen, während der zweite Apparat Hinweise zu den Quellen, Erklärungen, Wechsel der Leithandschriften usw. enthält.

Es handelt sich, wie in dieser Reihe zu erwarten, um eine schöne und aufschlussreiche Ausgabe, die durch ein Namenverzeichnis, S. 563-83, ein Wortverzeichnis, S. 585-89, und drei Farbtafeln der Handschrift H1, H3 und H15 in dankenswerter Weise ergänzt wird.

Arend Quak

Wörterbuch der mittelhochdeutschen Urkundensprache (WMU) auf der Grundlage des *Corpus der altdeutschen Originalurkunden bis zum Jahr 1300*. Unter Leitung von Bettina Kirschstein und Ursula Schulze erarbeitet von Sibylle Ohly und Daniela Schmidt. 23.+24. Lieferung: **verswîgen - vorder + vorder - wagen** (Veröffentlichungen der Kommission für deutsche Literatur des Mittelalters der Bayerischen Akademie der Wissenschaften). - Erich Schmidt Verlag, Berlin 2007, 2008. S. 2113-2208 und 2209-2304. (ISBN 978-3-503-02247-2).

Zwei neue Lieferungen des WMU sind erschienen. Damit nähert sich dieses Projekt allmählich dem Abschluss. Es gelingt dem Redaktionsteam, regelmäßig jedes Jahr ein neues Heft dem Publikum vorzulegen. Das ist leider wenig Wörterbuchprojekten gegeben. Auch jetzt kann man wieder feststellen, dass das Wörterbuch eine unumgängliche Ergänzung zum Material in Lexers 'Mittelhochdeutschem Handwörterbuch' bietet. In Lieferung 23 finden sich 55 Lemmata, die sich nicht bei Lexer finden, und auch die 24. Lieferung kennt 45 solcher Wörter. Wie schon bei früheren Besprechungen erwähnt, kombinieren die Herausgeber den Regelmaß der Ausgabe mit Genauigkeit und Gediegenheit. Alle Möglichkeiten werden erwähnt, so wenn z.B. bei *vierder* (S. 2152) bemerkt wird, dass es sich um eine Abkürzung für *vierde(n)zal* handeln könnte, was im Hinblick auf die Tatsache, dass alle drei Belege in derselben Urkunde stehen, nicht ausgeschlossen scheint. Nur wenige Bemerkungen kann man eventuell machen. So fragt man sich, ob bei *vet* (S. 2145) nicht ausdrücklich erwähnt werden sollte, dass es sich um eine niederdeutsche Form handelt, wie auch aus dem Zitat hervorgeht. Interessant ist es zu sehen, dass dieselben Vokabeln im Mittelhochdeutschen und im Mittelniederländischen manchmal sehr unterschiedliche Bedeutungen haben können. So bedeutet mhd. *volklagen* 'eine Klage zu Ende führen' (S. 2193), während mnl. *volclagen* 'sich ordentlich beklagen' (MNW IX, 845) bedeutet. Beide Bedeutungen lassen sich ohne weiteres aus dem Textzusammenhang ableiten. Es ist manchmal faszinierend, die Überlieferungen in so nah verwandten Sprachen wie Mittelhochdeutsch, Mittelniederdeutsch und Mittelniederländisch zu vergleichen. Dieses Wörterbuch kann eine Hilfe bei der Interpretation mittelniederländischer Ortsnamen und Wörter bilden. So z.B. bei mhd. *vrihte/ vrehte* 'Ackerstück von bestimmter Größe' (S. 2246), das nur im Elsass vorkommt. Dies findet eine Entsprechung in anl. *frehtena* 'bestimmtes Flächenmaß': *Et apud Hillenhoven XV frethenas dedit etiam huic cum quadam curte* [1170-80], die Latinisierung eines Maßes, das als *vrecht* noch bis in die Neuzeit in der Gegend von Sittard (Provinz Limburg) benutzt wurde. Aus dem elsässichen Raum stammt auch *vurch* in der Bedeutung 'Furche, Grenzfurch; Vertiefung, Senke' (S. 2286). Da dies im Alt- und Mittelniederländischen als *for-* bzw. *vor-* erscheinen müsste, wäre zu erwägen, ob sich so nicht einige Ortsnamen erklären ließen. So kann das Wörterbuch auch für Forschungen in anderen Sprachen nützlich sein.

Arend Quak

Claudine Moulin & Michel Pauly (Hrsg.), *Die Rechnungsbücher der Stadt Luxemburg*. Erstes Heft 1388-1399 (Schriftenreihe des Stadtarchivs Luxemburg. Band 1). - Luxemburg 2007. 146 S. (ISBN 2-919979-16-7).

Im Archiv der Stadt Luxemburg lagern u.a. die Kontenbücher der Stadt, die von 1388 bis 1796 geführt wurden. Diese ziemlich vollständige Sammlung ist doch eine Seltenheit und es wundert deshalb nicht, dass dieser Text als erster herausgegeben wird in einer neuen Reihe mit Editionen luxemburgischer Texte. Es handelt sich hier um den ersten Band einer voraussichtlich zehn Bände umfassende Ausgabe, die dieses Corpus einem größeren Publikum zugänglich machen will. Wie die Herausgeber in ihrem Vorwort (S. 6) sagen, liegt die Bedeutung solcher Rechenbücher in den Einsichten in das tägliche Leben, die sie verschaffen, und in der Sprache, von der man annehmen darf, dass sie die Alltagssprache im Ort vertritt, wie sie damals gesprochen und geschrieben wurde. In diesem ersten Band finden sich die Kontenbücher für die Jahre 1388-1399.

In der Einleitung von Michel Pauly wird die Überlieferung beschrieben (S. 12). Das älteste erhaltene Buch vom Jahre 1388 war nicht das ursprünglich älteste, wie aus einer Eintragung hervorgeht (S. 13); man vergleiche die Bemerkung *in der lesten rechenonge der stedde* (S. 27,11). Die Ursprünge des Kontenbuches dürften in der Notwendigkeit liegen, die öffentlichen Bauarbeiten zu kontrollieren, wie aus der traditionellen Bezeichnung "Comptes de la baumaîtrie" hervorgeht. Claudine Moulin gibt dann eine Einführung in die Sprache des Raumes, aus dem der Text stammt. Der luxemburg-moselfränkische Raum bietet zwar die frühesten althochdeutschen Glossen (aus Echternach vom Anfang des 8. Jahrhunderts), aber die Quellen der frühen Neuzeit seien noch weitgehend unerforscht. Damit kann diese Ausgabe der Kontenbücher eine Lücke wenigstens teilweise schließen. Erstaunlich sei übrigens auch, dass die Rechenbücher der Frühzeit nur in deutscher Sprache geführt wurden (S. 19).

Die Ausgabe bemüht sich, eine detailgetreue Dokumentation des Textes zu geben. Abkürzungszeichen werden dabei aufgelöst, um dem Leser die Lektüre zu erleichtern. Auch die Textgliederung hält sich weitgehend an der Handschrift. Vielseitige Informationen auf dem Gebiet der öffentlichen Bauarbeiten stehen jetzt zur Verfügung. Dieser Band etwa gibt viel Auskunft über die Arbeiten an den Türmen und Mauern der Stadt. Für den Einblick in das tägliche Leben einer spätmittelalterlichen Stadt bietet der Text also große Möglichkeiten. Man kann nur hoffen, dass die weiteren Bände dieses interdisziplinaren Projekts in absehbarer Zeit erscheinen werden.

Arend Quak

Per Vikstrand, *Bebyggelsenamnen i Mörbylånga kommun. Ortnamnen i Kalmar län 7* (Skrifter utgivna av Institut för Språk och Folkminnen, Namnavdelningen. Serie A: Sveriges ortnamn). - Institut för Språk och Folkminnen, Uppsala 2007. 239 S. (ISBN 978-91-7229-048-8).

Das Buch behandelt die Ortsnamen in der südlichen Hälfte der Insel Öland in der Ostsee. In der Einleitung werden kurz die Geographie und Geschichte dieses Gebiets skizziert. Bewohnung ist seit dem zweiten Jahrhundert nach Chr. mit Sicherheit belegt. Die Ortsnamen deuten darauf hin, dass manche Orte schon vor der späteren Dorfeinteilung aus dem 14. Jarhhundert an der heutigen Stelle lagen, so dass die Annahme, die definitive Lage sei erst damals festgelegt worden, für eine Reihe von Orten nicht stimmen kann (S. 11). Außerdem gebe es Unterschiede in den Namen zwischen der Westküste der Insel mit einer größeren Variation in Namentypen und der Ostküste, die eher etwas jüngere Namen zu enthalten scheine. Es folgt dann ein kurzes Kapitel über die Sprache auf der Insel Öland (S. 19-23). Im dritten Kapitel wird dann der Name der Insel behandelt, der bekanntlich schon im 9. Jahrhundert in Wulfstans Reisebeschreibung in der altenglischen Form *Eowland* belegt ist. Der Name entspricht u.a. nl. *eiland* 'Insel' und wurde vermutlich aus der Sicht der Bewohner der Festlandküste gegeben. Im Mittelalter war die Insel in zwei *mot* eingeteilt, die wahrscheinlich auf eine alte kirchliche Einteilung zurückgehen. Kapitel 4 behandelt die Einteilung in *härader* 'Distrikte' (S. 26-33), die hier ausschließlich primäre Namen umfasst. Im nächsten Kapitel werden mit verdeutlichenden Karten einige Namentypen vorgeführt: *-by, -inge, -lunda, -lösa, -löv, -rum, -stad, -säter* und *-torp*. S. 51-214 finden sich dann die einzelnen Ortsnamen dieser Gegend. Dabei werden in der guten schwedischen Namenforschungstradition die örtliche Aussprache, die ältesten Belege, die Einwohnerbezeichnung und eine Deutung des Namens gegeben. Die Behandlung erfolgt nach der Einteilung in *socken* in alphabetischer Reihenfolge. Die Erläuterungen werden durch Karten und Abbildungen verdeutlicht. Der Verf. scheut auch anekdotische Bemerkungen nicht. So etwa bei *Övetorp* (S. 62), das sogar von offizieller Seite versehentlich als Övertorp geführt wird und sogar 40 Treffs im Internet hat! Die Deutungen der Namen sind vorsichtig, wobei manchmal mehrere Möglichkeiten erwähnt und beargumentiert werden, vgl. etwa Glömminge (S. 65-67). Lobenswert ist auch der Versuch, den Namen mit der faktischen Situation vor Ort zu verbinden. So wenn Kvigerälla mit altschwed. **rydhil* 'Höhe, felsiger Boden' verbunden wird, wobei dann bemerkt wird, dass das Dorf "ligger på en låg men tydlig förhöjning i det här mycket flata landskapet" (S. 69). Alles in allem handelt es sich um ein gediegenes und hübsches Buch.

Arend Quak

Klaus von See & Julia Zernack (Hgg.), *þú ert vísust kvenna*. Beatrice La Farge zum 60. Geburtstag (Skandinavistsische Arbeiten B d. 22). - Universitätsverlag Winter, Heidelberg 2007. Geb. 147 S. (ISBN 978-3-8253-5433-6).

Wie es sich für eine Festschrift gehört, wird sie mit einer Lobrede auf das Geburtstagskind eröffnet, in der Klaus von See mit Recht weit ausholt (S. 9-20). Das passt zum Inhalt dieses Buches, das sehr unterschiedliche Beiträge zur Nordistik und Verwandtem enthält. Katja Schulz schreibt in ihrem Beitrag über eine "amerikanische Edda" (S. 21-47), Longfellows 'Song of Hiawatha'. Obwohl die Bezeichnung zunächst abwegig erscheint, zeigt Schulz, wie sich die Bezeichnung 'Edda' zu einer allgemeinen Genrebezeichnung entwickelt hat, wie auch das Wort *Saga*. Longfellow selbst - der sich in der skandinavischen Literatur inklusive in der 'Kalavala' auskannte - sprach von einer "Indian Edda". Aus dem Aufsatz wird deutlich, wie es dazu kam und sich ein amerikanischer Stoff einem europäischen Erzählmatrix angepasst hat (S. 41). Debora Dusse liefert einen Beitrag zur Rezeptionsgeschichte der altnordischen Überlieferung über Wieland den Schmied in der europäischen Literatur und Kultur (S. 49-64). Julia Zernack geht auf die Reminiszenzen des Baldermythus bei Stefan George ein, einem Autor, bei dem man solches eigentlich nicht erwarten würde (S. 65-83). Matthias Teichert zeigt in seinem Beitrag 'Sigurds magische Schachspiele' (S. 85-102) an Hand der 'Sigurðar saga þǫgla' aus dem 14. Jahrhundert, wie narrative Elemente aus den übersetzten Riddarasǫgur mit einheimischen und anderen Traditionen kombiniert werden. Klaus von See ('Sippe. Einige Bemerkungen zur Geschichte von Wort und Begriff', S. 103-116) schildert die Entwicklung des Begriffs 'Sippe' namentlich im 19. Jahrhundert in "germanentumelnden" Kontexten bis zur politischen Hochkonjuktur im Dritten Reich. Er liefert eine kritische Betrachtung zu den verschiedenen Auffassungen der ursprünglichen Bedeutung des Wortes. Als Abschluss des schönen Bandes bietet Helena Lissa Wiessner einen Auszug aus dem Briefwechsel zwischen Axel Olrik und Andreas Heusler geboten mit einer Einleitung (S. 117-47).

Arend Quak

Proceedings of the 21st International Congress of Onomastic Sciences. Uppsala 19-24 August 2002, 4. Ed. Eva Brylla & Mats Wahlberg in collaboration with Dieter Kremer & Botolv Helleland – Institutet för språk och folkminnen, Uppsala 2008, 420 S. (ISBN 978-7229-054-9).

Die Herausgabe von Kongressabhandlungen erfordert Zeit, viel Zeit, nicht zuletzt wenn die Organisatoren sich dazu entschlossen haben, die Vorträge in gedruckter Form zu veröffentlichen. Der vorliegende Band ist der vierte in der Reihe von fünf geplanten Bänden der Akte des 21. Internationalen Kongresses für Namenforschung, der im August 2002 in Uppsala gehalten wurde. Er enthält die Vorträge zweier ziemlich verschiedenartiger Sektionen, nämlich der Sektion 4, *Name dictionaries and name projects*, mit 24 Beiträgen, und der Sektion 5, *Name treatment and name planning* mit 21 Beiträgen. Die Vorträge stammen aus sehr verschiedenen Sprachgebieten, und hier möchte ich auf einige aufmerksam machen, die den Lesern der Amsterdamer Beiträge vielleicht interessieren könnten. Wie sich schon aus der Überschrift schließen lässt, betrifft es zunächst die Beiträge in der Sektion 4. Hier geht es, nach den Worten von Dieter Kremer in seiner Einleitung um die Vorstellung von aktuellen Forschungsvorhaben oder den Bericht über laufende Projekte. Sieben der Vorträge beschäftigen sich mit anthroponymischen Themen, dreizehn mit toponymischen, während in den restlichen vier Beiträge sowohl Personen- als Ortsnamen im Mittelpunkt stehen. Unter den letzten möchte ich besonders den Vortrag von Angela Bergermayer erwähnen, „Das namenkundliche Forschungsprojekt „Die Sprache des mittelalterlichen Slaventums in Österreich"", der interessante Beispiele der Interaktion von slawischen und germanischen Eigennamen bietet.

Unter den anthroponymisch geprägten Vorträgen sind drei Beiträge hervorzuheben, die alle ihren Ausgangspunkt im interdisziplinären Projekt *Nomen et gens* haben. In „Probleme der Lemmatisierung frühmittelalterliche Personennamen im interdisziplinären Projekt Nomen et gens" erörtern Dieter Geuenich und Heicke Hawicks das Problem, dass die Historiker Personen zunächst prosopographisch erfassen wollen, während die Philologen zumal ihre Namen sprachhistorisch und sprachgeographisch analysieren wollen. Auf dasselbe Thema stoßen wir im Vortrag von Andreas Schorr „Konflikte und Probleme in der interdisziplinären Zusammenarbeit von Historikern und Philologen. Ein Erfahrungsbericht aus dem Projekt Nomen et gens". In „Probleme der ethnischen Identifikation. Der Beitrag der Geschichtswissenschaft zu einem interdisziplinären Personennamenlexikon am Beispiel der Namen des Frankenreichs (Hagiographie/Historiographie)" geht Steffen Patzold näher auf die Frage ein, in wie weit es möglich sei, Aussagen zu machen über die Ethnizität von Personen, die in frühmittelalterlichen Quellen auftreten. Seine Konklusion lautet, dass ethnische Zugehörigkeit nicht eine Frage des Blutes, sondern von Eigen- und Fremdzuschreibungen war.

Ulf Timmermann zeigt in seinem Beitrag „Auf dem Weg zu einem Lexikon nordfriesischer Vornamen" wie schwer es ist, einen Vornamen gerade als nordfriesisch zu deuten. Die oft unfreiwillig komischen Titel von Vornamen- und Familiennamenbücher geben Ken Tucker Anlass in „A new approach to personal names dictionaries. The proposed Canadian forenames and surnames dictionary" nach brauchbaren Aufnahmekriterien für solche Nachschlagewerke zu suchen.

Bei den Vorträgen, die sich auf die Toponymie konzentrieren, geht es einerseits um mehr oder weniger allgemeine Projektbeschreibungen, andererseits um die Erörterung von Sonderproblemen, die im Laufe eines Ortsnamenprojektes auftreten können. Zu der erstgenannten Kategorie gehören drei schweizerische Beiträge, von Martin Hannes Graf „Das Nationalfonds-Projekt Datenbank der Schweizer Namenbücher. Der Kanton St. Gallen", von Eugen Nyffenegger „Thurgauer Namenbuch. Die Siedlungsnamen des Kantons Thurgau" und von Viktor Weibel „Orts- und Flurnamenbuch des Kantons Nidwalden. Projekt Orts- und Flurnamenbuch des Kantons Schwyz". Aus dem nordgermanischen Sprachgebiet stammt der Vortrag von Svavar Sigmundsson „Dictionary of Icelandic Place Names".

In der letztgenannten Kategorie sind zwei Beiträge zu erwähnen, die sich trotz ihrer Titel teilweise auch mit Ortsnamen germanischen Ursprungs befassen, nämlich von Laimute Balode „The historical dimension of toponyms in Latvian onomastic dictionaries" und von Inge Bily „Die Vorkarten im Atlas altsorbischer Ortsnamentypen". In „Field-names in the Achterhoek, province of Gelderland. A regional research project" zeigt Louise H. Maas auf die vielen Übereinstimmungen in der Mikrotoponymie der östlichen Niederlanden und des angrenzenden Deutschland. Zuletzt soll hier auch der interessante Beitrag von Maria Vòllono erwähnt werden, ‚Nordwörter' und ‚Südwörter'. Alte Wortschichten in Siedlungs- und Flurnamen und ihre Aussagefähigkeit für die Stellung des Saar-Mosel-Raums innerhalb der ‚Westgermania' – eine Projektpräsentation".

Die Themen der Sektion 5, *Name treatment and name planning* liegen den Lesern der Amsterdamer Beiträge in ihrem wissenschaftlichen Leben vielleicht etwas ferner als diejenigen der Sektion 4, im Alltag begegnen sie ihnen aber oft. Ein Teil der Vorträge beschreibt nämlich die Probleme, die sowohl national als international mit der Standardisierung und Rechtschreibung von Ortsnamen verbunden sind, andere beschäftigen sich mit der Frage, wie Recht and Eigenname sich zu einander verhalten, und mit der Rolle der Namengebung in der Werbung.

Zusammen bieten die 45 Vorträge dieses vierten Bandes der Akte des 21. Internationalen Kongresses für Namenforschung einen deutlichen Einblick in die Problematik der beiden Sektionen. Dabei soll man natürlich bedenken, dass seit 2002 bereits viele Jahre verlaufen sind. Wer gerne wissen möchte, was letztendlich aus all diesen schönen Vorhaben geworden ist, kann vielleicht versuchen das mit Hilfe von Google herauszufinden.

Rob Rentenaar

Thomas Neukirchen. *Die ganze aventiure und ihre lere. Der „Jüngere Titurel" Albrechts als Kritik und Vervollkommnung des „Parzival" Wolframs von Eschenbach.* – Universitätsverlag Winter, Heidelberg 2006. 388 S. Geb. (ISBN: 3-8253-5231-5)

Obiges Werk, Habilitationsschrift des Aachener Germanisten Th. Neukirchen, gilt als Fortsetzung und Ergänzung der langen Reihe von wissenschaftlichen Untersuchungen der letzten hundert Jahren zum Thema „Jüngeren Titurel" und dessen Verhältnis zu Wolframs „Parzival". Laut dem Inhaltsverzeichnis gliedert sich die Monographie in elf Kapitel, zusammen mit dem Vorwort. Diese verlaufen so: I. Einleitung; II. Prolog und Programm des „Jüngeren Titurel"; III. Vorfahren und Geburt Titurels und sein Leben bis zur Geburt Sigunes; IV. Vom Beginn der Liebe Sigunes und Tschinotulanders bis zu Tschinotulanders Orientzug; V. Tschinotulanders Ende und die Zerstörung des Brackenseils; VI. Die Bedeutungslosigkeit der „Titurel" –Fragment für die zwei Erzähler des „Jüngeren Titurel" und die grundsätzliche Kritik Albrechts an Wolfram; VII. Kritik der sogenannten Hinweisstrophen; VIII. Mutmaßungen über „Verfasserfragment" und „Parzival"; IX. Die aventiure und ihre lere; X. Anhang: Genealogie;

XI. Bibliographie. Subkategorien befinden sich unter jeder Überschrift.

Der Autor beginnt mit Einleitung und einem detaillierten Abriß der Forschung, der eine exzellente Skizze des bisherigen Forschungsstandes hervorhebt. Zu betonen ist freilich die Feststellung, daß es sich prinzipiell um ein „epigonales" Werk handelt, welches im Laufe der Zeit als Zielscheibe der Kritiker fungieren mußte. Dies will auch der Autor - wie seine jüngsten Vorgänger - schrittweise ändern. Der Leser gewinnt somit Übersicht der Tendenzen und nimmt zugleich Stellung des Verfassers bezüglich der umstrittenen Entscheidung des Wolf/Nyholm-Gespanns, das sich für die Wahl der Leithandschrift A entschied, wahr. (Neukirchen steht der Entscheidung kritisch gegenüber, was auch seine eigenen Leistungen hier z. T. beeinträchtigt.) Positiv zu bewerten ist die Beobachtung von dem Autor in bezug auf den Gesamttext: „Eine umfassende textkritische Untersuchung der Hss. des „Jüngeren Titurel" ist und bleibt nach wie vor ein Desiderat der Forschung". (S. 16) Die darauffolgenden Seiten werden der bisherigen Forschung gewidmet (S. 17-35). Teil 2 von diesem Eingangskapitel gilt dem eigenen Thesenvorgang (Prospekt, S. 35-40), wo der Autor etliche Fragen aufwirft. Dabei wirken jene Fragen mal fokussiert, und mal tendenziös. Der Geist Wolframs und dessen „Parzival" liegen obigen Fragen zugrunde.

Kapitel II (Prolog und Programm des „Jüngeren Titurel") setzt sich mit Pro- und Epilog auseinander. Hier zeigt sich der Verfasser souverän in Sache Forschungspointe, vor allem im Sinne Wolframs „Parzival" und „Willehalm". Die Zusammenhänge mit Bertold von Regensburg wirken überzeugend; Neukirchen betont absichtlich „Willensfreiheit des Menschen" und „Tugendhaftigkeit des Menschen". Albrecht, so Neukirchen, verschafft neue Horizonte des Wolframschen, indem er als lebendiger „Wolfram-Erzähler" auftritt. Damit besagt Albrecht, so die These, Verbesserungsvorschläge. Dabei tauchen laut dem Autor kritische Töne auf, die die damalige (und heutige) Leserschaft zur Kenntnis nehmen sollte („... wer anders als Wolfram von Eschenbach hätte gegen die eigene mächtige Autorität wirkungsvoller ins Feld geführt werden können", S. 63). So wirkt von Scharfenberg, so Neukirchen, total souverän, auch in Sache Wolframkritik. Der Autor will hier sagen, daß das Rollenspiel seines Albrechts mit und gegen den Strich zu lesen ist, d. h. Albrechts „Wolfram" ist ein Bejahungsinstrument des „neuen" Wolframs. Textuell ist aber zu merken, daß der neue Wolfram viel wortreicher ist; manches zieht sich lange hin, was auch an den vielen „Titurel"-Zitaten zu sehen ist. Laut Neukirchen wirkt Albrechts „Titurel" als „Ergänzung, Korrektur und Umgestaltung bestimmter wesentlicher Passagen des *Parzival*"; in mancher Hinsicht muß man ihm Recht geben.

Kapitel III (Vorfahren und Geburt Titurels uns sein Leben bis zur Geburt Sigunes) wird, wie der Titel selbst suggeriert, dem Leben des Gralkönigs gewidmet. Bis auf gewisse von dem Autor selbst vorgenommene Textänderungen (siehe unten) ist dieses Kapitel eine Erläuterung des „Jüngeren Titurel" selbst. Wolframs Urwerk kommt seltener in Frage; statt dessen lernt man von dem durchaus faszinierenden Leben Titurels, seinen Fehlern und seiner Abdankung. Dazu kommt eine Resümierung Neukirchens der Gralgesetze (S. 130ff.), die sowohl für die Scharfenbergforschung als auch für die Wolframforschung von Interesse sind. In mancher Hinsicht steckt hier das Geheimnis der Leistung dieser Habilitationsschrift: Albrecht zeigt in der Tat, wie im Kap. IV, geniale Fähigkeiten, die Neukirchen nicht zur Kenntnis nimmt. Auch die Gralsippe kommt unter die Lupe, und laut Albrecht und dem Autor schneidet sie relativ schlecht ab.

Kapitel IV (Vom Beginn der Liebe Sigunes und Tschinotulanders bis zu Tschinotulanders Orientzug) setzt sich mit dem Text weiterhin stark auseinander, indem der Autor sich mit Text und bisherigen Textanalysen befaßt. Der Verfasser zeigt sich hier ebenfalls souverän mit dem Text und der passenden Forschung, etwa W. Schröder, Heinzle, Zatloukal, Parshall, Guggenberger, usw. Wichtige JT-bezogene Themen der Beziehung zwischen Sigune und Tschinotulanders, deren Liebe und die Basis der Brackenseilgeschichte werden untersucht und ausgewertet. Gelungen ist auch das Verbinden der obigen Tugenden (vgl. Kap. II) mit Tschinotulanders selbst, so Neukirchen. Hier verschafft der Autor neue Perspektive in Sache JT-Forschung, was zu loben ist. Der „Parzival"-Leser bekommt auch neue Impulse, da man diesen Hintergrund wohl kaum kennt. Auch der Willehalmforscher kann von den z. T. neuen Zusammenhängen lediglich profitieren, da die Ruckschlüsse aufschlußreich wirken. Aktuell wirkt auch die detaillierte Erläuterung des Orientzuges, dies im Sinne der neugewonnenen Faszination mit dem Konfikt zwischen Orient und Okzident. Hervorzuheben sei insbesondere der Aufenthalt in Bagdad und Umgang mit dem „Anderen", was auch Stoff für weitere Untersuchungen liefert. Abstecher Richtung Edelsteinsymbolik und Oriluskonflikt schließen das Kapitel ab.

Kapitel V (Tschinotulanders Ende und die Zerstörung des Brackenseils) wird von den jeweiligen Strängen textuell dominiert. Der Verfasser fokussiert auf die Gründe obiger Zerstörung - Rache, die Neugier Sigunes, ihre dominierende (und zerstörerische) Position vis-à-vis Tschinotulanders (S. 235) und den kommenden Tod selbst, wo Albrecht wieder Kontakt mit dem „Parzival" aufnimmt. Interessant wirkt auch die Rolle der Saelde, die in anderen „epigonalen" Werken wie Heinrichs „Diu Crone" auftaucht, allerdings unter einem anderen Blickwinkel und Textposition. Dies hat m. E. Neukirchen völlig außer acht gelassen. Richtig beurteilend wirkt die Diskussion von dem Tod des Tschinotulanders (S. 244ff.); mit Recht spricht der Autor von Tschinotulanders' „willekür", eine Stelle, wo Neukirchen vielleicht seinen Favoriten von dem alten Meister differenzieren müßte.

Kapitel VI (Die ganze *aventiure* des „Parzival") befaßt sich mit den „Titurel"-Fragmenten für den Text und JT-Forschung schlechthin. Nach der Auslegung Neukirchens zeigt sich Albrecht selbstständig, kritisch und distanziert von Wolfram (S. 260). Die Klage über mangelhafte Unterstützung des Dichters selbst mag überzeugend klingen, wirkt aber gegen eine Selbstverherrlichung des Scharfenbergschen Schaffens (Fazit: wäre es so bahnbrechend, wie Neukirchen behauptet, so hätte man ihn vielleicht nicht im Stich gelassen). Die letzten Worte fallen zugunsten des Dichters und seiner Leistung. Albrecht, so der Autor, wirkt souverän in Sache Parzivalfortsetzung und -verbesserung; ihm sollte man den Lorbeerkranz gönnen. Mit Recht stellt der Autor fest, daß die obigen Fragmente Wolframs gar nicht hineingehören. Wegen Tschinotulanders Tod (und Schuld, die dadurch subsumiert wird) aber bleibt zu fragen, ob sich der hier suggerierte moralische Wert des „Jüngeren Titurel" wirklich bewahrheiten läßt. Die Frage nach dem „Besitz der *aventiure*" wirkt daher gegenstandslos (S. 271), da alle beide Dichter ein Gesamtbild verschaffen.

Es folgen die Kapitel VII (Kritik der Hinweisstrophen) und VIII (Mutmaßungen über „Verfasserfragment" und „Parzival"). Kapitel VII bringt eine ergiebige Anzahl von wichtigen Beobachtungen zum Thema Hinweisstrophen, deren Bedeutungen und die möglichen Benutzungsformeln, die dazu passen. Gemäß der eigenen Verbesserungsthese des Autors wirken jene Strophen kritisch und nützlich. Wichtig zu merken ist auch die Auswertung der Überlieferungszweige (vgl. S. 278ff.; 286ff.), wo Neukirchen mit Recht von den recht mangelhaften Qualitäten der jeweiligen Textströmungen schreibt (I befaßt sich mit Wolfram/Albrecht; II mit Erzähler Wolfram). Eine bevorstehende Aufgabe, so der Autor, wäre Festlegung einer repräsentativen Texttradition, die sich auf solider Manuskriptenbasis stützt. Das Ende jenes Kapitels setzt sich mit der Schröderfassung der Handschrift „H", die mangelhaft ist, und mit Deutungskonstanten auseinander. Die Mutmaßungen über das sogenannte „Verfasserfragment" handeln sich um obige Tendenzen der Forschung, wo „Wolfram"-Segmente (vgl. Kap. VII) mit Wolfram/Albrecht-Erzählertendenzen zu kontrastieren sind. Daher gilt dieses Kapitel als Fortsetzung und Verteidigungsinstrument des vorigen Kapitels, wo sich jene Tradition der Mehrströmigkeit manifestiert. Die wissenschaftlichen Argumentationsformen sind solid, geistreich und kenntnisvoll; sie untermauern die Grundthese(n) der ermahnenden, verbessernden Dichtung, wirken selbstständig und überzeugend.

Kapitel IX (Die *aventiure* und ihre *lere*), das letzte Kapitel, ist das *summa theologiae* des Werkes, der Versuch, alles unter Dach und Fach zu bringen. [L]ere gilt laut dem Autor als Grundeigenschaft und Substrat des Albrechtschen Schaffens: sie setzt die „Parzival"-Tradition richtig fort, moralisiert, fokussiert und verbessert die Wolframsche Tradition, die man bestens gekannt hat, damit die Gralsage ein korrektes Ende findet. Überzeugend und lehrreich wirkt das Ende; Neukirchen agiert souverän mit den von ihm angesammelten Punkten zugunsten der eigenen These. Das Kapitel schließt mit Beobachtungen über *prodesse et delectare* (Bildung und Genuß), zusammen mit Kommentaren zur Form der narrativen Ethik.

Kapitel X (Anhang: Genealogie) bietet dem Leser eine exzellente Skizze des „Clan-Mapping" des Gralgeschlechtes; Kapitel XI bringt eine hervorragende Bibliographie.

Schlußbemerkungen: Neukirchens Monographie ist zweifelsohne eine exzellente Leistung, die neue Wege in der „Jüngeren Titurel"-Forschung schafft, die m. E. notwendig sind. Der Autor präsentiert luzide Argumente zugunsten seiner These der Differenzierung und Untermauerung der Scharfenbergschen Argumentationsformeln, d.i. die Fortsetzung als *lere*, als Abbruch mit der „Parzival"-Unterwürfigkeit und zugleich als *continuatio* der Gralgeschichte, allerdings mit Vorbedacht. Gelungen ist diese Monographie in dem Sinne, auch mit etwas Skepsis seitens des heutigen (und vielleicht auch damaligen) Lesers. Defizite an Talent findet man nicht. Kritisch steht dieser Beobachter dem absichtlichen Versuch des Autors gegenüber, der viele Wolfschen Textstellen kontinuierlich umgestaltet hat nach eigenem Wunsch und Bedarf, z.

B. S. 117, wo man „begen si icht sunden // da mvz_ si vur vil herte b_z erkiesen" liest, statt Wolfs „vur sunde werk und willen m_zen si dem libe b_z" (515). Diese oftmals willkürlich vorgenommenen Textänderungen wirken verwirrend, lenken vom besseren, textbezogenen, standardisierten Textverständnis ab, und sind unnötig. Neukirchen ist aber nicht der erste oder letzte, der solches macht. Erwünschenswert wäre aber der Wolftext pur. Ansonsten findet der Leser hier ein hervorragendes, informatives und wichtiges Werk, welches in die Forschungsbestände unserer Bibliotheken gehört.

Gary C. Shockey

Claudia Lauer, *Ästhetik der Identität. Sänger-Rollen in der Spruchdichtung des 13. Jahrhunderts*, Universitätsverlag Winter, Heidelberg 2008.

„Literatur diskutiert und beschreibt Identitätsmodelle. Im Gegensatz zum höfischen Roman, der neben der Frage nach dem Ich-Erzähler v.a. die Möglichkeit narrativer Figurenanalyse bietet, konzentriert sich die Frage nach Identität innerhalb der Lyrik ausschließlich auf die Frage >Wer spricht?<. Damit sind zwei der umstrittensten Bereiche innerhalb der mediävistischen Literaturwissenschaft aufgerufen: >Ich< und >Rolle<."

Diese Zeilen eröffnen das reichhaltige Buch das, nach dem Vorwort (S.5-6), fünf Kapitel umfasst: 1. Einleitung (S. 11-27), 2. Zu einer Ästhetik der Identität (S. 29-41), 3. Die ästhetischen Handlungsrollen (S. 49- 285), unterteilt in 3.1 geistliche Lehre, 3.2 weltliche Lehre, 3.3 politische Lehre, 3.4 Kunstlehre, 4. Zu einer Ästhetik der Identität - Zusammenfassung und Ausblick (S.287-317), 5. Schlussbemerkungen (S. 319-325), und einen Anhang (S. 327-355). Der Leser muss sich auf ein verwickeltes Problemgebiet von Dichtung und Wahrheit in der Sangspruchdichtung vorbereiten.

Im Vorwort weist die Verfasserin auf den Kern ihres Buches: „Ich" und „Rolle" in der Sangspruchdichtung" hin und sie erwähnt als Basis Ciceros Betrachtungen (106 – 43 v. Chr.) über die *persona*, in der die Einheit „Ich" als eine Vielfalt von „Rollen" erkannt ist.

Nun geht das lateinische Wort *persona* zurück auf das schon bei Homer (8. Jh. v. Chr.) vorkommende Wort *prosoopon*, 'Antlitz', später ‚Maske des Schauspielers', von Cicero gebraucht für die ‚Rolle' die der Mensch in unterschiedlichen sozialen Verhältnissen hat. Es handelt sich hier m.E. um ein allgemeines menschliches Verhalten. Jeder Mensch - in der Antike, im Mittelalter und auch heute – ist eine Bündelung sozialer Rollen. Wir reagieren heute auch unterschiedlich, je nach der Situation, in der wir uns befinden: zu einem Kind sagen wir „Du hast eine schöne Zeichnung gemacht" (Rolle des Erziehers), zur Nachbarin, die oft Klavier spielt „Sie spielen ganz schön" (Rolle des Friedensapostels), zu einem Freund der eine dicke Wange hat „Geh' mal zum Arzt oder Zahnarzt" (Rolle des Ratgebers). Jean Fourquet, hat schon 1954 in seinen *'Thèses sur le Minnesang'* auf die Rolle der *persona* in der deutschen mittelalterlichen Lyrik hingewiesen: *L'auteur conçoit un personnage, placé dans une situation - pour fin d'exprimer ce que ressent et pense son personnage placé dans cette situation.* Claudia Lauer recherchiert jetzt das Problem ausführlich für die Sangspruchdichtung. Der Aufbau ihrer Untersuchungen ist folgender: Die unterschiedlichen Rollen, die das Ich spielt, werden ausgehend von zwei „früheren" Dichtern – Herger/Spervogel und Walther von der Vogelweide - bei „späteren" Dichtern, wie dem Marner, Reinmar von Zweter und Heinrich von Meißen, untersucht.

Kapitel 1. Einleitung, bietet eine Übersicht über die Entwicklung der Forschung der Sangspruchdichtung seit ihren Anfängen. Im 19. Jahrhundert suchte man in der Sangspruchdichtung die biografische Wirklichkeit des Dichters. Dieses Interesse setzte sich im 20. Jahrhundert fort, aber „wohl nicht zuletzt auf grund des Mangels an realhistorischen Hinweisen innerhalb der Dichtung selbst" (S. 18) - und, würde ich sagen, weil wir über das Leben der Dichter so wenig wissen – wurde die biografische Methode verlassen und wandte man sich einer abstrakteren Betrachtungsweise zu, die diese Dichtkunst u.a. „als *ars* von Gott bezieht, an ethische und religiöse Grundwahrheiten erinnert" (S. 19). Diese Forschungsentwicklung erinnert in hohem Maße an die Skizze die Joseph Ratzinger, der heutige Papst Benediktus XVI. in dem Vorwort seines Buches ‚Jesus von Nazareth' (Herderverlag, 2008, S. 10-13) gibt. Er beschreibt die Wendung in der Theologie seit den 50er Jahren des 20. Jahrhunderts als den immer größer werdenden Riss zwischen, „dem historischen Jesus" und dem „Christus des Glaubens". Der Papst bekämpft die Auffassung der biografischen Theologen, dass „die Evangelien den geheimnisvollen, auf Erden erschienenen Gottessohn gleichsam mit Fleisch umkleiden" wollen mit dem Argument: „Sie brauchten ihn nicht mit Fleisch zu ‚umkleiden', er hatte wirklich Fleisch angenommen". Die vom Papst angegriffene Forschung könnte antworten: „Quod esset demonstrandum".

Die germanistische Literaturwissenschaft ihrerseits wurde nach dem Verlassen der biografischen Richtung allmählich durch die vielen Rollen des „Ichs" gefesselt: an diese Forschungsrichtung schließt Claudia Lauer an. Sie bespricht die Grundfrage „Wer spricht?", dargestellt an Hand von den Rollen die das „Ich" in zwei Strophen von Heinrich von Meißen spielt. Diese Problematik, die auch als Rückgriff auf den ‚Sitz im Leben' verstanden wird, nennt die Verfasserin „Ästhetik der Identität".

In Kapitel 2, ‚Zu einer Ästhetik der Identität' geht die Verfasserin von der doppelten Prämisse aus, dass Sangspruchdichtung pragmatische und ästhetische Kunst zugleich ist und legt ihre Ausgangspunkte klar dar (S. 29): „Es handelt sich so gesehen um kommunikatives Handeln, das situativ gebunden und zugleich relativ situationsabstrakt ist, das gleichzeitig als poetische Kommunikation und soziale Interaktion verstehbar ist, und dessen übergeordnetes Wirkziel in der überzeugenden inhaltlichen wie ästhetischen Vermittlung bestimmter Werte und Normen besteht". Das alles dürfte richtig sein: ‚kommunikativ' weil die Sangspruchtexte im Mittelalter für Zuhörer oder Leser gemeint sind, ‚situativ' weil sie sich auf eine vorhandene Situation beziehen, ‚situationsabstrakt' weil sie auch allgemeingültige Aussagen enthalten, ‚poetische Kommunikation' weil die Texte allgemeine poetische Merkmale haben, ‚soziale Interaktion' weil sie sich zu bekannten sozialen Verhältnissen äußern. Nur ist es für die heutige Forschung eine schwierige Frage welche dieser Möglichkeiten in einem bestimmten Spruch vorliegen.

Kapitel 3 ‚Die ästhetischen Handlungsrollen'. Bei dem Vergleich früherer und späterer Dichter ist m.E. Vorsicht geboten, so in der Abteilung ‚Sündenklage' wo die Verfasserin (S. 50-52) zunächst eine Strophe des frühen Spervogel (um 1170) analysiert und anschließend eine Gebetsstrophe des späten Marner (1230-1265), die ähnliche Motive aufweist, von denen sie (S. 52) sagt: „Die Sündenklage des Marners nimmt Motive, Strukturen und Topoi des Spruchs von Herger/Spervogel auf". Hier – und an anderen Stellen – kann der Leser irrtümlicherweise den Eindruck bekommen, dass es eine durchlaufende Linie von Vorbild und Nachfolge in der Sangspruchdichtung gegeben hat, was so wohl nicht gemeint ist.

Im Abschnitt ‚Weltliche Lehre' behandelt der Teil ‚Armutsklage' S. 88/89, Herger/Spervogel, der MF 29,13 als hungernder fahrender Sänger in einem Garten vergebens nach Obst sucht. Von hier aus entwickelt die Verfasserin ihre Betrachtungen über die Armutsklage beim Marner *Dû teilest ungelîche, lieber hêrre got, dîn guot* und in Walther von der Vogelweides Tegernseespruch L 104,23, wo der Dichter im Kloster nur Wasser zu trinken bekommt. Überzeugend ist auch das Nacheinander der Reaktionen auf materielle und soziale Armut in Strophen vom Spervogel, Walther von der Vogelweide (Tegernseestrophe), dem Marner und vom Meißner (S. 93-99). Die Analysen der Verfasserin legt die Rezeptionsmöglichkeiten unterschiedlicher Gesellschaftskreise klar.

Ob Walther in L 31,13 *Ich hân gemerket: von der Seine unz an die Muore, von dem Pfâde unz an die Trâbe* das Gebiet abgrenzt, das er als fahrender Sänger kennengelernt hat (S. 156) oder vielleicht als hochgeschätzter Mitreisender des Bischofs Wolfger von Passau, der wiederholt in Italien *von dem Pfâde unz an die Trâbe* war – man denke an die Reiserechnungen des Bischofs aus den Jahren 1203/4 nach denen Walther einen nicht zu unterschätzenden Betrag bekommen hat, was ein anderes Licht auf diesen Spruch werfen würde -, bleibe dahingestellt.

Überzeugend ist wieder die Interpretation der ersten Strophe von Walthers Reichston (S.158), wo Claudia Lauer - neben gelehrten Elementen wie das Wortspiel auf den Topos *êre ist bezzer danne guot*, der Dreifaltigkeit *guot, êre, gotes hulde*, der Haltung des Nachdenkenden, die schon seit dem 9. Jahrhundert in der bildenden Kunst bekannt ist für den Heiligen Joseph, der nach Matthäus 1:19-24, zweifelnd nachdenkt über die jungfräuliche Schwangerschaft der Maria, bevor ein Engel Gottes ihn eines Besseren belehrt (Köln, Schnütgenmuseum, italienischer Reliquienschrein aus Elfenbein aus dem 9. Jahrhundert, siehe Wolfgang Braunfels, Die Welt der Karolinger und ihre Kunst, München 1968, S. 286, Abbildung Nr. 194), - eine Negation von Walthers Rolle als Ratgeber (*dô dâhte ich mir vil ange wie man zer welte solte leben*) erkennt zugunsten seiner praktisch-poetischen Identität als Fahrender (*stîge und wege sint in genomen: untriuwe ist in der sâze, gewalt vert ûf der strâze*).

In der Abteilung 3.4 Kunstlehre interpretiert die Verfasserin sehr schön die Sängerklagen (S.229ff.) bei Walther von der Vogelweide, Reinmar von Zweter, dem Marner und dem Meißner. Durch das Auftreten der unhöfischen Sängerkonkurrenz droht Walther auch selbst die Rolle eines unhöfischen Sängers zu übernehmen um sich am Hofe behaupten zu können, wendet sich aber abschließend an Herzog Leopold um höfische Hilfe, bei Reinmar von Zweter findet die „zunehmende Entbindung vom Hofherrn" statt, beim Marner das ‚Zurücktreten der engen sozial-höfischen Abhängigkeit des Sängers' und beim Meißner schließlich wandelt sich die Kunstklage in eine Gesellschaftsklage.

Der Marner lobt in seiner Totenklage (S. 235ff.) seine verstorbenen Vorgänger (u.a. Walther) sehr, aus deren Garten er seine Blumen liest. Ähnliche persönliche Rückgriffe kennen auch andere Spruchdichter.

In der Abteilung Publikumsschelte 3.4.4. (S. 238 ff) gibt Walthers schwierige Strophe L 84,22 *ich drabe dâ her vil rehte drîer slahte sanc*, in der er die drei, bei den *rederîchen*, d.h. den Redegewandten, beliebten Arten des Gesanges, nämlich den hohen, niederen und mittleren Gesang behandelt, der Verfasserin Anlass zu hochinteressanten Betrachtungen über Walthers Dichtungsart. Walther bezieht diese uns aus der mittellateinischen Poetik als *grandiloquus, humilis* und *mediocris* bekannten drei Stilarten, auf sein eigenes Dichten und bittet den *edelen künig* um Rat, wie er sie in ein allgemein akzeptierbares Lied zusammenbringen kann (vgl. Hendrik Sparnaay, Zu Walthers ‚*Drîer slahte sanc*', in: Neophilologus 19, 1934, S. 102-107). Er möchte *ein ungehazzet liet*, d. h. ein für sein Publikum geeignetes Lied zusammensetzen. Ein ähnliches Problem kennt der Marner wenn er sagt *wer kann dirre werlte nâch ir willen nû wol sprechen?* Sowohl bei Walther wie beim Marner wird das Publikum als dumm dargestellt.

In Konkurrentenschelte , Abteilung 3.4.4 (p. 242ff.) behandelt die Verfasserin in genauen werkimmanenten Interpretationen die Polemik der sich als legitim betrachteten Sänger - Walther von der Vogelweide, Reinmar von Zweter, der Meißner - gegen lärmende Sängerkonkurrenten und *lotterritter* und enthüllt damit „eine christlich-anthropologische Verallgemeinerung" des „eitlen, hoffärtigen und falschen Menschen".

Im Kapitel 4 unterscheidet die Verfasserin (S. 315) für die mittelalterliche Sangspruchdichtung drei Ebenen :
1. die Wirklichkeits- und Gesellschaftsebene
2. die Aufführungsebene: Sänger, Publikum, Text-Ich und textinneres Gegenüber,
3. Textebene, die sich in den uns jetzt vorliegenden Textausgaben realisiert.

Mit diesem ‚sangspruchspezifischem Kommunikationsmodell' will die Verfasserin die Integration in die mittelalterliche Lebenswelt darstellen. Dazu wäre folgendes zu sagen. So wie das literarische Ich des Dichters nicht sein biografisches Ich ist, so ist die in der Lyrik hervorgerufene literarische ‚Wirklichkeit' nicht die historische Realität. Ein Beispiel: In Walthers Ottenton heißt es L 11,37 ff. *Die fürsten sint iu undertân und habent mit zühten iuwer kunft erbeitet. und ie der Missenaere, der ist iemer iuwer âne wân, von got wurde ein engel ê verleitet.* Aus der Geschichte ist aber bekannt, dass der Markgraf von Meißen gegen Otto komplottiert hatte, so dass Walthers ‚Wirklichkeit', aus welchem Grunde auch, unrichtig ist.

Was uns als Philologen heute vorliegt, ist die Textebene. Ein allgemeines Problem das in vielen Studien auftaucht ist die Beziehung zwischen Dichtung und Wirklichkeit. Wiederholt werden in vielen Studien, auch im vorliegenden Buch, literarische Aussagen auf eine Realität bezogen, deren Wirklichkeitswert problematisch ist. Noch ein Beispiel: in der Behandlung des Herrscherlobes analysiert die Verfasserin „im politisch aktualisierten Kontext" die Lobgesänge von Walther von der Vogelweide (S. 170) und von Reinmar von Zweter (S. 173) auf Kaiser Friedrich II. (*der edel künec, der milte künec, ein wahter Cristentuomes, der triuwen triskamer hort, vrides hant*). Aber in Wirklichkeit war Friedrich II. ein Unmensch. Seine Grausamkeit war schrecklich. Den Verschwörern von Capaccio ließ er 1246 die Nase abschneiden, die Hände und Füße abhacken, und die Augen ausstechen. Auch hat er sie von Pferden auseinanderzerren, lebendig verbrennen und ertränken lassen (Benoist-Mechin, Frédéric de Hohenstaufen, Paris 1983, S. 297). Diese bittere Diskrepanz zwischen Dichtung und Wahrheit mahnt zur Vorsicht bei Schlussfolgerungen aus der Literatur auf die Wirklichkeit. Die Verfasserin glaubt (S. 319ff.), dass ihre Untersuchung der Texte sich auf die sozial- und kulturhistorische Ebene zurückbeziehen lässt. Hier ist m.E. Vorsicht geboten, weil über das Leben der meisten Dichter wenig bekannt ist – fast alles was die Forschung über ihr Leben zu berichten weiß, stammt aus den Dichtertexten selbst, so dass die Gefahr einer Zirkelargumentation lebensgroß ist (vgl. ihre Anmerkung 1 auf S. 29) und die „exogene Ausdifferenzierung" (S.320) der sozialen Rollen in der Schwebe bleibt. Die Bezeichnung ‚Rolle' ist doppeldeutig, denn ‚Rolle' bezeichnet neben dem Verhalten innerhalb der Gesellschaft - „Angela Merkels Rolle in der Regierung ist groß" -, auch die von einem Schauspieler zu verkörpernde Gestalt - „Peter Keitel hat in dieser Aufführung die Rolle des ‚Faust'". Leider gehen diese beiden Bedeutungen von ‚Rolle' in der mediävistischen Sekundärliteratur oft durcheinander. In der Sangspruchdichtung, im Minnesang, wie in der Literatur überhaupt, haben wir es an erster Stelle mit Peter Keitel zu tun, denn dessen Worte hören und lesen wir: der Dichter hat die Freiheit mit seinen angeblich gesellschaftlichen Rollen zu schalten und walten, wie er will. Die ‚Ästhetik der Identität' ist an erster Stelle eine ästhetische und nicht eine praktische Angelegenheit. Und eben diese Ästhetik hat die Verfasserin mit ihren Interpretationen hervorragend herausgearbeitet.

Die Verfasserin unterscheidet die Spruchdichtung von dem eigentlichen Minnesang und unterbaut diese Trennung mit einer ausführlichen Fußnote (S.15, Nr. 24). Ein Hauptunterschied wäre die Vielzahl der Ich-Rollen der Sangspruchdichtung. Aber auch der Minnesang verfügt oft über viele Ich-Rollen; darauf hat die Forschung schon früh hingewiesen (Paul Kluckhohn: Der Minnesang als Standesdichtung. In: Archiv für Kulturgeschichte 11,1914, auch in: Der deutsche Minnesang. Aufsätze zu seiner Erforschung, von Hans Fromm. Bad Homburg 1961, p.58-84 und der obengenannte Jean Fourquet 1954). Nun ist die Situation in die der Minnesänger sein ‚Ich' platziert zwar weniger verwickelt als in der Spruchdichtung, das verhindert aber nicht, dass auch der Minnesang Rollendichtung ist. In Walthers Lied L 74,20 *Nemt frouwe disen kranz* etwa lassen sich vier unterschiedliche Rollen des Ichs unterscheiden.

Albrecht Dürers weibliche ‚Melancholie' auf dem Umschlagbild des schönen Buches sitzt auf einem Stein, den Kopf in die linke Hand gestützt, und schaut nachdenkend in die Ferne. Worüber denkt sie im Jahre 1514 nach? Hat die ‚Melancholie' vielleicht auch über die gesellschaftlichen Rollen nachgedacht? Oder über die Frauenemanzipation? Da hat sie zwar lange warten müssen, aber in unserer Zeit ist es endlich so weit: in dem Vorwort zu ihrem Buch aus 2008 dankt Claudia Lauer zehn Personen für ihre Hilfe und Unterstützung, acht Frauen und zwei Männern. Die Haltung der ‚Melancholie' ruft natürlich auch Reminiszenzen auf an das Bild des mittelalterlichen Denkers, wie seit dem frühsten Mittelalter an den Heiligen Joseph, der auch Stoff zum Nachdenken hatte. Claudia Lauer hat ein wichtiges, zum Nachdenken über essenzielle Probleme mittelalterlicher Dichtung anspornendes Buch geschrieben.

Zu welchen überraschenden Resultaten die biografische Interpretation literarischer Elemente führen kann, möge eine Betrachtung aus dem kolonialkritischen Roman ‚Max Havelaar' des niederländischen Schriftstellers Multatuli (Eduard Douwes Dekker) (1860) zeigen:

Droogstoppel sucht den jungen Stern auf den Pfad der Tugend zurückzuführen.

Wenn ich auch, wo es sich um Prinzipien handelt, niemand fürchte, habe ich doch begriffen, daß ich mit Stern einen anderen Weg einschlagen muß als mit Fritz. Und da zu erwarten steht, daß mein Name (die Firma ist Last & Co.; aber ich heiße Droogstoppel, Batavus Droogstoppel) mit einem Buche in Berührung kommen wird, in dem Dinge stehen, die mit der Ehrerbietung, wie sie jeder anständige Makler vor sich selbst haben muß, nicht zusammenstimmen, so achte ich für meine Pflicht, mitzuteilen, wie ich diesen Stern auf den richtigen Weg zurückzuführen versucht habe. Ich habe ihm nicht von dem Herrn gesprochen, weil er lutherisch ist, aber ich habe auf sein Gemüt und seine Ehre gewirkt. Sieh hier, wie ich das angelegt habe, und merk dabei auf, wie weit man es in der Menschenkenntnis bringen kann. Ich hatte ihn hören sagen: »Auf Ehrenwort«, und fragte, was er damit sagen wolle? »Nun,« sagte er, »daß ich meine Ehre verpfände für die Wahrheit dessen, was ich sage.« »Das ist sehr viel,« erwiderte ich. »Sind Sie denn so überzeugt, die Wahrheit zu sprechen?« »Ja,« erklärte er, »die Wahrheit sage ich immer. Wenn die Brust mir glüht ..« Der Leser weiß den Rest. »Das ist wirklich sehr schön,« sagte ich, und ich that so, als ob ich es glaubte.

Aber das war gerade die Feinheit des Strickes, mit dem ich ihn fangen wollte, um, ohne Gefahr, den alten Stern in die Hände von Büsselinck und Waterman fallen zu sehen, doch das junge Kerlchen einmal recht zum Bewußtsein seiner Stellung zu bringen und ihn fühlen zu lassen, wie groß der Abstand ist zwischen einem, der eben erst anfängt, wenn auch sein Vater große Geschäfte macht, und einem Makler, der zwanzig Jahre die Börse besucht hat. Es war mir nämlich bekannt, daß er allerlei Zeug von Versen aus dem

Kopfe wußte (er sagte »auswendig«), und da Verse immer Lügen sind, so war ich sicher, ihn sehr bald auf Unwahrheiten zu ertappen. Es dauerte denn auch nicht lange. Ich saß im Seitenzimmer, und er war in der »Suite,« denn wir haben eine Suite; Marie strickte, und er wollte ihr etwas erzählen. Ich hörte aufmerksam zu, und als es aus war, fragte ich ihn, ob er das Buch hätte, wo das Ding drin stand, das er soeben hergedröhnt hatte. Er sagte Ja und brachte es mir; es war ein Band der Werke von einem gewissen Heine. Am folgenden Morgen gab ich ihm, Stern meine ich, die nachfolgenden ‚Betrachtungen über die Wahrheitsliebe jemandes, der das folgende Machwerk von Heine einem jungen Mädchen vorträgt, das in der Suite sitzt und strickt'.

»Auf Flügeln des Gesanges,
Herzliebchen, trag ich dich fort.«

Herzliebchen ... ? Marie, Ihr Herzliebchen? Wissen die alten Leute davon? Und Luise Rosemeyer? Ist es brav, so etwas einem Kinde zu sagen, das durch dergleichen sehr leicht seiner Mutter gegenüber ungehorsam werden könnte, weil sie sich in den Kopf setzen könnte, sie sei mündig, weil man sie »Herzliebchen« nennt? Was bedeutet das »Forttragen auf Ihren Flügeln?« Sie haben keine Flügel, und Ihr Gesang auch nicht. Probieren Sie es einmal über die Lauriergracht, die nicht einmal sehr breit ist. Aber wenn Sie wirklich Flügel hätten, dürften Sie dann so etwas einem Mädchen vortragen, das noch nicht eingesegnet ist? Und wäre sie auch, angenommen, was bedeutet dies Angebot von »zusammen wegfliegen?« Pfui!

»Fort nach den Fluren des Ganges,
da weiß ich den schönsten Ort.«

Dann gehen Sie doch allein hin und mieten Sie sich eine Stube, aber nehmen Sie nicht ein Mädchen mit, das seiner Mutter in der Hauswirtschaft helfen muß. Aber Sie meinen das ja auch gar nicht. Erstens haben Sie den Ganges nie gesehen und wissen also gar nicht, ob da gut leben ist. Soll ich Ihnen sagen, wie die Sachen stehen? Es sind alles Lügen, die Sie darum erzählen, weil Sie sich mit dem Geverse zum Sklaven von Versmaß und Reim machen. Hätte die erste Zeile geendet auf Lug oder Trug, so hätten Sie Marie gefragt, ob sie mitginge nach Broek und so weiter. Sie sehen also, daß Ihre angebliche Reiselinie nicht ernst gemeint war, und daß alles auf einen Klingklang von Worten ohne Sinn und Verstand hinausläuft. Wie wäre es nun, wenn Marie wirklich Lust bekäme, die Reise zu machen? Ich spreche noch nicht einmal von der unbequemen Manier, die Sie vorschlagen; doch sie ist, Gott sei Dank, zu verständig, um nach einem Lande zu verlangen, von dem Sie sagen:

»Dort liegt ein rotblühender Garten
im stillen Mondenschein,
die Lotosblumen erwarten
ihr trautes Schwesterlein.
Die Veilchen kichern und kosen
und schaun nach den Sternen empor,
heimlich erzählen die Rosen
sich duftende Märchen ins Ohr.«

Was wollen Sie in dem Garten mit Marie im Mondschein thun? Ist das sittlich, ist das brav, ist das anständig, Stern? Wollen Sie, daß ich mich schämen muß, wie Büsselinck und Waterman, mit denen kein anständiges Haus etwas zu thun haben will, weil ihre Tochter davongelaufen ist, und weil sie Pfuscher sind? Was sollte ich antworten, wenn man mich auf der Börse fragte, warum meine Tochter so lange in jenem Garten geblieben ist? Denn das begreifen Sie doch, daß kein Mensch mir glauben würde, wenn ich sagte, daß sie da die Lotosblumen besuchen mußte, die, wie Sie sagen, schon lange auf sie gewartet haben. Ebenso würde jeder verständige Mensch mich auslachen, wenn ich närrisch genug wäre, um zu sagen: Marie ist da in dem roten Garten (warum rot und nicht gelb oder lila?), um auf das Kichern und Kosen der Veilchen zu horchen, oder auf die Märchen, die die Rosen sich heimlich ins Ohr flüstern? Und könnte so etwas wahr sein, was hätte Marie davon, wenn es doch so heimlich geschieht, daß sie nichts davon versteht? Aber es sind Lügen, fauler Schwindel, und häßlich ist es auch; denn nehmen Sie einmal einen Bleistift und zeichnen Sie sich eine Rose mit einem Ohr, und sehen Sie, wie das aussieht. Und was bedeutet das, daß die Märchen duftend sind? Soll ich Ihnen das einmal auf gut holländisch sagen? Das will sagen, daß ein Lüftchen an dem Märchen ist ... so ist es!

»Es hüpfen herbei und lauschen
die frommen klugen Gazell'n,
und in der Ferne rauschen
des heiligen Stromes Well'n ...
Dort wollen wir niedersinken
unter dem Palmenbaum,
und Liebe und Ruhe trinken
und träumen seligen Traum.«

Können Sie nicht in den zoologischen Garten gehen, wenn Sie durchaus wilde Tiere sehen wollen? Müssen es gerade die Gazellen am Ganges sein, die doch in der Wildnis nicht so gut zu betrachten sind, wie in einer netten Umzäunung von geteertem Eisen? Warum sind diese Tiere fromm und klug? Das letztere lasse ich gelten, sie machen wenigstens nicht solche thörichte Verse - aber fromm? Was heißt das? Heißt das nicht einen Mißbrauch treiben mit einem heiligen Wort, das nur gebraucht werden darf von Menschen, die den wahren Glauben haben? Und dann der heilige Strom? Wollen Sie Marie Dinge erzählen, die sie zu einer Heidin machen können? Wollen Sie ihren Glauben erschüttern, daß es kein heiliges Wasser giebt als das Wasser der Taufe, und keinen heiligen Fluß als den Jordan? Ist das nicht ein Untergraben von Sittlichkeit, Tugend, Religion, Christentum und Anstand? Denken Sie einmal über das alles nach, Stern! Ihr Vater ist ein achtungswürdiges Haus, und ich bin sicher, er findet es gut, daß ich so auf Ihr Gemüt wirke, und er wird gern Geschäfte machen mit einem, der Tugend und Religion aufrecht erhält. Ja, Prinzipien sind mir heilig, und ich scheue mich nicht, gerade heraus zu sagen, was ich meine. Machen Sie also kein Geheimnis von dem, was ich sage, schreiben Sie es ruhig Ihrem Vater, daß Sie hier in einer soliden Familie sind, daß ich Sie auf das Gute hinweise, und fragen Sie sich selber, was aus Ihnen geworden wäre, wenn Sie zu Büsselinck und Waterman gekommen wären? Da hätten Sie auch solche Verse aufgesagt, und da hätte man nicht auf Ihr Gemüt gewirkt, weil es Pfuscher sind. Schreiben Sie das getrost Ihrem Vater, denn wo Prinzipien im Spiele sind, fürchte ich niemand. Da wären die Mädchen auch mit Ihnen mitgegangen nach dem Ganges, und dann lägen Sie nun da unter jenem Baum im Grase, während Sie nun, weil ich Sie warne, bei uns bleiben können, in einem anständigen Hause. Schreiben Sie das alles Ihrem Vater, und sagen Sie ihm, daß Sie so dankbar sind, daß Sie zu uns gekommen sind, und daß ich so gut für Sie sorge, und daß die Tochter von Büsselinck und Waterman weggelaufen ist, und grüßen Sie ihn sehr von mir, und schreiben Sie, daß ich noch 1/16 Prozent Courtage unter deren Gebot ablassen werde, weil ich die Schleicher nicht leiden kann, die einem Konkurrenten das Brot vom Munde stehlen durch günstige Offerten. Und thun Sie mir den Gefallen, in Ihren Vorlesungen bei Rosemeyers etwas Tüchtigeres zu bringen. Ich habe in Shawlmanns Paket Aufstellungen über die Kaffee-Erzeugung der letzten zwanzig Jahre gesehen: lesen Sie einmal so etwas vor. Und Sie müssen auch die Mädchen und uns alle nicht so als Kannibalen hinstellen, die etwas von Ihnen aufgefressen haben. Das ist nicht anständig, mein Sohn; glauben Sie doch jemand, der weiß, was in der Welt los ist. Ich habe Ihren Vater schon vor seiner Geburt bedient (die Firma, meine ich, Last & Co., früher war es Last & Meyer); Sie begreifen also, daß ich es gut mit Ihnen meine. Und spornen Sie Fritz an, daß er besser aufpaßt, und lehren Sie ihn keine Verse machen, und wenn er Gesichter schneidet gegen den Buchhalter, und dergleichen mehr, thun Sie, als ob Sie es nicht sähen. Geben Sie ihm ein Vorbild, weil Sie so viel älter sind, und bringen Sie ihm Ernst und Würde bei, weil er Makler werden soll.

Ich bin Ihr väterlicher Freund

Batavus Droogstoppel

(Firma Last & Co., Makler in Kaffee,

Lauriergracht Nr. 37, Amsterdam)

(Quelle: Multatuli, Max Havelaar. Halle a. d. S[aale] [o. J.], S. 134-139).

A. H. Touber

Bernhard Anton Schmitz, *Gauvain, Gawein, Walewein. Die Emanzipation des ewig Verspäteten*. Max Niemeyer Verlag, Tübingen, 2008. IX + 342 pp. (ISBN 978-3-484-15117-8).

Gawein, the delayed knight

I met Bernhard Schmitz in 2002 at the twentieth international Arthurian Congress in Bangor. He was then working on his PhD dissertation concerning Gauvain (Gawein or Walewein in the German or Dutch romances). I was particularly interested in his work as Gauvain formed my own field of interest all be it from another perspective. I studied the irony in the 'Roman van Walewein'.

Bernhard was a very enthousiastic discussion partner, but apart from this one conversation, I had no further contact with him. Later on, I heard that he had died in 2006 just before Easter on Good Friday. He had finished his research by then, but had not yet defended his thesis. Bernhard died much too young at the age of 43, but thankfully his scientific heritage won't be lost. In 2008 his dissertation 'Gauvain, Gawein, Walewein. Die Emanzipation des ewig Verspäteten' was published posthumously by Niemeyer Verlag.

In the introductory chapter, Schmitz makes clear that he wants to investigate the function of Gauvain (Gawein or Walewein) in a number of French, German and Dutch romances of the 12th and 13th century. This demarcation also explains the lack of Middle English romances in this study. Schmitz states that Gauvain may be a well discussed Arthurian figure but that there still lacks a systematic functional description of this famous Arthurian knight. Most studies concentrate on the character (in the sense of personality) of Gauvain or are limited to a functional description of Gauvain in as far as he forms a standard of value for other knights: "Bislang galt Gauvain nach funktionalen Kriterien allenfalls als der Vergleichsmaßstab, an dem die Qualifikation bzw. die Würde anderer Ritter abgelesen werden kann, die sich mit ihm im Zweikampf messen oder die Ehre haben, sich zu seinen Freunden rechnen zu können." (p. 3)

Schmitz argues that his approach solves the typical inconsequences that have often been associated with the character of Gauvain. An example may clarify this statement. Gauvain's actions in Chrétien de Troyes's 'Yvain, le chevalier au lion' have often been described as quite negative (for instance by Uitti, Kelly, Busby and Lacy): Gauvain is found guilty of delivering poor advice to his companion Yvain, he is absent from the court during the crucial moments, he defends the unjust claim of the eldest sister de la Noire Espine ... Schmitz however shows that in all these cases Gauvain behaves as a representative of the court who defends the courtly standards and by doing so also possibly thwarts the protagonist in his personal ambitions. On the basis of Chrétien de Troyes's romances, Schmitz presents the following action scheme: Chrétien's novels characteristically show an initial crisis at Arthur's Court (Initialkrise, Provokation). The knights - Gauvain included - cannot react in an adequate way (Stasis, Inertia der Gauvainfigur). The crisis is followed by a maladjusted action by the Seneschal Keu which opens the way for the protagonist (Negative Intervention Keus – Intervention des Protagonisten). Keu is then punished for his brutal intervention (Bestrafung Keus). Eventually also Gauvain comes in action (Intervention Gauvains) and although his attitude may seem contradictory with his excellent reputation, his proceedings are always in harmony with the desired standards of Arthur's court. For instance his advice to Yvain not to give in to *recreantise*, may seem unlogical and/or selfish, but from the viewpoint of the court, Gauvain certainly has a point. At least this is Schmitz's opinion. I think that indeed it cannot be denied that 'recreantise' and the sometimes conflicting interests of the individual and society form an important theme in Chrétien's oeuvre. Chrétien however does never claim that personal welfare and relationships should be given up because of communal interests. On the contrary, he promotes a delicate balance between individual and society. This is certainly not what Gauvain has in mind; it is his doing that his friend Yvain completely forgets his wife Laudine and loses her loyalty in endlessly fighting tournaments. I think that Chrétien wants to make it clear that Gauvain's advice does not lead to a harmonious situation which makes it hard to think of Arthur's nephew as the ideal representative of the courtly interests.

Schmitz includes all the romances of Chrétien de Troyes in his investigation except for Cligès, which is a bit of an outsider in Chrétien's oeuvre. He then turns to the Middle High German and the Middle Dutch Arthurian romances. Successively Schmitz discusses the oeuvre of Hartmann von Aue and Wolfram von Eschenbach. He ends with an analysis of the post-classical romances the 'Roman van Walewein' (Middle Dutch) written by Penninc and Pieter Vostaert and 'Diu Crône' (Middle High German) by Heinrich von dem Türlin.

Regarding Hartmann, Schmitz determines that in his attempts to rationalize his sources, the German author prefers a psychological approach of his characters to a functional one: "Der Vereindeutigungsprozess zeigt sich insbesondere bei Hartmann von Aue, der die Figuren Gawein und Keie ihre ursprünglichen Funktionalität entkleidete und mit dem Ziel größerer Plausibilität psychologisierte" (p. 147). Wolfram von Eschenbach on the other hand pays more attention to functionality than his colleague

Hartmann, especially when Keie is concerned: "Insbesondere die für deutsche Autoren problematische Keiefigur wird bei Wolfram in ihrer Funktion (durch ihr Amt) erklärt" (p. 205).

Schmitz then turns to the post-classical romances the 'Roman van Walewein' and 'Diu Crône'. The fact that Walewein/Gawein has become the protagonist in these romances has some far reaching consequences that have in some research been indicated as inconsistencies in the story or in the characters. In the following paragraphs I especially want to focus on Schmitz's findings on the Middle Dutch 'Roman van Walewein', which has been the core-romance of my own research on irony.

Schmitz elaborates on the initial crisis with the arrival of a magical chess-set at Arthur's court at which the assembled knights react as paralised. The sudden interruption of a courtly assembly, the passive reaction of the knights and Walewein's inertia, that all reminds of Chrétien's model; Arthur's triple summons and his promise to hand over the sovereignty to the deliverer of the chess-set however deviates from it. Also the typical, rude intervention by seneschal Keie who traditionally induces the protagonist to action, is lacking. According to Schmitz, the role of Keie has been taken over here by the king himself. The intervention of King Arthur completely turns upside down the courtly order and this is closely connected with one of the main themes Schmitz attributes to this novel: the harmoniously coexisting (or the lack of it) of men and women. According to Schmitz it is significant that at the initial description of Arthur's court, only the king and his men seem to be present as Guinevere and her ladies are not mentioned at all. If this is correct, this is a serious violation of the courtly ideals. Every court Walewein calls at on his quest for the flying chess-set is in its own particular way an illustration of how men and women should or should not live together. The court of King Amadijs stands out positively but everywhere else the equilibrium is thoroughly disturbed: at king Wonder's court, the women live in complete separation, at Ravenstene, King Amoraen's court, there is no queen at all and in Endi, king Assentijn keeps his daughter like a bird in golden cage. I admire Schmitz's keen observations but I doubt part of his analysis concerning the situation at Arthur's court. It is not because Penninc does not mention the presence of Guinevere and his ladies in the beginning that they were absent. When Walewein bids his farewell at the beginning of his quest, he takes leave of the king, the queen and all who were with them in the great hall. In my opinion the queen had been present all the time only Penninc didn't mention that explicitely (after all, Penninc is a male author for whom 'men' simply may have meant 'all the inhabitants of the court, male and female alike'). The fact that Walewein wonders at the situation at Wonder's court is proof enough that back home men and women do not live in separate quarters. Schmitz does cite the passage where Walewein's amazement at the situation is expressed: *Maer hine sacher vrouwe no joncfrouwen/ Dat dochte hem ene vremde saken* (vs. 1060-61) but he does not associate this scene with the apparently different situation at Arthur's court (see p. 230-231).

In conclusion, I want to have a closer look at Schmitz's discussion of Walewein's particular function in the 'Roman van Walewein'. The fact that Arthur's nephew has now become the protagonist of the novel has, according to the German researcher, a great influence on how Walewein has been depicted. He turns from a knight who defends the needs and the values of the king's court to a character who acts for his own benefit. Walewein sets out to fulfill king Arthur's wish (in his traditional role of courtly character) but he ends up looking for a bride for himself (in his new role of protagonist). According to Schmitz, this switch explains for an number of ambivalences concerning Walewein that keep turning up in the research. For instance, how come that Walewein as an example of courtliness carries on like a madman in fight scenes and shows no mercy for his opponents? Or what to think of the peculiar way the love motive has been treated in this novel? Walewein promised the love-stricken king Amoraen to fetch Ysabele so that the lonely king could marry her but he ends up falling in love with her himself. This however does not mean that Walewein forgets his former promise. He still intends to turn Ysabele over to Amoraen but fortunately the old king very conveniently died before that could happen. This certainly is not the most consistent part of the novel.

In each of these cases, Schmitz argues, we are confronted with attempts of the authors to combine the conflicting functions of Walewein as a character: the representative of the court on the one hand and the protagonist with his own personal motives on the other hand. Again, I think Schmitz makes some very fine observations but in his analysis he confines himself to the process of creating the novel. He tries to look over the shoulder of the authors but he does not take into consideration the effects their choices must have had on the reader or on the audience. This is a similar kind of criticism that has been formulated about Maartje Draak's dissertation on the 'Roman van Walewein' and more specifically concerning her discussion of the fairy-tale backgrounds of the story. Draak discusses the opening scene of the Middle Dutch romance in regard to the underlying fairy tale. She concludes that some of the fairy tale motives break through the courtly layer several times. The greed of the king for the richly decorated chess-set, his promise to abdicate his throne, Walewein's repeated demand for the validity of this promise ... Draak all explains them as typical, uncourtly fairy-tale motives without ever considering what the audience must have thought of all these inconsistencies.[1]

This audience of course does not care about editorial interventions, but it does undergo the effects of them. I think this is where irony comes in and in this respect I think Schmitz's research complements very well with my own findings. It cannot be denied that combining two antipodal functions had some effect on the character of Walewein. In my opinion there are a lot of indications that he must have been depicted as an ironically pictured hero. I am also convinced that the emerging irony is not merely an unintentional side-effect of Walewein becoming the protagonist of this novel. Penninc and Pieter Vostaert were perfectly acquainted with the conventions of the courtly genre and they were both quite capable writers as has been pointed out fre-

---

[1] Draak 1975, p. 60-62. For a discussion of Draak's ideas see Uyttersprot 2004, p. 199 and following. See also there for further reading.

quently by several researchers (and confirmed by Schmitz's own study) who must have elaborated on the imago of their hero. When Walewein is only willing to set out on a quest in the prospect of a reward, it is very well possible that this leads back to the fairy tale source (Maartje Draak) or that in this way the danger of the prospective adventure is emphasized (thesis of Besamusca and confirmed by Schmitz)[2], but at the same time this unmistakably raises questions about the integrity of Walewein as the absolute hero, as *der avonturen vader* (the father of adventures) as he is called in the same scene.

On the whole Bernhard Schmitz has presented himself as a versatile and accurate researcher who has demonstrated a thorough approach coupled with balanced discussion with his colleagues. He has been very direct and successful in getting his opinion to paper, it is such a pity that any further dialogue with this talented researcher about his opinions of the figure of Gauvain/Gawein/Walewein is no longer possible because of his untimely death. A further discussion certainly could have been very fruitful.

Veerle Uyttersprot

Bibliography

Besamusca 1989: B. Besamusca, *'Walewein', 'Moriaen' en de 'Ridder metter mouwen': Intertekstualiteit in drie Middelnederlandse Arturromans*. Hilversum,.

Draak 1975: A.M.E. Draak, *Onderzoekingen over de 'Roman van Walewein'* (met aanvullend hoofdstuk over 'Het Walewein onderzoek sinds 1936'), Groningen/Amsterdam.

Uyttersprot 2004: V. Uyttersprot, *'Entie hoofsche Walewein, sijn ghesellle was daer ne ghein'. Ironie en het Walewein-beeld in de Roman van Walewein en in de Europese middeleeuwse Arturliteratuur*, Katholieke Universiteit Brussel.

Cordula Kropik, *Reflexionen des Geschichtlichen. Zur literarischen Konstituierung mittelhochdeutscher Heldenepik* (Jenaer germanistische Forschungen, Neue Folge, Band 24). - Universitätsverlag Winter, Heidelberg 2008. 404 S. (ISBN 978-3-8253-5408-4). Euro 54,-.

Ausgehend von der Annahme, dass Heldensage in einer schriftlosen Gesellschaft die Funktion hat, die Geschichte dieser Gesellschaft von Generation zu Generation weiterzugeben, stellt die Verfasserin sich die Frage, welche Funktion die Heldensage bekommt, sobald eine Gesellschaft alphabetisiert wird. Aufgezeichnete Heldensagen, d.h. Heldendichtungen, erheben bekanntlich den Anspruch, Wahrheit zu übermitteln, obwohl diejenigen, die diese Heldendichtungen aufgezeichnet haben, sicherlich wussten, dass die Ereignisse, von denen sie berichten, nicht immer historisch wahr sein können, weil sie von den Darstellungen in lateinischen Quellen abweichen.

In ihrer Einleitung zitiert die Verf. aus der Vorrede zur 'Heimskringla' von Snorri Sturluson, der einräumt, dass man nicht wisse, was Wahres an den Geschichten, die er

---

[2] Besamusca 1993, p. 79-80.

aufzeichnet, sei, dass aber "kundige Männer aus alter Zeit diese Überlieferung für wahr gehalten haben" (S. 9). Von seiner schriftlichen Hauptquelle, der Chronik des Ari Þorgilsson, sagt Snorri, dass Ari ein so hohes Alter erreicht habe, dass er die meisten der von ihm berichteten Ereignisse selbst miterlebt habe, und was vor der Zeit stattgefunden habe, habe er von anderen zuverlässigen Gewährsleuten gehört, die ihrerseits Augenzeugen gewesen seien. Was er aus mündlichen Dichtungen übernommen habe, stamme von Skalden, die ihre Dichtungen an den Höfen der Könige vorgetragen haben, so dass auch ihre Berichte auf Wahrheit beruhen dürften. Mit anderen Worten: Snorri geht davon aus, dass mündliche und schriftliche Quellen sich weder durch ihre Zuverlässigkeit noch durch ihre Nähe zu den dargestellten Ereignissen unterscheiden. Im Folgenden versucht die Verf. nun, die aus Snorris Argumentation hervorgehende Reflexion des Geschichtlichen auch in der deutschen Heldendichtung, die sich ja ihrer mündlichen Wurzeln bewusst ist, aufzuzeigen.

Der erste und umfangreichste Teil ("Inszenierung und Kommentar") ist dem 'Nibelungenlied' und der 'Klage' gewidmet, von denen die Verf. annimmt, dass sie gleichzeitig und in der gleichen "Nibelungenwerkstatt" entstanden seien, so dass die beiden Texte "als Teil eines Konzepts zu sehen [seien], dem es darum geht, verschiedene Arten geschichtlicher Überlieferung inszenierend [einander] gegenüberzustellen" (S. 147).

Ebenso wie die altnordische Dichtung beruht auch im 'Nibelungenlied' der Wahrheitsanspruch auf Augenzeugenschaft, aber anders als in der altnordischen Dichtung wird nicht erzählt, was jemand, der dabei war, einst gesehen hat, sondern dass, was berichtet wird, "gesehen werden kann" (S. 53). Die sehr frequent vorkommende *man sach*-Formel spielt in dieser Argumentation eine entscheidende Rolle. Im Gegensatz zur Isländersaga ist, so schließt die Verf., der "Ton des Augenzeugen" im 'Nibelungenlied' nicht natürlich, sondern gemacht. Das 'Nibelungenlied' erzeuge die Illusion, mündliche Dichtung zu sein, es sei aber nicht die Wiedergabe einer mündlichen Dichtung, sondern eine "schriftliterarisch erzeugte Simulation tradionellen Erzählens" (S. 60). Deswegen werden auch widersprüchliche Elemente aus der mündlichen Tradition bewusst eingesetzt. Sie machen den Eindruck, abweichende Beobachtungen von verschiedenen Augenzeugen zu sein und verstärken somit die Illusion, es handle sich um die Aufzeichnung einer mündlichen Dichtung. Hier werden Gedanken ausgearbeitet, die die Verf. schon vor einigen Jahren in einem Aufsatz veröffentlicht hat.[1]

Es würde im Rahmen dieser Besprechung zu weit führen, alle folgenden Abschnitte genauso ausführlich zu besprechen. Die Verf. behandelt noch die 'Außensicht' auf die berichteten Ereignisse, d.h. die Tatsache, dass der Erzähler zumeist völlig schweigt über das Innenleben der Figuren; nur äußere, sichtbare Zeichen werden mitgeteilt. Allerdings ist die Interpretation einiger Strophen m.E. nicht überzeugend. Wenn z.B. von Str. 285 gesagt wird, dass der Erzähler aus der Tatsache, dass Siegfried *vil dicke bleich unde rôt* wird, auf seinen Gemütszustand schließe, könnte man auch das Umgekehrte behaupten, schließlich werden die Gedanken Siegfrieds ja in der ersten

---

[1] Kropik 2005, 141-158.

Zeile explizit mitgeteilt. Kritische Bemerkungen wie diese ließen sich zweifellos auch zu anderen Stellen machen, aber im großen und ganzen ist die Arbeit so gediegen und minutiös und die Zahl der beigebrachten Beispiele so groß, dass Detailkritik kaum ins Gewicht fällt.

Sodann geht die Verf. ausführlich auf das Verhältnis zwischen 'Nibelungenlied' und 'Klage' ein. Auch die 'Klage' will den ursprünglich mündlich überlieferten Stoff "über die Schwelle zur Schriftlichkeit heben" (S. 185), nur versuche sie dies nicht zu erreichen, indem sie Mündlichkeit simuliere, sondern indem sie den Stoff in der Form historiographischer Buchdichtung darbiete. Die 'Klage' erweise sich so als konzeptuell notwendige Ergänzung zum 'Nibelungenlied', da sie aus historiographischer Perspektive erkläre, was das 'Nibelungenlied' "aus der Sicht seiner Sageninszenierung heraus nicht erzählen und erklären" könne (S. 380). Wie man sich aber die "Nibelungenwerkstatt" vorzustellen hat, in der 'Nibelungenlied' und 'Klage' gleichzeitig entstanden sein sollen, wird nicht deutlich. Die Verf. geht auf jeden Fall von (mindestens) zwei Dichtern aus - in dem Abschnitt "Nibelungenwerkstatt" (S. 136-141) ist die Rede von einem "Nibelungenepiker" und von einem "Klage-Dichter" - und von einer "Werkstattgemeinschaft", in welcher der eine mit dem anderen sozusagen "den Schreibtisch teilt" (S. 139). In einer Anmerkung (S. 140, Anm. 305) erwägt die Verf. sogar die Möglichkeit, dass der Nibelungendichter seinen Text "von vornherein auf die 'Klage' hin konzipiert und erzählt." Diese Möglichkeit haben auch andere in der Vergangenheit schon erwogen.[2]

Was sich im Fall des 'Nibelungenliedes' und der 'Klage' zum erstenmal vollzieht - der Übergang von der Mündlichkeit zur Schriftlichkeit und die Reflexion über die Frage, wie schriftliche, d.h. literarische Heldendichtung auszusehen hat und was sie zu leisten hat, ist einmalig und braucht in folgenden Fällen nicht mehr wiederholt zu werden. Der Weg der nachnibelungischen Heldendichtung beginnt denn auch "bei 'Nibelungenlied' und 'Klage'; sie denkt, von diesen ausgehend, weiter und nutzt sie als Folie für die eigene Reflexion" (S. 186). Im zweiten Teil ("Übersetzungen ins Literarische") behandelt die Verf. 'Dietrichs Flucht' und 'Rabenschlacht', zwei Epen, die einige Generationen später als 'Nibelugenlied' und 'Klage' entstanden sind, aber ebenfalls einen ursprünglich mündlich überlieferten Stoff schriftlich bearbeiten. Sie seien sich der "Geschichtlichkeit ihres Gegenstandes zwar noch bewußt, doch erscheint sie als unproblematisch" (S. 305). Sie simulieren nicht Mündlichkeit, sondern berufen sich auf schriftliche Quellen.

Im dritten Teil ("Brechungen und Neubesetzung in der 'späten' Heldendichtung") geht die Verf. zunächst auf 'Ortnit' und 'Wolfdietrich' D ein. In beiden Dichtungen spiele das Problem der Geschichtlichkeit im Grunde keine Rolle mehr: "Traditionsbezug und beglaubigende Quellenfiktion sind vom Instrument der Reflexion heroischen Erzählens zum Gattungssignal geworden" (S. 383). An Hand des 'Biterolf' und des 'Eckenlieds' versucht die Verf. anschließend darzulegen, dass die späte Heldendichtung, obwohl die Stoffe jeglicher historische Relevanz entbehren, die Reflexion der

---

[2] Voorwinden, 1981, 276-287.

Geschichtlichkeit trotzdem nicht aufgibt, sondern als gattungstypisches Merkmal beibehält. Die Verf. schließt sich der in der Forschung gängigen Auffassung an, dass es sich bei jenen Dichtungen, in denen Dietrich in den Tiroler Bergen gegen Riesen und Zwerge zu kämpfen hat, um späte Heldendichtung handelt. Merkwürdig ist allerdings, dass schon in einer der ältesten Dichtungen, in der Dietrich auftritt, dem altenglischen 'Waldere', ein Kampf mit einem Riesen erwähnt wird.[3]

Abgesehen vom eigentlichen Thema, den Reflexionen des Geschichtlichen, enthält das Buch, sozusagen als Nebenprodukt, sehr lesenswerte und anregende Interpretationen der behandelten Dichtungen: 'Nibelungenlied', 'Klage', 'Dietrichs Flucht', 'Rabenschlacht', 'Ortnit', 'Wolfdietrich' D, 'Biterolf' und 'Eckenlied'. Die fast tausend Anmerkungen enthalten oft sehr wesentliche zusätzliche Informationen. Die Bibliographie zählt mehr als dreihundert Titel, die offensichtlich auch alle gründlich studiert worden sind, denn sie werden ausnahmslos im Text oder in den Anmerkungen zitiert und kommentiert. Besonders gründlich aber befasst setzt sich die Verf. mit den Arbeiten von Michael Curschmann, Walter Haug, Joachim Heinzle, Michael Mecklenburg und Jan Dirk Müller. Alles in allem ein sehr anregendes Buch, das den Leser über den neuesten Forschungsstand, insbesondere über den Stand der Nibelungenforschung, informiert, das aber letzten Endes auch nicht die endgültige Antwort auf alle bisher umstrittenen Fragen bietet. Was es wohl bietet, ist die Grundlage, von der die Nibelungenforschung in Zukunft auszugehen und mit der sie sich zunächst einmal auseinanderzusetzen hat.

Das Buch ist die überarbeitete und ergänzte Fassung einer Dissertation, die im Wintersemester 2005/2006 von der philosophischen Fakultät der Friedrich-Schiller-Universität Jena angenommen wurde und 2007 - nicht zu Unrecht - einen Promotionspreis empfing. Die sorgfältige Textgestaltung ist auffallend. Beim Lesen sind mir nur zwei unbedeutende Druckfehler aufgefallen (zweimaliges "*man*" auf S. 74 und "Heldendepen" auf S. 377).

Norbert Voorwinden

Literatur

Kropik 2005: Cordula Kropik, Inszenierte Sage. Überlegungen zum Traditionsverständnis des Nibelungenepikers, in: Nibelungenlied und Nibelungenklage (Neue Wege der Forschung), hg. von Christoph Fasbender, Darmstadt.

Schwab 2000: Ute Schwab, Dietrichs Flucht vor den Ungeheuern im ae. Waldere. Eine Episode aus der märchenhaften Dietrichdichtung als Legitimation eines Schwertes samt der Genealogie desselben und ihre Funktion in der ae. Walther-Dichtung, in: 5. Pöchlarner Heldenliedgespräch. Aventiure-/märchenhafte Dietrichepik, hg. von Klaus Zatloukal (Philologica Germanica 22), Wien.

Voorwinden 1981: Norbert Voorwinden, Nibelungenklage und Nibelungenlied, in: Hohenemser Studien zum Nibelungenlied. Unter Mitarbeit von Irmtraud Albrecht hg. von Achim Masser, Dornbirn 1981, 276-287.

---

[3] Vgl. Schwab 2000, 131-155.

Mai und Beaflor. Herausgegeben, übersetzt, kommentiert und mit einer Einleitung von Albrecht Classen (Beihefte zur Mediaevistik, Bd. 6). – Peter Lang, Frankfurt am Main, Berlin, Bern, Bruxelles, New York, Oxford, Wien 2006. 500 S. (ISBN 3-631-54303-4).

Der höfische Versroman *Mai und Beaflor* eines anonymen mittelhochdeutschen Dichters des späten 13. Jahrhunderts, eine dramatisch-bewegte und bewegende Familiengeschichte mit Happy-End (Max Wehrli) wird hier erstmals in einer ausführlich kommentierten Edition vorgelegt. Nach einer informativen Einleitung, die in den Text einführt, motivgeschichtliche Assoziationen registriert, zur Gattungsfrage und zum historischen sowie literarischen Hintergrund des Romans Stellung nimmt, die bisherige Forschung über die Protagonisten Mai erörtert und politische Recherchen anstellt, befasst Classen sich mit emotions- und mentalitätsgeschichtlichen Aspekten, mit didaktischen Intentionen der Sozial- und Kirchenkritik, mit der fiktionalen Quellenberufung und der literarästhetischen Beurteilung des Versromans. Die Erörterungen zur handschriftlichen Überlieferung von *Mai und Beaflor* sind dem Text und der Übersetzung des Romans vorangestellt. Classen entscheidet sich für einen weitgehend diplomatischen Abdruck der Handschrift A (München, Staatsbibliothek, cod. germ. 57, fol. 1r-52v). Den Text der Handschrift A ergänzt Classen dort durch den Textbestand der Handschrift C (Codex C 6, Landesbibliothek Fulda), wo die Handschrift A Lücken aufweist. Fehler der Überlieferung werden dadurch korrigiert, dass die richtige Form in eckigen Klammern erscheint. Verschreibungen, die in den Handschriften durchgestrichen sind, erscheinen im Text und werden durch runde Klammern gekennzeichnet. Classens Übersetzung der Neuausgabe von *Mai und Beaflor* versucht, das mittelhochdeutsche Original so nahe wie möglich entsprechend der Versstruktur ins Neuhochdeutsche zu übertragen. Sachkundliche und sprachliche Erklärungen in Anmerkungen am Ende des Textes erschließen den Versroman in mehrfacher Hinsicht.

Albrecht Classens sehr verdienstvolle Publikation wird der *Mai und Beaflor*-Forschung neue Impulse verleihen.

Fritz Wagner

Jörg Schwarz, *Stadtluft macht frei. Leben in der mittelalterlichen Stadt* (Geschichte erzählt Bd. 15). Primus Verlag, Darmstadt 2008. 143 S. (ISBN 978-3-89678-364).

Die mittelalterliche Stadt gehört zu den beliebtesten Forschungsobjekten der deutschen Mediävistik. Das Thema hat nicht nur Anlass zu zahllosen detaillierten Studien über vielerlei Teilbereiche des städtischen Lebens gegeben, sondern auch eine Menge allgemeine Überblicke und Einführungen zur Geschichte der mittelalterlichen Stadt ergeben, die innerhalb und außerhalb des deutschen Sprachbereichs als grundlegend betrachtet worden sind, wie zum Beispiel Edith Ennens 'Die europäische Stadt des Mittelalters'. Der Titel des Buches von Jörg Schwarz lässt auf den ersten Blick vermuten, dass sich der Autor in diese Tradition einzureihen versucht, aber es wäre verfehlt, *Stadtluft macht frei* als ein akademisches Handbuch zu betrachten. Der Autor hat, ganz den Zielsetzungen der Reihe 'Geschichte erzählt' entsprechend, vor allem ein sehr anschauliches Buch über das Leben in der mittelalterlichen Stadt geschrieben, das die Thematik einem breiten Publikum zugänglich macht.

In 8 Kapiteln, die zusammen nur 130 Seiten umfassen, führt Schwarz seine Leser in großen Sprüngen durch die Stadt des Mittelalters. Das erste Kapitel ist ein buntes Durcheinander. Der Autor geht sehr kurz auf sehr verschiedene Aspekte des Alltaglebens ein, wie Märkte, Turniere, Brandgefahr und Hospitäler. Welche Systematik diesem Abschnitt zugrunde liegt bleibt aber völlig unklar. Im nächsten Kapitel folgt eine mehr systematische aber keineswegs vollständige Beschreibung verschiedener Stadttypen.

Es folgen zwei Kapitel über die Organisation der Städtegemeinschaft. Zum ersten wird die Entstehung der städtischen Kommunen oder ‚Schwurgemeinschaften' behandelt, hier ganz in traditionellem Sinne: Die Errungung kommunaler Freiheit wird als Kampf gegen feudale Gegenkräfte wie z.B. den Erzbischof Kölns verstanden. In der jüngeren internationalen Literatur aber wird dieser schroffe Gegensatz zwischen kommunalem Freiheitsstreben und feudaler Unterdrückung im Frage gestellt und weitgehend nuanciert. Schwarz räumt diesen neuen Einsichten leider keinen Platz ein. Der nächste Abschnitt hat die Selbstregierung der spätmittelalterlichen Stadt zum Thema und zeigt sehr schön wie das theoretisch harmonische und (annähernd demokratische) Gesellschaftsmodell der Stadt immer wieder internen Spannungen und Machtkämpfen ausgesetzt war. Das Beispiel Augsburg zeigt, dass solche Auseinandersetzungen sogar zu einer Diktatur in der Form eines Stadttyrannen führen konnte.

Die Selbständigkeit der Stadt wurde durch Stadtmauern, das Thema des folgenden Kapitels, verkörpert. Mauern grenzten die städtische Gemeinschaft ab von der feudalen Umgebung, praktisch, symbolisch und rechtlich: Innerhalb der Mauern galt städtisches Recht und bürgerliche Freiheit, außerhalb der Mauern nicht. Wiederum Köln und jetzt auch Nördlingen (wo die Stadtmauern bis heute noch in ihrer mittelalterlichen Form stehen) sind die Beispiele, die zeigen wie die städtische Gemeinschaft seine Mauern baute, unterhielt und zur Verteidigung der Stadt gebrauchte. Die letzten drei Kapitel befassen sich mit Reisen und Migration (ein Kapitel von nur 6 Seiten!), Außenseitern und Randgruppen wie Bettlern, Kranken und Juden, bzw. mit der städtischen Geschichtsschreibung im späten Mittelalter.

Die Stadt des Mittelalters heißt in diesem Band übrigens eigentlich das Köln des (vornehmlich späten) Mittelalters. Die Stadt am Rhein bildet im ganzen Buch jedesmal den Ausgangspunkt der Betrachtungen; für verschiedene Themen werden dann weitere Städte wie Nürnberg, Nördlingen und Regensburg zur Ergänzung oder zum Vergleich herangezogen. Das Buch handelt also in erster Linie von *deutschen* Städten. Die Hansestädte des Nordens bleiben aber weitgehend außer Betracht, wie auch zum Beispiel die brabantische Städtelandschaft, die immerhin während des ganzen hohen und späten Mittelalters zum Reich gehörte. Nur sehr selten richtet der Autor seinen Blick über die Grenzen des deutschen Sprachraums hinaus. Zwar werden Marseille und Genua als Beispiele frühmittelalterlicher Handelsstädte angeführt und geht eine Darstellung der Entstehung der bürgerlichen Kommune in Mailand der Beschreibung einer ähnlichen Entwicklung in Köln voraus, aber dabei bleibt es. Sehr stark urbanisierten Regionen wie Norditalien und Flandern, oder sehr große Hauptstädte wie Paris und London werden kaum berücksichtigt.

So macht Schwarz die Großstadt Köln zum Maß aller urbanen Dinge. Diese Vorgehensweise ist aus rhetorischer Sicht gut zu verstehen, weil sie dem Autor die Möglichkeit verschafft, alle unterschiedlichen Themen an einem festen Punkt aufzuhängen und so eine mehr oder weniger einheitliche Geschichte zu erzählen. Das Problem ist aber, dass Köln eben nicht das Maß der Dinge war. Als Stadt mit über 40.000 Einwohnern, mit riesigen Bauwerken und Stadtmauern, mit völliger Autonomie, mit großem Einfluss auf ihre Umgebung war die Rheinmetropole eher Ausnahme als Regel. Man kann Köln schwer als repräsentativ für „die mittelalterliche Stadt" betrachten, weil die mittelalterlichen Städte im Westen Europas zwar viele ähnliche Merkmale aufwiesen, aber zugleich viele verschiedene Erscheinungsformen kannten. Es gab schließlich auch Kleinstädte, die kaum von Dörfern zu unterscheiden waren. Es gab Regionen, wie zum Beispiel England, wo viele Städte keine Stadtmauern besaßen, weil sie die einfach nicht brauchten. Die Beziehungen zwischen Landesherrn und Stadt gestaltete sich in verschiedenen Gebieten auf unterschiedliche Weise; so haben die Städte (Ost- und West-)Frieslands bis weit ins 15. Jahrhundert hinein überhaupt keinen Landesherrn anerkannt, dahingegen konnten die preußischen Städte sich dem weitgreifenden herrschaftlichen Einfluss des Deutschen Ordens kaum entziehen. Die Liste ließe sich einfach erweitern, aber der Kern ist klar: Schwarz verspricht mit dem Titel dieses kleinen Buches vielleicht einiges zu viel.

Für einen mit der Stadtgeschichte bekannten Leser reicht dieses Buch darum nicht aus. Es ist dazu einfach zu dünn. Gezwungenermaßen kann der Autor die einzelnen Forschungsgegenstände nur sehr knapp behandeln und Raum für Vertiefung oder Problematisierung gibt es nicht. Wohl aus demselben Grund fehlen einige wichtige Themen aus der Alltagsgeschichte, vor allem das religiöse Leben der mittelalterlichen Stadtbewohnern. Tatsache ist aber dass Jörg Schwarz *Stadtluft macht Frei* nicht in erster Linie für Historiker, sondern für ein breit interessiertes Publikum von Nicht-Experten geschrieben hat. Für jene weniger eingeführten Leser ist dieses anschaulich und flott geschriebene Buch eine reizvolle Einladung zu einem weiteren Streifzug in der Geschichte der mittelalterlichen Stadt.

Job Weststrate

MITARBEITER AN DIESEM BAND

Dr. Elżbieta Adamczyk, Department of Older Germanic Languages, School of English, Adam Mickiewicz University, Al. Niepodlegosci 4, 61-874 Poznan, POLEN

Prof. Elena Afros, Department of Languages and Literatures, Wilfried Laurier University, 75 University Avenue, Waterloo ON, N2L 3C5, CANADA

PD Dr. Helmut Beifuss, Kirchenweg 1, 69168 Wiesloch, DEUTSCHLAND

Prof. Dr. Albrecht Classen, Department of German Studies, 301 Learning Services Building, 1512 E. First Street, University of Arizona, Tucson, AZ, 85721 USA

Michel van der Hoek, University of Minnesota, Dept. of German, Scandinavian, and Dutch, 205 Folwel Hall, 9 Pleasant Street, Minneapolis, MN 55455, USA

Prof. Dr. John M. Jeep, Director, Medieval Studies, Dept. of GREAL, Miami University, Irvin Hall 152, Oxford, Ohio 45056-1848, USA

Yasushi Kawasaki, Kyoto University, 7-11 Nakanoshima, Fukakusa Fushimi, Kyoto 612-0049, JAPAN

Prof. Dr. Frederik Kortlandt, VG Vergelijkende Taalwetenschap, Universiteit Leiden, Postbus 9515, 2300 RA Leiden, NIEDERLANDE

Dr. Guus Kroonen, VG Vergelijkende Taalwetenschap, Universiteit Leiden, Postbus 9515, 2300 RA Leiden, NIEDERLANDE

Dr. Cobie Kuné, Prof. Pelstraat 31, 2035 CP Haarlem, NIEDERLANDE

Dr. Erika Langbroek, Beethovenstraat 80^I, 1077 JM Amsterdam, NIEDERLANDE

Dr. Michael P. McGlynn, Dept. of Modern and Classical Languages, Wichita State University, Wichita, KS 67260-0011 USA

Prof. Valentine A. Pakis, Dept. of German, Scandinavian, and Dutch, College of Liberal Arts, University of Minnesota, 205 Folwell Hall, 9 Pleasant Street S.E., Minneapolis Minn. 55455-0124 USA

Prof. Dr. Arend Quak, Instituut voor Oudgermanistiek/Scandinavisch Seminarium, Universiteit van Amsterdam, Spuistraat 134, 1012 VB Amsterdam, NIEDERLANDE

Prof. Dr. Rob Rentenaar, Åtoften 28, 2990 Nivå, DÄNEMARK

Drs. Annelies Roeleveld, Zuiderweg 29, 1461 GM Zuidoostbeemster, NIEDERLANDE

Prof. Dr. Gary T. Shockey, Dept. of Foreign Languages, Tawson University, 8000 York Road, Tawson MD 21252-0001, USA

Prof. Dr. A. H. Touber, Leeuweriklaan 9, 5561 TP Riethoven, NIEDERLANDE

Dr. Veerle Uyttersprot, Vakgroep Nederlandse Literatuur, Universiteit Gent, Blandijnberg 2, 9000 Gent, BELGIEN

Dr. Elly Vijfvinkel, Varenhof 37, 3069 KG Rotterdam, NIEDERLANDE

Dr. Norbert Voorwinden, Rembrandt van Rijnlaan 20, 2343 SV Oegstgeest, NIEDERLANDE

Prof. Dr. Fritz Wagner, Johann-Sigismund-Straße 8, 10711 Berlin, DEUTSCHLAND

Dr. Job Weststrate, VG Geschiedenis, Archeologie en Regiostudies, Universiteit van Amsterdam, Spuistraat 134, 1012 VB Amsterdam, NIEDERLANDE

Rosmarie Zeller (Hrsg.)
Morgen-Glantz 17/2007
Zeitschrift der Christian Knorr von Rosenroth-Gesellschaft

Bern, Berlin, Bruxelles, Frankfurt am Main, New York, Oxford, Wien, 2007. 274 S.
ISBN 978-3-03911-457-3 br.
sFr. 69.– / €* 47.60 / €** 49.– / € 44.50 / £ 28.90 / US-$ 57.95
* inkl. MWSt. – gültig für Deutschland ** inkl. MWSt. – gültig für Österreich

Der vorliegende Band der Zeitschrift Morgen-Glantz (17, 2007) enthält die überarbeitete Fassung der Vorträge, die bei der 16. Tagung der Christian Knorr von Rosenroth-Gesellschaft im Juni 2006 in Sulzbach-Rosenberg gehalten wurden. Thema der Tagung war «Knorrs *Conjugium Phoebi & Palladis* im Kontext alchemistischer Symbolik und barocker Festkultur». Es werden außerdem Rezensionen im Band veröffentlicht, die zum Aufgabenbereich der Gesellschaft und ihrer Zeitschrift gehören.

Aus dem Inhalt: Rosmarie Zeller: Einleitung – Philipp Theisohn: «[...] was Kunst sey / sey durch Ihn». Knorrs *Conjugium Phoebi et Palladis*, die Friedensspiel-Tradition und die Alchemie des Krieges – Monika Flür: Multimedialität im *Conjugium Phoebi & Palladis*. Theatralische Elemente zur Inszenierung von Chaos, Ordnung und Harmonie – Marie-Thérèse Mourey: Knorr von Rosenroths *Conjugium Phoebi et Palladis* im Kontext der Planeten-Ballets des 17. Jahrhunderts – Pierre Béhar: Alchimistische Symbolik im dramatischen Werk Lohensteins – Sibylle Rusterholz: Alchemie und Dichtung. Johann Valentin Andreaes *Chymische Hochzeit Christiani Rosencreutz. Anno 1459* – Rosmarie Zeller: Metaphorische Verschlüsselung alchemistischer Prozesse. Zur Bildlichkeit in Knorrs *Conjugium Phoebi et Palladis* und Monte-Snyders *Metamorphosis Planetarum* – Manfred Knedlik: Die Inszenierung der Liebe. Zum Theater bei den Sulzbacher Hochzeitsfeierlichkeiten des Jahres 1692 – Herbert Seifert: Die Feste zu den drei Hochzeiten Kaiser Leopolds I. – Irmgard Scheitler: Festmusik am Hof Kaiser Leopolds I. – Maria Goloubeva: Hofrepräsentation Kaiser Leopolds I. und ihre Wirkung außerhalb von Wien – Thomas Lau: «Des 'Edlen Tütschlands' Zierde». Die Kaiserin und die Deutsche Nation - die Inszenierung weiblicher Tugend im Zeichen bourbonisch-habsburgischer Rivalität – Bernhard Jahn: Lieto fine - Überlegungen zur Funktion der Hochzeit in barocken Opern – Rosmarie Zeller/Gerd Geismann: Zum Rücktritt von Italo Michele Battafarano – Dietrich Blaufuß: Seitensynopse zum *Apokalypse-Kommentar*.

Bitte senden Sie Ihre Bestellung an:

Peter Lang AG · Internationaler Verlag der Wissenschaften
Moosstrasse 1 · Postfach 350 · CH-2542 Pieterlen · Schweiz
Tel.: +41 32 376 17 17 · Fax: +41 32 376 17 27
e-mail: info@peterlang.com · Internet: **www.peterlang.com**

To access international literature on linguistics and language that speaks volumes, start here.

ProQuest Linguistics & Language Behavior Abstracts

offers a world of relevant, comprehensive, and timely bibliographic coverage. Thousands of easily searchable abstracts enhance discovery of full-text articles in thousands of key journals published worldwide, books, and dissertations, plus citations to reviews of books and other media. This continuously growing collection includes over 410,000 records, with monthly updates and backfiles to 1973—plus browsable indexes and a thesaurus through the ProQuest Illumina™ interface.

So whatever your quest, start here with ProQuest Linguistics & Language Behavior Abstracts.

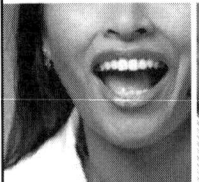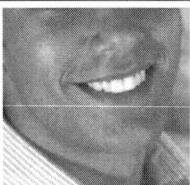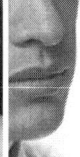

ProQuest Linguistics & Language Behavior Abstracts

For a free trial, contact pqsales@proquest.com or log onto www.proquest.com/go/add today.

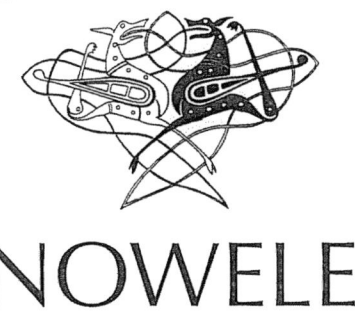

NOWELE

NORTH-WESTERN EUROPEAN LANGUAGE EVOLUTION

NOWELE publishes articles dealing with all aspects of the (pre-)histories of Icelandic, Faroese, Norwegian, Swedish, Danish, Frisian, Dutch, German, English, Gothic and the Early Runic language.

Contributors to **NOWELE** vols. 50-55 (2007-2009) include:

> Elmer H. Antonsen, Alfred Bammesberger, Hans Basbøll, Rolf H. Bremmer Jr, Bernard Comrie, Bernhard Diensberg, Gillian Fellows-Jensen, Peder Gammeltoft & Jakob Povl Holck, Erik W. Hansen, Jón Axel Harðarson, John Hines, Michel van der Hoek, Jarich Hoekstra, Adam Hyllested, Guus Kroonen, Frederik Kortlandt, Susanne Kries, Klaske van Leyden & Norval Smith, Anatoly Liberman, Thomas L. Markey, Bernard Mees, Laurits Rendboe, Michael Rießler, Jørgen Rischel, Berit Sandnes, W. Wilfried Schuhmacher, Michael Schulte, Krzysztof Tomasz Witczak.

'In der kurzen Zeitspanne, in der NOWELE veröffentlicht wurde, hat sich die Zeitschrift zu einem wesentlichen Organ der sprachwissenschaftlichen Diskussion insbesondere im Bereich der germanischen Sprachen und ihrer unmittelbaren Nachbarschaften entwickelt.'

Historische Sprachforschung 103 (1990)

Subscriptions: **NOWELE** appears twice a year, each issue containing c. 120 pages. Subscription rates, two issues (one year) D.Kr. 320.00, single issues D.kr. 190.00, plus postage (and sales tax). All subscription orders should be sent to:

**University Press of Southern Denmark
Campusvej 55 DK-5230 Odense M**

35,- C44787